The Forgotten Nature of New England

The Forgotten Nature of New England

A Search for Traces of the Original Wilderness

Dean B. Bennett

Photographs and Illustrations by the Author

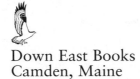

Down East Books
Camden, Maine

Copyright © 1996 by Dean B. Bennett
ISBN 0-89272-374-2
Book design by Write Angle Communications
Cover design by Phil Schirmer
Color separation by Roxmont Graphics
Printed and bound at Capital City Press, Montpelier, Vt.

5   4   3   2   1

Down East Books, Camden, Maine

Library of Congress Cataloging-in-Publication Data

Bennett, Dean B.
        The forgotten nature of New England : a search for traces of the
original wilderness / Dean B. Bennett.
            p.   cm.
        Includes bibliographical references and index.
        ISBN 0-89272-374-2 (pbk.)
        1. Natural history—New England.   2. Natural areas—New England.
3. New England—History   I. Title.
QH104.5.N4B46   1996
508.74—dc20   96-5724
                                                            CIP

Cover: Lake Winnepesaukee, N.H., from C. T. Jackson, *Final Report on the Geology and Mineralogy of the State of New Hampshire*, 1844.

To my parents,
Elsie and Donald Bennett,
who gave me a love for the outdoors.

Contents

Preface

The favor of a continental edge and the good fortune of a midlatitudinal position contribute a natural richness to this country of New England such that it is admired by great numbers of inhabitants and visitors. But in the past four hundred years this land and its waters, forests, and creatures attracted those who saw in them a utility much different from the view of the country's native inhabitants. Thus, much of its original character has disappeared or has changed; removed from sight and sound, it is forgotten. However, it is precisely this circumstance that presents a unique opportunity—a chance to rediscover the nature of New England, for the remnants of that earlier time are reminders of that which was known by the early natives, explorers, and settlers of this region. Herein lies the challenge of a work such as this: to impart to you the sense of excitement, mystery, and challenge that comes with an effort to discover the early traces of New England's wild nature and its myriad details.

The search was painstaking, spanning nearly two and a half years, and although many have documented the changes in New England's landscape over the centuries, information about the remaining, relatively undisturbed natural areas and features was scattered among many sources and often not readily obtainable. I looked for clues left by Native Americans; for written descriptions, maps, and other images among papers, letters, journals, and reports of early visitors and settlers; for scientific documents of geologists, botanists, and other naturalists; for information stored in the memories of people still living; and for actual, surviving remnants of the early New England wilderness, itself—historic features of land and water and communities of plants and animals and natural phenomena still with us today.

My travels over land and water covered the length and breadth of New England, from the Allagash in northern Maine to Block Island off the Rhode Island coast, from the barren Province Lands of Cape Cod to the mountains of the Berkshires, from the coast of eastern Maine to Grande Isle in Lake Champlain. In the end, I found more than one hundred remnants. Not unexpectedly, approximately half are in Maine, for that state is as large as the other five New England states together and, even to this day, contains large, unsettled areas.

The search was not without difficulties. Some descriptions were sketchy or incomplete; references were unavailable; memories were unclear; directions were inaccurate or missing; maps were unobtainable or incorrect; roads were gated and areas fenced; signs warned of no trespass; litter and graffiti were in evidence; developments and disturbances were present. But these impediments were minor compared to the information uncovered and the enthusiastic support from people throughout New England. Time after time I followed the footsteps of early New Englanders to the vestiges of the wilderness they had seen. Revealed to me were sights, sounds, and smells the Native Peoples and first Europeans had encountered. Perhaps I even experienced the same insights and feelings they experienced.

I also learned that the surviving remnants of our original wild nature, by their rarity and fragility, are vulnerable to the effects of human visitation and use, however innocent and caring the intent. This book, therefore, is meant as a journal of discovery—a means whereby you may experience satisfaction from merely knowing, vicariously, about the unspoiled examples of nature documented in the pages that follow. In keeping with this intent, the would-be explorer who desires to see these remnants firsthand must exercise her or his own exploratory skills, for this book offers little guidance to precise locations. Rather, like the early reports on which it is based, it offers verification of the existence of places and things, but its maps are crude approximations and its names are sometimes derived from the whim of the writer. This approach in part reflects a desire to respect the privacy of those in whose possession some of these remnants now reside and who are well aware of the fragility of these features and, as such, care for them so that they will continue to survive.

I hope in the pages ahead you will capture a sense of discovery and some of the mystery and wonder experienced by those who first encountered the New England wilderness. There are lessons to be learned, too, in the diminishment of the region's original natural character. This book will have served its purpose if you come away with a vision of what we may gain by the preservation and restoration of that which, to our good fortune, remains.

Dean Bennett
Mt. Vernon, Maine

Acknowledgments

Special recognition and appreciation are given to Fred H. Dearnley, photographic specialist at the University of Maine at Farmington, who applied his considerable photographic talent to the making of black-and-white prints from my photographs and slides as well as to the reproduction of illustrations from historic references and who gave me much advice on black-and-white photography.

This book would not have been possible without substantial help from others. The breadth of topics investigated, the scope and depth of historic research, and the extent of geographic coverage were at times nearly overwhelming. Two years of literary research were required, followed by six months of travel throughout New England for firsthand study and photographic documentation, and another nine months of writing. Letters and phone calls ran into the hundreds as I sought information on the status and locations of sites. Meetings and field studies were arranged throughout the region with individuals knowledgeable of special areas as I made preparations to visit the more than one hundred sites. On several occasions individuals volunteered to guide or accompany me on my trips. People were universally generous with their information, assistance, and encouragement, making my work on this project truly pleasurable and rewarding. I must add, however, that my acknowledgment of the individuals below in no way removes me from assuming responsibility for any errors of fact nor do my interpretations and judgments imply their concurrence.

I wish to express a special thank-you to my wife, Sheila, who is a pillar of support throughout all of my projects and who accompanied me on many of my trips across New England. Other members of my family who helped were my son, Richard, who accompanied me into the Caribou–Speckled Mountain Wilderness, and my brother, Jim, and his wife, Julia, who provided a base for my Vermont trips. Jim and I spent a very pleasant spring day together visiting sites in western and northern parts of that state.

Others from my university campus to whom I express appreciation for support are the members of the Academic Council, who granted me a Libra Professorship, members of the Faculty Development Committee, who granted funds for some of my work, and the following individuals who helped me in various ways: Alfred Bersbach, Janine Bonk, Diana Duffy, William Geller, M. Alan Hart, Stacey Hodges, Sylvia Hodgkins, Shirley Martin, and James B. Petersen.

I also thank those who reviewed sections of the manuscript: James B. Petersen, Barbara Vickery, and Lyle Wiggin.

Foremost among the organizations that assisted me are the New England state chapters and field offices of The Nature Conservancy. I owe them a special debt of gratitude, for time and time again, as I searched for a remnant piece of our wilderness heritage, I discovered it intact and protected, thanks to one of the state chapters. Among the staff of the

Conservancy's state organizations, I thank the following: **Maine**—Julie S. Henderson, Janet McMahon, Nancy Sferra, Kyle Stockwell, and Barbara Vickery; **New Hampshire**—Krista M. Helmboldt; **Vermont**—Marc DesMeules; **Massachusetts**—Tim Simmons; **Rhode Island**—Kevin M. Doyle and Chris Littlefield; **Connecticut**—David Gumbart; and the Eastern Regional Office—Lesley Sneddon.

Others whom I thank for information of a general nature or for their knowledge of sites and subjects relating to more than one state are the following: Charles Cogbill, Mary Byrd Davis, David R. Foster, James G. Geiger, John A. Lutz, Robert N. Oldale, John B. Pearce, Charles Roth, and Craig L. Shafer.

For information and assistance relative to sites in the New England states, I thank the following: **Maine**—Acadia National Park, Linda Alverson, Walter A. Anderson, James Bernard, Patty Bouchard, Mike and Rhonda Brophy, Jasper Cates, Irvin C. Caverly, Susan Caverly, Tim Caverly, Robert Chute, Tom Cieslinski, Michael Cline, Philip W. Conkling, Carroll Cutting, Michael Doyle, Diana Dudley, Don Dudley, Tabitha Dudley, Katrina van Dusen, Bill Foley, Olcott Gates, Carolyn Haddon, Daniel J. Harrison, Mark Hedden, George G. Herrick, Stanley Howe, Julia A. Hunter, Malcolm L. Hunter, Jr., Fred Hurley, Alan Hutchinson, Peter Jones, Van King, Ernest Knight, Eric Lahti, Alan Larson, Arthur Libby, Robert G. Marvinney, Mark McCollough, Susan Miller, Tad Miller, Maurice Mills, Jr., Caroline M. Pryor, Small Point Association, Earle G. Shettleworth, Jr., Susan Moulton, John Richardson, David Sanger, Steve Selva, Thomas Squiers, Jym St. Pierre, Steve Swatling, Craig Tenbroek, Woodrow B. Thompson, Harry R. Tyler, Jr., Regina Webster, Marshall Wiebe, and Betsy Wyeth; **New Hampshire**—Lee Ellen Carbonneau, David T. Funk, Carl F. Gebhardt, Thomas C. Miner, Richard Ober, H. Sharon Ossenbruggen, Ned Therrien, Ann Valpey, Daniel Valpey, and Peter Wellenberger; **Vermont**—Juanita I. Blaskowski, Diane Harlow Burbank, Art Cohn, Diane L. Conrad, Bill Crenshaw, Marjorie Drummond, Christopher Fichtel, Jay Hughes, Charles W. Johnson, Steve Parren, Giovanna Peebles, Carolyn Shapiro, Gwenda Smith, Diane L. Vanecek, Vermont Division for Historic Preservation, Vermont Historical Society, George M. Wallace, Stephen W. Weber, and Kathren B. White; **Massachusetts**—Carolyn E. Banfield, LeBaron Briggs, Richard Callaghan, Peter W. Dunwiddie, Fred Dunford, Barbara Flye, Richard Foster, Marsha L. Goldstein, Anne Harding, Kevin Hollenbeck, Jack Lash, Robert T. Leverett, Rob Leverett, Rob MacArthur, Austin B. Mason, Ed Moses, Glenn Motzkin, John O'Keefe, William A. Patterson, III, Tom Sanker, and Patricia Swain; **Rhode Island**—Donald D'Amato, J. Allan Cain, Nathan A. Fuller, Michael Hebert, Mary Newhouse, Christopher J. Raithel, Paul Robinson, and Jennifer Simmons; **Connecticut**—John Anderson, Nancy Phelps Blum, Starling Childs, Frank Egler, Robert E. Freedman, Nancy W. McHone, Ken Metzler, Moodus Cave Hill Resort, Nancy M. Murray, David B. Prezyna, Curtis Rand, Margaret Thomas, and Gordon W. Thomson.

Finally, I wish to thank Thomas A. Fernald and Karin Womer of Down East Books for their continued faith, support, and encouragement.

Chapter 1
Of the Wilderness

A cool, brisk wind greeted me the morning I arrived on Morris Island after crossing the roadway from the mainland of Cape Cod. I had come to visit a wilderness—one of dunes, marshes, and smells of salty air. It's New England's southernmost protected wilderness—the Monomoy Islands Federal Wilderness Area. Later that day, I was scheduled for a guided trip to North Monomoy Island but at the last moment decided to come early for a preview. I was fortunate: the tide was low and the trail along the beach had been opened.

Standing on the wooden stairway leading down the steep embankment to the shore, I was first struck by the flat plain of sand and water that stretched out for miles before me. To my right, down Morris Island beach, I could see the white slivers of North and South Monomoy islands. Long, thin, white bands of beaches and sandbars interrupted the blue, wind-whipped waters between me and the islands. Somewhere out there, at a point where the islands end, Samuel de Champlain, on October 3, 1606, had found his ship "entangled" among the shoals and sandbars of a "very dangerous place." He named the point Cap Batturier; today, it's known as Monomoy Point.

Few people were on the beach that early morning in mid-May as I sauntered across the freshly washed and cleaned sand, following the trail markers. Ahead, fading, tide-washed human footprints strayed off the trail to the water's edge. Fresh gull tracks zigzagged next to them. Parts of shells, seaweed, and dead fish littered the wet sand. Far in the distance, the low dune escarpment of North Monomoy cut a brilliant white line above the blue waters. Masses of white gulls fluttered over and around it. The island did not project a common view of wilderness—of dense forests and unbroken shorelines—but a feeling of wilderness was there in its isolation, its remoteness, and its barrenness.

At last we succeeded, by the grace of God, in getting by a sandy point which juts almost three leagues into the sea, south southeast, a very dangerous place.

—Samuel de Champlain, 1606[1]

The trail turned towards the dunes along the shore and soon became lost in loose, tractionless sand. Forward movement became more difficult. Surrounded by beachgrass, I treadmilled into a dune scrubland of bayberry, blueberry, weathered and stunted pitch pine, and red oak. My trail guide identified beach heather and pointed out red cedars browsed by white-tailed deer.

The trail led to a small salt marsh. Here a pool of open water surrounded by cordgrass is resupplied with nutrients twice a day. Marshes were once considered

Beyond a salt marsh at the edge of Morris Island, across shallow waters and sandbars, the steeply faced, high dunes of North Monomy Island project the open, barren expansiveness of a different kind of wilderness area.

wastelands, but we now realize the ecological importance of these places to shorebirds and waterfowl and their role as nurseries to fish and other aquatic creatures. From this marsh I looked across the open water and sandbars to the high dunes of North Monomoy, steeply facing the open Atlantic and on the bay side gradually tapering to the gentle line of the horizon.

Whether these islands were connected to the mainland in Champlain's time is open to conjecture, for they have been both islands and peninsula since their formation by deposition of eroding glacial deposits from outer

Cape Cod. From the 1930s to the 1950s, they made up a ten-mile-long, land-tied barrier beach system. In 1958 they became one island when the connecting bridge of land was breached. Twenty years later, a storm severed the island into two islands, North Monomoy and South Mon-omoy. Because of continuing wave erosion and the addition of new sediments, the configurations and sizes of these barrier islands are continually changing. In 1984 the islands encompassed about 2,750 acres. North Monomoy is the smaller of the two, being about two and a-half miles long and about a mile wide at its widest point, including tidal flats. South Monomoy is about five miles long and nearly one and a-half miles wide. The islands display a long escarpment of eroded sand dunes, upwards of perhaps forty feet high in places and parallel to their eastern shores. Behind are back dunes that level out to include freshwater ponds, salt marshes, and mud flats.

Monomoy Islands

In 1944 the Monomoy National Wildlife Refuge was established, encompassing the islands and a forty-five-acre portion of Morris Island, where the refuge's headquarters is located. Ninety-four percent of Monomoy was designated as federal wilderness in 1970. Today, it still remains southern New England's only wilderness area. Although inaccessible by roads, the area may be reached by boat at many locations. For this reason, a caution to visitors is in order, for its dunes and stabilizing vegetation may be easily destroyed by heavy foot traffic and overuse.

Vegetation on the sandy dune areas is understandably limited to those plants that are able to grow in the shifting sands and withstand the assault of storms. About one-third of the islands' upland areas are unvegetated. The most common plant is the tenacious beachgrass. Other plants, scattered through the beachgrass, include seaside goldenrod, dusty miller, beach pea, sea rocket, false heather, poison ivy, bayberry, and beach plum. South Monomoy is also home for a few small pitch and black pines and beaked willows. The western sides of both islands contain salt marshes of grasses typical of these areas—saltwater cordgrass, saltmeadow cordgrass, and blackgrass. South Monomoy contains freshwater ponds and marshes.

Among the islands' animal life are small mammals, of which the meadow vole is the most abundant. Harbor seals winter here by the thousands. Among the invertebrates are quahogs and softshelled clams. But perhaps most interesting are the thousands of horseshoe crabs that migrate into the shallow waters to breed. Other fauna include Fowler's toad, diamondback terrapin, Atlantic Ridley turtle, and leatherback sea turtle.

Many birds are also attracted to the islands' variable habitat conditions and remoteness. The islands are well known as stopover and resting sites for migrating shorebirds and as a breeding habitat for waterfowl and colonial seabirds. During cold weather, as many as 100,000 common eiders converge in the nearby waters. Here, too, are the beautiful snowy egret and the endangered piping plover and roseate tern.[2]

My planned trip to North Monomoy Island that day was cancelled because of rough seas. Though it was a disappointment, my visit that morning to Morris Island and the views it provided of the Monomoys were surprisingly fulfilling. Like Champlain, I had experienced an irresistible urge to learn more about this strange, fascinating environment. Exploration is a drive we humans have, although few probably have Champlain's will and drive to face the unknown. Yet, as I thought about it, I had received a lesson. Satisfaction can be found by *not* visiting an area so vulnerable to human intrusion. That takes a different kind of will—one that may ultimately ensure the future of a few wild areas, like the Monomoy Islands, on this earth.

EARLY ACCOUNTS

The Countrey all along as I sailed, being no more than a meer wilderness.

—John Josselyn, 1638[3]

We begin to acquire a picture of New England's "original" wilderness (original in the sense that most of it was unaltered by human hands) when we sift through the historic accounts left by those who first described it—the early explorers, settlers, and visitors. John Josselyn was one who visited the settlements soon after their establishment. What was that wilderness he saw in 1638 on his way from Boston to Black Point (now Scarborough) in the province of Maine? What of it remains where we can experience, as did Josselyn and his contemporaries, the mystery, solitude, and beauty of its primeval character? Where can we gain some understanding of our place in a natural world that in too many cases is obliterated by our imprint? And from these remnants of New England's forgotten nature, what insights can we gain into ourselves and our obligation to preserve this natural heritage for future generations? It is with these questions that our search begins.

The early Europeans left us many firsthand accounts of the natural character of the new world in a rich collection of diaries, letters, journals, reports, business papers, books, maps, and art. Be aware, however, that it is undoubtedly an imperfect view that they gave us. The descriptions they passed on are limited by the selection of subjects and by the information-gathering tools and methods available. These, in turn, were influenced by the state of their science, technology, and communications; the cultural climate and social values that surrounded them; and the superstitions, beliefs, and preconceptions they carried with them. We know, for example, that strong economic motives influenced many of the choices of subjects they wrote about, and their descriptions often favored that which promoted exploration and settlement for financial gain. We also know that early religious beliefs, especially among the Puritan settlers, influenced their attitudes towards the wilderness. More subtle was how their view of this new land and its future was influenced by the pastoral, domesticated European landscape they had left behind. Nevertheless, in spite of their biases, we are fortunate that today we have at our disposal a rich historical record that allows us to draw back, at least partially, the curtain of time that obscures the secrets of that wild landscape.

Although Viking sagas may suggest that early Scandinavian mariners visited New England, hard evidence of this is almost nonexistent. A notable exception is a Viking coin discovered on the Maine coast. It wasn't until European explorers arrived in the early 1500s and issued written reports to their sponsors that details of the New England wilderness began to emerge. Such reports are invaluable to us, for they are made by those who translated their firsthand observations into the written word. While their writings are at times detailed and perceptively descriptive, they tend to avoid reference to feelings they must have experienced in seeing this continent for the first time. One has to look closely for any emotional impact that accompanies their encounters with the new world—the anticipation, excitement, exhilaration, anxiety, and fear that must have been felt. Though these feelings were seldom mentioned directly, they may be easily inferred from some of the writings.

Giovanni da Verrazzano, sailing for France in 1524, gave us perhaps the first, most accurate account of the New England coast. The historian Lawrence Wroth described him as "a well-educated, imaginative, and aggressive man of the sea" who "must have been educated in the high tradition of the Florentine Schools" in Italy.[4] Verrazzano's reports were descriptive and detailed. Of the wilderness he saw off the Maine coast near Casco Bay, he communicated to the King of France that he "found another land high full of thicke woods, the trees whereof were firres, cipresses, and such like as are wont to grow in cold countreys."[5] His accounts helped fan the winds of exploration, and throughout the century other notable explorers sailed along the continent's edge, including Estevan Gomez in 1525, Simon Ferdinando in 1579, and John Walker in 1580.

The 1600s saw increasingly detailed reports coming from the explorers and learned men who accompanied them; the mists of uncertainty surrounding the mysterious character of this new land were being swept away. On May 14, 1602, Bartholomew Gosnold arrived on the New England coast, possibly at Cape Elizabeth or Cape Neddick on the shores of what is now Maine. He explored the coast to the Elizabeth Islands at the southwest end of Cape Cod. Two men who sailed with him left written accounts— John Brereton and Gabriel Archer. Brereton described their point of arrival as "being full of faire trees, the land somewhat low, certeine hummocks or hilles lying into the land, the shore ful of white sand, but very stony or rocky."[6] Gosnold sailed for Cape Cod, encountering unmapped land and uncharted waters with dangerous shoals. Archer described the frequent soundings they made and, at one point, a place of shallow depth between Nantucket Island and Martha's Vineyard that he named "Tucker's Terror, upon his [shipmates'] expressed feare."[7]

Martin Pring followed Gosnold the next year in 1603, arriving with two ships, probably near the Fox Islands in Penobscot Bay off the Maine coast. It is thought that he sailed southwestward to Plymouth Harbor, exploring inlets where, he wrote, "we beheld very goodly Groves and Woods replenished with tall Oakes, Beeches, Pine-trees, Firre-trees, Hasels, Wich-hasels and Maples. We saw here also sundry sorts of Beasts, as Stags, Deere, Beares, Wolves, Foxes, Lusernes [lynx] and Dogges with sharpe noses."[8]

We are fortunate that the early 1600s ushered in two explorers who were also mapmakers—Samuel de Champlain and Captain John Smith. Their maps were among the first to provide a realistic view of New England's coastal features. Thus, they initiated a visual conception of the region that profoundly influenced how the resources of the coast and inland areas were henceforth understood and valued.[9]

Champlain, by all accounts, was a remarkable man. His reports of the explorations he made along the New England coast and farther north, including the St. Lawrence River, reveal an educated and talented man of stamina, determination, and resourcefulness, with an ability to lead others. One historian described him as being "at once sailor and soldier, writer and man of action, artist and explorer, ruler and administrator."[10]

Champlain, in 1604, was probably around thirty-four years old when he accompanied a French gentleman, Sieur de Monts, who hoped to establish a settlement and trading post on the Acadian coast, an area which included what is now easternmost Maine. During that year, Champlain visited Mount Desert Island and sailed up the Penobscot River as far as Bangor. The following year he made a more ambitious exploration of the coast from eastern Maine to Nauset Harbor on Cape Cod. In 1606, he made yet another trip to the outer eastern side of Cape Cod. Later, in 1609, he journeyed up the Richelieu River from the St. Lawrence to Lake Champlain.

Not only did Champlain leave us with maps and illustrations, but he gave us many written images of this land as it existed some four centuries ago. He wrote of a land that, to the Europeans, was unknown and uncharted and, therefore, presented difficulties and risks, such as he

The head of Somes Sound on Mount Desert Island. Explorer Samuel de Champlain visited the island in 1604. Illustration from Samuel Adams Drake, *Nooks and Corners of the New England Coast* (New York: Harper & Brothers, Publishers, 1875).

encountered while exploring Maine's Kennebec River. When he attempted to penetrate the maze of streams and islands that make up the mouth of this river, he was fortunate to have had natives to guide him. He met a group at Wiscasset Harbor after sailing up the Back River and along Westport Island several leagues (a league is roughly three miles).[11] Champlain gives the following account of the subsequent events:

They guided us down the river by Another than that by which we came, to go to a lake; and [passed] some island . . . near a cape [Hockomock Point]. Beyond the cape we passed a very narrow rapid [Hell Gate], but not without great difficulty; for, although we had a good, fresh wind and filled our sails with it as much as possible, we could not get through in that way, and were obliged to fasten a hawser [large rope] to some trees and to pull on it. Thus we managed to get through by strength of our arms, aided by a favorable wind. The savages who were with us carried their canoes on the land, as they could not get them through with paddles. After having cleared this rapid we saw some beautiful meadows.[12]

During the year of 1605, when Champlain was making his first exploration along the New England coast, another explorer arrived on the scene, Captain George Waymouth. An Englishman, he was sent to the Maine coast to find a place for settlement. In his company was a gentleman, James Rosier, who appears to have been employed by one of the trip's sponsors for the purpose of making a report. The expedition had left England on March 5,

1605, and arrived in the vicinity of Monhegan Island on May seventeenth. With supplies of water and wood exhausted, Waymouth looked for a safe, wind-protected harbor in deep water, from which he could send a party ashore. As Rosier told it:

Our Captaine manned his ship-boat and sent her before with Thomas Cam one of his Mates, whom he knew to be of good experience, to sound & search for a place safe for our shippe to ride in; . . . he found a convenient Harbor; which it pleased God to send us, farre beyond our expectations, in a most safe birth defended from all windes, in an excellent depth of water.[13]

The harbor and islands Waymouth found were at the mouth of the St. George River off present-day Port Clyde.

The first English attempt to settle in Maine came in 1607. The ill-fated Popham Colony, as it is now known, was established the previous year by members of the first Virginia Company under a charter from King James. The expedition consisted of two ships and was led by George

Early explorers and settlers sailed into the mouth of Maine's Kennebec River, seen here from Popham Beach.

Popham and Raleigh Gilbert. They arrived in early August at an island they named St. Georges Island where they found a cross which they supposed was left by Waymouth. After enduring a storm, they eventually entered the mouth of the "Sagadeocke River" (Kennebec River) and explored it for a distance of fourteen leagues. On August 18 they chose the site of their settlement on the west shore at the mouth of the river. At the end of that month, a group of fourteen set out with Gilbert to explore the coast westward into Casco Bay, a venture from which we obtain the following rare view described by one of the officers:

We Sailed by many gallant Illands & towards nyght the winde Cam Contrary against us So that we wear Constrained to remain that nyght under the head Land called Semeanis [Cape Elizabeth] whear we found the Land to be most fertill the trees growing thear doth exceed for goodnesse & Length being the most part of them ocke & wallnutt growing a greatt spaced assoonder on from the other as our parks in Ingland and no thickett growing under them. . . .

Sondaye beinge the 30th Auguste retornynge beffore the wynd we sailled by many goodly Illands for betwixt this head Land called Semeanis & the ryver of Sagadeockm ys a great baye [Casco Bay] in which Lyeth So many Illands & so thicke and neare together that yo Cannott well desern to Nomber them yet may yo go in betwixt them in a good ship fo yo shall have never Lesse Watter the 8 fethams these Illands ar all overgrowen with woods very thicke as ocks wallnut pyne trees & many other things growinge as Sarsaperilla hassell nuts & whorts in abundance.[14]

The colony spent a hard winter on the shore of the Kennebec. Many died, including George Popham. In the spring the survivors abandoned the place and returned to England. Permanent colonization would have to wait.

Other explorers ventured along the New England coast during the intervening years. Henry Hudson, under sail for the Dutch East India Company, arrived in eastern Maine in 1609 and sailed along the fishing banks to Cape Cod and on to Virginia. Samuel Argall, sent by the English, visited the coast of New England in 1609 and 1613. But it wasn't until Captain John Smith, at the age of thirty-five, surveyed the New England coast for eleven weeks in 1614 that the world was provided with its most accurate map of New England's complex coastal edge. His accompanying book, published in 1616, was perhaps one of the more truthful early descriptions of the economic potential of the region. It was also the first book to name this region New England. Smith came to know the New England coast in enough detail for him to single out "the remarkablest Iles and Mountains for Landmarkes" and "the cheefe headlands."[15]

Captain John Smith's survey of the New England coast in 1614 allowed him to produce the most accurate map of the time.

Other explorers followed Smith, but within a decade the wilderness of New England was no longer an object of simply coastal reconnaissance and survey: the establishment of colonies had begun in earnest. The well-known arrival of the Puritans to the shores of Massachusetts in 1620 serves as a popular point in time, marking the beginning of permanent European settlement. Among the settlers were learned people who became intimate with the land and its flora and fauna and left us a legacy of written materials, including books that further enlarged our concept of this early wilderness.[16]

One of the earliest was *Mourt's Relation*, published in 1622—the first printed book about the Plymouth Colony. Although it is not clear who wrote the various chapters, scholars suggest the names of Edward Winslow, Robert Cushman, and William Bradford. Other publications of the period include *Good Newes from New England* by Edward Winslow, printed in 1624, and *New England's Plantation* by the Reverend Francis Higginson, issued in 1630.

We are fortunate, however, that three Englishmen who came to these early New England settlements left us books in which they catalogued and described in some detail the natural history of that long-ago wilderness. One was Thomas Morton, who arrived in 1622 with an entourage to start a plantation. Although he was educated and practiced occasionally as an attorney, he gained notoriety for the reckless and carefree life he led. His irreverence and dishonesty constantly irritated the Puritans to a point where they once sent him back to England and to jail. To their dismay, however, Morton returned to continue his picturesque and, to them, sinful life. It's reported that he died a drunken reprobate but not before he wrote his book, *New English Canaan* or *New Canaan*, which was published in 1637. In the second part of his book, he included a description of the land and waters in and around the settlements, commenting on the plants, animals, and other natural features.

The second individual who gave us some insight into the character of the early New England wilderness was William Wood, who arrived in the Massachusetts colonies in 1629 and stayed four years. There is some speculation

The south part of New England in 1634. From William Wood, *New-England's Prospect* (London: Tho. Cotes, 1634).

The South part of Nevv-England, as it is Planted this yeare, 1634.

that he may have returned in 1635 and settled in the colonies. Although educated, he, like Morton, was not a scientist. However, his book, *New-England's Prospect*, published in 1634, was the first to focus directly on the natural history and resources of the region.

The third was certainly no ordinary visitor. He was John Josselyn, an English physician and botanist, who was an accurate observer of nature. His accounts were especially colorful and at times poetic. He entertained his readers with incredible stories about creatures in this strange, "new" world, arousing their curiosity and enlarging their knowledge of the region's multifaceted natural history. Josselyn's two books, *New-Englands Rarities Discovered* and *An*

Account of Two Voyages to New-England, both published in the 1670s, were based on two visits he made to the Province of Maine. The first occurred from 1638 to 1639 and the second from 1663 to 1671.

New England's early visitors, travelers, settlers, and explorers experienced the wilderness on both physical and psychological levels.

Physically, the Europeans were impressed by the *vastness* of the wilderness—a quality that separates it from the wilderness areas in New England today. Their writings are sprinkled with words, such as infinite, spacious, abundance, ample, multitude, and great plenty:

> *[The land beyond the White Mountains is] full of rocky Hills, as thick as Mole-hills in a Meadow, and cloathed with infinite thick Woods.*

> —John Josselyn, 1672[17]

It was also a predominantly *wild* land that the Europeans encountered—a place where untouched nature prevailed:

> *[The land had] a weather-beaten face, and the whole countrey, full of woods and thickets, represented a wild and savage hue.*

> —William Bradford, 1620[18]

But there were also areas that showed human influence, where Native Peoples had burned and cleared away the understory of the forests, leaving open woods:

> *In many places, divers Acres being cleare, so that one may ride a hunting in most places of the land . . . for it being the custome of the Indians to burne the wood in November, when the grass is withered, and leaves dryed, it consumes all the underwood, and rubbish, which otherwise would over grow the Country, making it unpassable and spoile their much affected hunting.*

> —William Wood, 1634[19]

Another quality of this wilderness was an absence of people. It offered unlimited opportunities for *solitude*—to be alone. One could easily wander away from the settle-

COLONIAL IMPRESSIONS

ments and be on one's own, totally reliant on one's own abilities. Without landmarks, it was also easy to become lost:

A neighbor got lost looking for strayed cattle and coming . . . near the head spring of some branches of Black-point River *or* Saco-River, *light into a Tract of land for God knowes how many miles full of delfes and dingles [valleys and clefts between hills], and dangerous precipices, Rocks and inextricable difficulties which did justly daunt, yea quite deter him from endeavoring to pass any further: many such like places are to be met with in* New-England.

—John Josselyn, 1674[20]

Away from the settlements the wildness and solitude were accompanied by a deep blanket of *silence*, broken only by natural sounds:

[There are] cleare running streames that twine in fine meanders through the meads, making so sweete a murmering noise to heare, as would even lull the sences with delight a sleepe.

—Thomas Morton, 1637[21]

Saturday the third of March, *the winde was South, the morning mistie, but towards noone warme and fayre weather; the Birds sang in the Woods most pleasantly; at one of the Clocke it thundred, which was the first wee heard in that Countrey, it was strong and great claps, but short, but after an houre, it rayned very sadly till midnight.*

—William Bradford, 1622[22]

The *economic* value of the wilderness as a source of goods that could provide comfort and wealth was a driving force among many who came to live in the region and among those who promoted its settlement:

The next commoditie the land affords, is good store of Woods, & that not only such as may be needful for fewell, but likewise for the building of Ships, and houses, & Mils, and all manner of Water-worke about which Wood is needefull.

—William Wood, 1634[23]

Even the Puritans, who arrived with different motives, soon recognized and exploited the natural wealth of the country:

A vast, mysterious wilderness "full of woods and thickets" and "cleare running streams" with "sweet murmuring noises" confronted New England's early settlers. Illustration from George B. Emerson, *A Report on the Trees and Shrubs Growing Naturally in the Forests of Massachusetts*, vol. 2 (Boston, Mass.: Little, Brown, and Company, 1875).

The commodiousnesse of the Countrey . . . and . . . the foure
Elements, Earth, Water, Aire and Fire . . . and convenient use
of these, consistith the only well-being both of Man and
Beast in a more or lesse comfortable measure.

—Reverend Francis Higginson, 1630[24]

Psychologically, the wilderness also had a powerful
effect on the early European explorers and settlers and influenced their attitudes towards it. But the relationship
was two-way, for the settlers also arrived with their own
set of attitudes and values towards the land. Their perceptions of this wilderness were influenced by those beliefs,
attitudes, and values rooted in their culture.

To the early Europeans the region was unknown and
had a *mysterious* and *frightening* quality about it:

But all this Coast to Pennobscot, and as farr I could see
Eastward of it is nothing but such high craggy cliffy Rocks
and stony Iles, that I wondered such great trees could
growe upon so hard foundations. It is a Countrie rather to
affright, then [sic] delight one. And how to describe a more
plaine spectacle of desolation or more barren I knowe not.

—Captain John Smith, 1616[25]

The Country beyond these Hills [White Mountains] North-
ward is daunting terrible.

—John Josselyn, 1672[26]

The wilderness also created in the minds of the early
settlers a *challenge*, and in many ways, it still is today. For
the Puritans, especially, it was perceived as a spiritual challenge—a place to prove their worthiness in the eyes of
God by overcoming temptation and hardship and removing the wasteland.

We must . . . pass through a Wilderness of Miseries e're we
can arrive at the heavenly Canaan.

—Increase Mather, 1677[27]

This countrey of New-England is destitute of all helpes,
and meanes, by which the people might come out of the
snare of Satan.

—John White, 1630[28]

In a wilderness there is not only want of many comforts,
but there is danger as to many positive evils.

—Thomas Shepard, Jr., 1673[29]

Great Head on Mount Desert Island exemplifies the "high
craggy cliffy Rocks" Captain
John Smith described along the
coast of eastern Maine. Illustration from Samuel Adams Drake,
Nooks and Corners of the New
England Coast (New York:
Harper & Brothers, Publishers,
1875).

As for the colonies . . . replenishing wast and voyd . . . they have a cleare and sufficient warrant from the mouth of God.

—John White, 1630[30]

Finally, the wilderness represented *freedom* and the opportunity to *escape* from the constraints of society. This was the case with the Puritans.

They should transport themselves into America, there to enjoy the liberty of their own persuasion.

—William Hubbard, 1680[31]

With that freedom, however, one faces the challenge of self-responsibility—of using one's own abilities to deal with the surrounding world and of realizing that one is on her or his own.

When we came to Nantasket, Capt. Squeb . . . put us ashore and our goods on Nantasket Point; and left us to shift for ourselves in a forlorn place in this wilderness.

—Captain Roger Clap, 1630[32]

Such were the beliefs and attitudes towards the wilderness that permeated the psychological fabric of the early colonies and influenced the profound change of the wilderness that followed. It is against this background that we now explore the nature of what this wild land was really like.

A WILDERNESS REVEALED

When the Puritans landed at Plymouth in 1620, Massachusetts was 90 percent forested, according to estimates, and each of the other New England states was 95 percent covered by forest.[33] Nonforested areas included marshes, interval lands, meadows, bogs, beaches and sand dunes, and mountaintops. Though the land undoubtedly appeared stable and unchanging to the settlers, as it does to many today, its character was essentially the product of ongoing natural processes. It had undergone thousands of years of environmental change due to climatic fluctuations, glacial assaults, sea invasions, earthquakes and land movement, wind storms, fires, pathogens, and effects of animals. The most disruptive natural disturbance to the vegetative cover was fire, which was more frequent in the drier, warmer sections of New England's southern coast and less frequent in western and northern sections where cooler, wetter conditions exist. Burning of vegetation by Native Peoples altered the forest in some locations. Major hurricanes occurred periodically with devastating effects on the forest in some areas. From time to time, outbreaks of disease nearly decimated certain species of trees, such as the eastern hemlock. Thus, viewed in the scale of geologic time and in the length of time that it takes for biospheres and ecosystems to respond to natural events, it was a dynamic landscape that the settlers encountered and one with many subtle variations, not all of which were readily apparent.

We are able to make this assessment of the early New England wilderness through the reports and works of many individuals, spanning a time from exploration to the present. Some of the evidence they have provided is direct, coming from writings of those who, like John Josselyn, engaged in firsthand observation and study. Some information, however, is less direct, such as that from reports of those who have undertaken research in the natural, social, and behavioral sciences and in the arts and humanities. But in all cases, as we shall now see, the view that has emerged is fascinating and the methods of inquiry not only interesting but sometimes romantic.

Surveyors of Ancient Forests

If any one element characterized the early New England wilderness and exerted a profound influence on the lives of its settlers, it was the deep, mysterious blanket of forest that covered much of the landscape. Among the first to report the nature of this forest were the boundary surveyors. They came ahead of the settlements, establishing the boundaries of each new tract of land granted or sold. Equipped with theodolite, tripod, iron measuring chains (a full chain measures sixty-six feet), and other necessary equipment, such as axes, the surveyors mapped and recorded the distinctive features of the land. Even as late as the early 1800s, government surveys in northern New England states, sections of which were still being settled, resulted in records of trees that are now useful in determining the nature of the pre-European-settlement forest. Timber cruisers also left records of the character of the uncut forests. They were hired to ascertain the potential economic value of the woodland in preparation for cutting. They used a variety of methods, such as sampling areas or examining trees along predetermined lines. Their reports included comments on kinds of trees, quantities, topography, soils, and streams.

Using such historic evidence has proven to be an important means of reconstructing the early character of New England. However, these kinds of records are scattered and incomplete. For example, while government land surveys have given us valuable information about northern New England, they came too late to be useful in southern New England where colonization and clearing of the forest occurred early.[34] Other procedures were needed.

In the twentieth century we turned to the tools and methods of modern science for new views of primeval forests. Scientists analyzed existing vegetation, topographic position, soils, and plant associations to reconstruct probable climax forests. They used pollen analysis, or palynology, to show both the composition of the forests and the effects of disturbance before and after settlement. They studied live and dead plant materials and the nature of old-growth forests. They explored ancient forests and bored into old trees to take cores for the purpose of examining annual rings. They learned the ages of the trees, fluctuations in growth rates, fire damage, injury from insects and disease, effects of storms, and climatic and weather changes. They found that major hurricanes likely occurred every fifty to one hundred years and were more severe in southeastern sections of New England than in northeastern areas.[35] They investigated the extent of burning by Native Peoples through historic accounts, analysis of fire scars in tree ring studies, pollen studies, and charcoal counts. They studied archaeological evidence of native population density and discovered, in some locations, parallels with fire frequency. From these studies they were able to conclude with a fair degree of certainty that burning was carried on by natives; however, they still are not sure of the extent of their burning.[36]

Scientific Investigators of the Land

Although the forests dominated the early landscape and occupied much of the attention of the commodity-oriented settlers, they were also interested in rocks, such as slate and granite, and the ores and minerals, such as copper, gold, and mica, for use and profit. The science of geology, however, developed slowly and was still in its infancy in the late 1700s. In fact, as late as 1776, the term "geology" had not yet been coined. At the turn of the eighteenth century, problems relating to geologic time, the relationships of fossils to specific strata, the classification of minerals, the causes and effects of volcanoes, and the mapping of geologic features were still being worked out. A number of concepts, such as the idea of glaciation, were still to come.[37]

By the 1820s the United States had expanded economically and advanced socially, educationally, and technologically to a point where the need for a greater understanding of nature and the nation's natural resources was recognized. The practical values of science were being discovered by a changing society. Federal and state governments were increasingly lobbied to support research. In this climate the need to gather information about the location, quantity, and value of economic resources and to evaluate opportunities for land and water development was increasingly acknowledged and promoted, especially related to public lands.[38] Geology was becoming a "new, exciting, and fashionable science" that was altering our ideas about the structure and history of the earth.[39] State governments began to employ geologists to survey mineral and agricultural potential and to determine the possible locations of dams, canals, and transportation routes. Some of these scientists were also broadly concerned with the natural history of the regions they surveyed, and in some instances, scientific teams were formed, consisting of geologists, botanists, entomologists, and scientists of other disciplines.

Charles Hitchcock, who was a key figure in surveys of Maine, New Hampshire, and Vermont, reviewed the utility of a geological survey in an 1861 report:

*In the first place, the geological survey of a state develops its
mineral wealth. . . . In the second place [it] points out . . .
where no valuable mines or quarries can be worked. . . . In
the third place . . . It furnishes data from which to judge the
character of the soil. . . . [and] In the fourth place, . . . [it]
encourages the study of the works of nature.*[40]

The state surveys conducted in New England added
much to our knowledge of the region's wilderness. Although the surveys were begun in the early to mid-1800s,
the geologists, especially in northern New England, were
able to give us many first views, for they penetrated areas
still wild and undeveloped. These scientists looked at the
landscape differently from the land surveyors and woods
cruisers. The way the geologists documented phenomena
such as caves, fossils, mountains, rock formations, lakes,
rivers, and streams was done in a manner heretofore un-
recorded.

When the first state-funded geological survey was
begun in Maine in 1836, field geology was in its romantic
period, carried out by rugged, educated outdoorsmen. Typ-
ically, beginning in early spring, members of a scientific
team would spread out over a state to inspect outcrops
and make other observations along the coast and rivers
where rocks were exposed by the action of wind and
water. They followed predetermined routes in bateaux and
birch bark canoes, using hired guides. They searched for
mines, examined the soil, looked for fossils, commented
on the effects of storms and fires, climbed hills and mountains to measure their heights, and recorded their findings
on maps and in journals. They endured black flies and
mosquitoes and ice and snow of late spring storms and
early fall freezes. They lost supplies in rapids and waterfalls. They hunted for food and encountered deer, caribou,
and bear.

Maine employed Charles T. Jackson to carry out its
first geological survey. A graduate of Harvard with a doc-
torate in medicine, Jackson followed his interests to become
a well-known geologist, completing surveys for Rhode Island and New Hampshire as well as for Maine.[41] He
worked three field seasons in Maine, from 1836 to 1838,
and issued a number of reports on the state's geology with

Charles T. Jackson leads an expedition into Maine's Mt. Katahdin region in 1837, one of New England's early state geological surveys. From Charles T. Jackson, *Atlas of Plates Illustrating the Geology of the State of Maine* (Boston, Mass.: Dutton and Wentworth, 1837).

comments also on forests and wildlife, including the "venomous" insects he encountered. He sprinkled his reports with thoughts about scientific, economic, and social concerns. He described graphically the difficulties encountered while engaged in this work. The following incident occurred on October 4, 1837, at Grindstone Falls on the East Branch of the Penobscot River:

While we were engaged in exploring the rocks, our men tried to shove the boat up the falls, but the violence of the current prevented their effecting their object, the boat being instantly filled and sunk in the attempt; while all our baggage and provisions that remained on board were swept off and carried down the stream. A scene of unwonted activity now ensued, in our endeavors to save our articles as they were rapidly borne down the foaming waters. The boat fortunately, was not much injured, and we succeeded in hauling it upon a rock, and bailed out the water, after which we gave chase to our lost articles, and succeeded in saving those that were most essential to our safety. The bread barrel, although scuttled, was but half full of bread, and floated down stream, with its opening uppermost, so that but little of it was injured. Our bucket of rice burst open, and was lost. The tea-kettle and other cooking apparatus sank in the river, and were fished up by a hook and line. The tent was found about a mile down the river, stretched across a rock. The map and charts were all soaked with water, so that it required almost as much labor and patience to unroll them, as the papyry of Herculaneum. Our spare boots and shoes were irrecoverably lost. Having rescued

*the most important articles from the water, we carried by
the falls, camped and dried our papers and provisions,
being thankful that no worse an accident had befallen us.
Fortunately we had taken the precautions to remove our
surveying instruments and blankets from the boat, before
the falls were attempted. Having kindled a camp fire and
dried ourselves, a storm of rain began to pour around us,
but our great fire was not easily damped, and we passed a
comfortable night beneath the shelter of a waterproof
tent.*[42]

During Jackson's last field season in Maine, the naturalist Ezekiel Holmes conducted a survey up the East
Branch of the Penobscot River to Matagamon Lake where
he portaged overland to explore the Aroostook River

Haskell Rock distinguishes one
of the many rapids Ezekial
Holmes and other scientists negotiated on the East Branch of
the Penobscot River during early
scientific expeditions into the
interior of northern Maine.

watershed. His wide-ranging observations and recom-
mendations, published in 1839, covered everything from
opportunities to build canals, dams, and roads to assess-
ing the value of rocks and minerals, forests, and soils. His
broad interests are illustrated in his discussion below of
the climate of that section of the country in which he speculated on the effect of lightning on the soil:

*The electrical state of the atmosphere must be very different
in such a dense forest, from what it is in an open country,
and how far this may influence the productions of the soil,
in hastening or retarding their growth and maturity, or vary
the results of agricultural operations, cannot, in the present*

state of science, be determined. . . . That electricity also, has
a powerful influence upon soils, is also beyond a doubt; but
by what laws, special or general, it acts, or how the various
effects which may be attributed to it, are brought about, is
yet almost wholly unknown to even the most scientific.[43]

Between 1830 and 1839, Edward Hitchcock, a professor and later president of the University of Massachusetts,
conducted a comprehensive survey of the geology of
Massachusetts. His four-part report, published in 1841,
covered the topics of economical geology, scenographical
geology, scientific geology, and elementary geology. His
treatment of scenographical geology dealt with, in his
words, "striking features of our scenery, that are the result
chiefly of geological changes, and which produce landscapes abounding in beauty and sublimity."[44] He described
scenic views, mountains, cliffs, valleys, coastal features,
rivers, gorges, waterfalls, and caverns, to name a few. Not
only were many of his descriptions vividly and elegantly
expressed, he engaged artists to accompany him on his excursions and their work resulted in fine drawings of many
of the features he selected for inclusion in his report.

In this same time period of the 1830s and 1840s, James
G. Percival completed a geological survey of Connecticut.
The bulk of his report dealt with the rocks and minerals of
the bedrock geology, but he included a brief section on
physical geography in which he commented on topography, drainage, scenery, and routes of communication. The
most extensive view, he wrote, "is from the summit of Ivy
Mountain, in Goshen, a short ridge, but little elevated
above the general level of the plateau. From that point, the
view extends, on the East, . . . commanding nearly the
whole extent of its Eastern main Trap range to the range
of Bolton Mountain and Haddam Hills . . . and on the W.
to the Catskill Mountains, while in a N.–S. direction, it extends from some of the hills near the Sound, to Saddle
Mountain, in the N. part of Berkshire County."[45]

During the last half of the eighteenth century the geologists conducted another round of surveys and once
again scoured untouched and little-visited areas of Maine,
Vermont, and New Hampshire. These, too, added to our
knowledge of the unaltered character of the New England

wilderness. Two scientific reports on the natural history and geology of Maine were published in 1861 and 1862, both authorized and funded by the Maine Legislature. These were headed by Ezekiel Holmes and Charles H. Hitchcock, who appointed teams of assistants with specialties in botany, entomology, and marine zoology. Holmes, in the preface of their first report, described the task they faced:

> The careful exploration and critical scientific examination of a tract of country covering more than thirty-one thousand square miles and a great part of those miles still covered with a dense forest which can be traversed advantageously only through its water channels by canoe or batteau, cannot be the work of a single summer nor a single year, however propitious may be the weather or however favorable all other attendant circumstances and requirements may be.[46]

Ezekiel Holmes also gives us insight into the motivations of these scientists in this following comment about Charles Hitchcock's discovery and collecting of unknown fossils on the shores of Telos Lake in the Allagash region of northern Maine:

> Professor H. [Hitchcock] arrived with his trophies from Lake Telos. He had found a large harvest of fossils, and some of them he exhibited triumphantly as "not being in the books," and therefore new to science. In these days of fratricidal warfare and bloody victories, it may seem small business to feel jubilant over a shell in a rock, and count the discovery of a hitherto unknown mollusk or defunct species of lizard or fish, a triumph; but, after all, there are no victories so really and lastingly beneficial to the world, and so productive of good to the brotherhood of man, as the sinless and noiseless triumphs of mind over matter, as manifested in the scientific developments of the mysteries of nature.[47]

The curiosity about the "mysteries of nature" these men shared was evident throughout their reports. Within the world they explored, there were no bounds for their interest. They reported on plants, mosquitoes and other animals, minerals, rock formations, rivers, the weather and climate, even meteors, as in the following:

> Black heavy masses of metallic iron called meteors have sometimes been seen to fall from the sky. . . . There is no value attached to such specimens other than what interest is

connected with them on account of their source. They must be fragments of other worlds, or each entire meteor may be a world by itself.[48]

While the Maine survey was being undertaken, Charles Hitchcock; his father, Edward; and brother, Edward, Jr., were also a part of another survey in Vermont, under the direction of Albert Hager. Their report appeared

Picturesque Willoughby Lake in northeastern Vermont was featured in a survey of the state's scenographical character. From Albert D. Hager, et al., *Report on the Geology of Vermont*, vol. 2 (Claremont, N.H.: The Claremont Manufacturing Company, 1861).

in 1861 in two volumes. A well illustrated section on the scenic character of the state is especially valuable in identifying and describing interesting features of landscape that had avoided alteration by the encroachment of settlement. In a descriptive passage about Willoughby Lake and the view from nearby Mount Pisgah, which the geologists climbed on August 16, 1860, we glimpse the dualism of values, still prevalent today, between wild nature and development. From the summit they were moved to remark on the "wild, picturesque, and beautiful" scene they saw. But they also saw to the south the "land of promise in Vermont, and the openings in the forest, and occasional farmhouses that dot the landscape, [giving] evidence that the work of developing this valuable portion of the State is already commenced."[49]

Later, Charles Hitchcock was again employed by the state of New Hampshire to conduct a geological survey of that state. This was a broad study, published in 1874 in three volumes. Not only did he include historic facts, topography, forests, animals, and areas of scenic interest, along with the state's geological character and economic potential, but he gave an intimate view of the unbroken "continuous primeval forest" in a section of northern New Hampshire that was, and still is, wild and remote—Coos County. And in so doing he also let us inside the mind of a scientist with a passion for his work, speaking eloquently about the joys and hardships experienced in exploring an undisturbed part of New England:

The difficulties encountered in traversing an unbroken forest are many and varied. At times the experience is most pleasurable, and, again, obstacles are encountered that are almost insurmountable. To-day we cross a beautiful lake. The clear, sparkling waters reflect the bright sunlight, while along its borders are mirrored the trees that stand in stately grandeur on its shores. To-morrow its waters roll in tumultuous wave, and the clouds rest almost on the bosom of the lake. To-day we traverse its shores, and walk upon the soft green moss that lies spread under the trees of evergreen like a carpet, so soft and elastic to the tread, while the rays of the sun, shining through the thick foliage, give a genial light, and the fresh green moss covers even the fallen trunks of the trees, as if to conceal every sign of decay;—and here, where a stream trickles over its mossy bed, one is carried away in elysian dreams, and forgets all else save that some enchantment binds him here. But to-morrow we become entangled in the undergrowth and shrubs, in what seems to be an illimitable morass; while the gently descending rain adheres to every spray of the foliage, and every touch brings down an additional shower to add to our discomfiture, until every thread of our apparel is saturated. . . . Then, retiring within our shelter, we steam until we are dry. So, day by day, the experience is ever new; but at no time is it an easy task to travel through the unbroken forests.[50]

Recorders of Wild Beasts

We know much about the early wildlife of the New England wilderness from several sources. The earliest evidence comes principally from the work of archaeologists, who looked for ancient clues left by the first human inhabitants in this region. They probed shell middens, investigated burial sites, and examined ledges containing rock art, or petroglyphs, and through their painstaking, time-consuming work, we enlarged our knowledge of the animal life that

Petroglyphs on an outcrop on the bank of the Kennebec River in central Maine. These stylistic representations of animals were carved by a Native American shaman before European settlement.

was part of the early wilderness. Coastal shell middens on the Maine coast, where Native People discarded shellfish remains after their meals, have yielded preserved bones of animals no longer here. These include the bones of the woodland caribou, now removed to the north. Here, too, are the skeletal parts of more unfortunate creatures—the extinct sea mink and the great auk.[51] Their demise leaves our world emptier and our ecosystems different than they might have been. Just how, we do not know. Artifacts from aboriginal cemeteries provide another source of evidence. The Boucher Cemetery in Highgate, Vermont, has yielded a number of clues, dating between 900 and 100 B.C. These include bones of the wild turkey and timber rattlesnake.[52] Today, neither of these creatures range over New England's landscape in the numbers they once did.

Of special interest are the petroglyphs. They are considered the work of shamans, Native American "medicine people," who were considered to possess the power of magic and especially the ability to be transformed into animals. Many of the figures that were carved into soft sandstone hundreds or thousands of years ago still survive today. Some appear to represent wild animals, but they are perhaps more symbolic of magical powers. Though archaeologists may question whether a wolflike canine pictured in a rock carving represents a wolf or a source of power, some petroglyphs readily identify animals, such as the coastal Maine moose depictions made between 1400 and 1600 A.D.[53] Another source of information from Native Americans lies in their oral tradition of storytelling.

Among the Wabanakis of Maine, the legends of Gluskap, their creator and hero, included many references to animals, for example, the eagle, wolverine, beaver, and moose. These suggest the presence of these animals in the early wilderness of New England.[54]

After the first contact by the Europeans, we have an increasingly detailed record of the wildlife here. Several explorers left us lists, such as James Rosier's in 1605, which included the following:

Fowles. Eagles [bald eagle], Swannes [whistling swan], Penguins [like the great auk], Mews [mew gull], and Turtledoves [passenger pigeon]; Beasts. Rain-Deere [caribou], Fallow Deere [white-tailed deer], Wolues [wolf], Polecats [skunk] and Beauer [beaver]; Fishes. Whales, Seales, Tortoises, and oisters.[55]

Following settlement, as the Europeans became more familiar with the wildlife, their descriptions became more detailed—some colored by the folklore of the time as in William Wood's description of a wildcat:

The Ounce or the wilde Cat, is as big as a mungrell dog, this creature is by nature feirce, and more dangerous to bee met withall than any other creature, not fearing eyther dogge or man; he useth to kill Deare, which hee thus effecteth: Knowing the Deares tracts, hee will lye lurking in long weedes, the Deare passing by he suddenly leapes upon his backe, from thence gets to his necke, and scratcheth out his throate; he hath likewise a devise to get Geese, for being much of the colour of a Goose he will place himselfe close by the water, holding up his bob taile, which is like a Goose necke; the Geese seeing his counterfet Goose, approach nigh to visit him, who with a suddaine jerke apprehends his mistrustlesse prey.[56]

The lynx, shown here in an early engraving, may have been the wildcat William Wood described as inhabiting southern New England in 1634. Illustration from Oliver Goldsmith, *A History of the Earth and Animated Nature* (n.p., 1774).

We also have other kinds of clues to the wildlife here at the time of European settlement. For example, records of the fur trade give us some insight, as we see in a letter dated June 24, 1633, in which a gentleman by the name of Ambrose Gibbins reported to his company, "I have delivered . . . 76 lbs and 4 ounses of beaver, 10 otters, 6 musquashes [muskrat] and on [one] martin more, that Captain Neale had 358 lb and ii ounses of beaver and otter, 17 martins, on black fox skin, on other fox skin, 3 racoon skins, 14 musquashes. . . ."[57] Records of this kind were often uncovered through the research of historians, who compiled and analyzed the information they collected to give us a more complete picture of the wildlife present in New England when the Europeans arrived.

Chroniclers of the Historic Wilderness

The work of historians is a crucial element in discovering New England's past wilderness. Historians of the time were a special breed of scholars, who compiled and chronicled information about the history and character of the New England landscape when the settlement of some areas was still underway—a time when fresh evidence still existed of the region's unaltered features and the populations of many plant and animal species were still intact.

Of special interest are the early state histories. They began to appear at the end of the eighteenth century and early nineteenth century. One of the earliest was the product of Jeremy Belknap, who published the first volume of his *History of New-Hampshire* in 1784. His third volume contains a geographical history with sketches of natural history. It provides a comprehensive view of New Hampshire's natural environment at the turn of the eighteenth century. He painted a picture not only of the state's physical character but of its effect on the senses.

In the same period, an early history of Vermont was written by Samuel Williams, of which a second edition was published in 1809. His treatise, *The Natural and Civil History of Vermont*, also includes a comprehensive picture of that state's environment less than twenty years after it had received statehood. His detailed descriptions range from insects to mountains and provide fascinating information, such as the following:

The following relation was given to me, by one of the earliest settlers at Cendon: "The number of pigeons [passenger pigeons] was immense. Twenty five nests were frequently to be found on one tree. The earth was covered with these beech trees, and with hemlocks, thus loaded with nests of pigeons. For an hundred acres together, the ground was covered with their dung, to the depth of two inches. Their noise in the evening was extremely troublesome, and so great that the traveller could not get any sleep, where their

Early historians chronicled the demise of the passenger pigeon. Illustration from S. G. Goodrich, *Recollections of a Lifetime*, vol. 1 (New York: Miller, Orton and Mulligan, 1857).

nests were thick. About an hour after sunrise, they rose in such numbers as to darken the air. When the young pigeons were grown to a considerable bigness, before they could readily fly, it was common for the settlers to cut down the trees and gather a horse load in a few minutes."[58]

Over a half-century later Zadock Thompson published his *Natural History of Vermont*. T. D. Seymour Bassett, writing of Zadock Thompson in the foreword to a reprint of the book, described him as a man close to nature, who grew up on a farm "cleared only a few years before he was born," who "saw nature little disturbed," and who "counseled conservation."[59] Thompson described many objects of nature that still exist today, including caves and swamps, and many that are now gone, such as the wolverine and wolf. He gave us yet another insight into the character of the northern New England wilderness before those of European descent arrived to settle.

In southern New England in 1797, the year after Zadock Thompson was born, a historian by the name of Benjamin Trumbull produced a brief description of Connecticut's natural history. In particular, he described the Connecticut River at the time and recounted its history, including the following: "The first discoveries made of this part of New-England were of its principal river and the fine meadows lying upon its banks." Trumbull credited the English with discovering the river, writing that "Mr. Winslow, the governor of Plimouth went to Connecticut in 1631 and discovered the river."[60]

An early history of Maine appeared in 1832, written by William D. Williamson. He took the attitude of other historians that "in perusing the History of a country, it is desirable to have a previous acquaintance with its geography and natural productions." But he was also careful to make it known that he was "exploring . . . difficult and untrodden grounds and that facts and fidelity without perfect description, are all which ought reasonably to be expected."[61] With that caveat, he proceeded to describe many aspects of Maine's natural history with brief descriptions of their human history as well. He, of course, was right about exploring untrodden paths: his 365 islands on the coast are in reality 3,000 or so. And, as we shall see later, we are fortunate today to still have a few relatively untrodden paths to take.

The Mapmakers

Historians were not the only ones compiling information of use to us today in obtaining a glimpse at the early wilderness; so were the statisticians and mapmakers. Moses Greenleaf was one of the first in Maine to document the state's geographical features. Almost ten years before the first geological survey was published, his 1829 map and book, *A Survey of the State of Maine, in Reference to its Geographical Features, Statistics, and Political Economy*, presented the most up-to-date description of the state at that time. Greenleaf not only conveyed what was known about the resources of Maine, but also showed what was not known. He raised the idea that the wealth and strength of Maine depends on having an adequate conception of the development opportunities the state's natural resources present and, further, that perhaps this conception at that time was very inadequate. He suggested that the time had arrived to commence an examination of the state's wildlands.[62] It is likely that his published survey exerted some influence in edging the state towards authorizing its first geological and natural history surveys. Indeed, Greenleaf's map was used by Charles Jackson during his first surveys.

Moses Greenleaf knew well the power of maps in conveying an understanding of the landscape. Maps have a profound influence on our conception of location, shape, and spatial relationships of features, and they provide a record of how our concepts of the land change and of the changes in the land, itself. Cartographers, or mapmakers, are among those who left a visible record of the wilderness character of New England. Among the earliest were Samuel de Champlain and John Smith, who produced maps in the early 1600s, and Willem Blaeu and John Seller, who produced exquisite maps of New England in 1635 and 1676, respectively. Many of these maps also included pictures of animal life, vegetation, and Native Peoples.[63] Much later, beginning in the early 1800s, the geologists employed in state survey work produced useful maps.

Artists of the Landscape

The geologists also included in their reports hundreds of illustrations of the features they studied. Many drew their own sketches, which were later redrawn by artists in the form of woodcuts and engravings. After the development of the camera, photographers sometimes accompanied them. The mid-1800s was also a time when landscape painters were creating a significant body of work. Many were collectively known as the Hudson River School, primarily because they painted in large studios at the mouth of the Hudson River in New York City, and many painted the scenery surrounding the Hudson River. These painters documented the character of our unspoiled wilderness. One of the most famous was Thomas Cole, credited with founding the school's philosophy. Among the many works he created is a famous 1836 painting of the Connecticut River Valley, *View from Mt. Holyoke, Northampton, Massachusetts, after a Thunderstorm (The Oxbow)*. There is the interesting possibility that Cole represented a link between science and art at the time through connections of one of his friends, Daniel Wadsworth, an amateur artist and geologist whose brother-in-law and close friend was Benjamin Silliman, a leading scientist of the time.[64]

There were many other noted artists, as well. One was the landscape painter Frederic E. Church, who painted Maine's Mt. Katahdin in the course of several trips to that mountainous area as early as the 1850s. In the 1870s, he took the Bangor photographer James C. Stodder with him, resulting in early photographs of the region. Other early artists rendered the still undisturbed wilderness scenery in finely detailed drawings. Isaac Sprague was one. He produced most of the dramatic mountain scenes in the 1848 book *Scenery of the White Mountains*, written by the botanist William Oakes.

Thus, we have seen that the original character of the New England wilderness was documented in many ways, from the early Native Peoples to present-day scientists. We have also seen that the land was not immune to human influence, and the attitudes of its new human inhabitants were such that they immediately sought to remove its wildness. But as we shall now see, the changes they brought about not only affected the land but influenced the very attitudes and values they held towards it.

Although the land the early Europeans came to was a dynamic one, the changes were almost imperceptible compared to what was to occur in a few hundred years. The assault against the wilderness began with the ax and plow, the gun and trap, and the seine and net. The wave of girdling, cutting, burning, plowing, trapping, hunting, and fishing moved from the coast inland and northward. By 1660 a band of settlements stretched along the coastline from the New York–Connecticut border to Penobscot Bay in Maine. Although slowed by the wars with the natives, 1760 saw settlements encompassing all of Connecticut and Rhode Island and most of Massachusetts, except the northern Berkshires. By 1820 settlements had swept through all of Vermont and most of New Hampshire and had moved northward to central Maine. Large portions of northern Maine, however, were never settled due to the sales of large blocks of public land by the state land agent to private owners who have since managed their lands for timber harvesting.

What was the effect of this invasion on the New England wilderness? Most noticeable was the removal of the forests, which reached its greatest extent between 1820 and 1865. By 1860, for example, some uplands in many hill towns of central New England were only 25 percent forested.[65] Maine was an exception because extensive harvesting did not begin in that state until the late 1700s. By

Changes in Land and Mind

The cutting of trees began in earnest at the time of settlement, with deforestation reaching its height in New England between 1820 and 1865. Illustration from John S. Springer, *Forest Life and Forest Trees* (New York: Harper and Brothers, 1851).

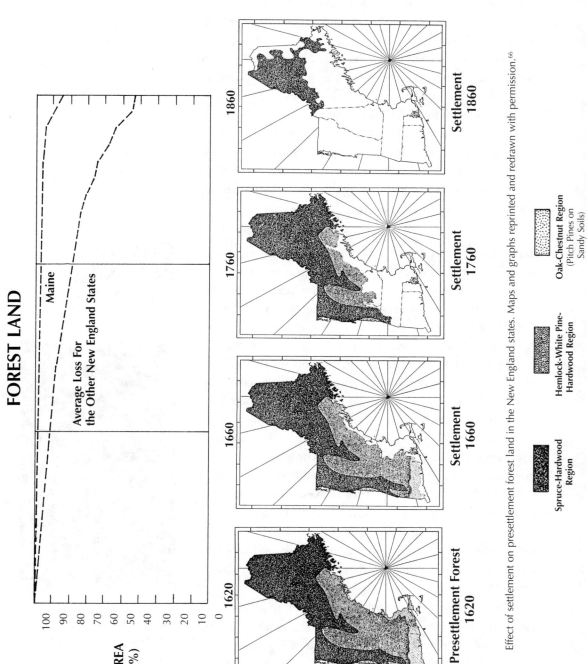

Effect of settlement on presettlement forest land in the New England states. Maps and graphs reprinted and redrawn with permission.[66]

1880 only 40 percent of Massachusetts' forests remained, 27 percent of Connecticut's, 34 percent of Rhode Island's, 50 percent of New Hampshire's, and 74 percent of Maine's.[67] A study of census records by Roland M. Harper graphs the trend and shows similar percentages for 1880.[68] Lamenting this loss of forest, Henry David Thoreau wrote in the mid-1800s, "We shall all be obliged to let our beards grow at least if only to hide the nakedness of the land and make a sylvan appearance."[69]

The clearing of the forest was devastating to normal ecological processes. As Charles F. Carroll pointed out, "when trees are destroyed en masse . . . the severe and sudden changes affect all living things in the forest. Shade-loving plants die, food chains are interrupted, birds and [other] animals migrate, and new microbes and insects invade. The relation of sun, land, vegetation, and fauna is drastically changed, and in the struggle for existence only those things that can adapt to the new environment will survive."[70] Additionally, the opening of the ground to the sun and winds creates problems of wider impact. In winter the exposed land freezes to deeper levels, and in spring, without a forest canopy to retain the blanket of snow for a longer period of time and to allow a slower warming, the snow melts more rapidly. Because the ground is still frozen and the trees that normally slow the flow of runoff are now removed, streams and rivers are more likely to overflow their banks, and destructive flooding can occur. Timothy Dwight, who traveled extensively throughout New England in the late 1700s and early 1800s when he was president of Yale University, wrote that the Connecticut River was "often fuller than it probably ever was, before the country above was cleared of its forests: the snows in open ground melting more suddenly, and forming much greater freshets, than in forested ground."[71]

When the rivers and streams surged with unchecked pulses of water, widespread erosion of the soil occurred on the cutover land. On the cleared agricultural land, plowing reduced the soil's ground cover, and cattle grazing compacted the soil and close-cropped the plants, further reducing the soil's water-holding capacity. Soil particles and nutrients were washed away, and over time huge quantities of sediments were carried by streams and rivers into ponds and lakes. This result has been borne out by researchers who have found that sedimentation rates increase significantly in ponds after human settlement occurs in their watersheds.[72]

The denuding of the landscape, followed by cycles of reforestation and harvesting, turned the unbroken wilderness into a patchwork of even-aged stands of trees and other managed communities, such as blueberry barrens, pine plantations, and cultivated fields. Surprisingly, there are few studies linking the effect of this removal of New England's wilderness on the healthy reproduction of trees, shrubs, and herbaceous plants. One Connecticut study in 1913 suggested that the following shrubs occur most often in forest areas that have never been cleared: common witch-hazel, mountain laurel, alternate-leaf dogwood, striped maple, hobblebush, and American yew.[73] However, it still remains unclear how many plants may have been lost due to the effects of clearing. We do know, for example, that in Massachusetts a total of 50 native species of plants are now extirpated (no longer living within the state's borders) and 116 are endangered in the state.[74] There are likely many causes that we still do not fully understand, such as the role of air-borne pollutants.

More information is available about the loss of some animal species. Loss of habitat, unregulated hunting and trapping, and overfishing have removed forever six animals from Massachusetts and extirpated eleven others. Those now extinct are the eastern elk, sea mink, heath hen, great auk, passenger pigeon, and Labrador duck. Among those extirpated are the mountain lion, lynx, wolverine, and timber wolf. Seven animals, including six whales, five birds, six reptiles, and one fish are on the Federal Endangered and Threatened Species List. The beaver and wild turkey are examples of the few species that have returned to Massachusetts.

The loss of even one species is a sobering thought. Fortunately, the realization that something is rare or becoming so moves people to become concerned and protective. This happened in the case of our diminishing wilderness, according to Roderick Nash, a leading wilderness historian, who pointed out that the simple scarcity theory of value underlies the modern wilderness philosophy that civilization needs wilderness and must protect it.[75]

Concern for the wilderness first appeared among the Puritan leaders—not for the wilderness per se but for the contradiction with the Puritan ethic against greed. Roger Williams worried about the "depraved appetite after the . . . great portion of land, land in this wilderness."[76] This, however, did not stop the relentless clearing of the landscape. Even so, the settlers were not unaware of the inexhaustibility of the supply of natural resources. As early as 1698, they began to pass laws against cutting trees on private and common land. By the early 1700s restrictions in Massachusetts and New Hampshire applied to mining as well as to timber. Laws were also extended to wildlife. A deer season was implemented in New Hampshire in 1741, and in 1755 the state passed laws to protect alewife and herring runs.[77]

Concerns were also afoot in the settlements for other than the loss of material resources. Other values were beginning to creep into the American mind. In the late 1700s and early 1800s, the botanists John and William Bartram were among the first of many artists and writers who espoused the romantic notion that wild nature was beautiful and awe inspiring; in short, it was sublime. Their contemporary, the painter George Catlin, called for the establishment of "a nation's Park containing man and beast, in all the wild and freshness of their nature's beauty!"[78] Some fifty years later Catlin's concern for the preservation of wildness found a supporter, Henry David Thoreau, who wrote: "To preserve wild animals implies generally the creation of a forest for them to dwell in or resort to."[79] Thoreau was one of the transcendentalists, about whom the geographer Michael Williams commented in an insightful comparison: "Unlike the Puritan pioneers who thought that morality stopped on the edge of the clearing, the transcendentalists thought it began there, for man was inherently good not evil and perfection could be maximized on entering the forests."[80]

Still, attitudes changed slowly, as Alexis de Tocqueville observed during his trip to America in the early 1800s:

Man gets accustomed to everything. He gets used to every sight. . . . [He] fells the forests and drains the marshes. . . . The wilds become villages, and the villages towns. The American . . . does not see anything astonishing in all this. This incredible destruction, this even more surprising growth, seem to him the usual progress of things in this world. He gets accustomed to it as to the unalterable order of nature.[81]

The voices for wilderness, however, continued to grow in number and, perhaps more notably, in clarity and forcefulness. One was the Vermonter, George Perkins Marsh, who, in the 1874 edition of *Man and Nature* recognized the interrelationships between nature and people. He argued that "a large and easily accessible region should remain, as far as possible, in its primitive condition."[82] By 1890 appreciation and concern for our remaining wilderness was growing into a national movement, and the public was hearing from one of the most influential voices of the time, John Muir. An ardent wilderness hiker, writer, and advocate as well as one of the founders of the Sierra Club, Muir devoted his life to the cause of wilderness preservation and made a powerful presence during the late 1800s and early 1900s. He once wrote, "There is a love of wild nature in everybody, an ancient mother-love showing itself whether recognized or not and however covered by cares and duties."[83]

Through the first half of the twentieth century the cause of wilderness was taken up and advanced by others, including Aldo Leopold, Bob Marshall, Siguard Olson, Howard Zahniser, and David Brower. In 1935 the Wilderness Society was formed for the purpose of protecting wilderness and stimulating appreciation for its emotional, intellectual, and scientific values. Aldo Leopold, through a series of eloquent essays, advanced the idea of a land ethic, an ecological conscience that provides to this day a philosophical statement for wilderness preservation and our conduct with respect to the rest of nature.[84]

As a result of these efforts, the high point of the century regarding preservation of the American wilderness took place in the Rose Garden of the White House on September 3, 1964, when President Lyndon B. Johnson signed the Wilderness Act into law. On that day we became the first country ever to make the preservation of wilderness a national policy. Wilderness was now defined as an area where the earth and its community of life are "untrammeled" by humans, where we are only visitors who do not remain. The act went on to further define wilderness as:

an area of undeveloped Federal land retaining its primeval character and influence, without permanent improvements or human habitation, which is protected and managed so as to preserve its natural conditions and which (1) generally appears to have been affected primarily by the forces of nature, with the imprint of man's work substantially unnoticeable; (2) has outstanding opportunities for solitude or a primitive and unconfined type of recreation; (3) has at least five thousand acres of land or is of sufficient size as to make practicable its preservation and use in an unimpaired condition; and (4) may also contain ecological, geological, or other features of scientific, educational, scenic, or historical value."[85]

One of the distinct achievements of the Wilderness Act was a definition of wilderness as a place—a physical entity that we could identify and so protect. As a further clarification of this definition, Joan Elbers wrote that there is implied "the presence of wild animals and plants carrying out their ecological roles within an ecosystem that maintains itself or undergoes natural succession without human control."[86]

We had come a long way from Josselyn's time when wilderness was considered a threat, a source of evil, and a wasteland to be removed if settlement and prosperity were to occur. We were beginning to find that what we were trying to destroy was part of ourselves—that we are, indeed, deeply connected, not only physically but psychologically, to a natural world that has evolved and works in ways that still elude our complete understanding. Perhaps wilderness preservation was our acknowledgement of this lack of understanding, and perhaps, more significantly, it was a collective sign of a humbler attitude toward nature—a recognition that we are not complete masters of our environment.

The Wilderness Act was a public expression of a different set of values from those brought to this land by those early Europeans centuries before, but clearly the conditions we face today do require a different set of values if we are to have a relationship with the rest of nature that will sustain our existence on this earth. And as we look for symbols of these new values, what could be more fitting than areas of wilderness we have consciously preserved, some of which contain remnants that have survived the changes we have brought to the New England landscape.

ISLANDS OF WILDERNESS

When John Josselyn observed the wilderness of the coast of Maine in 1638, little did he—or any European, for that matter—know that 1.9 billion acres of unbroken wild land stretched across a vast continent behind that eastern shore. In fact, it was a common idea then that the land Josselyn saw was an island. Indeed, Josselyn wrote:

New England is . . . judged to be an island, surrounded on the North with the spacious River of Canada [St. Lawrence River], on the South with Mahegan or Hudsons River, having their rise, as it is thought; from two great lakes not far off one another, the Sea lyes East and South from the land.[87]

An island New England is not, but the wilderness Josselyn saw is now reduced to "islands" in a sea of human development. Today, only a tiny fraction of roadless wilderness remains in our six New England states. Of that only fragments have survived relatively untouched—places where we may experience something of what the early explorers and settlers knew and discover for ourselves the naturalness and wildness of early New England. But development continues to threaten even those few fragile remnants that are left. Fortunately sixteen wilderness areas under public ownership in New England have been rescued from the relentless, increasing pressure of development humans have exerted on the landscape. Fourteen are federally owned areas, now protected by the Wilderness Act.

Two others, under state ownership in Maine, are also included among the sixteen because they represent significant acreage and are specifically managed to maintain wilderness character in perpetuity while allowing controlled outdoor recreation. Baxter State Park is one of the two and is the largest wilderness area in New England, containing 173,000 acres managed under a "forever wild" mandate. The other state-owned area in Maine is the Allagash Wilderness Waterway, which also carries a federal designation as a National Wild and Scenic River. It consists of 23,000 publicly owned acres of land surrounding the river and its headwaters in a narrow 100-mile-long corridor. In addition, there are three federal wilderness areas in Maine: the Caribou–Speckled Mountain Wilderness in the White Mountain National Forest and two in the Moosehorn National Wildlife Refuge. The other federally designated wilderness areas in New England are Great Gulf, Pemigewasset, Presidential Range–Dry River, and Sandwich Range in New Hampshire; Big Branch, Breadloaf, Bristol Cliffs, George D. Aiken, Lye Brook, and Peru Peak in Vermont; and North and South Monomoy Islands in the Monomoy National Wildlife Refuge in Massachusetts.

Altogether the sixteen areas cover about 360,000 acres, accounting for less than one percent of the total 42,629,120 acres in New England. However, by their very

Bristol Cliffs Wilderness in Vermont is one of six federally designated wilderness areas in the Green Mountain National Forest.

existence, they provide proof that citizens do have the will to create what Aldo Leopold termed "blank spots" on the map. Within each perhaps we can capture the mystery of a wilderness past. Although their history includes human use, they have hidden pockets of New England's original nature that have escaped the ax, plow, and other implements of the utilitarian mind. Here perhaps we can experience firsthand what the Native Americans and Europeans saw. Here we can discover some of what these wildlands can tell us about the land of John Josselyn's time, and, perhaps more importantly, here we can find values only wilderness can give us.

Baxter State Park, Maine

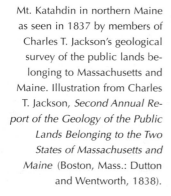

The Indines say that this Hill is the highest in the Country. . . . It is curious to see—Elevated above a rude mass of Rocke large Mountains—So Lofty a pyramid.

—Joseph Chadwick, 1764[88]

Captain Joseph Chadwick, a surveyor for the General Court of Massachusetts, made the first known recorded sighting of Satinhungemoss Hill, now called Mt. Katahdin—the centerpiece of New England's largest protected wilderness area, Baxter State Park. When I first sighted Katahdin in 1962, on my way to the Allagash River, I didn't realize that I was privileged to be provided a view not unlike Chadwick's of two hundred years earlier nor did I appreciate

Mt. Katahdin in northern Maine as seen in 1837 by members of Charles T. Jackson's geological survey of the public lands belonging to Massachusetts and Maine. Illustration from Charles T. Jackson, *Second Annual Report of the Geology of the Public Lands Belonging to the Two States of Massachusetts and Maine* (Boston, Mass.: Dutton and Wentworth, 1838).

how rare an opportunity I had to see firsthand, so untouched, one of New England's highest mountains. It was only after I had traveled to view the high mountains of New England's other states that I realized Katahdin was a singular mountain, distinguished by an absence of bristling antennas, towers, and buildings and without the scars of roads, ski trails, and gondola pathways.

Credit for the preservation of the Katahdin wilderness goes to one man, Percival Baxter. With this one gift to Maine, Baxter, a former governor of the state, demonstrated the value of bequesting wild land for the benefit of future generations. When he commenced fulfilling a dream that had formed in his mind by the year 1917, it took him from 1931 to 1963 to acquire the land and transfer it to the protective custody of the state. He required most of the land to be managed under the concept of "forever wild." Because of his vision and mandate, I and countless others are now able to make periodic visits to this park and see most of its 200,000 acres relatively unchanged, except for the occurrence of natural events. For those unable to do so, satisfaction may be gained from the knowledge that a part of our wilderness still remains. For all of us, there is in this vast, wild land the opportunity to rediscover qualities and features of an original Katahdin wilderness and relive the impressions of those who described them first.

It is not known whether Joseph Chadwick actually ascended Katahdin, but we do know that Charles Turner, Jr., did in 1804. He canoed up the West Branch of the Penobscot and probably followed what is now the Hunt Trail. I didn't realize at the time that the route I first followed in 1969 was the same route Turner used for his trip to the top. Unlike Turner's successful expedition, my first attempt up the mountain was thwarted by bad weather. We were above the tree line when tentacles of dark rain clouds dragged over the ridge above and dangled threateningly over us. I developed an instant respect for mountain weather, but when we turned to go back down and I looked out over the cloud-shadowed Maine landscape and saw hundreds of lakes, mirroring the shafts of sunlight squeezing through the stormy sky, I knew that I would be back.

My first experience was not uncommon in the history of Katahdin mountain climbing. The Reverend Joseph Blake's first attempt up the mountain in 1836 was also unsuccessful due to wind, mist, and a cold rain. Twenty years later he succeeded, as I did also on my second attempt. Blake left us with the following description of the Katahdin wilderness that he saw from the mountaintop:

Now standing on the summit, let us look around. But I cannot describe the prospect, nor tell how greatly we enjoyed it.

Not more extensive, nor more sublime, but far more beautiful is it than the view from Mount Washington. What a wonderful panorama of woods and mountains, lakes and streams!

"The eye is not satisfied with seeing." You look on a world of woods in every direction, with here and there a mountain or a mountain range lifting itself up, rivers and brooks winding through the forests shining like strings of pearls or ribbons of glass in the sunlight, and on all sides lakes and lakelets, one for every day of the year, many of them dotted with islands, reposing in the embrace of the woods. You would look until it is daguerieotyped [sic] within you, a picture that will not fade, nor you tire of gazing upon it while life shall last.

Most interesting is the mountain itself. It stands comparatively alone, an immense mass of white granite crowned with red thrown up through the overlying rocks. When? Who can tell? Not crumpled, but split into fragments of all sizes, thrown up five thousand or more feet above the sea, by that mighty force that "setteth fast the mountains." What among the White Hills has power like that basin to hush and awe the heart, whether you look down into its depths, or from within it lift your eyes three thousand feet to the summit of those almost perpendicular walls![89]

The South Basin, to which the Reverend Blake referred, is, indeed, a feature to inspire humbleness and awe, and to look into it is to look into the heart of the mountain. I remember first seeing it from the Knife Edge, as did Blake 120 years before, and being fearfully transfixed on the thin rim of this bowl—a feeling described by the geologist Charles Hitchcock in the report of his 1861 survey expedition:

Having gained the top [of Chimney Peak] . . . We travelled at least three-fourths of a mile along a very narrow ridge, whose top was only a foot wide, while on both sides of us we could look down for 3,000 feet over precipices too steep to be descended with safety. So awe-inspiring was the sight that some of the party crawled upon their hands and knees over a large part of the distance. We never imagined that in our New England mountains, localities could be found so nearly resembling the peaks and ridges of the Andes.[90]

The Reverend Blake on a return trip across this narrow mountain ridge described a similar feeling: "It is a dizzy height, a fearful way to one who has no company. There is little danger of being precipitated into the depth

Mt. Katahdin's Knife Edge is well known for its ability to weaken knees and fearfully transfix some of its hardiest climbers.

below. I had passed over it once, why could I not pass over it again? And yet a feeling of awe which I know not how to describe held fast to my heart as if it would still its beating."[91]

Other features here impart a feeling of wildness. Once, while traversing the Tableland and the Northwest Plateau, I left the trail and walked a short distance west

Klondike Pond, bounded by mountains of the Katahdin Range, drains into the mysterious, little-explored Klondike, a peat bog of virgin spruce seen here in the distance.

and peered over the edge. Below me I gazed into the clear waters of Klondike Pond, second only in elevation to Speck Pond in the Mahoosuc Mountains. Its height, however, is not its main attraction: it's the Klondike, an intriguing, mile-square peatland of virgin black spruce lying a thousand feet below in a remote, difficult to access, mysterious, and little-explored valley into which the pond drains.

The first sighting of the Klondike by non-native people was probably in 1825 by Joseph Norris, Sr., and his son who were employed by the Maine Boundary Commission to run an east–west base line across Maine from a monument on the St. Croix River. Such a line would provide a reference for surveying Maine's unsettled wildlands to the north. On November 10, with winter fast approaching, they arrived on the edge of the Northwest Basin and saw before them ledges and cliffs dropping perpendicular to the basin's floor twelve hundred feet below. Beyond they saw the almost impenetrable tangle of dense sub-alpine spruce–fir forest. At this point they gave up and, remarkably, considering the lateness of the season, were able to make their way over Baxter Peak and down Abol Slide and out.[92]

Myron Avery, writing in *The Maine Naturalist* in 1930, described the Klondike and his trip into it the previous year via Wassataquoik Stream:

The Klondike is the least known of the many features of Katahdin. It is shrouded in an atmosphere of mystery. Its very name provokes interest. A quarter of a century ago it was the moose-hunting grounds of a famous Penobscot Indian, Joe Francis. He called it his Klondike because of its isolation and loneliness, suggesting the Alaskan Klondike. . . .

The eastern wall of the Klondike is formed by spurs from Fort Mountain and from the Northwest Plateau, perhaps originally a continuous ridge through which the Middle Branch cut its way. From the brook bed the dark wooded slopes rise steeply, shutting out the sun and creating an atmosphere of intense wildness and loneliness. For the first hour we climbed over enormous boulders in the brook, where a misstep would mean a severe fall. Intermittently we would try to make our way along the slope above the brook, only to be driven back to the boulders. Nowhere does the Wassataquoik have distinct falls. For the first hour's travel that morning the stream cascaded over and sometimes around the enormous granite boulders that choked its bed. Then we passed beyond these spurs and the valley widened. We waded knee-deep on gravel in the cold waters of the brook, quite free from boulders.

At the end of the second hour we came to an open bog. Here the brook forked and became so overhung as to prevent further travel in its bed. We crossed the open spruce bog with its scattered growth of tamarack and spruce and in a short time found ourselves in the inevitable spruce and fir, not quite scrub but surely a dense tangle. Soon we came to windfalls and the timber increased in size. At

10:30 A.M. we had reached the low divide between the Owl and Barren.[93]

More recently, in 1984, a team of botanists led by Donald Hudson, Jr., bushwacked from Mt. Coe into the Klondike to describe its vegetation and other features of its natural history. In their report, they noted:

The reference to the Canadian and Alaskan wilderness is a compelling epithet, and fits this wild stretch of forest in all respects. Botanists, zoologists and geologists have been intrigued by the potential for exciting discovery in such a remote and unknown place, luring the interested party by lying so close at hand—yet out of touch.[94]

A relatively short distance from my viewpoint overlooking Klondike Pond and over the west rim of the Northwest Plateau, the trail plunges steeply into the Northwest Basin. This remote, glacial cirque and the Klondike were described by two experienced outdoor enthusiasts and authors as "two of the loneliest and most interesting pieces of landscape in New England."[95] Over the years, I have stayed two nights in the Northwest Basin, enclosed on three sides by high rock walls and separated by high mountains and distances measured in miles from the nearest habitation. This place delivers the strongest feeling of remoteness of any other place I've visited in New England. It's the silence that one notices most. It is here that one can truly capture the isolation undoubtedly felt by Joseph Norris and his son when they first looked down into this basin.

Of course, many places in this vast park allow an authentic feeling of our early wilderness to be captured. My trips have brought me into the valleys of the Wassataquoik lakes where the rare blue-backed trout survives and to Green Falls, so named because of the large moss-covered boulders over which a small mountain stream flows. The trails have also led me through forests of old-growth, virgin trees and past spectacular geologic features. I have visited pockets harboring rare plants, such as the male fern, whose only location in Maine seems to be here in this park. I have not discovered all the secrets of this wilderness nor will any individual in our limited lifetimes. I find satisfaction in just knowing that some areas and objects exist, though I may never see them, such as the oldest documented red spruce tree in Maine, aged at 423 years—a tree that began its life in 1569 when exploration of the New England coastline was still in its infancy.[96]

The story of the preservation of this largest of New England's protected wilderness areas is an inspiration for all who wish to safeguard a natural legacy.[97] It took Governor Percival Baxter over thirty years to acquire the more than 200,000 acres that he deeded to the state of Maine. Thanks to his vision, persistence, wealth, magnanimity, and longevity, he showed what is possible. The number of visitors and, especially, the number turned away because of a lack of room show how much we need and value areas such as this.

We could have easily lost the opportunity to preserve and protect this wilderness area since a popular appreciation of wilderness in our culture is a relatively recent phenomenon, occurring within the twentieth century. One has only to read the 1861 state geological report by Charles Hitchcock to gain some insight into the historic vulnerability of this area. It was the eminent geologist's view that "if a good carriage road could be built from the Hunt farm to Chimney Pond in the Basin, and a good foot or bridle path from there to the summit, an immense number of visitors would be attracted to Mt. Katahdin, especially if a Hotel should be built at Chimney Pond, the most romantic spot for a dwelling-house in the whole State."[98]

For those of us who appreciate the remote wildness of this basin, Hitchcock's view is a sobering reminder of what it might have been. I will remain forever indebted to Governor Percival Baxter, as Baxter State Park will remain forever wild.

The Allagash Wilderness Waterway, Maine

At the falls the . . . rock [is] gullied full of deep potholes. . . . the river is divided by a small island, on each side of which it pitches over the rough slate rocks 25 feet nearly perpendicularly. The banks just below are precipitous, and of about the same height. The Country in the vicinity has been burnt over, and the rough ledges of slate appear every

where above the soil. Through these the portage extends on the southern side.

—James T. Hodge, 1838[99]

The sound of this falls, now called Allagash Falls rather than the Grand Falls of Hodge's time, was my first experience with them. I heard them some three miles away on an approach during a windy, sunny morning in early July

Allagash Falls, an outstanding natural feature in Maine's Allagash Wilderness Waterway, continues to awe visitors with its power and scenic beauty.

1962. The party I was with was nearing the end of a ten-day trip beginning at Telos Lake some eighty miles upstream. Since that time, I have made numerous canoe trips in this wild and scenic river system. Today, its shorelands are protected by state ownership and are managed to maximize their wilderness character, though public ownership extends only an average of five hundred feet from the high water mark.

Like so many of our protected wilderness areas, we owe it to luck that some proposed development didn't occur to alter its wild character severely and irreversibly. Almost a hundred years ago Maine's forest commissioner suggested in his annual report that

a dam could be built at the head of the falls twelve feet high and about 100 feet long on solid ledge. This would increase the available head to forty-five feet. Above the falls the river is quite rapid, then almost dead water for three miles. It is quite wide and filled with islands. It can be flowed several feet and would make a secure storage for many millions of logs. A canal could be cut through the ledge for a distance of about 500 feet, or the water could be conveyed in pen-

stocks to the lower basin, or better still mills could be located near the head of the falls and the logs taken from the pond above. . . . There is little doubt that the Allagash falls when fully developed will furnish the best water power in the whole county of Aroostook.[100]

This wasn't the only time a vision of hydropower would threaten the waterway. In the 1970s, a strong case was made for building a dam on the St. John River that would inundate a large area of the river. Fortunately, this, too, was averted.

The Allagash Wilderness Waterway provides an avenue nearly one hundred miles long through the north woods of Maine. Here one can experience again and again, without the unexpected intrusion of development, some of the wildness the geologist James Hodge and others first saw. Along its course one has the opportunity to encounter a semblance of the natural diversity of the north woods as it once was—the intimate streams, unbroken shorelines, undisturbed marshes and peatlands, outcrops of fossils and bedrock, falls and rapids, old forests, and thick clouds of blackflies and mosquitoes in spring. Other animal life of Hodge's time, rare today, has been reported in recent years: a wolf on Long Pond in the winter of 1972, a mountain lion in the lower river region in 1994, a woodland caribou on Chamberlain Lake in 1990—the last of an unsuccessful reintroduction effort.[101] My wife and I tentatively identified a lynx on a road near Telos Lake in 1993. Only the wolverine has not appeared in reports, though it is probable that it was once present here.

Often, when I have entered the waterway, I have come by way of upper Allagash Stream and down into Allagash Lake, a remote and beautiful body of water with no road access and restrictions on motorized travel. The lake is undammed and ledges along its forested shoreline display the marks of naturally fluctuating water levels. Near the outlet of the lake, I never cease to marvel at the beaches of dark gray, glaciated slate that emerge ramplike along the lakeshore. Here one can still share the same fascination for these ledges that Oliver White expressed in 1862:

Just south of the outlet . . . and forming the southern shore of this cove is perhaps the finest exhibition of the smooth-

Glaciated slate ledges, backed by the unbroken forested shoreline of Allagash Lake, appear today much as they did to Oliver White when he described them in 1862.

ing striating effect of the drift movement easily found. It consists of a surface shelving down under water at an angle of 12°, 500 feet long and over 50 feet wide, as smooth and regular as a floor, and covered with fine scratches [from the effect of glacial movement] running 50° west.[102]

Allagash Stream below the lake flows swiftly over a rocky, ledgy bed between dense growths of overhanging trees and shrubs. Halfway, on its five-mile course to Chamberlain Lake, it is interrupted by Little Round Pond and Little Allagash Falls. I first visited this picturesque, remote falls in 1965, following Oliver White's route upstream from Chamberlain Lake and took satisfaction that little had changed, including the difficulty of the trip as White described it:

June 3d, . . . we rowed directly for the upper end of the lake [Chamberlain], and entering upon Alleguash River soon began to discover ledges. . . . For nearly three miles these slate ledges are almost continuous . . . producing a series of very difficult rapids, and in three places a perpendicular descent of from two to six feet. . . . Half way up from Chamberlain lake, we came to the Grand falls [today, Little Allagash Falls], where the water descends twenty feet over a ledge. . . . To the east of the falls the drift has been washed away, exposing a surface beautifully levelled and striated, the scratches having a direction of north 50° west.[103]

Below Allagash Stream lie a series of large lakes. In 1938 when Hodges first surveyed the area these were drained totally by the Allagash River, but four years later a drainage area was dug out at the end of Telos Lake and dams installed on Telos and Chamberlain Lakes to divert some of the flow down the East Branch of the Penobscot

River. The water level was, thus, raised, so when Henry David Thoreau came into Chamberlain in 1857, he saw a lake somewhat larger than that seen by Hodges in 1838 and similar to my view of it a hundred years later.

Thoreau entered the Allagash by way of Mud Pond Carry. If he hadn't become separated from his guide and taken a wrong turn, he would have found Mud Pond in a similar condition as I did in 1976—only inches deep, filled with brown ooze, and offering little clearance for the draft of a canoe. It hasn't changed much since Hodge came into the Allagash by the same route in 1838. He wrote that, "Mud Lake, as its name indicates is low and muddy."[104] As a result, he was forced to portage his bateau almost a quarter of a mile around the pond to a point near the shallow outlet at Mud Brook. Today, because of the dams, Mud Brook is only a quarter of a mile long instead of the two-mile length to Chamberlain Lake that Hodge described:

The outlet of Mud Pond . . . down which we passed on the 23rd, is very small and shallow for the first mile, almost filled with rounded boulders. . . . Its banks abound with juniper and hackmetack, and rise the height of small hills. For the last mile above Chamberlain Lake, the stream is easily navigated.[105]

Some natural features that these early visitors saw remain relatively unchanged around the Allagash lakes. Fossils still may be found imbedded in the outcrops on the shore of Telos Lake. Ezekiel Holmes, in his 1861 report, wrote, "an examination of some of the ledges on different parts of the shores of this lake led to the discovery of very interesting fossils. . . ."[106] At one location near the fossils, red pine still grow on a dry, south-facing slope where, on Wednesday, July 29, 1857, Thoreau noted that "We landed on a rocky point on the northeast side, to look at some Red Pines, the first we had noticed."[107] I first viewed these pines on a cold, snowy January day, and they looked stark and grim against the deep snow of the hillside. High overhead, the sun made a bright, haloed spot in the clouds, casting a mystical spell of light on the snow-covered lake. When I returned the next summer, the bark of the trees was the brightly reddish color that undoubtedly attracted Thoreau.

Another feature upon which one can depend to be ever present in this lakes region of the waterway is the backdrop offered by the Katahdin range. It dominates the scenery and creates a remote, wild feeling, projecting many moods, depending on the position of the sun, the weather, and one's location. It was one of the first observations Thoreau made when he awoke after his first night on the shore of Chamberlain Lake: "It was a pleasant sunrise, and we had a view of the mountains in the southeast. Ktaadn appeared about southeast by south."[108]

Here in the Allagash Waterway, as in many other of our protected wilderness areas, pockets of forests are still undisturbed, containing trees alive when the first timber cruisers surveyed the region. One is the Eagle Lake Old-Growth White Pine Stand. It was first surveyed by the Critical Areas Program of the Maine State Planning Office in 1978. It is possible that some of these very pines may have been included among those Hodge referred to in his 1838 report: "Our route was through dead water, mostly lakes. The country continues low, and scarcely any hills are to be seen. Pine timber is abundant and large, mixed with spruce, fir, maple, &c."[109] It is more certain, however, that Thoreau passed by them on his way to Pillsbury Island, his farthest point north in 1857.

Today, some of the pines in the Eagle Lake stand are more than 3 feet in diameter at breast height and over 130 feet tall.[110] On two occasions I explored the forest beneath these pines—both during times when a nearby bald eagle's nest was inactive and probably when an alternative nest was being used. Only from one vantage point was I able to see the giant nest of sticks beneath the shaggy top of one of the old pines. This is one of New England's northernmost nesting sites for bald eagles. As I walked in this forest, I came across places where the understory is open, and I felt the humbling forces of age and size associated with the old trees. In other places the remains of trees lie on the forest floor—prostrate and decaying—overcome by age and wind, soon to disappear beneath the rising tide of young trees and shrubs responding to the sunlight now let in. I had a difficult time making my way through the forest in those places, but here and there a giant stood

The author inspects a giant white maple in an old-growth forest near Eagle Lake in the Allagash Wilderness Waterway. Some of Maine's largest white pines are also located in this stand and were growing here when Henry David Thoreau passed by in 1857.

defiantly over the jumbled mass of roots, trunks, and limbs. This mixture of young and old, of openness and closeness, of shade and light is characteristic, I learned again and again during my visits to remnant forests of New England's wilderness.

Eagle and Churchill Lakes drain into the Allagash River, which flows uninterrupted for sixty-two miles to the St. John River. Along its course, one is still able to capture

A white-tailed deer crosses Chase Rapids, a wild stretch of the Allagash River.

many of the sensations and feel some of the emotions quite likely experienced by early visitors, though there have been changes in the interim—primarily related to timber harvesting and road construction. A notable feature of the river—one of the first to be encountered on a trip downstream and one that appears in the early literature—is Chase Rapids, called Chase's or Long Falls by Hodge. Chase Rapids is the most thrilling and challenging of those in the waterway. In 1861, Hitchcock and his party reported that, "we found it necessary to carry our luggage over a portage of nearly a mile and a half in length, but after lifting our boats around the dam, they were run down the rapids to the end of the portage."[111] Today, many who run these rapids still do so in empty canoes, having had their luggage transported to a safer point downstream.

This wild stretch of river at Chase Rapids is also notable in another way. It was near here in 1901 that hunters reported seeing a herd of seven caribou, said to be one of the last authenticated sightings of these animals in their

wild native state in Maine.[112] Today, while caribou have
not been seen again in this area, other wildlife encounters
may be had. I remember maneuvering around a cow
moose neck-deep in a pool at the lower part of the rapids.
And most thrilling, a winter trip on skis to these rapids
found my wife and me in the middle of a coyote's attempt
to run down a deer along the snow-covered bank directly
across the river from us. In our twenty years of visits to
this waterway, we had never before seen a drama of this
kind enacted.

The Allagash Wilderness Waterway is one of the
northeast's premier examples of a protected wild and
scenic river. Its existence is a credit to Maine people, and
in one respect it serves as an inspiration for future efforts
to protect elements of the state's natural heritage that contribute to its unique cultural identity. The act creating the
waterway called for the preservation of its natural beauty
and wilderness character. But this is proving difficult to
accomplish, for the waterway is a fragile strip of river corridor, and part of the lesson to be learned lies in the difficulty to establish a suitable buffer zone and adequate control over roads, access, timber harvesting, development,
and use. It is my hope that one day the Allagash Wilderness
Waterway will have a wide zone of roadless forest truly
buffering its shores, fewer access points, and appropriate
management policies so that future generations might find
here, as did Thoreau, a refuge from civilization.

Baring Wilderness Area, Moosehorn National Wildlife Refuge, Maine

*Going west northwest, . . . one enters a river, almost half a
league wide at its mouth, in which there are two islands one
or two leagues further up: one very small, near the mainland
on the west; and the other in the middle. The latter . . . was
named by De Monts, St. Croix Island. Going farther up, one
sees . . . a large one [river], flowing in from the west: that is
the River Etechemins [St. Croix River]. Two leagues up this
there is a rapid. . . . The soil is of the finest, and there are 15
or 20 acres of cleared land. . . . All the rest of the country is
covered with very thick forests. A settlement was made in
this place in the year 1604.*

—Samuel de Champlain, 1604[113]

When Champlain sailed into the mouth of the St. Croix River in the early summer of 1604, he was possibly the first non-native visitor to see this easternmost river of New England. The exploring party chose an island in the river, St. Croix Island, as a site for a settlement. Plagued by swarms of black flies and mosquitoes, they set about making it habitable for the winter. The object was to establish permanent settlements in the wilderness and profit from its resources. The settlement lasted one unusually severe winter, during which nearly half of the seventy-nine members of the party died.

Three hundred and ninety years later, in early summer and a mere eight miles almost directly west of that fateful island settlement, hordes of mosquitoes and blackflies, following the same genetic predisposition as their ancestors, swarmed around another explorer in search of the best remaining untouched example of Champlain's "very thick forests." I was in one of the two federal wilderness areas in the Moosehorn National Wildlife Refuge—the Baring Wilderness Area. This most easterly of the federal wilderness areas, which I was exploring on that overcast June day, contains 4,680 acres. Nearby to the south lies the Edmunds Wilderness Area, totaling 2,782 acres.

The refuge in which these two wilderness areas are located consists of glaciated, rolling hills, rocky coastal shoreline, and a great number of brooks, streams, lakes, ponds, and wetlands. Under the cooling influence of cold ocean currents, forests of spruce and fir, as well as northern hardwoods and scattered stands of white pine, dominate the landscape. Migrating and breeding waterfowl and other birds associated with lakes, ponds, and wetlands are found on the refuge, and the common woodcock is a subject of special study and management. Ospreys and bald eagles also nest here, as well as other birds of prey. Large terrestrial mammals include deer, moose, black bear, coyote, and bobcat. Once heavily logged, the wilderness areas are now protected to preserve their wilderness character. It was, therefore, of special interest to me to learn that in the Baring Wilderness Area there exists an old-growth forest and one containing an eagle's nest.

An overcast sky threatened rain on the morning of my mile-long hike on the gravel road to the old pine forest.

Topping a small, eskerlike ridge, I could see in the distance the mountain on which the old pines reside. I passed near the edges of two ponds connected by a small stream meandering through a marsh. An old beaver house sat in the middle of one. Something swirled in the water at the periphery of my vision—perhaps a beaver, I thought. At the edge of the larger pond, beaver scat littered the shore. In the water near the shoreline, the bright blue of a blue flag plant caught my eye. I looked at it more closely; it was the more rare slender-leaved blue flag. Across the pond I now had a clear view of the small mountain. The ragged tops of the old pines gave the mountainside an appearance that an artist would describe as scumbled. I checked the course I had plotted and proceeded on the gravel road around the pond. A small sign announced the boundary of the wilderness area.

I paced my distance along the road at the foot of the mountain. By compass I entered the forest in the direction of the old white pines. The lower part of the mountain presented an almost impenetrable barrier of small spruce and fir. A few hundred feet up the steep slope I began to see scattered, old pine trees, forming the overstory above the smaller red spruce, fir, red maple, striped maple, and ferns closer to the forest floor. A red-eyed vireo sang monotonously as I inspected the trees—once mere seedlings when Charles Jackson passed through this region on his 1836 survey. The road he followed from Calais to Houlton was, he wrote, "through the woods" and "in many places almost impassable, and the traveller is constantly obliged to have recourse to his axe, in removing fallen trees that obstruct his progress."[114]

I stood 300 feet above sea level. Above me were ledges, and around me boulders littered the forest floor. One nearby rock was covered with moss and the delicate, pinkish blossoms of the tiny twinflower, a creeping boreal plant. The sun broke through and spattered the mountainside with its light. The pines are large; I measured one at twenty-eight inches in diameter—an average size for these eighty-to-eighty-five-foot-high trees. Some are over three feet in diameter. Many were double-topped, perhaps caused by an opening of the canopy by fire or logging over a hundred years ago.[115] I saw no sign of the

Delicate blossoms of twinflower grow on a moss-covered boulder in an old pine forest in the Baring Wilderness Area of Moosehorn National Wildlife Refuge.

eagle nest, although I knew from experience that they are difficult to see from below. Later, a biologist informed me that the eagles had abandoned the nest in the spring for an unknown reason.

As I left the mountain and returned to my truck later that morning, the gravel access road led me back over a dike constructed to improve the attractiveness of the ponds to beaver and waterfowl. I passed small cleared areas that I presumed were cut to enhance the diversity of habitats. A nesting platform for osprey rested on a pole in a small pond. Coming over a ridge near the road, the sounds of heavy trucks became louder. I was thankful that within this magnificent refuge there are areas set aside as wilderness where the sounds of human activity are limited by distance and terrain and where in the future one might return to still find old forests. It is likely that someday the big pines will be gone, replaced by the small spruce and fir that now wait in the understory for their day in the sun. Outside the world will continue to experience the more direct effects of human influence, but for those who wish to take compass in hand and hike into this wilderness area, there will be an opportunity to gain another perspective on the changes occurring in the familiar, everyday world they left behind.

Caribou–Speckled Mountain Wilderness, Maine

While on Mt. Caribou the other day we had a grand view of the Wild River Valley which appeared like a vast unbroken forest.

—Anonymous, *Bethel Courier*, August 3, 1860

On September 30, 1993, the view from Caribou Mountain was still grand—almost unlimited in the clear fall air. A strong, cool breeze buffeted the two of us as we gazed directly west over the sparkling, mica-flecked gray granite knobs of the mountain and the top of Mt. Hastings to the Wild River Valley. In the distance the blue peak of Mt. Washington, wreathed in low white clouds, poked above the mountainous terrain. Nearer, the mountains and valleys displayed the fall colors in pointillistic style. That day the view still contained the appearance of an unbroken

From atop the granite ledges of Caribou Mountain, one may still capture the feeling of New England's wild mountain landscapes of the past. This peak is located in the Caribou–Speckled Mountain Wilderness in the White Mountain National Forest.

forest. No sign was left of the town of Hastings that once thrived on the logging of that valley, nor could we see any evidence of the extensive railroad system with its wood-hauling locomotives that rattled through the hills. Gone were the stripped mountainsides, the dams, and scars of the disastrous fires of 1903 that ended the logging in Wild River Valley.[116] No, that day we saw a breathtaking view of nature, only as can be seen from a peak in the foothills of western Maine. The Mahoosucs and Old Speck Mountain lay directly north. South, Speckled Mountain, the rugged companion of Caribou Mountain in this wilderness area, could be seen guarding one side of Evans Notch, and beyond to the west, East Royce stood protectively over its westerly counterpart.

I crisscrossed the exposed mountaintop between dwarfed red spruces on its easily traversed, granite-paved avenue, festively colored by the red-tinged leaves of low-bush blueberry plants. The rocks are covered with lichens—species of hollow-branched, free-growing reindeer moss, forms of *Cladina* and *Cetraria*, and a member of the genus Cladonia. I saw tufts of the moss *Polystrichum piliferum* with leaves ending in white or colorless, long bristles. In summer, the white blossoms of three-toothed cinquefoil show up in patches on the rocky slopes. Mountain ash, mountain holly, sheep laurel, and alpine bilberry fill the gullies between the ledges. In wetter areas on this mountaintop, one finds leatherleaf, Labrador tea, small cranberry, cotton grass, and sundew—all characteristic of cool, northern bogs. It was, in fact, a beautiful mountain rock garden that I explored that day, with the added comfort that this mountain is surrounded and protected by 12,000 acres of federal wilderness land.

Wilderness designation was conferred on the area around Caribou and Speckled Mountains in the fall of 1990, after a long struggle between environmental groups and business interests. Rugged, relatively remote and isolated, and practically undisturbed for almost a century, the area is well suited to the promotion of wilderness values, such as the increasingly precious opportunity for solitude and quiet. Here it is recognized that management goals may include "allowing the area to serve as a refuge from the civilized and often stressful environment many people find themselves living in today."[117]

On that fall day, the two of us were in search of quiet isolation in undisturbed nature as we left the trailhead at Caribou Trail for a seven-mile, round-trip hike. Here mountain streams would provide us avenues of entry and exit. I looked forward to seeing two undisturbed features of this wilderness: Kees Falls on Morrison Brook and the top of Caribou Mountain.

The trail led us quickly into the woods and away from the sound of traffic on the Evans Notch Road. Frequent

Kees Falls, reduced to a trickle in a dry fall season, is in the Caribou–Speckled Mountain Wilderness.

encounters with the small, noisily gushing brook reassured us that we were still on the right trail. About a mile into our gradual ascent, we came to the wilderness boundary marker. Along the steep side of Morrison Brook's ravine, we passed well-rooted, large, old yellow birch trees. Farther along we heard the sound of a falls below. In this season, it is often reduced to a trickle. The setting around the large pool in the steep-walled basin was shadowed and secluded, and we lingered there peacefully for half an hour.

Another mile, along small cascades and falls, brought us to the col between Caribou and Gammon Mountains where we turned to ascend Mud Brook Trail to the summit of Caribou. There we met a work crew with llamas on the way to dismantle the lean-to above. This, I learned, was in keeping with the Wilderness Management Plan's goal to "move the area as close as possible to 'absolute wilderness,' that is, an area that has no human influences modifying the area."[118]

After a short, steep climb, we reached the summit, explored the top, and ate lunch while enjoying the splendid view. The trail down gave tantalizing views of Speckled Mountain with its intriguing dark patches of thick spruce and fir. Here we knew that opportunities for future trips along secluded trails were now preserved. Between us and Speckled Mountain lay Haystack Notch deeply incised by mountain streams.

We continued down the trail, leaving the stunted spruce behind. Once again we found ourselves in stands of old hardwoods. Giant white maple and huge yellow birch towered over us. We stopped frequently to look up at the kaleidoscope of yellow and red patterns against the brilliant blue sky. Maturity for these trees did not mean their transformation into wood products. They could live out a full life and make their contribution to humans in other ways while continuing to play a role in the ecosystem they inhabited. I knew, too, that other plants in this wilderness are now protected: rare plants, such as the silverling, a low, tufted plant with showy, silver-haired modified leaves under its flowers, and the tiny white-petaled mountain sandwort—both of which live on the rocky mountain summits. In the dark, damp lower areas, other rare plants reside, such as Goldies fern, Brauns holly fern, and yellow jewelweed.

As we continued down Mud Brook, I wondered if it was named by loggers who first saw it muddy from carrying sediment in the runoff from logging or land clearing operations. Today, it is as clear as any mountain stream could be and will probably remain so now that its headwaters are located in this protected wilderness.

We left satisfied that we had experienced the isolation and the quiet we had come for. These qualities, it seems, are not new values. I remembered the story of John Brickett who, sometime around 1803, built a log cabin in this valley just south of Speckled Mountain. Employed as a surveyor for a potential railroad route that would pass through Evans Notch, he tried to discourage its construction by surveying from the lowest point in the notch to the highest peak of the Royce mountains and thus show that the railroad grade would be too steep for practical consideration. He wanted to protect the quiet of his farm from the loud sounds of trains that would pass by.[119]

The Sandwich Range Wilderness, New Hampshire

White Face mountain is one of the most remarkable of the Sandwich group. It is very abrupt, and its summit is a naked rock, while its sides have been deeply scored by immense land falls or slides, which have denuded its rocky surface, and formed the beds of mountain torrents

—Charles T. Jackson, 1844[120]

When Charles T. Jackson conducted his geologic survey of New Hampshire in the early 1840s, Mt. Whiteface was surrounded by a pristine wilderness. Today, it is the core of one of New Hampshire's four federally designated wilderness areas—the Sandwich Range Wilderness. In the interim, most of this area was logged.[121]

The area is located within the White Mountain National Forest in central New Hampshire. It encompasses 25,000 acres of mountains with glacial cirques, valleys, and high mountain passes. Mountain streams cascade down the slopes of long ridges covered with spruce and fir at high elevations and northern hardwoods at lower levels. In this wild setting one may find moose, now increasing in number, and perhaps lynx, which may be an infrequent visitor. And for people who might visit this wilderness, the topography and vegetation combine to provide a feeling of solitude.[122]

Within the boundaries of the Sandwich Range Wilderness is the Bowl Research Natural Area, a small, high-elevation valley, which is "not known to have ever been disturbed and gives every appearance of being in a natural state."[123] This is "indicated by the large size of the hardwoods and red spruce as well as the absence of old logging roads."[124] Located on the eastern slope of Mt. Whiteface, this 500-acre, irregularly shaped virgin forest extends about a mile in a north/south direction and a mile and a quarter at its widest east/west dimension. One of its oldest hardwood trees began its life perhaps as early as 1732, over a hundred years before Charles Jackson surveyed the area.[125] The eastern boundary is formed by the Wonalancet River, a mountain stream originating in the Bowl.[126]

Within this area, the high slopes above 3,000 feet are dominated by old red spruce and balsam fir, intermingled with a sprinkling of paper birch. On the lower slopes, red spruce is the primary species with specimens growing to twenty-eight inches in diameter. On the floor of the Bowl grow northern hardwoods. One forester found a yellow birch that measured three feet in diameter and a sugar maple almost as large.[127] Other researchers looking specifically at the spruce and fir suggest that some spruce may reach at least three hundred years in age.[128] Here it seems is a prime example of a remnant mountain forest of the "original" New England landscape.

One late spring day, two of us arrived at the Diceys Mill Trailhead to begin our hike to the Bowl. The day was cool and the clouds from a recent low-pressure system were being swept away. The trail was well marked with newly routed signs. The one-and-a-half-mile hike angled up the contours on the west side of Mt. Wonalancet, at times steep and rocky, and passed through beautiful woods of northern hardwood trees growing among large boulders. The Wonalancet River, well below us and out of

our sight and hearing, paralleled our direction. At the Tom
Wiggin Trail cutoff, the trail dropped steeply down to the
stream. Finding a place to ford the high waters, with sticks
to help maintain our balance, we crossed and left the trail
to follow the tumbling, rocky stream into the secluded valley of the Bowl. We advanced slowly through the thick
vegetation and downed trees and around the large boulders that lay strewn on the forest floor to the stream's edge
and often out into it. Swarms of black flies followed us, always seeming to find us again after we had ducked under
some thick, shrubby area.

We traversed the low, wet pockets along the stream
and steep slopes above it. On a small terrace, nestled
among the trees on a hillside, we found a wet seep filled
with mosses, liverworts, and blue violets. Beyond, a large
uprooted tree exhibited the development of pit and mound
topography so characteristic of old forests. On the ground,
beneath the large hardwoods and scattered red spruce,
grew bunchberry, Canada mayflower, wood sorrel, and
clintonia—a plant whose tall stalk supported delicate yellow blossoms in full flower. The sky, now cleared, allowed
bright sunshine to dapple the forest floor and understory.

In an interesting twist, the old forest we entered that
day represented the future of the Sandwich Range Wilderness. That remnant virgin woodland allowed us to see and
experience what had been set forth by the planners of the
wilderness as its desired condition in years ahead:

*The forest will appear natural and evolve without direct in-
terference by humans, a product of natural succession. . . .
Stands of trees will contain a mix of sizes from seedling to
maturity. . . . There will be opportunities for foot travel into
areas with and without trails. . . . Opportunities to experience solitude and remoteness from external influence will be
available. . . . Evidence of people will be reduced by management and the passage of time.*[129]

Lye Brook Wilderness, Vermont

We have here met to dedicate and consecrate this extensive wilderness to God manifested in the flesh, and to give a new name . . . which new name is Verd Mont, in token that her mountains and hills shall be ever green and shall never die

—the Reverend Hugh Peters, 1763[130]

Almost one hundred years after the Reverend Peters' ceremonial christening of the Green Mountains, Albert Hager wrote in the Report of the Geology of Vermont: "The most striking and characteristic feature in the scenery of Vermont is the range of mountains that extends the entire length. . . ."[131] Thus, it is easily understood why Verd Mont, French for Green Mountains, became, with the omission of the letter d, the name of the new state of Vermont—a designation that occurred in the late 1700s. This mountain chain, with its peaks exceeding 4,000 feet in height and tens of miles wide, was and still is a powerful force on the ecological character and economic development of the state. The mountains are responsible for east–west biological differences, and their steep slopes made the streams vulnerable to the widespread stripping of trees and other vegetation that took place in the early 1800s. Charles Johnson writes that:

Under the combined effects of farming and heavy logging, 70 to 75 percent of Vermont by the 1850s was open land, in the form of clear-cut areas, pastures, or croplands, and the hills and mountains, stripped of their protective trees could no longer hold the soil—the streams and rivers became muddy with the run-off. . . . Hunting and trapping continued unabated, with few conservation laws. . . . Wildlife of the forests grew scarce, and fish that depended on clear, cold streams diminished or vanished completely. The Green Mountains of Vermont, in short, had become a biological wasteland, offering little for people to live upon— a dramatic change from the bounty of a century earlier.[132]

Today, the forest has returned to many of those once barren landscapes of Vermont, admittedly a different kind of forest in age and pattern. Now approximately 75 percent is forested as compared to the 70–75 percent of the land that was once denuded a century and a half ago. The lessons of earlier years; the emergence of a conservation ethic, forged in large part by the Vermonter George Perkins Marsh; the recognition of new needs for the land; and changes in patterns of land ownership—these among other reasons were responsible for the change.

One of the changes responsible for a greener Vermont was the establishment of the Green Mountain National Forest in 1932. Today, at over 300,000 acres, it represents about half of Vermont's publicly owned land, or 5 percent of the state's land area. Though much of the land is managed for multiple use, six areas, encompassing almost 60,000 acres, have been set aside as wilderness. Two lie north of Rutland: Bristol Cliffs and Breadloaf, the latter being the largest among the six areas. The four to the south are Big Branch, Peru Peak, George D. Aiken, and Lye Brook. At 15,680 acres, the Lye Brook Wilderness is the second largest in the state.

At 7:00 A.M. on an early June day, after navigating ten miles of steep, narrow, twisting, gravel mountain roads, I arrived at the Branch Pond Trailhead near the southern end of the Lye Brook Wilderness. I had chosen this wilderness area to visit because of Bourn Pond, one of Vermont's secluded and undeveloped bodies of water. The botanist Hubert Voglemann, who has extensively traveled the state conducting surveys of its natural areas, called it "one of the most picturesque of Vermont's backwoods areas."[133] The day was very windy and dark clouds were threatening rain showers when I began my two-and-a-half-mile hike to the pond. No one else was parked at the trailhead, and no one had recently registered: I would be alone.

The trail was fairly level with low ridges and occasional wet areas as I skirted the east side of Branch Pond. Three-quarters of a mile in, I came to a sign that marked the boundary of the wilderness area. The trail was resplendent with the blooming of spring. I walked past large numbers of painted trillium, profuse patches of clintonia, and masses of goldthread and unfurling ferns. The understory was thickly spotted with the clustered flowers of hobblebush beneath white birch and very large, old yellow birch. In some places, the hobblebush was replaced in the understory by dense stands of young balsam fir.

Soon I began to notice that I was not alone here. Fresh tracks indicated that a small moose was ahead of me,

Painted trillium brightens the edge of a trail in Vermont's Lye Brook Wilderness in the Green Mountain National Forest.

going my way. I changed a camera lens and prepared
for a quick photograph in case I met the moose. The trail
took me by old beaver ponds and their cuttings, onto a
boardwalk over wet swampy ground, and along an old
corduroy road—a sign of long-ago lumbering. An oven-
bird flew into a nearby thicket.

I first saw the waters of Bourn Pond glistening
through the trees. I left the trail and followed a path to its
boggy southern shore, where I wouldn't have been sur-
prised to see the moose. What greeted me was the sun and
patches of blue sky among the windswept clouds. Blossoms of leatherleaf, a bog-building heath plant, livened the
bog mats around a small group of dead, gray-bleached
trees, which imparted a primitive look to the scene. Low
hills offered a backdrop. They are drained by Bourn
Brook, which begins at the outlet of this pond. Three and
a half miles to the northwest, the brook flows through a
deep gorge in a place named Downer Glen. Here researchers might someday confirm that the hardwoods and
hemlocks along this gorge are part of a long-ago forest.[134]

The forests at the edge of Bourn Pond, however, are
younger. Where I stood, the mixed hardwoods and conifers come right to the shore. Red maple, white and yellow birch, and balsam fir are abundant in these woodlands, and beneath them one finds hobblebush, mountain
maple, and mountain ash. On the forest floor near the
pond, yellow clintonia and painted trillium are joined by
bunchberry, star flower, Canada mayflower, and wild sarsaparilla. Ferns and club moss add their greenery.

I lingered on the shore for some time. Only the wind
made a sound. No other humans were present. Reluctantly, I started back on the trail. Almost as soon as the
pond had disappeared from sight, I was startled to hear
what I thought was a human voice. I paused—only a tree
creaking in the wind. I noticed that dark clouds had
once again closed the sky. Moose tracks reappeared in
the trail, again going my way. I never saw the animal, but
I left satisfied, knowing that for a time we had shared a
trail through a wilderness where we were both free to
privately pursue our respective activities.

Secluded, undeveloped
Bourn Pond is protected within
Vermont's Lye Brook Wilderness.

New England's large areas of wildland let us sense the vast earlier wilderness. They allow us to experience feelings of solitude, isolation, tranquillity, and intimacy with wild nature, as well as feelings of excitement, anxiety, and exhilaration. Smaller remnants of this wilderness can be rediscovered along New England's long and crooked coastline, in its back country, and among hidden places that house creatures now gone and others that barely survive. It is for these remnants that we now search.

Chapter 2
Of the Isles, Bays, and Coastal Lands

For a moment, as I stood atop one of those hills on that triangular-shaped island that Verrazzano saw 470 years ago, the darkening shoreline appeared to burn with fires again as the sharply cut peaks of Mohegan Bluffs caught the last rays of a setting sun.[2] One hundred and forty feet below, waves gently lapped the rock-covered beach, as if to soothe the ravages of previous, storm-driven assaults. A long, winding, wooden stairway snaked down the steep bluff to the beach, clinging to the edge of a sharp ravine where grasses and maritime shrubs maintained a tenuous foothold. Two deer, at first hidden in the shadowy gully, jumped at the sound of steps on the stairs. Ghostly white tails lurched up the slope and disappeared.

At the bottom of the stairway beneath the wildly contoured bluffs, the waves worked noisily, asthmatically, sorting the jumble of granitic rocks and large boulders they have released from this hill of sands and clays during wilder, stormy times. For 11,000 years since glacial times, the waves have worked these materials. Their excavation reveals the island's relationship to Long Island to the southwest and Martha's Vineyard and Nantucket Islands to the northeast—all part of a sinuous ridge of earth materials scoured from the mainland by the last glacier and left at its melting edge.

Amid the jumble of boulders strewn along the shore, under the darkening shadows of the high peaks above, cut off from all signs of human life, one experiences waves of loneliness here. The geologist J. B. Woodsworth once described this beach as "one of the most desolate tracts on the eastern coast of the United States."[3] Cool air settled down from the top of the bluffs with the disappearance of the sun, and mists rose up by the island's profiled edge silhouetted against the distant horizon. A light pink colored

We discovered an island in forme of a triangle, distant from the main land 10 leagues about the bignesse of the island of the Rhodes; it was full of hils covered with trees, well peopled, for we saw fires all along the coast.

—Giovanni da Verrazzano, 1524[1]

69

the sky above the Atlantic. These bluffs undoubtedly appear much the same as they did in Verrazzano's time, protected, as they are, from human development by the nature of their instability. But Verrazzano never had this view: unfavorable weather prevented his landing and he passed by.

The silhouetted, ragged edge of Block Island's Mohegan Bluffs.

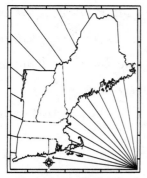

Block Island, Rhode Island

Two months after my visit to Block Island and 350 miles directly northeast of that sea-bounded landmass, I stood beneath a different set of bluffs, not made of the sediments that compose Mohegan Bluffs nor aged in mere thousands of years, but cliffs of rocks created more than 400 million years ago. The place is Quoddy Head, New England's easternmost coastal point and the termination of the region's most undeveloped section of coast. From a high trail along the rim of these cliffs, I eased down a steep ravine between rock walls into a small cove beneath vertical cliffs, towering one hundred feet high. Here, tidal extremes and hard storms keep the rocks barren and the cove's tiny beach well-cobbled. The scene differs little from the lithographic image Charles Jackson included in the atlas of plates that accompanied his 1838 report on the geology of Maine. The toll of weathering is seen in the surf-pounded rubble of rocks at the base of the cliffs and in the wind-stunted spruce clinging to the rocky headland above.

The day I was there, a spring freshet cascaded over the face of one of the cliffs at the back of the cove. Round cobblestones on the floor of the three-sided canyon, only recently left wet and dark by the outgoing tidal waters, were now dry and whitened from the hot sun. Seawater, clear and blue-green, sloshed in and out of the cove, and long strands of seaweed swished on the rocks. The sound of a lobster boat and a spattering of plastic litter washed up on the beach were the only differences Jackson might have observed could he have returned. Otherwise, the impression of Charles Hitchcock, written in 1861, is still accurate: "There is a wilderness about the spot which is greatly increased by the fogs so frequently settling down over the ocean adjacent to the shores."[4]

Jackson and Hitchcock were latecomers to the New England coast compared to Verrazzano, Champlain, Smith, and the other early explorers who first described it. Verrazzano came from the south, it is believed, and explored as far north as Penobscot Bay. After passing Block Island, he discovered Narragansett Bay and "a passing good haven," now Newport, Rhode Island. After a visit there he "departed from the said coaste, keeping along in the sight thereof, and . . . the land somewhat higher with certaine mountains." He rounded Cape Cod and proceeded northeasterly up the Massachusetts and Maine coasts. Somewhere near Casco Bay he landed and saw "very great wood and certaine hils." Continuing northeastward, Verrazzano found "high mountains within the land." Along the Maine coast he counted thirty-two islands, "lying al neere the land, being small and pleasant to the view, high, and having many turnings and windings between them, making many fair harboroughs and chanels."[5]

It was almost a hundred years later, in the first decades of the seventeenth century, before we acquired the comprehensive and accurate images of the coast of New England given by Samuel de Champlain and Captain John Smith. From 1604 to 1606, Champlain led three voyages along the New England coast from the St. Croix River in eastern Maine to Nantucket Sound just south of Cape Cod. Smith surveyed the coast in 1614 from Penobscot Bay to Cape Cod. From their words we learn about this edge of the continent at a time when only Native Peoples inhabited it and its features were relatively untouched.

Champlain's description begins at forty-five degrees latitude at the St. Croix River in easternmost Maine:

West Quoddy Head, as seen by the geologist Charles T. Jackson in 1836, differs little from what visitors see today. Illustration from Charles T. Jackson, *Atlas of Plates Illustrating the Geology of the State of Maine* (Boston, Mass.: Dutton and Wentworth, 1837).

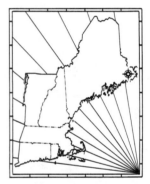

Quoddy Head, Maine

From the St. Croix River along the coast about 25 leagues, we passed a great quantity of islands, banks, reefs, and rocks, which project more than four leagues into the sea in some places. . . . Among these islands there are a great

Areas along the eastern coast of Maine still appear as undeveloped as they were nearly four centuries ago when the explorer Samuel de Champlain commented on the "great quantity of islands" and the "great many good, fine harbors."

many good, fine harbors. . . . [Passing Mount Desert Island and Isle au Haut and coming] opposite the River of Norembegue [Penobscot River]. . . . the quantity of islands, rocks, shallows, banks and breakers is such everywhere that it is strange to see. . . . Skirting the coast westward one passes the mountains of Bedabedec [Camden Hills]. . . . Going about eight leagues, running westward along the coast, we passed a number of islands and rocks jutting out a league into the sea, and went as far as an island ten leagues from Quinibequy [Kennebec River].

Smith began his voyage along the New England coast farther south than Champlain:

The most northern part I was at, was the Bay of Pennobscot. . . . The Bay is full of great Ilands, of one, two, six, eight, or ten miles in length, which divides it into many faire and excellent good harbours.

Continuing to Saco Bay, Smith provides the following description:

Westward of this River [Kennebec] is the Countrey of Aucocisco [Casco Bay], in the bottome of a large deepe Bay, full of many great Iles, which divides it into many good Harbours. Sawocotuck [Saco] is the next, in the edge of a large Sandy Bay, which hath many Rocks and Iles, but few good Harbours.

Champlain also comments on the sandy nature of the shore in this area: "This coast is sandy in most places from Quinibequy."

Leaving present-day Maine, the explorers passed the Isles of Shoals and the New Hampshire coast. In the vicinity of Ipswich or Newburyport, near the mouth of the Merrimack River, Smith saw "many rising hilles, and on their tops and descents many corne fields, and delightful groves." And beyond to Massachusetts Bay "are many Iles, and questionlesse good Harbours . . . the Coast is for the most part, high clayie sandie cliffs [Point Allerton and Peddocks Island]. The Sea Coast as you passe, shewes you all along large Corne fields." He also noted the large population of natives. This is what Champlain also reported seeing in the area around Boston Harbor ten years before: "All along the shore there is a great deal of land cleared, and planted with Indian corn. The country is very pleasant and agreeable, with a great many beautiful trees."

Beyond Boston Harbor, Smith came "to Accomack [Plymouth Harbor], an excellent good Harbor, good land. . . . Cape Cod is the next presents it selfe. . . . This Cape is made by the maine Sea on the one side, and a great Bay on the other in forme of a sickle."

Of Cape Cod Bay and the cape, Champlain reported: "We were so engulfed that we had to turn completely about to round the cape we had seen." Proceeding on to Nantucket Sound, he saw "low and sandy lands, which are not lacking in beauty and fertility, although hard to reach. There are no shelters, very many reefs, and there is little water for nearly two leagues from the land."[6]

The value of these written reports to the Europeans across the Atlantic and the maps that accompanied them is not difficult to imagine. And their value continues to grow because they provide us a firsthand glimpse of a coast and land from which we are able to make some assessment of change—a kind of a baseline, if you will. To be sure, the land and waters were not completely untouched, for there were fires, clearings, villages, and the taking of animals by the natives. But the air and waters were unimpaired. No roads, docks, breakwaters, transmission lines, buildings, planes, vehicles, and powerboats existed. No sounds from engines could be heard—only the wind and waves.

Except for the smoke from native fires, the air was unpolluted by human activities. Only natural smells wafted over the land and water. In fact, scents peculiar to certain areas were carried over long distances by the winds and breezes and easily discerned by the discoverers and early settlers. Thomas Morton observed that "shipps have come from Virginea where there have bin scarce five men able to hale a rope, untill they have come within 40 Degrees of latitude, and smell the sweet aire of the shore, where they have suddainly recovered."[7] Morton had a penchant for such stories and when advocating the superiority of Massachusetts' climate, according to one scholar, was led into making "ludicrously wild statements."[8] Still, there is likely some element of truth in the observation, for Verrazzano wrote that he smelled the "sweete savours [of the trees] farre from the shoare."[9]

In some respects, it is difficult to believe that the unaltered, natural qualities of the New England coast existed less than four hundred years ago, only two hundred and fifty years before the birth of my great grandmother, who I remember well, perhaps a mere eight generations before those with whom she was personally acquainted. Cast in this light, we have in a very brief time drastically changed much of what those explorers experienced. Questions relative to the changes the New England coast has undergone have been thoroughly explored by others; the question addressed here, however, is what remains today that is relatively untouched?

THE ISLES

And when the days appeared we saw we weare environed Round about with Illands you might have told neare thirty illands.

—James Davies, 1607[10]

Most often the islands were the first parts of the continent encountered by the European explorers in their voyages to the new world. This was especially true for those who arrived first off the Maine coast, since some three thousand islands occupy the offshore waters here. It is no wonder, then, that James Davies and the others on their way to establish a colony at the mouth of the Kennebec River found themselves surrounded by islands when they arrived in Georges Harbor in 1607.

If he could return, Davies would see few, if any, undisturbed New England islands. There are, however, many that still retain elements of their previous character and a few that are noteworthy in this respect. On these islands we can still capture a rich flavor of their past.

Monhegan and the Georges Islands, Maine

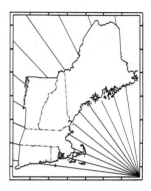

Friday, the 17 of May, about sixe a clocke at night, we descried the land. . . . It appeared a meane high land, as we after found it, being but an Iland of some six miles in compasse, but I hope the most fortunate ever yet discovered.

—James Rosier, 1605[11]

Monhegan Island was the island identified by Rosier when his ship, commanded by Captain George Waymouth, made landfall. This island, Isle au Haut, and Mount Desert Island have been called the greatest island landmarks on the coast of Maine.[12] One writer called Monhegan Island "the sentinel of New England," and it probably already had experienced a long history of European involvement before Rosier saw it.[13] It might well have been one of the three "high, pleasing" islands Verrazzano saw and named after the three princesses in the court of the King of France.[14] It is also likely that Monhegan was used by fishermen for drying fish years previous to Champlain's and Waymouth's encounter with it.

I first saw Monhegan from a nearby island. It lay six miles directly south and from my perspective was long, low, and blue-gray, reflecting, in part, the clearing sky. The view might well have been the same in 1605 when, almost to the day in mid-May, 389 years earlier, Waymouth's *Archangel* lay along that island's north shore. "This Iland is woody, growen with Firre, Birch, Oke and Beech, as farre as we saw along the shore; and so likely to be within," wrote Rosier.[15]

Today, behind the rugged, rocky shore of that distant island, a virgin remnant of Rosier's "woody" land possibly exists. About fifteen acres of almost pure red spruce grow in a dense stand on the northern half of the island. Severe growing conditions in this coastal environment and competition keep the trees small (about ten inches in diameter). The effects of storms and other destructive weather-related factors appear to hold the trees to around a hundred-year rotation, or cycle of replacement. One eleven-inch-diameter spruce, for example, showed about ninety growth rings.[16] However, from my vantage point, miles away, these details escaped me and I saw only a forested shore on the island.

My view of Monhegan that day was from a graveyard of ghostly-white skeletons of dead spruce, a wreckage of twisted trunks and severed limbs and flaking bark. Wind, salt, ice, and freezing spray had kept this high, rocky, seaward end of the island barren. Spots of sunlight played on the ocean's surface between me and Monhegan as I traced mentally the route Captain Waymouth might have taken past this point, around the island to the protected north end, and into the sheltered harbor where I had been left off earlier in the morning for the purpose of steeping myself in history.

A trail led past the dead trees into a dark forest of second-tier spruce. It followed the edge of the island, over damp, moss-covered ground on top of high ledges. A pair of osprey cheeped. Through the trees the dark form of

A stand of hundred-year-old yellow birches fills a sunlit glen on one of the Maine islands described in 1605 by James Rosier, who accompanied Captain George Waymouth in his exploration of the St. George River.

their nest appeared, silhouetted against the ocean. The shaded forest suddenly opened into a bright, skylit glen. The opening seemingly glowed from the brightly hued bark of hundreds of branches spreading from the short trunks of hundred-year-old yellow birch trees.[17] Branches, fringed with strands of unraveling, papery bark, splayed from short chunky boles, reaching out forty feet and nearly as high. The contrast of this opening, filled with long crisscrossing branches and new, yellow-green, sunlit leaves, against the surrounding dark spruce forest was stunning. Soft tan leaves of previous years covered the forest floor. An occasional fern, still unfurling, added another touch of spring.

Nearby, I found another grove of yellow birches, where three-foot boles stood in a field of thickly sprouting wood ferns, long beech ferns, and hay-scented ferns, their fronds yet unfurled on stems poking through a heavy mat of the previous year's crop. Above the ferns, the trees branched six to twenty times. Several old trees, long uprooted by strong winds, lay prostrate, sprouting rows of new stems, each sprout on its way to becoming a new tree. I suspected that this forest covered an old pasture, but, even so, it took me one step closer back to that time when Rosier described this island.

A trail, rutted by sheep, led back to the north end of the island and to the boat that would transport me to the mainland. On this western side of the island, occasional openings in the trees and side trails offered views of the harbor at the mouth of the St. George River. Rafts of eider ducks bobbed in the waters and loons and black guillemots swam and fished. This edge of the island was a jumble of rocks amid numerous ledges—little changed, I imagined, in four hundred years.

Mount Desert Island, Maine

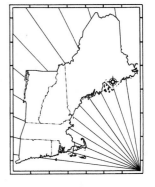

I went near an island about four or five leagues long. The distance from this island to the mainland on the north is not a hundred paces. It is very high with notches here and there, so that it appears, when one is at sea, like seven or eight mountains rising close together. The tops of most of them are without trees, because they are nothing but rock. The only trees are pines, firs and birches. I called it the Island of the Desert Mountains.

—Samuel de Champlain, September 5, 1604[18]

William Williamson, in his *History of the State of Maine*, wrote that these "high and rugged mountains may be seen the distance of twenty leagues [at sea], and are remarkable for being the first landmark of seamen."[19] But these barren, desertlike mountains are striking when seen from any

direction, as many a motorist will attest who has seen
them from Route One in Sullivan looking across Frenchman Bay. Standing on their summits of coarse-grained
pink granite, they offer an equally spectacular panorama.
Here one can see many of the hundreds of islands that dot

Looking across Frenchman
Bay from Sullivan, the
mountains of Maine's Mount
Desert Island still appear as
barren and desertlike as they
did to the explorer Samuel de
Champlain who described
this "Island of the
Desert Mountains."

the coast of eastern Maine. Here, also, one soon comes
to appreciate the amazing natural diversity of the island,
with its fascinating mountains and ridges, beaches and
tidal flats, wetlands, rocky outcrops and cliffs, forests of
spruce and fir and northern hardwoods, and ponds and
lakes. From these vantage points atop the mountains, the
surrounding steep-sided valleys still retain an ageless,
mysterious quality of their own, often filled with shadows, dense fog, or swirling mists. One hears the deep
stillness or the sound of an echoing call. Exploring this
island offers snatches of what it was like during an earlier
time.

On one of the island's western mountains in a small
notch, protected from wind and human disturbance, lies a

Sunlight spatters an old forest of
red spruce in a small protected
notch near the top of one of
Mount Desert Island's western
mountains. Some of the spruce
date back to the mid-1700s.

small forest of old trees. Some of them began their lives as early as the 1740s, a time when the French and Indian wars were disrupting European settlement. Aged red spruce dominate this stand, which also includes yellow birch and red maple. Those trees that fell victim to the ravages of wind left openings now filled with young fir and spruce and, beneath them, wood ferns. On the shaded forest floor lie beds of liverworts and delicate feathermoss. Nearby, northern white cedar grow along a small stream.[20]

At the northern end of the island in the lowland near Salisbury Cove, an old forest of much different character suggests changes in the land caused by its settlement. White pines, dating to the late 1700s, started their lives on a small plot of land once cleared for pasture or crops. Walking among these towering, three-foot-diameter trees, one wonders why this grove has remained uncut for so long. Openings left by the few large trees that have died and fallen are filled again with young white pine. Pine are known to have difficulty in tolerating a northern, ocean-side environment. Here, perhaps, grows a genotype of this species that is able to adapt.[21] If so, one sees in this forest both its past and its future. With prophetic insight, Samuel Drake wrote in 1875, "In the neighborhood of Salisbury Cove there are still to be seen, in inaccessible places, trees destined never to feel the axe's keen edge."[22]

The future of Mount Desert Island's old forests is ensured. Today, about one-half of the island is within the boundaries of Acadia National Park, which had its beginnings in land-protection efforts undertaken in the early part of the twentieth century. The park now protects many of the features of New England's early landscape. Of special note is Somes Sound—a glacially-cut trough, penetrating well into the island and nearly cutting it in half. This feature is the only fjord, albeit a poorly developed one, on the east coast of the United States.

One clear day from the top of Flying Mountain, I gazed down on this long, narrow bay, taking in its length from one end to the other. The small, spruce- and fir-covered mountain juts into the narrow mouth of the sound, and its northeastern side slopes steeply down to the water's edge. This side is part of the roughly three and one-half miles of shoreline along Somes Sound that is now protected by the park and would probably appear little changed if seen by the members of the Jesuit colony who settled near here in 1613.

Somes Sound, seen here from the top of Flying Mountain, is a glacially cut trough leading into the heart of the island. Portions of its shoreline are protected by Acadia National Park.

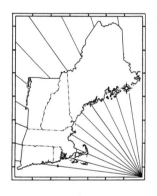

Great Wass Island, Maine

Coasting along . . . we came to one [island] at . . . which we anchored, where there was a large number of crows of which our men captured a great many, and we called it the Isle aux Corneilles.

—Samuel de Champlain, June 18, 1605[23]

Eastward from Mount Desert Island and off the mainland town of Jonesport lies the Great Wass archipelago, a group of more than thirty islands. The historian Samuel Eliot Morison suggests that it was in a sheltered harbor of this archipelago that Champlain anchored and named Head Harbor Island, the Isle aux Corneilles.[24] Southwest of Head Harbor Island lies the largest island in the group, Great Wass. This island dominates the center of the cluster of rocky knobs rising above the surface of Eastern Bay, the tip of an ancient granitic formation called the Great Wass Pluton. The fifteen hundred acres of the preserve portion of the island is owned by the Maine Chapter of The Nature Conservancy.[25]

One spring day on Great Wass Island, I followed a secluded trail that led directly into a damp, cool, shadowy envelope of spruce and fir. Branches thick and heavy with evergreen needles and carpets of soft and spongy mosses intercepted sounds from without and absorbed those from within. Inside, it was damp and moist. The mosses and liverworts absorbed more than sound; precipitation collects here, too, and it is said that more falls here than any other place in Maine. The air was misty and cool. Outside, the temperature hovered in the eighties. Inside, rays from the hot sun filtered through the dense woods, splashing patterns, silhouetting, lighting, reflecting—making it difficult to distinguish the path I followed. Mosses and lichens luxuriated in incomparable richness, as perhaps exists in no other place in this state. Laid out before me was a complex carpet showing hues of green, brown, blue, and yellow.

The trail wove, rose, and fell, controlled by granite ridges and boulders. More colors and patterns appeared. In wooded areas, I walked between patches of bunchberries—bright green, parallel-veined leaves surrounded pure, flat-white flowers—and beneath the repetitious patterns of mountain ash leaves.

In open areas, heath plants, chest high, closed the trail from sight. White puffs of blooming Labrador tea dotted the trailside. Then the trail moved up to open rocks on a granite ridge. Stunted jack pine clung to thin acid soils—a

A granite ridge in the heart of Maine's Great Wass Island overlooks a coastal peatland, undoubtedly as undisturbed as it was in 1605 when Samuel de Champlain is thought to have sought shelter in a nearby harbor.

pine of northern areas lured here by the cool temperatures, now in such numbers as to comprise eastern Maine's largest population. The trail moved higher up onto the ridge and lost itself on the rocks. A view opened to the south. A peatland, sprinkled with bright greens of spring foliage, extended towards the open Atlantic, a thin sliver of blue over the tops of black spruce ringing the wetland.

On an island off the eastern coast of Maine, a small stand of virgin red spruce towers above a deep mat of mosses and liverworts.

I was at the heart of Great Wass—a place where one can say, "No other area in the United States offers such insights into the character of the coastal subarctic."

One of the "Ranges" off the Coast of Maine

I called them [the islands] the Ranges. Most of them are covered with pines and firs, and other poor kinds of wood.

—Samuel de Champlain, September 21, 1604[26]

No one is certain which islands off the eastern Maine coast Champlain called the "Ranges." Remarkably, however, one island in this vicinity has trees that date back to the 1600s, perhaps within the lifetimes of some who knew this noted explorer.

I looked into this forest of ancient red spruce from the edge of a small stream, and though it was mid-May and the ground still wet from the winter's melt, only a trickle flowed—a seep, really, from the dense, moss-covered forest floor at its edge. The woods are primeval, in both age and appearance. Only ten acres have escaped the centuries of repeated cutting and fires on this island. I was hesitant: every footstep in the deep moss seemed a violation. A shallow brooklet led into the dark woods, its gully crisscrossed with rotting fallen trees and cramped with turgid moss, each leaf full and plump with water. I waded into the woods.

Along the seepage, shallow pools reflected the tops of the trees against a blue sky, and where the sun penetrated to a muddy bottom, the full height of the forest was revealed in a kind of double exposure. The sun's rays first touch this forest seventy-five feet above its floor, a distance of centuries. The rays filter through towering red spruce and down through the tops of smaller old balsam fir. Only 20 percent of the light reaches the deep moss and the few herbaceous plants that grow here.

Inside, on the forest floor, sphagnum mosses, feather moss, and dense tufts of the liverwort *Bazzania trilobata* sop up both water and sound, bringing a silence like the deep, soft snow of winter. The moss crawls up the dark, rough-barked, two-foot-thick trunks of old spruce. Canada mayflowers follow, finding a foothold on the mossy trunk. Even the trees' own seedlings live on these tree-trunk hummocks.

Throughout the forest understory another generation of spruce and fir waits—now a dense barrier to those who would enter. A few other species of trees have found small niches here—a red maple, seemingly out of place, and a lone white birch, noticeably bright. A gull cried overhead and the scent of a nearby tidal flat drifted into the forest, reminders of the nearness of this forest to the sea. What sea-faring person first set foot here? And when?

I came out of the woods and followed the stream, clogged with windblown debris and decaying roots and limbs. The stream flowed into a small pond, ringed with the mirrored reflections of the tall spruce. At the pond's outlet, the stream gained life as it dropped to the island's cove and into a marsh where the old forest ends. The stream slowed, seemingly disoriented, its route indirect, cutting deeply into the muck while the tidal waters were in retreat. In the distance I saw a sheltered harbor. Was this one of Champlain's Ranges?

Isles of Shoals, Maine/New Hampshire

Two leagues to the east we saw three or four rather high islands.

—Samuel de Champlain, July 1605[27]

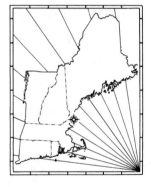

Champlain was perhaps the first to provide written reference to the Isles of Shoals, a cluster of seven islands situated seven miles off the coast of Maine and New Hampshire southwest of the Piscataqua River. Through them the boundary line of these two states runs. The islands are singled out for inclusion here because they represent so many islands along the New England coast that, despite a long history of human visitation and habitation, retain some features of their original nature. In some respects, these islands offer the opportunity to differentiate more sharply between the islands as they once were and as they are today. They are easy to traverse, and one can readily see the signs of habitation—the stone walls, cellar holes, and pathways—and explore the rocky bluffs, chasms, wetlands, and tidal ponds. These islands also have an explicit written history, dating back to human settlement, as well as a detailed description of their natural history.

Leaving Portsmouth Harbor one stormy evening for a three-day visit to the largest of these islands, Appledore, I gained respect for the forces that shape these tough granite knobs and for the people who settled them. The boat bucked its way across the open stretch of water, pounded head-on by the high waves. When I stepped off the boat onto the rocky shore, I had come to appreciate the words of Samuel Drake who visited these isles in 1875: "During violent storms, the savagery of these rocks, exposed to the full fury of the Atlantic, and surrounded by an almost perpetual surf, is overwhelming."[28]

Human use is amply evident on the island's trails, and much reminds one of its past. Mt. Agamenticus, in the county of York, Maine, still rests definitively on the low coastal mainland, twelve miles to the northwest beyond York Harbor. John Smith, in his description of New England, identified this mountain as a major landmark. He also named these islands after himself while orienting them to the mainland: "Smyths Iles are a heape together, non neere them, against Accomintycus."[29] One might suspect that Appledore's barrenness, the prevalence of low shrubs, and the lack of trees, characteristics all of the islands possess, result from overcutting, but these, too, were conditions of the past. As early as 1624, four years before the records of first settlement on the island, the Englishman Christopher Levett wrote:

The first place I set my foote upon in New England, was the Isles of Shoulds, being Ilands in the Sea, about two leagues from the Mayne. Upon these Ilands, I neither could see one good timber tree, no so much good ground as to make a garden.[30]

Two hundred and twenty years later, in 1844, the geologist Charles Jackson confirmed that little had changed: "They [the islands] are composed of ledges of rock, and but few of them possess any soil suitable for agriculture."[31] And so it is today; one still sees steep, rocky shorelines and the effects of glaciation—striations and

An 1875 drawing of the rocky shore of Smutty Nose, captures the character of the Isles of Shoals archipelago seven miles off the coast of Maine and New Hampshire. Despite centuries of human habitation, the islands retain the barren, sparsely vegetated appearance described by early explorers. Illustration from Samuel Adams Drake, *Nooks and Corners of the New England Coast* (New York: Harper & Brothers, Publishers, 1875).

chatter marks, rounded outcrops, oddly placed boulders, and land scraped of its soil, supporting a sparse but hardy vegetation.[32]

One early morning while the eastern sky slowly brightened, I followed a dimly lit trail, brushing against dense growths of huckleberry, bayberry, and other shrubby plants, all the while trying to avoid the thick stands of poison ivy. A stick held overhead protected me from a potential attack from aggressive great black-backed gulls, for their nests were scattered throughout the island. We can only guess whether these birds were present here during Smith's time, but on the other side of the island, black-crowned night herons, black guillemots, double-crested cormorants, and other water birds nest as they have done for centuries.

The trail led to the other side of the island and descended to a small, natural, rock-walled inlet—an extension of a wide ravine, extending from a cove on the landward side and almost severing the island in two. Without a doubt, this tiny cove for centuries has invited visitors, who, in the first rays of the morning sun, saw it as I did. The tide was out and the granite outcrops were covered with plant and animal life, each species attached by its own devices and adapted to its peculiar location where it could compete effectively for food when the nutrient-rich waters returned. What these organisms didn't know, however, is that cooperatively they produced a thing of great beauty. Samuel Drake, when he visited here a century and a quarter before, appreciated this, too:

Looking at the islands at low tide, they present well-defined belts of color. First is the dark line of submerged rock-weed. . . . next comes a strip almost as green as the grass in the rocky pastures; above these again, shaded into browns or dingy yellows, the rocks appear of a tawny hue, and then blanched to a ghastly whiteness, a little relieved by dusky patches of green.[33]

The click of my camera shutter, the soft shush of waves, and a distant cry of a gull were the only sounds while I recorded the spectacular display. We have in this pattern of colors a litmus test of the quality of our ocean waters. I left this tidal inlet feeling, for the moment, secure.

Block Island, Rhode Island

Block Island presents an irregular rolling surface of hills and valleys of gentle undulation. . . .

—Charles T. Jackson, 1840[34]

A northern harrier, endangered in the state of Rhode Island, skimmed over the fields and the shallow pond. Overhead a high sun shined through traces of windswept clouds and reflected brightly off the stone walls edging the fields. The tops of the walls made bright lines over the ground, revealing the rolling surface of the hills and giving limits to the fields. Once these walls lay scattered on a forest floor where a glacier had strewn them some eleven thousand years ago.

Today, at Dicken's Point, these fields roll back from the edge of crumbling bluffs where the roots of trees in a dense forest once struggled against waves and tides to keep the soil in place. According to one visitor, who explored this island in 1636, it "was all overgrown with brushwood of oak."[35] Studies of pollen in sediments of a nearby pond confirm that oak-dominated forests once resided here, along with lesser populations of elm, pine, hickory, ash, cedar, beech, maple, and tupelo.[36] By the early 1700s, however, most of the forests were harvested, and in 1840, Jackson reported, "There are no trees upon Block Island."[37]

The forest here at the edge of the field at Dicken's Point is but a narrow band of maritime shrubs, typical of the remaining vegetation on the island. Of the trees that once resided here, only their pollen remains, hidden in the sediments at the bottoms of the freshwater ponds and beneath the surfaces of the wetlands. But another remnant of past life is here, hidden in the field—an endangered two-inch-long insect, the American burying beetle.[38] This

Dickens Point, on Block Island, once covered by an oak-dominated forest, is one of the few remaining habitats of the American burying beetle in the United States.

beetle requires the carcasses of small dead animals for the propagation of future generations. The carrion provides food for the insect's larvae. Once it ranged across the eastern half of the continent to South Dakota and Texas, but today, it is found only on Block Island and in small areas of Oklahoma and Nebraska.

What caused its demise? One looks to ecological connections for answers. For example, one theory suggests that the removal of the forest that once played host to vast flocks of passenger pigeons and the unregulated hunting and trapping of these and other birds and mammals upon which the beetle depended for its food are to blame. Whatever the cause, it is a different environment compared to that visited by the navigator Adrian Block, who set foot on this island in 1614.

Most of the fields on Block Island are the result of clearing and cultivation. But a few knolls on this island have a climate, soil, and location that tend to prevent the growth of woody shrubs. These are morainal grasslands, which may have existed before settlement. From a distance one might suspect that one of these knolls was simply a clearing reverting back to a forest of shrubs and trees. Closer observation confirms the mixed up nature of the rocky-sandy-gravelly soil on which grows tufts of grass interspersed with cladonia and other kinds of lichens. Ecologists note that the higher percentage of native species might indicate that these grasslands are original features. Here one might also find rare species of plants, such as bushy rockrose, northern blazing star, and Maryland golden aster.

This morainal grassland on Block Island may still appear as it did before settlement.

At the north end of Block Island, where settlers are thought to have landed in 1661, small shrubs feebly hold wind-whipped sandy deposits of a relic dune system.

Approaching Block Island by ferry from Point Judith on the mainland, the route skirts a long, high, vertically gullied bluff. This is Clay Head, named after its blue-gray clays, which are mixed with colorful sands and gravels—another presettlement feature. Beginning at the north end of a long arcing beach, a sandy trail through scrubland ascends the bluff and winds along the edge of its steep face, at times more than a hundred feet above the sea. Bayberry, highbush blueberry, and other low shrubs provide a fencerow between the trail and the bluff's sheer drop. Bank swallows dart about their nesting holes. A rufous-sided towhee rustles beneath a tangle of shrubs. The path squeezes between the bluff and a small wetland and winds by small stands of exotic black Japanese pines. It comes again to the precipitous edge, and large areas of the embankment are seen slumping towards the ocean below. Near the end of the island, the trail circles and returns on itself.

Longshore currents sweep away the sand and other sediments from Block Island's bluffs. The stream of particles moves northward until the currents, unable to sustain their ability to carry the load, deposit the sediments at the end of the island. Here a long, sandy point builds outward toward the mainland. Winds and waves work the deposits, whipping them into dunes and small hills and isolating a small brackish pond. Seen from across the pond, saddle-shaped breaches in the dunes exhibit the unrelenting nature of these forces on them. Viewed from the south, down the length of the beach, a berm angles up steeply on its seaward side. On the landward side lies a back-dune wetland. Beach grass and shrubs, such as bay-berry, pepperbush, and wild rose, gather in this environment to make their advance to the dune ridge, as they have gone here for centuries. This is a relic dune system—one where the first settlers are said to have landed in 1661—and another relatively intact piece of our New England wilderness that still survives today.

With these words Verrazzano set forth the first detailed description of Rhode Island's Narragansett Bay. The bays and harbors were often the first places described in detail because the explorers sought them out, not only as safe refuges from the sea but for the opportunities they afforded for exploration over land and up rivers and for their possibilities as locations for settlements. Many early descriptions of bays along the New England coast exist. Progressing northward, we have Brereton's description of Buzzard's Bay at the southwest end of Cape Cod, discovered by the Gosnold expedition of 1602; Champlain's 1605 description of Cape Cod Bay, Plymouth Harbor, and Boston Harbor; Smith's 1614 observations of Saco Bay and Casco Bay; also accounts of Casco Bay in 1607 by Davies of the Popham expedition and Levett's in 1624; and Champlain's 1604 characterization of Penobscot Bay and Passamaquoddy Bay. Today, the effects of nearly four centuries of use and development are readily apparent in many of our harbors. Generally, we see less change as we move northeastward along the coast, and in this regard, one is of special note.

BAYS

The mouth of the haven lieth open to the south halfe a league broad . . . it stretcheth twelve leagues, where it wareth broader and broader, and maketh a gulfe about 20 leagues in compasse, wherein are five small islands very fruitful and pleasant, full of hie and broad trees. . . . In entering into the haven, on both sides there are most pleasant hils, with many rivers of most cleare water falling into the sea.

—Giovanni da Verrazzano,
1524[39]

Mill Cove, at the head of a small harbor on the western side of Rhode Island's Narragansett Bay, is part of the "haven" the explorer Giovanni da Verrazzano found when he sailed into the bay in 1524.

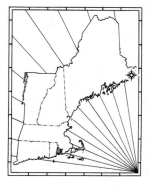

Cobscook Bay, Maine

I went to a river in the mainland called the River of the Ete-chemins . . . and we passed by such a number of beautiful islands that I could not count them. . . . They are all in a bay.

—Samuel de Champlain, 1604[40]

The bay Champlain sailed into that mid-June day was Passamaquoddy Bay. Champlain also passed the mouth of another, Cobscook Bay, a more complex extension of the Passamaquoddy Bay system. The bays in this region are the result of a pattern of sedimentary and volcanic rocks, much different from the long northeast-southwest oriented, drowned valleys that created many peninsulas and islands along the southerly coastal sections of Maine.[41] The orientations of rock belts and erosional processes have formed a curving, or arcing, pattern of valleys and ridges which, because of sea-level rise, became bays, peninsulas, and strings of islands. Identified as "the most extensive undeveloped embayment complex in Maine" and singled out for its "relatively pristine character" as late as the 1970s and 1980s, Cobscook Bay retains to this day the look of Champlain's time.[42]

I first saw this bay through swarms of mosquitoes and black flies when I arrived on the edge of a small cove one mid-June evening. It was a warm evening, and the air was clear and bright, not the cool, foggy, and damp atmosphere reputed to favor this region of the coast. At the time, the tide was low, but during my stay, the meaning of "Cobscook," Indian for boiling tides, revealed itself. One could see the tidal waters enter the cove, almost as small waves. They reversed the flow of meandering streams in the mud flats and filled the basin with twenty or more feet of seawater. Mainland peninsulas became islands. The streams, the wide flats over which they flowed, and high rocky shorelands all disappeared. At low tide the next morning, fingers of rocky outcrops reached out into the cove again. In the red light of the morning sun, rakelike shadows revealed scars of glacial encounters.

Later, on the edge of another part of this cove, I quietly contemplated a time when Maine was only a continental

fragment in a sea below the equator. Beneath the mud flats
that I saw before me, on the bottom of the intertidal zone,
lives a creature directly descended from ancestors who lived
in ancient Middle Cambrian seas, a lineage of over half a
billion years. It is a priapulid, a spiny, cucumber-shaped
animal, soft bodied and wormlike, and six inches long.

Another species living in the cold waters of this bay is
also a member of an ancient phylum, *Brachiopod*a, represented in the fossil record dating back to Early Cambrian
times, or around 600 million years ago. Like clams, this
organism has two hinged valves, or shells. However, they

An incoming rush of high tidal
waters at Reversing Falls in Pem-
broke, Maine, changes the direction of flow from the upper
reaches of Cobscook Bay.

are shaped differently, thus, their common name, lamp
shells. This species of brachiopod lives beneath the waters
off Crow Neck where cold, strong tidal currents prevail.

The Crow Neck area of Cobscook Bay is also the site
of one of Maine's outstanding reversing falls. I caught it at
low tide, and as I stood beneath a large red oak at the edge
of the tidal channel where the current drains the upper
reaches of the bay, it was easy to imagine I was beside the
rapids of a large river. The low falls rolled and frothed
noisily over ledges between the peninsula and an island.
But unlike our inland rapids, the rocky shores here display
the distinctive bands created by the algae, lichens, bar-
nacles, and other organisms of the intertidal zone. A
kingfisher flew by with a fish in its mouth. By the bird's
behavior I suspected a nest was nearby, deeply excavated
into a bank of soft earth. Upon reflection, the kingfisher's presence was not surprising: these fast currents

bring nutrients and attract fish. I thought about navigating these falls. Champlain had difficulty at one of these places when he attempted the Kennebec River. Today, we have overcome such obstacles. But for a moment in this place, where I saw no habitations or modern, high-powered boats, I could easily picture one of those shallops of 1600-vintage being pulled up through the fast waters of these falls.

Bays of the Piscataqua, New Hampshire

I found a great River and a good harbour called Pascat-taway. . . . *the* Sagmore *or* King *of that place . . . told me there was much good ground up in the river about seven or eight leagues.*

—Christopher Levett, 1624[43]

Christopher Levett spent about a month in the area around what is today Portsmouth, New Hampshire. While looking for a place to establish a permanent settlement, he "surveyed as much as possible" and saw "much good timber." He noted that the ground was "very rockey and full of trees and brushwood."[44] It is not known how far up the Piscataqua River he traveled, if he did at all. It seems likely, however, that he saw the bays a few miles inland that drain into the river. As early as 1647, a map shows them as Little Bay and Great Bay, names they still have today. At that time there were settlements around them. Belknap in 1792 describes several rivers that "empty into a bay, four miles wide, called the Great Bay [and] the water in its further progress is contracted into a lesser bay."[45] Current maps show the bays encircled by a maze of transportation systems, businesses, and residential areas. Yet, amazingly, after centuries of development, it was reported in 1960 that on a gentle slope at the edge of one of these bays a small woodland was discovered that "may be a remnant of the forest that originally bordered" its shore.[46]

I set out to find this presettlement forest of old hardwoods. Considering that it was reported to be only three acres in size and also that the estuary complex contains miles of shoreland covering thousands of acres, the likelihood of finding the woodland seemed small, indeed. But after many letters and phone calls, I arrived one day in late April at a possible site. Swollen leaf buds hung on the branches of old red oaks lined along the shore. Behind them on a shallow, rocky slope grew American ashes, red and white maples, and hickories.

At first I saw a lifeless forest floor beneath the trees; dry yellow-brown leaves from previous years crackled with every step. The land dipped into a sinuous depression—a shallow gully in which a small brook flowed. Moss-covered trunks of fallen trees, mud-bottomed pools, and bright-green tufts of new grasses marked the brook's weaving course to the edge of the woodland where it gushed over a low, blocky ledge of quartzite into the bay. On a knoll above the brook, a shagbark hickory stood, silhouetted against the waters of the bay; its long, loose strips of bark were dished and frayed. Puffs of green from the clustered needles of white pines softened the gray, vertical patterns of the trees.

A shagbark hickory grows in a small woodland on the shore of the Little and Great Bay complex near the mouth of the Piscataqua River. Located in a highly developed region, this tiny forested area, surprisingly, may be a remnant of pre-European-settlement times.

Beneath a large, old maple, cuddled next to its trunk, a patch of bloodroot sprung forth to capture the early season's sunshine before the canopy closes and shuts out the light. The bloodroot's stem and roots contain a red-orange liquid that flows out if they are broken. A single, deeply lobed, pinwheel-shaped leaf wraps protectively around each plant's white flower until it blooms. Already the flowers in this patch blossomed on long stems well above their leaves.

I left the bloodroots and continued my exploration. A stump or two casts suspicion on the presettlement characterization of the woodland. But large trees are growing here, and a few old decaying trunks of windblown trees lie on the forest floor. The site appeared to match the description of the report I had read. Further study might reveal its age and history, but for the moment, it seemed possible this woodland had somehow escaped the development one sees next to its borders and across the bay.

MOUNTAINS

*The remarkablest . . .
mountains for Land-
markes are these . . . .
them of Pennobscot:
the twinkling Moun-
taine of Aucocisco; the
greate mountaine of
Sassanou; and the
high Mountaine of
Massachusit.*

—Captain John Smith, 1614[47]

One of the first points of the mainland sighted by the early explorers approaching the New England coast was the mountains. Champlain noted the mountains of Mount Desert Island and, as did Smith, the Camden Hills and the White Mountains. Smith, in the introductory quotation, also singled out Mt. Agamenticus in York, Maine, and Great Blue Hill near Boston, Massachusetts. Today, the slopes and tops of most of these mountains display trails, roads, buildings, antennas, towers, and other encroachments that mar their natural appearance. However, each of these mountains still contains elements that survive from that time when the white sails of tall-masted wooden ships could be seen from their summits.

Mountains of the Penobscot, Maine

Ten of us . . . marched up into the country towards the Mountains, which we descried at our first falling with the land. Unto some of them the river brought us so neere, as we judged our selves when we landed to have been within a league of them. . . . In this march we passed . . . Oke like stands left in our pastures in England, good and great, fit timber for any use.

—James Rosier, 1605[48]

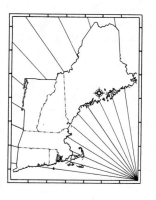

Seen from atop an island hill overlooking Georges Harbor and the string of islands leading into the St. George River, the "Mountains of the Pennobscot," so named by Captain John Smith, rise as low humps on the horizon, hued a slightly darker blue than the sky. Today, they are known as the Camden Hills. "There are five or six of them . . . and are clothed with forest," noted the historian Williamson in 1832, and "most of them are neither steep nor rugged. . . . the highest of them may be 1,500 feet above the level of the sea."[49] Their height and closeness to the coast prompted Smith to regard these mountains as coastal landmarks "whose feet doth beat the Sea: But over all the land, Iles, or other impediments, you may well see them sixteene or eighteene leagues from their situation."[50]

The trail I followed up Megunticook Mountain in these hills was slopped with mud from the spring runoff. Forest trees still clothe this mountain, and I looked for red oak—old oak—like those "oke stands" Rosier saw in 1605. I knew that above me such a stand has stood on this mountain for almost a century and a half.[51] The south slope was sunny and warm for April. Already the snow was gone, but the ground waterlogged and seeping quickly enough to fill the gullies with mountain brooks. Fresh deer tracks pointed upward. Large red oaks began to appear along the trail. I stepped from rock to rock across a fast stream and up into a shallow ravine beside a ledgy ridge that cuts across the mountain's slope. The oaks seemed taller on the ridge, and I climbed up.

Large oaks stretched down the mountainside beyond my sight. Tall, straight, gray columns, some two feet in diameter, rose to thirty feet or more before branching wildly to a height of ninety feet. American beech, sugar maple, and white ash also occupied the canopy. Other hardwoods and hemlock were scattered about at lower levels. The sun shined over the top of the mountain behind me and sent long shadows down the mountain. Through the open canopy's scribble of twisting limbs, I saw in the distance the deep blue waters of Penobscot Bay and the cold, white shore of Islesboro Island. I began to appreciate Williamson's opinion that "no place affords so commanding a prospect of the Atlantic, the Penobscot Bay, the numerous islands and the contiguous country."[52]

I walked along the ledge-topped ridge beneath the oaks, sidestepping light green mounds of pincushion moss and fallen limbs. A soft breeze brushed the brown litter of last year's leaves. It was quiet and even felt secluded here in these open woods. Last fall's crop of acorns still dotted the ledge, each accented and enlarged by its individual shadow. Splashes of green from an occasional red spruce or hemlock or Christmas fern added the only dashes of color.

I came off the ridge and followed a gushing mountain brook. The silence I had experienced was now replaced by the sound of falling water as the brook made its way over and around the many rocks that impeded its course. It bounced down the mountain by the feet of the big oaks and out of sight. I know that it has but a short way to go before it reaches the bay, but its course below me will re-

A mountain brook, invigorated by the spring melt, flows beneath one of many red oaks in a 150-year-old stand on Mt. Megunticook in Maine's Camden Hills. James Rosier commented on the "good and great Oke" he saw in these hills on an overland march in 1605.

spond to human influences. Here, where there is not a stump along its course, it is free; such is not the case with most of New England's brooks and streams.

Mt. Agamenticus, Maine

The remarkable mountain, Agamenticus, lies about four leagues north of the entrance of Pascataqua.

—Jeremy Belknap, 1792[53]

Almost two hundred years before Jeremy Belknap recognized the exceptional nature of Mt. Agamenticus, Captain John Smith singled it out as a prominent landmark for coastal voyagers. It is likely that it was seen much earlier by other explorers, for a number of them, including Gosnold in 1602 and Champlain in 1605, sailed along this section of the coast. The mountain also impressed the historian Williamson who, reinforcing Belknap's assessment, called it a "sightly eminence."[54] Still others have referred to it as a majestic hill.

I first noticed this mountain and the relief that it imparted to the southern Maine coastline when I saw it from the Isles of Shoals on a calm, clear day in May. Its status as a landmark was clearly etched on the low, flat horizon. The mountain stands well over 300 feet above the rest of the landscape and 691 feet above the level of the sea. Actually, the mountain's lofty presence is shared with two nearby lower hills, Second Hill and Third Hill.

I selected a clear day in April to drive to the top of this mountain. The snow had left this coastal region, and the road was bare as I negotiated the switchbacks. I parked in the near-empty lot at the top and stepped from my truck, gathered my equipment, and headed up to the recreation building, still closed from the winter season. From its deck, I saw little different from the description Williamson gave in 1832:

From its top the beholder has a view of the Atlantic, skirted with an indented shore; from Cape-Ann to Cape-Elizabeth. On the southwest, he sees a country adorned with buildings, fields of cultivation, and waters of the Piscataqua; and northwesterly, he has sight of the White Hills, in New Hampshire.[55]

As for the mountain itself, what is noticeably different is its top: Williamson's "large crowning rocks, which form the summit" are covered with towers, antennas, walkways, driveways, and assorted buildings. Still, looking down the slopes of the mountain and toward Second and Third hills, I saw much that, in Williamson's words, was "covered with woods and shrubs."[56] I know that in these woods an unusually large number of plant species occur due to the soils, the effects of the nearby ocean on the local climate, and the latitudinal position. Here, the northern and southern ranges of plants mix: plants to the north are at the southern edge of their range, and plants with southern affinities are at their northern boundaries.

In these woods, however, is a difference from Williamson's time: a few members of the plant kingdom find here one of their last outposts in Maine. It is not surprising that these species are ones that have lived a tenuous existence at the fringes of their northern ranges. Here are Maine's remaining stands of chestnut oak, a handsome tree growing up to sixty feet tall, and the last natural populations of flowering dogwood, a small but especially beautiful tree when it flowers around the last week in May. Here also grows one of Maine's few stands of the threatened Atlantic white cedar.

In spring and fall, these hills become quite a different kind of landmark—one that attracts thousands of migrating hawks, an event that still occurs from those days when this region was a "meer wilderness" in the eyes of John Josselyn when he passed by. And just as that wilderness was once a place of escape for many who came to these shores in our colonial era, so, too, is it today. In the words of the Maine Chapter of The Nature Conservancy: "For the people of southern York County and their visitors, Mount Agamenticus is a refuge in the sea of development that has flooded this part of Maine."[57]

Blue Hills, Massachusetts

This is the highest and most conspicuous range of hills in the vicinity of Boston. . . . All these summits command extensive and most interesting prospects.

—Edward Hitchcock, 1841[58]

My route up the steep, smooth, granite ledges that pave much of the trail to the top of Great Blue Hill began easily enough in an open grove of tall hardwoods. The high canopy above was yet to close and hardly had begun to filter the bright sun. So heavily used was this particular area of woods that I had to look closely to find the trail going up. I walked with some uncertainty at first until I saw some hikers coming down from the ledges above. On the slope the trail cut deeply into the earth between the rock outcrops where others before me had walked, creating a series of steps up onto the granite shelving. It was an engaging hike—moving out onto open rocks exposing views to the west across Massachusetts and southern New Hampshire, then into wooded terraces of broken ledge and collected boulders among oaks and pines, up onto ramplike ledges, then into intermittent ditches dug by thousands of sneakers and hiking boots within the last century. Once I reached the top of Great Blue Hill, I anticipated being able to obtain an expansive view of this rugged terrain only fifteen miles from Boston. At 635 feet, this hill is the highest and westernmost of the twenty-two granite domes in the Blue Hill chain. The Native Americans who had once made this area their home called themselves the Massachusett, or "the people living near the high hills." There were few trails here then, I imagined.

Settlement of this region began in the 1620s. Even by then this mountain that I climbed had been named as Massachusetts Mount by Captain John Smith. With the expansion of settlements around Boston, these hills were increasingly looked to for their resources—granite for building material, forests for fuel and timber, and soil and space for agriculture. Less than three centuries later, the Metropolitan Park Commission reported that "it is not likely that a single acre of the [Blue Hills] reservation has escaped the woodcutters axe."[59]

These imposing, rocky hills were also seen in quite another way, more in keeping with the reasons for my own hike up the Great Blue Hill that day in mid-May. It had to do with their beauty and effect on the human soul, or in the words of Edwin Bacon, writing in 1922, their "wild rocky heights [and] widespreading views in all directions."[60] Or from the pen of Henry Maurice Lisle, more than a century earlier:

> Turning from the ocean's surface, next survey
> The fir-clad mountains, which behind you lay.
> There the GREAT BLUE HILL rears its
> cloud-capped head,
> And knotted oaks their verdant foliage spread.[61]

These hills continued to cast their spell on generations of people who lived and died within their sight. In 1893, the Massachusetts Legislature established the Metropolitan Park Commission, and within ten years the Blue Hills Reservation had been acquired.

The low observation tower I finally reached echoed the hollow-sounding, quiet talk of visitors. Through an elongated stone opening, I looked out over Lisle's "knotted oaks and verdant foliage," yellow-green and brilliant, rippling with every heavy gust of wind, randomly pierced by tall, dark-green pines. Their new leaves were not yet dulled by exposure to the elements, both natural and unnatural. I saw the tall buildings of Boston rising above the horizon—and beyond, the Atlantic, with long, white dashes where island shores cut the blue waters of Boston Harbor. Nearer are the low mounded hills, ledges slashing downward, not yet covered by the greening vegetation. Large patches of oaks dominate the forest—red, black, and chestnut—broken by smaller stands of hemlock and white and pitch pines. In the valleys are meadows, bogs, streams, and ponds. But it was the sea that kept drawing my attention, for in these places we always try to push to the limits of our vision. Edward Hitchcock noticed the sea, too, when he stood on the top of one of these hills:

> To look out upon the ocean is always an imposing sight; but when that ocean is studded with islands, most picturesque in shape and position, and the frequent sail is seen gliding among them, he must be insensible indeed, whose

soul does not kindle at the scene, and linger upon it with delight.[62]

Over a century and a half has passed since Hitchcock wrote his impression of what he saw from the Blue Hills. What impressed me most after gaining the summit of Great Blue Hill is that here, within the New England metropolitan area that has the longest history of settlement, I was able to see so much land still forested and know that a creature still lives here that is now absent from much of its former range: the timber rattlesnake.

CAPES, POINTS, AND HEADLANDS

And this is that headland which Captaine Bartholomew Gosnold discovered in the yeare 1602, and called Cape Cod, because of the store of cod-fish that he found thereabout.

—Henry Hudson, 1609[63]

Among the landmarks depended upon by the early navigators of the coast were the points and headlands. These were noted on maps and in logbooks. For example, from papers related to the Popham expedition of 1606, we find reference to "the head Land called the Semeamis," now known as Cape Elizabeth. Christopher Levett in 1623 located the mouth of the Saco River "one league to the North-east of a cape land," now Biddeford Pool. Martin Pring's account of his 1606 voyage makes mention of "shaping our course for Savage Rocke," probably Cape Neddick in Maine, and discovered "the yeere before by Captaine Gosnold."

Cape Cod, of course, was often mentioned, as in this 1610 journal entry by Samuel Argall: "About two of the clocke in the afternoone I did see an Hed-land, which did beare off me Southwest about foure leagues: so I steered with it, taking it to bee Cape Cod." Captain John Smith judged there were only two "chief Head-lands . . . Cape Tragabigzanda [Cape Ann] and Cape Cod."[64]

As one might suspect, the headlands and points along the New England coast have attracted the attention of people over the intervening centuries for many reasons. Yet, interestingly, some remain that retain features present when they were regarded as landmarks by the first Europeans.

Great Head, Maine

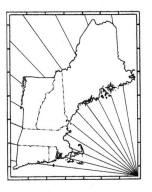

I looked up at the face of the cliff. It was bearded with icicles, like the Genius of Winter. Along the upper edge appeared the interlacing roots of old trees grasping the scanty soil like monster talons. Stunted birches, bent by storms, skirted its brow, and at sea added to its height. From top to bottom the face of the cliff is a mass of hard granite, overhanging its foundations in impending ruin, Slivered and splintered as if torn by some tremendous explosion.

—Samuel Drake, 1875[65]

From the top of Great Head on the eastern extremity of Mount Desert Island, I looked eastward past the mouth of Frenchman Bay to Schoodic Point and the peninsulas beyond. Champlain sailed by this bold promontory in 1604. The view from here is probably essentially the same as it was then, and so is this massive protuberance of resistant rock. The headland owes its longevity to diorite, a tough, dark intrusive rock, speckled black and white and related to both granite and volcanic basalt.

I made my way down a gradual slope of blocky ledges and pockets of grasses, small shrubs, and spruce seedlings to the northern margin of the bluff's sheer face. The rock is weathered gray, lichen covered, worn round in places, and fractured in others. Partway down, I looked past the rough profile of this headland to the south and the Cranberry Isles, some five miles distant. It was a clear day with large cumulus clouds drifting by. Far below, I heard the surf breaking on the rocks.

Drake believed that "to appreciate Great Head one must stand underneath it." From the shore, he observed, "you will stand in presence of the boldest headland in all New England."[66] He was right: rising 145 feet above the ocean, Great Head is one of the highest headlands on the eastern seaboard.

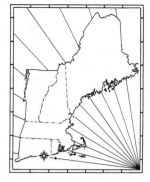

Bluff Point, Connecticut

[New London Harbor] opens to the south; from the light-house at the mouth of the harbour, to the town is about three miles . . . and as far up as one mile above the town entirely secure and commodius for large ships.

—Governor of the English Colony of Connecticut, 1774[67]

One can assume with some confidence that in the year before the American Revolution, New London Harbor was a place of brisk commerce, being one of two mentioned in that report to the King of England. Today, parkways and interstate highways, air traffic facilities, marinas and ports, business centers, and residential areas all bustle with activity of an intensity that would have been difficult to envision by those governmental officials in 1774. Amazingly, only two miles east of this harbor, one finds "possibly the only undeveloped and undisturbed coastal peninsula from New York City to Cape Cod." Its name is Bluff Point.

Walking the mile-and-a-half-long gravel roadway to the point one late afternoon in early May, I marveled at how quickly I had left the urban congestion and confusion I had just endured. The sounds persisted, though now muted, and a few walkers, joggers, and cyclists were getting their exercise, but the relative quiet, the fresh smells from the tidal waters and damp woods, and the change of pace joined to create a soothing effect.

The wide trail kept to a level terrace along the east shore of Poquonock River. To the west an airport separated this peninsula from the Thames River and New London Harbor. At first, the open woods of large oaks and sassafras trees captured my attention. In some places they lined the roadway and covered this western side of the peninsula's ridge, some 120 feet high to its top. Hickory, black birch, and gray birch grow here, too, I was informed, and along my route, I also passed a magnificent American elm in a clearing. Though the woods were open and the canopy not yet closed, the cloudy sky and lateness of the day created a dimness and mystical quality to the trailside forest. Occasionally, wildlife would reveal itself: a gray squirrel ran silently between the trees; a scratching

Bluff Point, on the coast of Connecticut, has been identified as perhaps the least disturbed peninsula from New York to Cape Cod.

turned out to be the beautifully colored and patterned rufous-sided towhee; an oriole provided a dash of orange to the forest. Deer tracks entered the road. I learned later that up to ten rare plants and animals have been discovered here.

The Bluff Point woods that I saw are not original. The peninsula probably experienced many cycles of clearing and revegetation. Along this coast, large open tracts of land cultivated by the natives were seen by early explorers. There are records and evidence of pasture land here in the early part of the twentieth century. Stone walls, old foundations, and existing vegetation suggest an agricultural history. Later, the point was populated by cottages and a mansion. The hurricane of 1938 destroyed most of the buildings, and a fire finished off another. In the early 1960s, the state began acquiring land. Today, the entire peninsula, over eight hundred acres, is now state owned.

I took a few steps off the road to the edge of the river which provided a view out to the point. I looked across a tidal marsh and a lagoon behind a beach system with sand flats and submerged beds of eelgrass. At different seasons of the year, these wet areas attract large numbers of greater and lesser scaups, muted swans, mallards, buffle-heads, and other waterfowl. When I reached the end of the peninsula in the light of early evening, I followed a trail down by the lagoon and up onto a pebble beach. A hundred clicks accompanied every step as the rocks rolled out from under my feet. My eyes followed the beach, which made a long, shallow arc to a half-mile, dune-covered sandspit that connected to a small island. Technically, this barrier beach and island combination is called a tombolo.

I turned eastward toward the rocky bluffs, climbing over huge boulders to their top. The bluffs are thirty feet high and steep faced. The bedrock here is 225-million-year-old gneiss and schist and is responsible for protecting the peninsula from the pounding waves. Erosion, however, continues to take place, and materials that are washed away maintain the beach system. The bedrock also forms the core of the peninsula over which layers of glacial material formed a drumlin—a long, rounded glacial hill—nearly two miles long.

On the east side of the point is another cove with a marshy area. Off the coast, some three miles, lies Fishers Island and, beyond, the expanse of Long Island Sound. The Sound was once a river valley before it was drowned by the sea following the melting of the last glacier.

As dusk settled over the peninsula, I followed the roadway back along the darkening woods. I recalled reading a report about the features I had just seen. It said that they "provide an excellent example of conditions that were once common along the Connecticut coastline." Then I remembered reading about a plan developed in 1965 that advocated high intensity use of this park. Still another plan in 1985 proposed turning it into a public beach with vehicle access. They were rejected![68]

Cape Cod, Massachusetts

We sailed around this headland, almost all points of the compasse, the shore very bolde . . . the land somewhat lowe, full of goodly woods, but in some places plaine.

—John Brereton, 1602[69]

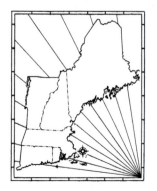

Henry Thoreau called Cape Cod "the bared and bended arm of Massachusetts." It is, without question, the most striking feature of the New England coast when seen from above or on a map. And Cape Cod has been inhabited for centuries, even thousands of years, first by Native Peoples and later by European settlers. Still, places exist here that are relatively unaltered, and that change primarily in response to natural influences. Perhaps the most unique of these features are to be found in the Province Lands.

The Province Lands

Cape Cod...is onely a headland of high hils, overgrowne with shrubby Pines, hurts [whortleberry bushes] and such trash.

—Captain John Smith, 1614[70]

I looked at the headland that Captain John Smith saw with profound wonder. About the only thing familiar to me that evening at the Province Lands' dunes was rapidly leaving—the sun. Dark shadows stretched over a strange, inhospitable otherworld of disfigured, humpbacked shapes, prostrate around me. They crept silently, carried by the wind grain by grain, dissected then reassembled. It was breezy, and vigorous gusts buffeted the dunes, but I saw no visible movement, for these were stealthy forms. A cluster of trees, once alive and vibrant, now stood stark—skeletons without bark or leaves.

I climbed onto the back of one of these humps. A tree or shrub once lived here; only a sun-bleached pile of dried and broken limbs remains. Yet, from this vantage point, I saw new shoots of beach grass, and nearby, low

The dunes of Cape Cod's Province Lands, first described by early explorers in the 1600s, are still considered the best and most spectacular sand dunes on the east coast of the United States.

shrubs—bayberry and beach plum—clinging to the tops of other humps. They looked dead, too, but it was May and new leaves had yet to show themselves. Only that morning I had left the Berkshires, where spring was already showing itself in the greening of the forested hills; the contrast here was striking.

That evening, I was at the "fist" of Cape Cod. Champlain observed these "lofty sand dunes, which are conspicuous viewed from the sea."[71] Today, they are still conspicuous, even stunning to the uninitiated, and those on the sandspit at the very tip of the cape are considered the best and most spectacular of any on the east coast of the United States. Historically, some dunes have exceeded one hundred feet in height.

Geologically, this is the youngest part of the cape, though it was created over a period of time measured in centuries.[72] Cape Cod, itself, is the product of glaciers. When the final ice sheet melted away fifteen thousand years ago, it had left a plain of deposited materials covering the south side of the cape close to the mainland and three moraines—ridges of clays, sands, gravels, and rocks of various sizes. These are the sandy materials that have been transported and shaped by ocean currents, waves, and winds to form the beaches, dunes, bluffs, and sand-spits that are now the fist and hook that form this end of the cape. Someday, scientists predict, the sea that created this environmental marvel will also reclaim it.

When the Pilgrims came ashore, possibly at Wood End near the tip of Cape Cod, the Province Lands' dune system had been long stabilized by vegetation. Beach grass, bayberry, beach plum, bear oak, and pitch pine all paved the way for sassafras, white and black oak, white pine, and the climax species that makes up the ultimate stage of forest succession on the cape—American beech. Previously, in 1602, Gosnold had reported taking on board "cypress, birch, witch-hazel, and beech" for fire-wood.[73] Champlain mentioned, too, that beyond an expanse of open shoreland "one enters the woods which are very agreeable and pleasant to see."[74] So when the Mayflower anchored here in 1620, it is not surprising that William Bradford also reported that this semicircular harbor was "compassed about to the very Sea with Okes, Pines, Juniper [red cedar], Sassafras, and other sweet wood."[75] Additional confirmation of the original, forested nature of the tip of Cape Cod comes from stumps of trees preserved in the sands and occasionally uncovered by the wind. Perhaps even more confirmatory is the existence of a surviving example of the Province Lands forest—a beech climax woods.

Hiking the trail to the Province Lands' old beech forest, I worked to gain traction in the deep, loose sand. The path skirts two shallow freshwater ponds, depressions

A climax forest of American beech at the "fist" of outer Cape Cod suggests the kind of forest that early explorers and settlers encountered here in the early 1600s.

among the dunes and choked with water lilies. Soon the trail was bordered by wooded slopes of high dunes, and it moved into a deep, ravinelike depression where cool, moist, shady conditions favored the growth of the beech. The gray, smooth-barked trees were short by northern standards and somewhat crooked and gnarled. Patches of Canada mayflower, starflower, and other plants familiar to this type of forest grew on its floor. A small sassafras tree beside the trail was now leafed out with soft-green, three-lobed leaves. A high sand dune had crept into the edge of the forest, slowly encircling the trunks of a few trees with a rising tide of sand.

Near here in 1791, a visitor was confronted with a similarly advancing sand hill that was burying the forest. He climbed the hill and saw "a desert of white sand. . . . The tops of the trees appear above the sand, but they are all dead. . . . [and] over the greater part of this desert the trees have long since disappeared."[76] Today, from the top of the encroaching sand hill, a vast plain of dunes still can be seen. Along its edge, near the beech forest, grow pitch pine that are not deterred by such conditions. The beech now depend on the pitch pine, it seems, to help protect them from the advancing flood of sand.

Sandy Neck and the Great Marshes of Barnstable

We observed a very low, sandy shore [and] sent the shallop to make soundings in the direction of some rather high land . . . where we thought there was an excellent harbor. . . . There were a great many oysters there . . . and we called the place Oyster Harbor.

—Samuel de Champlain,
1606[77]

Hauntingly, it appears low and long, levitating in the mists. Looking hard, one barely sees the low outline of Sandy Neck, only a shade darker than the gray horizon and lying two miles of salt marsh away. Everything lies flat here—almost six thousand acres of low, level land and water, except that distant ridge. Grain by grain the long-shore currents brought it here. Fashioned by wind and waves, the barrier grew, allowing the flat land and waters behind it to rest and develop, protected from the pounding waves. Things are slower here, quieter, more uniform. Even the mists hover peacefully.

John Brereton possibly gave the first description of Sandy Neck: "Captaine Bartholomew Gosnold, my self, and three others, went ashore, being a white sandie and very bold shore."[78] Four years later in 1606, Champlain also explored this shore and the harbor that lay behind it, calling it Oyster Harbor. Within three decades of these early explorations, the marsh that lay behind the neck and beyond the harbor waters was supplying colonial farmers with salt hay for fodder and bedding for cattle. Today, we know much about the value of this marsh and all salt marshes, for that matter, in supplying nutrients to other animals from which we benefit less directly than those early colonists did from their cattle.

The view I had of the Barnstable Marsh on that early, misty June morning, looking towards Sandy Neck and the ocean, might have been very similar to the one the Gosnold party saw. The new growth of *Spartina* grasses was well underway, bathed in nutrient-laden tidal waters that rise in the harbor over nine feet about twice a day. At low tide, only 10 percent of the water remains.[79]

Later in the day, I roamed the dunes of Sandy Neck, a six-mile-long sandspit that continues to build eastward into the harbor. It wasn't as prominent when Gosnold and Champlain saw it; in the last hundred years it has grown six hundred feet longer from sands brought by southward-moving currents from eroding cliffs along the Massachusetts coast all the way from Monomet Point. The dune ridge is also high—nearly a hundred feet at its maximum.

Among the rolling dunes, covered with spatterings of beach grass, the only shady place to find relief from the sun was some pitch pine in the back dune area. A wet depression was filled with old and new cattails. From it arose damp, swampy smells, mixed with the salt air from the bay. Up in the dunes, nearer the beach, one could look back towards the mainland and catch glimpses of the light-green marsh against the hills Gosnold hiked overland to climb so that he could see the area better. Near the beach, the dunes showed the effects of both wind and wave. Timothy Dwight, New England traveler and president of Yale, visited the cape in the early 1800s and saw at Sandy Neck "a long, lofty, wild and fantastical beach, thrown into a thousand grotesque forms by the united force of winds and waves."[80] Today, one sees the same.

Marconi Swamp

Cypres, of this is great plenty. . . . it is . . . to my minde, most bewtifull, and cannot be denied to passe for a commodity.

—Thomas Morton, 1637[81]

The beauty Morton saw in the "cypres," or Atlantic white cedar, is not easily described. I suspect that much of this beauty may be attributed to the environment in which it lives. I once visited such a place on Cape Cod, a swamp. I stood on a low hummock surrounded by dark, brown pools of water and a deep stillness. Faint, ghostly lines of the gray-barked trees were reflected in the deeper pools and merged with the sun-dappled bottoms of those that were shallower. The trees were tall and straight, with dense tops. Their trunks were patterned with narrow strips of bark, crossing to make elongated diamonds. Growths of lichens gave them a gray-green look.

The cedars grow in a swamp that developed in a kettle hole—a depression in glacial deposits created by a melting block of ice. Later, when the nearby ocean rose as a result of melting glaciers, the water table also rose and filled the depression. When I visited it, twenty-four feet of peat lay beneath me and the bottom of the kettle hole. A core pulled out of the peat in the late twentieth century yielded grains of pollen and charcoal that told part of the story of this forest. Its profile records three thousand years of cedar habitation in this area, which is sheltered from the wind and salt spray. Similarly, long, pencil-like cylinders, penetrating to the cores of some of the old trees, have also been extracted and analyzed for their annual growth patterns and deformities. We now know that an early fire once swept through the swamp, leaving it with fewer trees. The surrounding uplands were left barren and inviting to pitch pine.[82] It wasn't the last: five major fires,

Atlantic white cedars grow on hummocks in Cape Cod's Marconi Swamp, an increasingly rare forest type. Core samples from the twenty-four feet of peat beneath this forest attest to the cedars' presence in this area for three thousand years.

some perhaps set by the Native Americans, took their toll on the cedar, leaving no opportunity for the mature, dense stands, such as I saw from the hummock, to live for long.[83]

Permanent settlements came to this area of Cape Cod in 1640, and since then there have been few fires. Historic records from the settlement period confirm the existence of virgin cedar swamps in this region of Cape Cod. For example, sixteen miles away in the town of Chatham, its first colonial settler, William Nickerson, found a similar swamp filled with giant cedars.[84] Today, the old trees in that swamp, as well as in the one I visited, are now gone, probably harvested in the eighteenth and nineteenth centuries.

The swamp I wandered through that day in June is small, about seven and a half acres. And while it doesn't contain the huge cedars of colonial times, its trees are, nevertheless, old, beginning their lives in the late 1700s, and it is one of the better examples of this increasingly rare forest. There are perhaps thirteen thousand acres of Atlantic white cedar swamp left in the glacier-scoured regions of the northeastern United States.

It seems appropriate that this location is named the Marconi Swamp. Not far from it at the beginning of the twentieth century, the Italian physicist Guglielmo Marconi built the first transatlantic wireless telegraph and sent a historic message. Perhaps the time has come to send out a new message—that of protecting old swamps, such as this, as part of a larger effort to preserve our natural biodiversity.

Doane Rock

Now . . . I will come to speake of the Creatures that participate of earth . . . which is stones.

—Thomas Morton, 1637[85]

While the forests change, the dunes move and form, the peatlands grow higher, and the bays shallower, the stones that "participate of earth" still survive—some as they were first seen and described. Such is the case with Doane Rock, a lonely symbol of stability and resistance to change.

The rock eluded me when I first began to search for it. A small woods obscured it from the road. But then I glimpsed its large, greenish gray, weathered form through the trees and turned into the road that led to it. Soon, I stood facing what is perhaps the largest erratic, or glacially deposited rock, this far south in New England. Geologists hypothesize that it was plucked by the glacier from a volcanic ridge, which appears to lie under Massachusetts Bay, and then carried by the ice sheet a hundred miles before being dropped here on the uplands near Nauset Marsh in Eastham.[86]

This chunk of crystallized volcanic lava measures forty-five feet long by twenty-five feet wide. Its bottom is probably planted twelve feet below the ground, and its top rises eighteen feet above. It is, without question, a striking monolith. What better monument to the forgotten nature of Cape Cod?

COASTAL BEACHES

This coast is sandy in most places from Quinibequy.

—Samuel de Champlain, 1605[87]

From Quinibequy, or the Kennebec River, southward, the early explorers discovered stretches of sandy beach all along the New England shore. These are products of glacial outwash sediments, which continue to be brought down from the interior by the great rivers of the region like the Androscoggin, Kennebec, Saco, and the Merrimack. Other beaches are produced by the erosion of headlands and the transportation of their glacially deposited materials by longshore currents, such as we have seen at Province Lands, Barnstable, Block Island, and Bluff Point.

To the east of the Kennebec River, the explorers found a rocky coast where the sea level is rising, exposing and eroding new headlands. Freezing, thawing, and wave action loosen and dislodge fragments of the rocks and wash them into inlets and coves where they are tumbled and jostled until smooth and rounded. Here we find the greatest number of New England's pebble and cobble beaches. Today, along the Maine coast, a number of these beaches remain relatively pristine and one sand beach system exists that is still essentially undisturbed.

Gravel Beach of a Different Hue, Maine

The rocks are exceedingly beautiful along the whole coast. The jasper is mostly of a blood red color weathering brownish red.

—Charles H. Hitchcock, 1861[88]

The rocks rolled and rattled with every crunching step up the face of the steep ridge. From its top one sees almost a half mile of pebbles and small cobble-sized stones, smoothed and polished and spread in a softening arc across the end of a cove. The beach curves towards an undeveloped, ledgy shore along the cove's east side where spruce and fir rise above the rocks. Here the beach comes to an end in true barrier-spit style, allowing the sea to round its point and flood the tidal marsh it protects. Behind the gravelly barrier, a line of alders stabilizes its landward slope, and on the beach ridge, dense growths of beach pea reside.

These features are all taken in by the eye rather quickly, but what becomes most noticeable and draws one's attention is the unusual reddish hue of the beach.[89]

A relatively un-developed pebble and cobble beach on Maine's eastern coast, exhibits an unusual reddish hue due to the presence of the mineral jasper in many of its rocks.

Pick up these pebbles and look at them closely and in some you will see bright colored red veins of the mineral chalcedony, or jasper. Iron oxide impurities impart the rocks' reddish color. Collectively these lines of red in the rocks produce the beach's warm, brown-red color so pleasing to the eye. In much the same manner, these rocks moved the geologist Charles Hitchcock to comment on the beauty of this mineral when he examined nearby coastal outcrops in this section of Down East Maine.

Low tide exposes the beach in its entirety. Shadows reveal rhythmic patterns of spoon-shaped impressions, or cusps, in the beach, each a tiny embayment opening towards the sea's edge. On the top of the beach ridge the rocks, or clasts—a term given to rocks of pebble size and larger—tend to be disc-shaped. Moving down the beach's steep face, the rocks become finer and at the wave drenched shore, coarse again. Here on the lower beach the clasts are often spherical or rod-shaped from rolling down the face of the beach after each wave.

From the edge of the beach, steplike berms are visible on its face; a reminder that a beach continually changes its form and size. Slowly, the currents and waves carve away nearby glacial deposits and excavate bit by bit the surrounding 400-million-year-old volcanic ledges of rhyolite, carrying them to the beach. No early explorer saw the beach quite the way it appears today. This is true of all remnants of the New England wilderness. Yet, because these features continue to exist, relatively free of all but natural influences, we still can share the interest and excitement the early New Englander's felt in seeing them.

The Beaches of Sagadahoc, Maine

Capt. popham Sent his Shallop unto us for to healp us in So we wayed our anckors & beinge Calme we towed in our ship & Cam into the Ryver of Sagadehocke.

—James Davies, August 16, 1607[90]

A stormy night preceded the safe passage of the Popham party's entrance into the mouth of the Sagadahoc River, now known as the Kennebec. Here on a neck of rocky land, fronted by fine sandy beaches and nearby islands, the colonists elected to establish the first English colony in

Wave-washed sand laps the foot of a large granitic outcrop at a rare, relatively undisturbed beach near the site of the failed first attempt to establish an English colony at the mouth of the Kennebec River on the Maine coast.

Maine. It was, however, short-lived, abandoned after a fateful winter during which many died, including its leader, John Popham. Today, as one might expect on an attractive sandy waterfront such as this, there has been much human use. But, amazingly, there are still major portions of the beach system that survive in a relatively unaltered condition.

The water swirls by the rocky headland at the mouth of one of Maine's great rivers, the Kennebec, and carries with it new material washed from glacial deposits in the interior. Fine sands drift into the sea where unseen currents in the Gulf of Maine combine with the mysterious Coriolis force to move the sediments around the point and westward along the shore. Waves fling them onto the shore and leave the particles stranded to dry and blow to the wind, becoming yet another minute addition to a beautiful, complex sand-beach dune system. Its special attraction for our exploration is its status as the last remaining undeveloped beach system in Maine.[91]

Unlike the Popham expedition, I came overland to visit this sandy coastal area and chose my arrival on a day not marred by storms. The beaches and dunes are not as they were then, for beach building and erosion occur at drastic rates here. However, there are isolated, quiet areas here where one might easily capture the mood of that time. It is a place where untouched parabolic dunes migrate unhindered by fencing, buildings, and roadways; where new salt marshes still form as streams change their courses, and barrier spits change their size and shape with each storm; where American beach grass, beach heather, bayberry, and pitch pine grow naturally in response to changing water tables and drifting sands; where earthstar puffballs make their farthest trip north; where dune ridges move in response to a rising sea and other natural forces; and where least terns and piping plovers still nest on the open beaches.

I came in early morning on an April day. Soft sounds of songbirds and a gentle surf greeted me. Shadows cast by the low morning sun exposed the presence of the smallest bits of seaweed, shells, feathers, and other debris left by the receding tidal waters on the expansive beach. A veil of haze hung loosely around the low islands at the mouth of the river. Before me, a wide avenue of sandy land lay open to an island, a tombolo, one of two here. Footprints led across to a motionless, lone figure intent on the sunrise.

As the sun rose higher, I set out for a more remote part of this beach complex. A long, circuitous route skirted a double barrier spit and the salt marsh behind it. The narrow roadway crossed another secluded tidal marsh with a snakelike stream running between deep, mucky banks. The road led me up over a ridge on which grew tall red spruce. At the height of the land, a sunlit glen in firs and spruces beckoned me in to the foot of a mossy, lichen-covered ledge. A spotlight of sunshine touched a bright green tuft of moss on a jutting rock. The dark, angular ledge glistened with oozing dampness. There was a beauty, a closeness, and an isolation here totally different from the environment that I had just left. I returned to the road and followed it down the seaward side of the ridge through a corridor of gnarled pitch pine towards a lone barrier beach.

The trail dissolved to the soft sand of the beach, beside which rose another rock outcrop, a reemergence of the same granite and gneiss I had seen back on the ridge. Without looking closely at the rock, little suggested a similarity between the two. This one was weathered bare, rounded, and bleached—a smooth porcelainlike knob compared to the rough, dark, fractured rib of rock I saw in the forest. The beach below the bluff on its seaward side was low angled, expansive, and broad—four hundred feet from low tidal water to its dune ridge. It stretched toward the southwest to another rocky point in the far distance where some suggest that the explorer Verrazzano may have landed in 1524. Behind the dune ridge lay a field of dunes, curved in parabolic fashion, a hummocky land thickly covered with American beech grass and beach heather. Young pitch pine struggle here to hold the dunes. In back lay a marsh, a less chaotic place, quieter, but not less active, a place teeming with life, much of it hidden.

I left in the middle of the day with much of this rare, relatively undisturbed beach still unexplored. The dunes are too fragile. It's better to be a watcher here.

MEADS AND BOGGY SHORELANDS

The lowest grounds be the Marshes, over which every full and change the Sea flowes.

—William Wood, 1634[92]

The explorers and European settlers were very much aware of the wetlands along the coast, especially those that might yield grass for cattle. William Wood distinguished between meadows, or meads as some called them, and marshes: "Medow ground lies higher than Marshes. . . . There be places near the plantations great broad medowes, wherein grow neither shrub nor tree, lying low, in which Plaines growes as much grasse, as may be thrown out with a Sithe, thick and long, as high as a mans middle."[93] Others spoke of bottomlands, lowlands, and swamps. Little, if anything, was mentioned by Wood, Morton, or Josselyn of peatland, except in reference to "boggy ground." Peatland became more important, however, as the supply of wood diminished. The residents of Block Island, for example, turned to peat for fuel in the mid-1700s when they exhausted their supply of firewood.

Today, many of New England's coastal wetlands have been lost to development or other severe alteration. However, in the case of Barnstable Marsh on Cape Cod and Scarborough Marsh in Maine, some still survive with relatively large areas intact. Others are being restored, such as the Awcomin Marsh in Rye, New Hampshire. Some coastal wetlands, other than marshes, have also been identified for their special qualities. These include coastal raised peatlands. One which boasts national significance is Carrying Place Cove at West Quoddy Head at the extreme eastern end of the New England coast.

Carrying Place Cove, Maine

In the heaths or raised peatbogs which abound close to the sea in this outermost coastal strip of eastern Maine . . . vegetation climbs the rocky hummocks and slopes, thus forming a continuous undulating or even abruptly sloping boggy carpet.

—M. L. Fernald and K. M. Wiegand, 1910[94]

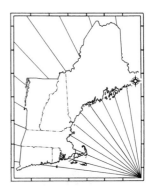

Within minutes the seawater came up over my sneakers. I moved the tripod again, still closer to the dark brown escarpment—so close that heath shrubs and sphagnum mosses hung out over me some ten feet above my head. But the rapidly rising tidal waters left no more room on the mud flat. Previous tides have so undercut this soft, dark edge that ahead of me it slumped raggedly. Chunks lay on the flat, disintegrating with each tidal wash. I have seen no other shore like what I saw at Carrying Place Cove.

Beside me the dark, partially decomposed remains of plants smelled wet and boggy. Layers were visible, revealing the history of this peatland. Those who have studied this unusually exposed edge see that this wetland began in an ancient, clay depression, perhaps a shallow pond or marsh, in a tombolo that connected West Quoddy Head to the mainland.[95] Over time sediments built up, and as the remains of roots reveal, a swamp developed. Deep moss and decayed matter accumulated on the wet, forest floor, eventually replacing the swamp with hummocks and hollows. Fires periodically swept through the developing peatland. Now, looking over its surface, one sees a raised plateau, built up over centuries by layers of dead vegetation. Small ponds now occupy the shoulders of the peatland, and communities of sedges, shrubs, and mosses populate its flattened top.

At the time this peatland first began to form, the isthmus here stood above high tidal waters that regularly sweep over vast areas of the coastal shoreline. However, changes in the elevation of the land relative to the ocean's level now allow the sea to eat away at the peatland's soft, vulnerable edge. Perhaps a century ago this edge extended a mile or more northward of its present location. Today,

Carrying Place Cove peatland, on the extreme eastern tip of Maine's coastline, crumbles into the sea as tidal waters continue to eat away at its edge.

the crumbling bank reminds us that, despite the significance we place on this natural feature, the rest of nature makes no value judgments. But we do, and the preservation of this forty-three-acre wetland provides an opportunity to learn more about the processes that continue to create it and also destroy it—processes that bear on our own future as well.

NATURAL CURIOSITIES

After exploring the shore and seeing . . . the deep gashes in its mailed garment, the basins hollowed out of granite and flint, and the utter wantonness in which the sea has pitched about the fragments it has wrested from the solid rock, the futility of words in which to express this confusion comes home to the spectator.

—Samuel Adams Drake, 1875[96]

The New England coast is a chaotic collection of bedrock types, infinitely varied in character and vulnerable to the influences in their environment. These outcrops emerge from beneath root-held soils along rocky shores of bays, headlands, and sea-bound islands. But as hard-edged and strong-willed as they appear, they are no match against the relentless assault of sea and weather. The power of waves and ocean currents can move objects of enormous size and weight during storm conditions. With jackhammer strength, air is driven into crevices, cracks, joints, or other breaks in the rocks, loosening blocks and fragments. In below-freezing weather, the water penetrating these fractures turns to ice, expands, and loosens the rocks. Currents and waves pick up the rock fragments and grind them against the shore, further shaping the features we see today. Some we have come to regard as unusual. "These natural curiosities," observed Samuel Drake, "are not infrequent along the coast."[97] Many still survive today, but others appear to have been lost and forgotten, their disappearance a mystery. We turn now to three examples.

Purgatory Chasm, Rhode Island

*The . . . Purgatory is seen to be divided by great fissures . . .
as if a Titan had slashed his scimitar through the mass.*

—Charles H. Hitchcock, 1861[98]

"It is said that a young man being challenged to prove his
love for a fair maiden, actually sprang across the ravine,
and declared his transit as one from Purgatory to Paradise."[99] The ravine, referred to by Charles Jackson in this
case, is a yawning cleft, 10 feet wide and 120 feet long, cut
into a high bluff of strange-looking rock. Sheer walls drop
50 feet into darkness from which comes the rhythmic
sound of washing waves.

With a great deal of anticipation, I walked up onto the
bluff overlooking the Atlantic and the white, sandy
beaches on the shore of Middletown, Rhode Island, near
Newport. What first attracted my attention is the unusual
rock of which the bluff is composed. Early visitors called
it puddingstone because of the pebbles and boulders
mixed in a finer stone matrix.[100] Geologists today call it
conglomerate, but what is so unusual is the shape of the
embedded rocks: they stretch or elongate in a north-south
direction, made more noticeable because they stand out in
relief due to the erosion of the surrounding softer rock.
Two hundred and fifty million years ago, when this mass
of rock was several thousand feet below the surface of the
earth, it experienced intense pressure from the east, which
created north-by-south folds. The heat and pressure softened the pebbles and boulders and squeezed them into the
elongated shapes that we see today.

I didn't see the great fissure at first and was startled to
find it only a few feet away. Looking across the bluff at a
low angle, the chasm was almost invisible. One had to
stand close to see into it. Its shore end, however, afforded a
dramatic view of its length and height. Here, the bluff once
had numerous closely aligned, east-west fractures. Water
from the spray of breaking waves and from precipitation
penetrated the openings and froze, loosening and prying
away the rock. Over thousands of years the excavation
continued in this weak zone, and the waves carried away
the dislodged pieces. Today, one sees a dark, forbidding

Purgatory Chasm, a great fissure
10 feet wide and 120 feet long
on Rhode Island's coast, was described by the geologist Charles
T. Jackson in 1840. Some of
New England's most enduring
and well-known features are
those composed of unusually
shaped bedrock that stimulated
a long history of folklore.

slot where some once believed punishment was meted out to purge of their mortal sins those who came here.

The Grottoes, Maine

The rocks . . . impart a cheerfulness to the walls of these grottoes.

—Samuel Drake, 1875[101]

The grottoes Samuel Drake described appear as a series of domelike openings in a steep cliff along the north shore of Mount Desert Island. Below is a slightly sloping pebble beach, only recently vacated by the tide the day I visited. The cliff rises up thirty-five feet above the bay and is topped by a ragged crown of spruce. When the sun is low, shadows reach out over the smooth shore, as if the cliff is trying to recapture the pieces it has lost to the waves.

At the foot of a steep cliff along the northern edge of Maine's Mount Desert Island, wave action has excavated a domelike sea cave, one of a series called The Ovens.

I entered the first of the caves and the deepest, perhaps thirty feet. Up close, the metamorphosed volcanic ash, called tuff, is iron-stained and gray-green in color and covered with hundreds of small breaks where the brittle rock shattered under the pressure of earth movement.[102] It is in these areas of fractured rock that the caves formed. The cave I was in is ten feet high, and through its rough, silhouetted opening, I looked across to the mainland on the other side of the bay. One could become trapped here by the incoming tide, I suspect. The floor was smooth and flat with neatly layered pebbles. The cave smelled damp and felt close. I heard only the swish of waves on the beach and an occasional drip.

There was more to explore. Passing a succession of shallower caves and barnacle-covered boulders strewn along the beach at the water's edge, I saw a high, narrow opening in the rock—a sea arch. Oriented to the length of the beach, it is large enough to allow a person to comfortably walk through. Here, in a greatly shattered section of rock, weathering has excavated the high rock outcrop and waves have carried the pieces away. Through the opening I saw the continuing face of the cliff and the shore along Frenchman Bay leading to Bar Harbor. For some reason, this sea arch is more interesting to me than the cave. Perhaps it's the sense of completion conveyed by this sculpting of the rock; here the sea has finally cut through to the other side. Or perhaps it's the symbolism of an arch—a freedom to pass through, a place of transition, or something of value upheld. Whatever, like Purgatory Chasm, it has become an object that has spanned human history and brought meaning and value to this coastline beyond its mere physical character.

Near Mount Desert Island's "ovens," the erosive effect of waves has created a rare and little-known sea arch. Illustration from Samuel Adams Drake, *Nooks and Corners of the New England Coast* (New York: Harper & Brothers, Publishers, 1875).

Pulpit Rock, Maine

One of the most remarkable of these isolated towers . . . is a single mass of red sandstone thirty-eight feet high, and worn at its base so that it is but eighteen feet in diameter. Its summit, which is 24 feet in diameter, is clothed with verdure, and supports a number of forest trees. This tower has received the appelation of the Pulpit Rock.

—Charles T. Jackson, 1837[103]

It has been more than a century and a half since Jackson described this unusual, crumbly, red-rock structure, obviously carved by the sea. But other than a brief reference to it by the geologist Charles Hitchcock twenty years later, I have found no mention of it. Jackson included two detailed

drawings of it in an atlas of plates accompanying his report, so we know how it appeared and the details of its
setting.

One day in mid-June of 1994, I set out to find this peculiar rock on the extreme eastern coast of Maine in the
town of Perry. Wading down a brook into a cove in which
it was supposed to be located, I passed pink-colored cliffs,
jutting out on the west side of the brook's wide ravine. The
contours of the rock cliffs are unusually rounded and
smoothed, presenting, in Jackson's words, "an appearance
of heavy, elephantine architecture."[104] The scene was exceptionally picturesque with the sunlit stream bordered by
soft-green marsh grasses and dark evergreens comple-
mented by the rose-colored rocks.

I sloshed around each corner in anticipation, Jackson's
drawings fresh in my mind. The tide was low, as pictured in
the old lithographs. I reached the mouth of the brook and
scanned the clearly visible shores of the cove. It was disap-
pointing, for no towers were to be seen.

I explored roads skirting the shores on both sides of
the cove. No trespassing signs turned me back on the first.
The second road was public, a through road, but private
residences also prevented access to most of the cove. I investigated three locations where the road passed close to
the water, but no tower was visible.

Later, I spoke with a geologist who specializes in
bedrock. We concluded that it is possible that the waves
and weather are responsible for its disappearance. Pulpit
Rock appears to be no more. Or is it? If Pulpit Rock has
given its final sermon, it is that nothing in nature is permanent, except, perhaps, the spirit of things. Still, I wonder if
it is more than a spirit. Perhaps someday I will return to
continue my search.

We end this chapter with a look at the longest and wildest remaining segment of the New England coast. The thirty-five miles from Cross Island in Cutler to Quoddy Head still retain much of the character seen by Charles Hitchcock when he surveyed this rough coastline in 1860. As late as 1994, a long-time resident of this section of the coast, one who knows it intimately, wrote: "Probably 60 percent of our seashore is still exactly as first seen by the earliest visitors."[106] This is a battered shoreline of tough, intrusive rocks and volcanics. Some have given it the name "bold coast," for numerous cliffs rise above the sea 90 to 150 feet. It holds a collection of headlands, including Great Head, Western Head, Fairy Head, Eastern Head, Jim's Head, Boot Head, and Quoddy Head. High tides and waves scour their high rock faces while a rising sea exploits new ground. Though relatively straight, possibly due to a parallel fault offshore, this stretch of coastline still contains a ragged configuration of inlets and coves that extends its straight-line measure by ten or more miles. Its variableness includes damp forests of spruce and fir, hidden heaths, pure brooks and streams, secluded estuaries, isolated marshes, unpolluted mud flats, and untrodden beaches.

Behind the rugged, ageless shore of Boot Head one can become privately aware of this coast's natural richness. On a secluded trail to Boot Cove, a startled family of grouse explodes in feather balls; only seconds before, it was too preoccupied to have heard the softly approaching steps of visitors. The chicks vanish into the dense surroundings where spruce and fir hang low and mossy rocks abound. The adult stays in the trail—plaintively whining to call attention to itself, crouching low, enticing one to follow—until the chicks are safe.

A boardwalk leads through a swamp and to a small heath. On the way, it passes a bank of sphagnum mosses at the edge of a wet depression on which grow pitcher plants in flower. Up the bank behind these carnivorous plants are the dainty, white flowers of Labrador tea and the pink blossoms of sheep laurel, crowding through the blue-green needles and purple cones of an overhanging tamarack tree. Farther along the edge of the heath, pure

THE "BOLD COAST," MAINE

There is often little soil over these hard rocks, and the effect produced by the great naked rough ledges upon the mind is that of a dreary inhospitable country suited for the wild beasts of the forest. A part of this country is uninhabited.

—Charles H. Hitchcock, 1861[105]

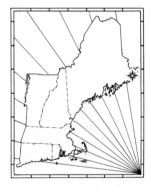

Pure white blossoms of newly flowered bunchberry plants nest in reindeer moss along Boot Cove Trail in Maine's longest and wildest stretch of coastline.

white blossoms of bunchberry lay settled in a patch of light-gray reindeer moss.

The path darkens, narrows, and smells of evergreens. It traces a route up the side of a hill where it is mossy, densely wooded, and most of all, quiet. The trail drops down again into lowland, through alders and high grasses. It emerges onto a beach inlaid with cobbles, fist-

Boot Cove's cobble beach is an outstanding example of undisturbed nature on Maine's "Bold Coast." The faint outline of Grand Manan Island in New Brunswick can be seen in the distance.

sized and larger. They look like soft, gray-green bubbles smoothed with wave-brushed strands of algae. The beach extends across the end of the cove to the steep-sided slope of Boot Head, now covered with the fresh, spring-green colors of newly leafed hardwoods. In the distance, the blue-gray outline of Grand Manan Island provides a sense of closure to the cove.

Ironically, this coast, which was one of the first to be explored, is, today, one of the first to have been protected from irreversible development. Several miles of this coastline, including Boot Head, are protected by conservation easement, state ownership, and private holdings for the purpose of preservation.[107] This provides an opportunity for future explorers to come to this wild, uninhabited coast in search of pleasure, scientific understanding, and other values an unspoiled environment provides. But perhaps more important, it will encourage exploration of the remaining New England coast for other remnants that we may wish to protect.

Chapter 3

Of the Country And Its Stones

John Josselyn recognized the varied character of inland New England early in the history of the region's settlement. Today, the title of Josselyn's little book, *New Englands Rarities Discovered*, could be appropriately applied to this book, for this is a discovery of the increasingly rare remnants of Josselyn's New England landscape. In the following pages we will scour New England, early descriptions in hand, looking for examples of those features still existent and intact that present themselves as those early discoverers found them. We will look first at some of our major mountains, then proceed to the mysteries within the earth beneath the surface—caves, minerals, relicts of ancient life, and other phenomena still with us today. Our survey will examine the landscape surface for examples of glacial features recorded by early observers— eskers, immense boulders, rocking stones, and other unusual evidence of the ice sheets that exerted such a profound influence on the shape and texture of the land. Finally, we will search for features, still existing, that have long aroused our interest and curiosity. We will not always be successful in our search, for as we shall see, some are now lost and by their absence tempt us to look further.

The Country generally is Rocky and Mountanous, and extremely overgrown with wood, yet here and there beautified with large rich Valleys, wherein are Lakes ten, twenty, yea sixty miles in compass, out of which our great Rivers have their beginnings.

—John Josselyn, 1672[1]

MOUNTAINS AND HILLS

In the formation of our mountains, nature has constructed her works on a large scale; and presents to our view objects, whose magnitude and situation, naturally engage our attention.

—Samuel Williams, 1809[2]

New England's many mountains and hills have long exerted an influence over the minds of the region's inhabitants. The largest of these mountains range slashwise across the top of New England where the most rugged and highest, the White Mountains, cluster in New Hampshire. Here, many are over four thousand feet high and extend above the tree line. Northeastward into Maine, they begin to scatter and divide into three major groups, the Boundary, Longfellow, and Katahdin ranges. Westward are the flat-topped Green Mountains, ranging north and south through central Vermont and changing into the lower, steeply cut plateau of the Berkshire Hills in western Massachusetts. Along the border between New York and the states of Vermont, Massachusetts, and Connecticut are the steep-sloped, sharp-peaked Taconic Mountains.

Legends of Native Americans show that some of northern New England's mountains were both revered and feared. The Wabanakis, for example, regarded Mt. Katahdin in Maine as the home of the Indian God Pamola, who would vent a terrible anger and exact frightening consequences if the natives ventured above timberline. When European explorers arrived, they depended upon the mountains for landmarks. Later, settlers and visitors often saw them as daunting, hostile, and hideous places, presenting danger and obstacles to settlement.

In the middle of the nineteenth century, those conducting the geological surveys to ascertain the economic potential of the states' resources cast a new eye towards the mountains. Couched in the language of reports, sometimes designed to put forth values state legislators and sponsoring agencies undoubtedly wished to hear, the scientists extolled the importance of mountains. Ezekiel Holmes, in an 1861 report, offered an opinion of their worth to the state of Maine:

They are conducive to the health of her people, to the fertility of her valleys and her plains, to the regular flow of her rivers, to the rains which irrigate her crops in summer, and to the snows that protect the herbage of her fields and her meadows in winter. A country that has no mountains is as a general thing, a dry and barren one.[3]

The geologists also expressed another view of the mountains, emphasizing scenic qualities. Some reports contained sections, entitled scenographical geology, in which they described, often in flowery terms, the aesthetic values of mountains, such as the following in the 1874 New Hampshire report:

Whether we stand upon the summit of one of our highest mountains in winter, when there is embraced in the view the whole country from the ocean to the Adirondacks, or, in summer, we stand by the side of one of our quiet lakes, which is entirely encircled by lofty hills, while the blue dome of the sky seems to rest just on the hill-tops, there is a charm and enchantment in the scene that draws the mind away from things terrestrial, and bears it away into the realm of thought and fancy.[4]

The coining of terms such as scenographical geology and the inclusion of scenic descriptions in geological reports was a reflection of the growing romanticism of the period. During this time, the painters of the Hudson River School were busy giving us spectacular panoramic views from the tops of mountains. It was also a time when the values of wilderness and the symbolism of mountains were the subject of literary works by Emerson, Thoreau, and others. The term "sublime" became common, expressing the awe-inspiring grandeur of the landscape.

The years of the 1800s were also a time when many first ascents of New England's higher mountains were made.[5] The geologists, themselves, are credited with some of them. Today, there are few mountains, if any, that do not have trails to their summits, and many are accessible by vehicles or by other motorized means. The tops of some of our more popular mountains and hills have lodging, restaurant, and skiing facilities. Others are sites for communication equipment. But just as we have seen with our coastal mountains, some features still remain undeveloped, where one may perhaps still experience some feeling of a first ascent.

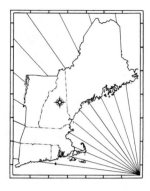

The White Mountains, New Hampshire

Fourscore miles (upon a direct line) to the Northeast of Scarborow [Maine], a Ridge of Mountains run Northwest and Northeast an hundred Leagues, known by the White Mountains, *upon which lieth Snow all the year, and is a Land-mark twenty miles off at Sea.*

—John Josselyn, 1672[6]

The White Mountains were noted as a landmark by both Samuel de Champlain and Captain John Smith in the early 1600s, well before Josselyn's first visit in 1638. Champlain saw them while passing Casco Bay, reporting that "from here large mountains are seen to the west."[7] Smith's account was included in his summary of landmarks, calling them "the twinkling Mountaine of Aucocisco."[8]

Forty-eight of these New Hampshire mountains are over 4,000 feet high. Mt. Washington is, at 6,288 feet, the highest in New England. It is the centerpiece of the White Mountains and the one that captured early attention. The first European known to have climbed this mountain was Darby Field, who made an eighteen-day trip to the top of the mountain in the summer of 1642.[9] He left no firsthand account of his trip, but details were recorded by two of his contemporaries, Governor John Winthrop of Massachusetts and Thomas Gorges, deputy governor of the Province of Maine. Based on these secondhand reports, it appears likely that his route took him by the Lake of Clouds.

The first ascent of Mt. Washington, of which we have a good descriptive account, occurred in 1784. It was made by a party of a dozen or more prominent individuals, including Jeremy Belknap and the Reverend Manasseh Cutler, who was a lawyer and scientist from Ipswich, Massachusetts. Belknap wrote extensively about this trip, even though he never actually reached the top himself. Others followed, and through their writing our understanding and appreciation of this unusual mountain grew. We have, for example, Dr. George Shattuck's letter of an 1807 excursion, published in the *Philadelphia Medical & Physical Journal*, and Dr. Jacob Bigelow's 1816 account of a trip, carried in the *New-England Journal of Medicine and Surgery*. An early and unusual documentation, incorporating words and visual images, was the beautiful book *Scenery of the White Mountains*, produced in 1848 by the botanist William Oakes and the artist Isaac Sprague.

On a clear spring day in 1994 when entering Crawford Notch, I stopped to admire these white mountains. The summit of Mt. Washington loomed above the snow-spotted glacial bowl of Oakes Gulf. Its blue shape, accented by shadows, presented a rugged but pleasing transition between the fresh green of the lower hills and the

Early descriptions of the White Mountains, including Mt. Washington and Mt. Jefferson seen here in this 1844 drawing, were documented in reports of the first state geological surveys. Illustration from Charles T. Jackson, *Final Report on the Geology and Mineralogy of the State of New Hampshire* (Concord, N. H.: Carroll & Baker, 1844).

billowing, white clouds floating overhead. I recalled my climb on the mountain as a boy up along the rim of Tuckerman Ravine—just out of sight of my view—above the tree line and into alpine country. And of another trip on the Auto Road beside the edge of the Great Gulf. Many of the features I saw then have changed little from the days of those early ascents in the 1700s and 1800s. Only the mountain summit, adorned with modern technological spires of communications and data-collecting equipment, showed the effects of human activity from my vantage point at the entrance to Crawford Notch. But viewed from distant Casco Bay, these distractions fade away and the mountain still "twinkles," as it did in 1614.

The Great Gulf I saw on the north side of Mt. Washington still retains its wild, primitive character. It is thought that this is the place to which Ethan Allen Crawford was referring when he related to Lucy Crawford sometime before 1845 that he had once become lost in clouds on the top of the mountain while leading a party. "I started toward the east," he said, "and we wandered about until we came near the edge of a great gulf."[10] It

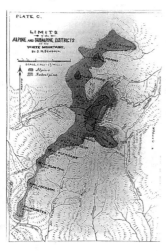

Surveyed and mapped in 1874, the Arctic alpine tundra areas on Mt. Washington and the tops of the surrounding mountains are still the most extensive in the eastern United States. Illustration from Charles H. Hitchcock, *The Geology of New Hampshire*, vol. 1 (Concord, N. H.: Edward A. Jenks, 1874).

also was here in 1774 that members of the Belknap-Cutler expedition saw that "the sides of the mountains are covered with spruce trees."[11]

Today, in remote parts of this large cirque, one can still find, at medium elevations, scattered remnants of that forest, containing large, virgin red spruce and balsam fir. On the higher slopes, ridges, and ravines, smaller-sized trees are considered to be entirely virgin. The headwall of the Great Gulf rises an impressive fifteen hundred feet. Above the tree line and the stunted evergreens of the krummholz, alpine tundra is present. In 1964 the 5,552-acre Great Gulf was designated as a federal wilderness area under the provisions of the Wilderness Act.[12]

Tuckerman Ravine is another spectacular glacial cirque—a bowl-like depression set into the high mountain slope. This is the most famous cirque in the Presidential Range, although at eight thousand feet its headwall is only half the height of the Great Gulf's. In 1848, William Oakes called this ravine a "wild and grand scene. . . . abruptly hollowed out of the side of the mountain, it is very long and deep, and its rough craggy sides are exceedingly steep, and in many places wholly inaccessible. A stream runs along the bottom through its whole length, and at the upper part several cascades are visible after a rain."[13]

The virgin forests of the Great Gulf aren't the only botanical features still intact from settlement times. On Mt. Washington and the tops of the surrounding mountains are the most extensive Arctic alpine tundra areas in the eastern United States.[14] As long ago as 1774, Jeremy Belknap, writing of the observations of scientists on his expedition, mentioned that "on the bald parts of the mountains the stones are covered with a short gray moss, and at the very summit the moss is of a yellowish color and adheres firmly to the rock."[15]

Some forty years later, Jacob Bigelow observed that "above the zone of firs . . . is a . . . bald region wholly destitute of any growth of wood. The predominance of rocks on this portion, leaves but a scanty surface covered with soil capable of giving root to vegetation; yet to the botanist this is by far the most interesting part of the mountain. Many of the plants of this region are rare, and not to be found in the region below."[16]

Today, this alpine zone is one of the most studied in the United States. In this harsh environment of freezing temperatures, fierce winds, deep snow, and swirling mists grow seventy-five alpine species of shrubs, sedges, rushes, grasses, lichens, and mosses. Influenced by snow depth in winter and such factors as humidity and soil moisture in summer, they arrange themselves into nine different plant communities, where they coexist with as many as ninety-five species of insects and spiders and other animals, such as the slate-colored junco and white-throated sparrow.

Associated with these "white hills" are the mountain passes, or notches, which, in themselves, contain a rich history. The notches provided access to and through the mountains. Two of particular note are Crawford, near Mt. Washington, and Franconia, farther to the west. Both contain features that, from the historic record, appear to remain essentially the same as they were when the region was truly wilderness.

I entered the Notch of the White Mountains, known today as Crawford Notch, from its south end. The precipitous mountains close in on the traveler until the floor of the notch accommodates only the tiny headwaters stream of the Saco River and the width of a road. Here, truly, one feels the past, for little has changed. Timothy Dwight's letter of nearly two hundred years ago demonstrates this: "When we entered the notch we were struck with the wild and solemn appearance of everything before us. The scale,

Called Notch of the White Mountains when the geologist Charles T. Jackson surveyed it in 1844, Crawford Notch still retains its awesome, wild character. Illustration from Charles T. Jackson, *Final Report on the Geology and Mineralogy of the State of New Hampshire* (Concord, N. H.: Carroll & Baker, 1844).

Naked scars of mountain slides in Crawford Notch bespeak of the ongoing natural processes that have periodically wreaked devastation on the soils and plants of New England's steeply sloped mountains.

on which all the objects in view were formed, was the scale of grandeur only. The rocks, rude and ragged in a manner rarely paralleled, were fashioned, and piled on each other, by a hand operating only in the boldest and most irregular manner."[17]

Dwight journeyed through the notch in 1797 and saw, as did I, the long, naked scars of past slides that had cut through the thin fabric of vegetation that clothes the steep slopes. Less than thirty years later, in 1826, the notch was the site of the most tragic slide in the White Mountains— a slide that blocked the very route Dwight had taken. It is known as the Willey Slide of August 28, 1826, and it occurred following heavy rains. A few days after the slide, the Reverend Carlos Wilcox, on a trip into the notch, viewed the devastation and wrote an account, which was published in the *Boston News-Letter*:

The steep sides of the mountains . . . had slid down into this narrow passage, and formed a continued mass from one end to the other. . . . it seemed almost certain, that the whole family were destroyed; and it soon became quite so. . . . There was no longer any room to doubt that they had been alarmed by the noise of the destruction around them, had sprung from their beds, and fled naked from the house, and in the open darkness had been so overtaken by the falling mountains and rushing torrents.[18]

Ironically, the house itself was spared, and if the family had not left it, they would have survived.

Edward Flaccus, who has researched the phenomenon of mountain slides, relates that the Willey Slide was one of the earliest avalanches about which we have historical information. In 1972, he reported that it was difficult to see the path of the slide because of its revegetation.[19] Some twenty years later, I also looked for evidence of the slide and could see little sign of it. However, as I traveled through this precipitous country, I saw the tracks left by many slides of lesser magnitude, graphic reminders that natural processes of the past continue to work and that, despite our technological advances, we still have little control over some of them.

Progressing northward and nearly through the notch, I came to a ravine, which cut deeply into the mountain slope on the right side of the road. Above me, on the side of Mt. Jackson in a shallow, rocky streambed, the long, white, ribbonlike Silver Cascade descended down the mountain. Reflecting the bright sun, the stream, indeed, assumed a silver appearance. Hiking upwards, stepping from rock to rock, I arrived at a shaded mountain pool into which the thread of water falls, splashing and foaming. There, the stream's wildness and provocative beauty ends, and it flows more subdued down the rocks and under the road to join the Saco River. William Oakes, in 1848, described this cascade as "probably the most striking and picturesque of any at the White Mountains."[20]

Today, Silver Cascade in Crawford Notch appears much the same as it did when the artist Isaac Sprague made this drawing of it in the mid-1800s. Illustration from William Oakes, *Scenery of the White Mountains: with Sixteen Plates, from the Drawings of Isaac Sprague* (Boston, Mass.: WM. Crosby and H. P. Nichols, 1848).

Fourteen air-miles directly west of Crawford Notch is another famous pass through the White Mountains, Franconia Notch. Charles Jackson gave his impression of this notch after his trip through it in 1844: "Although less imposing than the wild magnificence of the White Mountain Notch, it still may present attractions of another character which will prove equally interesting to the curious. The Basin, Flume and the Profile Mountain are the usual scenes admired by travelers who visit this place."[21]

I came into this mountain pass exactly a century and a half after Jackson's account and only a little more than two centuries after the first homesteaders arrived. I was one of Jackson's travelers, and my purpose was to see the three features he had singled out as scenic attractions. All three are now preserved in a state park, and I was curious to see if they were still as Jackson saw and described them.

The road dropped down into the notch, following the course of the Pemigewasset River, twenty-two hundred feet below the tops of the steep-walled, granitic Cannon Mountain on the west and Lafayette Mountain on the east.[22] The last glacier receives the credit for my route and for the extraordinary setting. Jackson came into this notch on a narrow dirt road by horse-drawn wagon, presumably seeing few if any other travelers. My arrival over a well-engineered, paved highway occurred in the midst of much traffic and many people, even though it was the first week in June and the beginning of the tourist season.

The Old Man of the Mountain greeted me first. "He" is the notch's most famous personality, still as stony-faced and defiant-looking as ever, despite the help he has received to reinforce his frost-ravaged, fractured, granitic countenance. Jackson called this striking rock feature "the most remarkable object seen from the Notch." I saw it by following a well-signed, paved walkway to an attractively designed, weatherproofed informational sign and display at a carefully laid-out viewing point. Jackson was directed by a "guide board on the road" to a point where he discovered a "stern visage of gigantic proportions on the brow of a rocky mountain, looking boldly upward."[23]

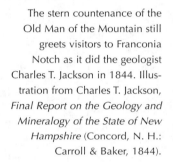

The stern countenance of the Old Man of the Mountain still greets visitors to Franconia Notch as it did the geologist Charles T. Jackson in 1844. Illustration from Charles T. Jackson, *Final Report on the Geology and Mineralogy of the State of New Hampshire* (Concord, N. H.: Carroll & Baker, 1844).

Jackson noted that it had only been discovered forty years before when the road was being laid out through the notch. But the "Old Man" would still have to wait six more years for immortalization by Nathaniel Hawthorne in his 1850 story, *The Great Stone Face*. Today, "he" still endures, and impressed those of us who stood silently that June day at the foot of a long, scumbled, forest-green cape that swirled up around his face. The expression projected by the shadows was rugged and had a look of firmness—not unpleasant but determined, and I had the distinct feeling that he was stubbornly making a point of some importance with the other mountains.

Four miles farther, I exited to the Basin, where the Pemigewasset River continues to smooth and shape this large granite pothole. Jackson wrote that "the diameter of this rocky basin is about 30 by 40 feet, and its depth appears to be in such proportion as to form a deep bowl. . . . On one side the rocks jut over the brim of the basin, forming a pretty grotto beneath, while the embankment, covered with green moss and wood flowers, presents a

The Basin, a large granite pothole, is an outstanding natural feature in Franconia Notch preserved for the enjoyment of visitors. Illustration from Charles T. Jackson, *Final Report on the Geology and Mineralogy of the State of New Hampshire* (Concord, N. H.: Carroll & Baker, 1844).

pleasant contrast to the foaming cascade."[24] Though a mere century and a half of scouring by the river has had little effect on this sculpted cavity, one must consciously ignore the encircling fences and walkways to see it as Jackson did. The Basin was not the first feature I had seen where provisions for human access and safety eroded the naturalness of a setting that had taken nature thousands of years to produce. Nevertheless, its inherently attractive and curious qualities still hold true, perhaps more in testimony to the tenacity of granite than to any efforts at human preservation.

For some reason, my visit to the Flume, another feature in this notch, seemed less diminished by the efforts to juggle safety and preservation. I suspect it is because of the intimate encounter one has with the powerful effects of geologic processes. A wooden walkway, built only inches above a wild, tumultuous stream, led me into the close confines of a narrow, four-hundred-foot-long granite gorge. It was enclosed by sheer and sometimes overhanging walls clad in lichen and moss. The granite rises seventy to ninety feet above the stream. The Flume lay undiscovered until 1808, and Jackson was one of the early visitors who saw it without a boardwalk and observed that in only the driest part of the year could one enter it. By the time the geologist Charles Hitchcock published his report on it

Geologist Charles T. Jackson visited the Flume in Franconia Notch some thirty-five years after it was discovered in 1808. Illustration from Charles T. Jackson, *Final Report on the Geology and Mineralogy of the State of New Hampshire* (Concord, N. H.: Carroll & Baker, 1844).

An 1877 heliotype of the Flume in Franconia Notch shows a boardwalk along its bottom and the absence of an immense boulder that previous drawings showed wedged between the chasm's walls. Illustration from Charles H. Hitchcock, *The Geology of New Hampshire*, vol. 2 (Concord, N. H.: Edward A. Jenks, 1877).

in 1877, a heliotype (an early kind of photograph) showed a boardwalk along the bottom of the chasm.

Unfortunately, the most remarkable feature of the Flume, in the opinion of Jackson and others, and one that shows in the early illustrations, is now gone. It was, in Jackson's words, "an immense rounded block of granite, which hangs over head, supported merely by small surfaces of contact against its sides. It appears to the traveler looking at it from below, as if ready to fall upon him."[25] The rock, ten feet by twelve feet in dimension, was swept away in a small landslide in June 1883 and never found. I'm sure that few who enter the Flume today know of that rock, which once captured so much attention, yet I'm also sure that most come away convinced they have experienced some of the still uncontrolled wildness of our landscape.

Dixville Notch, New Hampshire

It surpasses most other notches in the vertical height of its walls, one point being 560 feet above the highest part of the road. Some of the highest precipitous masses stand out in bold relief from the sides.

—Charles H. Hitchcock, 1874[26]

Dixville Notch, one of New England's wildest appearing notches, makes a narrow V-shaped gash between sharp, fanglike mountain ridges, and here one may find passage through the rugged country between Umbagog Lake and the Connecticut River in Coos County, northern New Hampshire. I passed through this deep mountain slot in complete awe of the spirelike, sheer walls of rock, seemingly untamed by the glaciers and subsequent erosion that humbled so many of New England's mountaintops. It looked unchanged from the descriptions left by the early geologists.

This notch attracted the attention of both Charles Jackson and Charles Hitchcock, both of whom were impressed by its unusual character. Said Jackson in 1844: "This notch may be regarded as one of the most remarkable exhibitions of natural scenery in the State, perhaps even surpassing the famous notch of the White Mountains [Crawford Notch] in picturesque grandeur. . . . and seems to come nearer to the scenery of the Alps than any thing else in New England."[27]

Hitchcock parroted these words thirty years later and added that "one can easily imagine that he sees here the turrets and spires of some ruined cathedral, or the battlements and towers of castles of the medieval age."[28] One hundred and thirty years later I saw something even more different: I saw only the shards of an embattled New England wilderness.

Dixville Notch, in New Hampshire's northern Coos County, attracted the attention of early geologists with its sharply pointed ridges. Illustration from Charles T. Jackson, *Final Report on the Geology and Mineralogy of the State of New Hampshire* (Concord, N. H.: Carroll & Baker, 1844).

Mahoosuc Notch, Maine

North of the Androscoggin [River] and the Lake at its source, and thence to Dead river, the country grows more mountainous, and attains a greater general elevation.

—Moses Greenleaf, 1829[29]

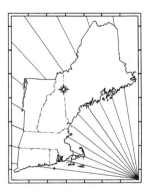

In Maine's Androscoggin River country, high in the Longfellow Mountains, one finds a section of the Appalachian Trail "considered the wildest and most difficult of any stretch of the Trail north of the Great Smokies in North Carolina and Tennessee."[30] This is truly wild, primitive, roadless country where a hiker may find solitude and scenic grandeur. At one time the torrential roar of glacial rivers carved the mountain's precipitous flanks, plucking huge boulders of granite and leaving them clogging a narrow trench between the mountains—a place now known as the Mahoosuc Notch.[31] Deep in the jumbled bottom of this cut, one feels the roots of mountains rising a thousand

Dixville Notch still evokes surprise from motorists unprepared for the impressive spirelike ridgetops that tower over the narrow highway passing through the notch.

feet on each side. Virgin spruce and fir hide some of the scars, and near the bottom, shadows obscure others, for this slot angles northeast by southwest and its depths receive little direct sunlight. A damp coolness pervades the numberless crevices where ice may linger throughout the summer and cold streams gurgle in unseen openings. Mosses proliferate, covering the boulders. One touches rough-hewn nature in these depths.

Remnants of an untouched wilderness also surround this notch. Entering the notch from the north, one passes beneath Mahoosuc Mountain on which grows an old forest of red spruce and balsam fir that began growing nearly a hundred years before Moses Greenleaf mentioned this region. Across the notch on its southeast side rises Fulling Mill Mountain, home for subalpine bogs and forests. To the northeast, nestled between Old Speck Mountain and Mahoosuc Arm in a glacially excavated depression, is Maine's highest pond, Speck Pond, a tarn 3,670 feet above sea level. A subalpine forest covers Old Speck Mountain, one of Maine's four-thousand-footers. Mahoosuc Arm, a broader, flat-topped mountain of subalpine heath and bogs and known as a "heath bald" because of its exposed openness, is also home for a subalpine forest of spruce and fir that contains one old spruce dating back to 1741.

Bigelow Mountain Range, Maine

It was our intention to have explored Mt. Bigelow, a lofty mountain upon Dead River, but the snow covered its surface and forbad any researches.

—Charles T. Jackson, 1839[32]

The old road follows along the top of a high, glacial riverbed to Stratton Brook Pond. A sunrise dusts the pond's misty waters with touches of gold. At the outlet, the pressure of flowing water has pushed aside the alders and allows a view of The Horns, rising two thousand feet and over two miles away directly north. To reach these peaks one must walk over three miles in a gigantic zigzag.

It was the middle of September when I hiked this section of the Bigelow Range—a ten-mile-long mountainous ridge with two peaks over four thousand feet high, mountain tarns, patches of uncut forest, and arctic alpine communities. Reddening maples splotched the edges of the pond and wetlands I passed. Another month and snow could turn me back, as it did Jackson. I followed the esker along the pond's north side and around its end. Across a wetland by the outlet of a mountain brook, the high peaks of West and Avery came into view. In the distance, I could see part of the band of undisturbed, subalpine balsam fir forest that stretches across this mountain range above the 2,700-foot mark. The trees cling to steep, rocky slopes. On the treeless tops above this high-elevation forest, over four thousand feet above sea level, eight species of alpine plants find a niche. Only twelve of Maine's mountains provide such an opportunity for these plants. Small and resilient, they are adapted to withstand severe effects of wind and temperature and sparse soil conditions. But where there is plant life there is also animal life. In the col between West and Avery peaks, among the rocks in mossy, moist crevices, is thought to live the rare yellow-nosed vole, a small, mouselike rodent of mountain environments.

Western Maine's Bigelow Mountain Range, seen here in the distance, is protected in the state-owned Bigelow Preserve.

The trail skirted the boggy edge of the wetland and turned directly towards the peaks and into rolling ridges of tall northern hardwoods. The open forest of stately trees allowed long views through dim, canopy-filtered light. I turned at a marker where the trail forked and zagged to the left towards The Horns Pond. The trail became steep, sloping steadily upwards through the hardwoods and, at one point, passed through a magnificent stand of red spruce, their slightly imperfect, steeplelike tops swaying in the light breeze a hundred feet above. A small mountain brook crossed the trail, then broke into a dozen tiny falls—each a rippling veil for the dark, wet rocks of a ledge. I paused for an enjoyable moment of rest before continuing. A beaver dam interrupted the trail, but a perfectly mirrored image of the mountain highlands I'd seen below compensated for the slight detour.

A few feet off the main trail an overlook provided a view of Stratton Brook Pond far below. Directly across Carrabasset Valley, the manipulated slopes of Sugarloaf Mountain graphically displayed the future once considered for this wild mountain range. I remembered an earlier trip in winter on the other side of this mountain range when I had cross-country skied to a lodge built in anticipation of developing the area as a commercial ski resort. However, the citizens of Maine voted to purchase the area and established the Bigelow Preserve. I also knew, as I looked across to the grassy swaths of trails on Sugarloaf, that I saw only half of the altered landscape that borders this range: if I climbed high enough, I could look northward over its top down to the dammed waters of Flagstaff Lake, which back up the full length of this mountain chain. The Bigelow mountains are, thus, squeezed between two massive works of engineering, and one's feeling of escape into a vast wilderness is tempered somewhat by the knowledge that it has its limits.

I pressed upward, passing through the undisturbed band of conifer forest I had seen from below—now revealed as mainly fir with some spruce and paper birch. Beneath the stunted trees, the once vibrant plants of spring and summer—wild sarsaparilla, wood sorrel, Canada mayflower, bluebead lily, starflower, and spinulose wood fern—now lay dried and withered.

At the top, my path joined the Appalachian Trail, which follows the peaks. Three miles to the west, the trail passes a nubble of spruce and fir where trees grow that had begun their lives before the mid-1700s. Protected by

steep slopes and the lack of nearby roads, they have escaped the ax and saw.[33]

The trail follows the south side of The Horns Pond,
and I took a short side trail that leads to the shore of this
high elevation pond. I looked out over the grasses, rushes,

The Horns Pond, located in a
tiny basin high in the mountains
of Maine's Bigelow Preserve, en-
velopes the visitor with feelings
of remoteness and wildness.

and sedges that inhabit the pond's shore to the rough outcrops of the ridge on its northwestern side. The tiny basin
had a remote and wild feeling about it. For the first time
that day, I had escaped the sounds of traffic and those of
the saws and skidders at work in the valley below.

Deboullie Mountain Region, Maine

*I find the town quite rough and hilly, particularly the North
East quarter, and damaged by hurricanes of Nov. 8th,
1872. . . . There is a large amount of cedar on this town.*

—John Shay, October 22, 1886[34]

On September 7 in the year 1886, John Shay, surveyor and
timber cruiser, traveled by railroad from Bangor, Maine,
to Presque Isle where he took a stage to Ashland. From
there he hired a wagon and team of horses to transport
him to the Fish River Bridge, probably in the town of
Eagle Lake or in Winterville Plantation. There he rented a
canoe and made his way to the east boundary of the township of Deboullie, near the northern border of Maine,
where he set up a camp. For the next month and a half, he
resurveyed the town, noting its timber and following the
field notes of a survey made by Noah Barker in 1848. A
copy of his journal reads:

Sept. 20. Rainy—Left E. Line 1½ miles from N. E. corner. Traced west 3 miles—most of the way large cedar & some good spruce.

Sept. 21. Snowing . . .

Sept. 22. Renewed North Line 2 miles West—find a small pond frozen over this morning.

Sept. 23. Renewed North Line 1½ miles West through a large quantity of cedar between ridges of rock maple and yellow birch. Ground very broken and hilly—Spruce very scattering.

On October 21, his work was completed, and he returned home.

Gardner Pond, in the township of Deboullie in a remote public lot in northern Maine, lies among glacially carved valleys and mountains.

Attuned to the land as he was, John Shay couldn't help but notice the unusual hilly nature and uncommon number of ponds in this township. On a bedrock map of northern Maine, the area appears as an anomaly—a small, isolated, irregular-shaped blob of granitelike rock surrounded by miles of slatelike rock. Erosion over millions of years has removed the softer slate, leaving the harder, granitelike rock protruding as mountains and hills above the generally low, rolling land. The highest of these is Deboullie Mountain, at almost two thousand feet in elevation. Nearby smaller mountains include Gardner, Black, and Whitman.

Flying over this region, one would see an abrupt change in landform, numerous steep cliffs, and huge rock slides, called talus slopes, all of which are intermingled with twenty-two spring-fed ponds that drain by different routes to the St. John River to the north. But what is of interest to us here is that these features are enclosed in a township that is relatively undeveloped. Within its boundaries are over a thousand acres of old-growth forests of spruce, fir, beech, and northern white cedar, including one forest that contains trees over four hundred years old, dating back to the 1500s.

One hundred years after John Shay made his survey, I paddled across one of the ponds near the center of this remote township to a point on its forested shoreline. I tied my canoe to an old cedar that was alive during all the

A stand of northern white cedars, some of which date back into the 1600s, grows on the shore of Gardner Pond.

early explorations of this town. Some of the northern white cedars in the stand that I saw that day were growing in the 1600s. Near the shore they leaned towards the pond's edge, as if groping for light, their trunks tapering upwards, twisting from huge hummocks rising from the low, swampy shoreland. Other trees lay rotting, haphazardly strewn on the humpy ground covered by thick, lush layers of mosses and herbaceous plants. Near the water, roots arched up above the forest floor and then twisted down into it again. It was a forest that showed its age and the rigors of a long life in this northwoods country.

A short paddle from the old forest brought me to the foot of Gardner Mountain's glacially sheared cliff and another of this country's spectacular, undisturbed features. I eased my canoe alongside huge granite boulders covered with lichens and polypody ferns, the edge of an immense apron of broken rocks stretching from the water's edge upwards to the base of the cliff 450 feet above me. All told, some six acres of talus covered the slope, the result of eleven thousand years of frost action prying the rocks out of the cliff. Though it was a warm July day, a cold breeze drifted out from the mossy crevices into which I peered; "ice-box talus" is a name some use to describe this phenomenon.

This isn't the only rock slide among these glacially carved mountains. Earlier I had visited a smaller but no less interesting one at the base of Deboullie Mountain's cliff. Here also, beautiful, lichen-patterned boulders come to the water's edge. For five hundred feet along the shore, boulders are piled to a height of eight feet.

I searched one of the cliffs for the Arctic sandwort, a tiny plant found only in one other place in New England. Looking at the cliff face through binoculars, I discovered the plant in an area darkened by seeping water. Highlights from the sun gave the low, sprawling plant and its

An Arctic sandwort, a small and very rare plant, clings to a narrow shelf of ledge in the face of a cliff on Deboullie Mountain.

tiny, white blossoms a bright, tufted appearance against the dark rock. It was a gleeful moment, finding this rarity, until I tried to approach it with my tripod and camera and discovered that a wide swath of very thick and tall and maleficent poison ivy separated me from the sandwort. Only after chopping some down and piling up a few dead trees for a bridge did I gain the access I wanted.

I hiked or portaged my canoe to several of Deboullie's roadless ponds, all quietly nestled among the hills and mountains. Some of the ponds are shallow and weedy, others deep and clear. A few support populations of blueback char. This is a rare fish, known only in a handful of deep, cold ponds in Maine. Slim and troutlike with a large mouth and a slightly forked tail, it perhaps evolved from Arctic char that became landlocked after the last glacier left this region. Its existence here today, like the few old forests, suggests that this region still retains some of its original nature and naturally evolving processes—characteristics that I now hope have a chance to continue in this remote area because the entire township is now publicly owned by the state of Maine.

Green Mountains, Vermont

Continuing our course in this lake on the west side I saw, as I was observing the country, some very high mountains on the east side, with snow on the top of them.

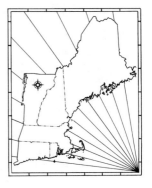

—Samuel de Champlain, July 1609[35]

A mere sixty miles north of the old cedar trees in Deboullie township flows the St. Lawrence River. Some of these trees were already a quarter of a century old when Samuel de Champlain sailed up that river in 1609. Later that summer he accompanied a party of Indians up a tributary of the St. Lawrence, the Richelieu River, and was the first European to see the great lake, now named after him—Lake Champlain, a huge body of fresh water one hundred miles long. Entering from the north, Champlain saw "four beautiful islands," and as he moved along the west shore, he looked across at very high mountains, which he observed as being snow capped.

Champlain's observation of snow on the mountains has provoked some speculation on the subject. A footnote in a 1904 history of Champlain's voyages suggests that Champlain mistook white limestone outcroppings on the Green Mountains for snow. The naturalist Zadock Thompson in 1853 interpreted the report as referring to snow on Mt. Mansfield. But the Vermont naturalist Charles Johnson, noting that limestone does not occur on Mt. Mansfield and questioning whether those outcrops that are quartz are large enough to give the appearance of snow, suggests that perhaps Champlain actually did see either snow or hoarfrost on the mountaintops or that in some light the barren rock summits might only have looked pale to him.[36] Indeed, on a recent early June day, as I looked across Lake Champlain to Mt. Mansfield from the Grand

Isle chain of islands, a line appeared at the summit that looked light enough to be snow, although when seen close up through my telephoto lens, it turned out to be only the light on the rocks.

From my vantage point on Grand Isle, looking across Lake Champlain toward the mainland of Vermont, distance and vegetation removed much of the visual evidence of human presence I had seen along the east side of the mountains. My view of the Vermont shoreline and the long chain of mountains, including Mt. Mansfield and Camels Hump to the south, was likely similar to the scene Champlain saw.

Mt. Mansfield is the highest in the state at 4,393 feet and is one of the few Green Mountain peaks that doesn't have a green summit: it extends above the tree line and contains the largest expanse of alpine tundra in Vermont. The alpine area covers about 250 acres and contains some of the rarest plants in the state, such as Lapland diapensia and bearberry willow. Some forty species of special interest to botanists are found in the summit area. Also along its ridgeline are alpine bogs, cliffs, and ledges, and on its upper slopes an isolated virgin spruce-fir forest grows. Over four thousand acres of the mountain are now designated as a National Natural Landmark, which also includes Smugglers Notch, one of New England's outstanding mountain passes.

When seen from the northern part of the Champlain Valley, the outline of Mt. Mansfield suggests a face-up profile of a human head. The "forehead" lies to the south and the "chin," which is the highest point, lies to the north. Between is the "nose," or the summit ridge. The superb views from the heights have long enhanced the mountain's reputation. These were probably first enjoyed by Ira Allen, a prominent figure in Vermont's early history, who is believed to have ascended the mountain in 1772. The survey geologists reported in 1861 that "the Chin furnishes one of the grandest and most extensive views of New England."[37]

Twenty miles to the south of Mt. Mansfield, another of Vermont's mountains rises above the skyline—Camels Hump. Over four thousand feet high, it is unmarked by the roads, ski trails, or other intrusions, seen on so many of the state's peaks. Eighteen thousand acres around the mountain are now state-protected. Its treeless summit is home for Vermont's only other community of rare arctic alpine plants, a mere ten acres in size. When hiking to this oasis of northern tundra land, one encounters the diversity of northern New England's mountain vegetation: a forest of very old northern hardwoods gives way to a scattering of red spruce and balsam fir, then, at 2,800 feet, stands a forest of mostly fir. Still higher, the trees become dwarfed and gnarled, and the forest is now called krummholz, after the German word for "crooked wood." Finally, one emerges into the open tundra, where, surrounded by populations of rare plants, one may still identify with the observation of a nineteenth-century Vermont scientist: "The same enchanting prospect of Champlain Lake and valley is here afforded that is seen from Mansfield Mountain, and to the east is outspread a rich and varied landscape that extends to the hazy summits of the White Mountains. . . . along the Green Mountain range may be seen a beautiful succession of peaks, that gradually fade out as they rise beyond each other in the blue distance."[38]

Taconics and Berkshires, Massachusetts

This mountain is the highest in the Commonwealth. . . . It presents a very grand appearance.

—Gentlemen in the County of Berkshire, 1829[39]

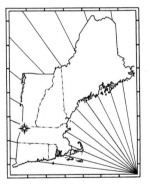

One clear day from atop Mt. Greylock, almost thirty-five hundred feet high, one sees to the east the deeply eroded plateau from which the beautiful Berkshire Hills are shaped and, in the distance, the valley of the Connecticut River. To the south, these hills range across western Massachusetts into northwestern Connecticut where northern hardwoods reach their southern extent. To the west the more roughly hewn Taconic Mountains edge the boundary between Massachusetts and New York. To the north the Berkshire range extends to central Vermont, and in the distance one sees the taller Green Mountains.

Below the summit of Mt. Greylock lies a small valley known as the Hopper, so named because the steep mountain slopes forming its sides give it a funnel-like shape.

Here, on the northwest slope of Mt. Greylock, about a thousand feet below its top, are three small stands of undisturbed old-growth red spruce—possibly remnants of a virgin forest. Together, they total about twenty acres.[40] Some trees in this forest are eighty feet tall and two feet through. The oldest, approaching two hundred years in age, were alive when this forested valley was described in an 1829 history of the Berkshires:

The Hopper is one of the wildest and most romantic spots in this section of our country. The patches of evergreens occurring on the sides of the mountain, are frowning with gloom on the spectator, whose eye is then relieved by resting on the bare cliffs, or the cultivated fields beside him.[41]

Today, this area is still wild and relatively inaccessible. Absent are signs of cutting—old logging roads, stumps, abandoned equipment. Penetrating the thick, tangled undergrowth beneath the densely growing spruce and climbing over and around the ledgy outcrops and fallen moss-covered trees—all on a steeply pitched, darkly shaded slope—can be a daunting experience.

I remember looking up at the cloud-shrouded slopes of Mt. Greylock from the valley on its western side. The Hopper was held in secrecy by the mists. It was in early May, and the road to the summit had not yet opened. Soon the crowds would come to enjoy the trails and the views. Much of the landscape they would see and experience has a human history of hard work and play, of happiness and sadness, of life and death—of change. Yet, a piece of land remains here with a history less affected by humans and perhaps more like the land as it was before people came—a place where, because of our absence, we might grasp some sense of our impact on the land.

Mt. Monadnock, New Hampshire

I saw Pigwackett lying one point from sd [said] mountain and Cusagee mountain and Winnipesockey laying north East of sd [said] Wannadnock.

—The Scout Willard, 1725[42]

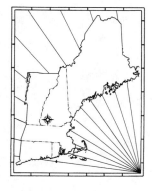

We end our survey of mountains that exemplify New England's early wilderness with Mt. Monadnock, not because it contains living remnants of that wilderness, but for the reason the Scout Willard sought it out in 1725—its presence is an imposing fixture of the landscape. Though its height is but 3,165 feet above sea level, this mountain is

Mt. Monadnock seen from Jaffrey, New Hampshire, during the mid-1800s when the naturalist and writer Henry David Thoreau climbed the mountain. Possibly one of the least forgotten features of New England's nature, it is included here because its imposing presence on the landscape has attracted generations of people who associate it with the wilderness legacy of the region. Illustration from Charles T. Jackson, *Final Report on the Geology and Mineralogy of the State of New Hampshire* (Concord, N. H.: Carroll & Baker, 1844).

regarded as the most prominent landmark in central New England. It appears as an anomalous bump in the surrounding landscape. It is the classic example of an isolated mountain rising from a plain and thus contributed its name, monadnock, to identify all such mountains.

Mt. Monadnock's promise of unexcelled views has drawn people to it for centuries. Of all the mountains that I have photographed in New England, this offers special opportunities. Today it is one of the most frequently climbed mountains in the eastern United States. From this mountain one can supposedly see six states on a clear day. The early geologists all visited it, fascinated by its glacially embossed and scarred ledges—a "remarkable scratching," wrote Edward Hitchcock in 1842.[43]

Perhaps even more remarkable, this mountain is now protected and will be available to future generations of hikers, who will journey here for the same reasons that brought the Scout Willard, Henry David Thoreau, Ralph Waldo Emerson, and others in the past.

UNDERGROUND MYSTERIES

Many parts of the country are yet unexplored; and of those which are known the knowledge is mostly confined to the surface and its vegetation.

—Jeremy Belknap, 1792[44]

We leave the surface of New England for a moment and explore what is hidden in its rocky depths. We shall look first at openings in the rocks that allow us access into mountains and under valleys—the caverns so prevalent in some regions and so scarce in others. Then we will look into the rocks themselves for their hidden treasures of minerals. Gold and semiprecious gemstones will be our focus, for these drove the imagination and determination of early collectors and entrepreneurs. We will also explore the signs of early life—shapes and patterns imbedded in the rocks—that mystified even the most eminent of our early scientists. Finally, we will consider the effects of the earth's restless movement beneath the surface of New England—the quakes and subterranean sounds that have figured in our historic relationship with this land and remain with us today. When we are through, you will likely agree with Jeremy Belknap's assessment in 1812 that many parts of the country remain yet unexplored, especially those underground.

Caves

Among the many rocky mountains and precipices, some openings appear, which are generally supposed to be the haunts of bears and rattle snakes; and are rather objects of dread than of curiosity.

—Jeremy Belknap, 1792[45]

People are drawn to caves, whether to enter them or merely to speculate on them. For some, caves invite adventure into unknown, dark, and foreboding places. They offer opportunities for true exploration, excitement, and personal challenge. In them one can demystify as well as face the fear of the unknown. Others have used caves as places of shelter for living and for hiding. Even for those who cannot or will not enter caves, these close and confining spaces are objects of curiosity. New England's caverns have long engaged its inhabitants in these pursuits, for caves are hidden throughout its countryside.

Generally, two kinds of inland caves are found in New England: slab caves, created among jumbles of boulders and haphazardly piled slabs of broken bedrock, and solution caves, created from water-dissolved limestone rock. Slab caves may be found scattered throughout the region, for example, among boulder fields and other glacial deposits and beneath piles of rocks left at the foot of mountains by glacial or frost action. Most of New England's solution caves, however, appear to be in a narrow belt along its western boundary, extending from northwestern

Connecticut through Massachusetts into central Vermont.[46] Elsewhere they occur randomly where limestone outcrops exist. The following examples allow us to capture the flavor of these often mysterious, little-changed, underground remnants of New England's historic landscape.

Moodus Cave, Connecticut

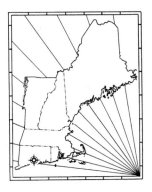

The awful noises . . . continue to the present time. The effects they produce are various and the intermediate degrees between the roar of a cannon and the noise of a pistol.

—A gentleman of Moodus,
1831[47]

Moodus, "the place of noises," or Morehemoodus, as the Indians called it.[48] From time to time, continuing into the present century, the mysterious sounds have been heard in and around the community of Moodus, located near the Connecticut River in south-central Connecticut. (See page 168.) It is not surprising to learn from explorers of Connecticut's caves that the "strangest and most mysterious of all the Nutmeg State caverns is the noisy Moodus Cave."[49]

One overcast day in early May, I met a geologist in Moodus for the purpose of visiting the town's intriguing historic cave. We followed a path at the edge of a field, then entered an open forest of hardwoods on a steep rock-strewn slope. Newly emerged herbaceous plants and budding tree leaves splotched bright green against the brown leaf-littered hillside. Delicate white flowers of wood anemone and rue anemone dotted the forest floor beside the path. Above us the opening of the cave showed black against the long, gray ledge that capped the ridge. A slight sprinkle of raindrops hurried us up the path. We paused at the entrance. The rocks around the opening are cracked, and the top of the entrance is arched, which, according to folklore, is possibly the result of attempts by local Indians to enlarge the entrance. I estimated the opening to be about five feet high and six feet wide, and beyond I could see that the leaf-littered earthen floor of the cave is flat.

We entered the mouth of the cave with flashlights ready and made our way back into the ridge along a damp passage. Bats, spiders, and mosquitoes supposedly live here, but we saw none. The cavern became smaller as we progressed until, at about twenty-five feet in, it was reduced to a small tunnel, hardly large enough to pass through. Some spelunkers, we learned, have crawled more than eighty feet along this tunnel to a room twelve by fifteen feet in size. Another report suggested that there was still more to explore.

The floor had begun sloping downward, and the wet sides and dripping roof of the cave were now rounded and somewhat smooth, taking on some of the characteristics of a solution cave, perhaps by the dissolution of feldspar. A

Moodus Cave, known for its strange noises, penetrates more than eighty feet into a Connecticut hillside, allowing one to explore another dimension of the New England landscape. Reports of earthquakes accompanied by thunderous sounds were first recorded in the 1700s around the town of Moodus.

layer of fractured rock in the side of the cave suggested a possible fault.[50] We listened; no noises could be heard. In fact, an absolute quiet prevailed. Through the opening of the cave's entrance, we could see across the valley to distant greening hills. A light rain had begun to come down. At that moment, I felt a strong sense of comfort. Contrary to its reputation, the cave imparted a calming peacefulness. Still more could be explored, I knew, but I decided against it. Although I had not heard the strange noises, I had, nevertheless, found what I had come for—to be immersed in and touched by an unusual part of New England's historic land.

A Southern Vermont Cave

Some time last year a hole was discovered in the side of the west mountain in Bennington . . . large enough to admit with some difficulty, the body of a man, widening in its descent, and apparantly of considerable depth, as was judged by the dropping of stones, &c., into it.

—The Nightingale, 1796[51]

I arrived in Bennington, Vermont, under cloudy skies. Scattered showers were punctuated by bursts of sunshine. Following a path along the edge of a field then up a wooded slope, I came into a large, open cut in the rocky side of Mt. Anthony. The path led directly into it. Vertical walls of fractured rock, covered with mosses and ferns, rose up on each side of the path to a height of perhaps twenty feet or more, then angled into the mountain, coming together at a large vertical crack in the face of a ledge. At the bottom of this large fissure, the path disappeared into a black, jagged hole, several feet wide at the bottom and sharply pointed seven or eight feet above. I approached cautiously, for I had learned that a bear had been seen very recently in the vicinity. I rattled around outside and listened. No sound came from within. A ruffed grouse drummed somewhere nearby.

I entered the cave. Water dripped all around. It has been suggested that some of the ledge in front of the entrance was blasted away to prevent water from accumulating here.[52] However, even if this were so, the floor by the entrance sloped slightly downward into the cave, allowing water to run in and create muddy conditions. A smooth, rippled pattern on one wall suggested dissolution of limestone by the water and the creation of new shapes as evaporation and deposition occurred.

The cave quickly narrowed into a small, low tunnel, requiring one to squat or crawl to progress farther. Beyond I could see a large chamber. In one corner, my light caught the smooth rippling of another dripstone formation near the base of a wall. I heard the hollow-sounding click of water dripping steadily into some unseen pool. It was wet and mysterious. I thought of the bear and strained to hear a step or movement. From early descrip-

Near the entrance of this southern Vermont cave a smooth, ripple pattern is created on the cave wall by the effect of water, evaporation, and mineral deposition on the limestone rock. A long history of exploration and rumor is associated with this cave, which was described as early as 1796.

tions, I knew that this dark room was the junction of several passages and rooms leading off into the mountain a distance of perhaps 150 feet. And it was once rumored that somewhere here is a tunnel that leads through the mountain to North Pownal three or four miles away.

I looked upward for any sign of light. That description in *The Nightingale*, nearly two hundred years ago, spoke of only one entrance through a hole above. Perhaps, the suspected blasting of the entrance now made it possible to enter directly from the mountain's side. Had I not been alone, I would have explored farther, for one particular passage of that early description piqued my interest:

The curiosities exhibited by the different degrees of petrifaction, baffle description. The walls are in many places the appearance of polished marble, and shine as if encrusted with ice: in many places the appearance of flowing curtains, folded below, appear peculiarly magnificent.[53]

I remembered that those early visitors found here the track of some kind of animal and the skull of a small creature. I listened again, hearing only the occasional hollow drip. I slid back out the tunnel and opening. The sun had taken over the sky. The spell was broken, and I came back from a two-hundred-year trip into the past.

The Forgotten Island Cave, Maine

Before starting on this expedition, we had received several vague accounts of an island in a lake somewhere . . . in which were sundry galleries and a cave of curious form and construction, "not made with hands."

—Ezekiel Holmes, 1861[54]

Buried within the pages of an 1861 report on a scientific survey of Maine lies a provocative account detailing the discovery of a solution cave. Such caves are rare in Maine. As late as 1976, a listing of the state's noteworthy natural features reported the possible existence of one, and that was only a rumor. So when I came upon the report by Ezekiel Holmes in which he described a limestone cave far to the north of the one reported in 1976, my interest perked up. Reading on, I learned that Holmes and his party were guided to the cave by a man who had discovered it in an unusual island while out hunting some thirty years previous—around 1830. Holmes describes the site:

At the westerly end of this lake, and a few rods from the shore, was the long sought for island. The water was sufficiently low to allow of our wading to the spot. It proved to be a portion of the limestone ledge we had just passed, rising up from the water about 20 feet, and say from 200 to 300 feet in circumference. Its top was covered with bushes and small trees. The caves talked about, proved to be large tubes or tunnels from three to four feet in diameter, worn smoothly, as if by running water, in a horizontal position, completely through or across the island. These tunnels are at the base of the island, and of course when the water in the lake is high, are nearly or quite submerged. They are at right angles to each other. The water was sufficiently low to allow us to creep through them. At the place where they cross each other, is a room, or cavity not quite eight feet in diameter and about five feet in height. There are but two main tunnels or tubes which perforate the island. There are three others commenced, but they pass only a little way before they run into one or the other of the main tunnels.[55]

My curiosity aroused, I decided to find this island with its complex of tunnels and a cave. Surely, if it still existed, it would be a prime example of New England's forgotten nature. I procured topographic maps of the general region described by Holmes and located what I thought was a likely candidate—a small, isolated pond with an island near a point of land. No roads penetrated the forest to the shore of the pond. I learned from a trapper who flies over the area that an old wood road, impassable for vehicles, does pass near the pond.

One sweltering August day, I hiked along the old road, which in some places was reduced to an overgrown path. After about a mile, I found a moose and deer trail in the dry bed of a small brook, which I followed through the woods toward the shore of the pond. Excitement from a year of anticipation translated into quickened steps. The dense woods allowed only glimpses of the pond and its distant shore, and it wasn't until I broke out into the open that I saw the island. The view through my telephoto lens revealed dark openings along the island's rocky shore just above the water level. The urge to explore the island was overwhelming, yet the difficulties in reaching it were apparent. Bogs and swamps cut off easy access from either direction, and the lateness of day precluded any attempt that afternoon.

A few days later, I made a second try. The plan was to bushwhack a mile and a half by compass to a stream that drained one of the wetlands near the island. After two attempts, I discovered an old trail leading to the stream and along its course in the direction of the pond. Unfortunately, the possibility of easily reaching the pond and island dissolved when I encountered a large beaver flowage that blocked the trail and required backtracking and then a considerable effort to skirt it. After searching for some time and realizing that the day was once again waning with no indication that the pond was nearby, I retraced my steps back out of the woods.

My third attempt came a month and a half later in fall when the moose were in rut. This time I portaged a small rubber raft the mile through the forest to the shore of the pond. There I pumped it up, assembled its oars, and loaded in my tripod and camera equipment. A light breeze created a small chop on the pond's surface as I rowed the half-mile to the island. The pond proved to be shallow and murky, and I looked carefully for sharp rocks and sticks that might puncture the raft. Nearing the island, I began to see more clearly the dark, rounded holes scalloping its rocky ledges at the water's edge. Centuries of dissolution by the pond's acidic water had worked on the rock. Small white cedars clung to the top of the island and crept down its crevices. It still looked as Holmes had described it.

One of the most curious forgotten natural features, discovered by the author after coming across its description in an early geologist's report, is this island honeycombed with solution caves in northern Maine. Such caves are extremely rare in the state.

Two kingfishers took flight as I approached. I rowed up to one of the tunnel openings. Peering in, I could see that the rounded sides of the tunnel were smooth. Light from around a corner at the far end indicated that the tunnel penetrated to another side of the island. Circling with the raft, I discovered much sculpting of the rock and small perforations and holes that were "eaten" through. For an hour I examined the island, and for a brief time as I looked into those dark holes, I'm sure that I felt the same excitement and curiosity as those geologists did over a century and a quarter before.

Unlike many of his contemporaries, Thomas Morton did not recklessly claim direct knowledge of gold in New England, although the same cannot be said for many of the other minerals he discussed. Most early writers overstated the presence of minerals, especially those that are metallic, such as zinc, tin, and copper, as well as silver and gold. Of course, precious metals were very much on the minds of early explorers and their backers, and rumors were rife about these riches in the New World. The sight of natives wearing copper ornaments only served to increase speculation. Although many of New England's minerals have attracted the economic interest of its inhabitants since settlement times, two in particular provide interesting examples—gold and semiprecious stones.

Hidden Treasures

They say there is a Silver and gold mine.

—Thomas Morton, 1637[56]

Gold

The Editor of the Boston Transcript, *speaks of having seen a fine specimen of gold recently in Dedham, found in examinations of quartz. . . . This is the first occurrence of gold being found in any place in New England.*

—The Naturalist, 1846[57]

Gold! The hope of finding this precious element has changed countless human lives. It holds the promise of power, wealth, and prestige. No wonder it engaged the imagination of those who explored the country and came here seeking their fortune and a new life. Today, places still remain where history records its discovery and where one may still find it and experience the quickening pulse of excitement from seeing a radiant yellow fleck of this precious metal.

From early times those who seriously sought gold agreed that it is a rarity in New England. Charles Jackson, reporting on the geology of New Hampshire in the mid-1800s, expressed the opinion that "although minute quantities of native gold have been found in the brown pyrites of Canaan and Grafton . . . still I apprehend that any who should undertake to extract the gold with a view of profit would suffer disappointment.[58]

Not all agreed on when and where the first discoveries were made. Contrary to the statement in *The Naturalist*, there were several reports before 1846. For example, a controversial discovery of an eight-and-a-half-ounce nugget in Newfane, Vermont, was reported in 1826. The same report went on to quote Professor Edward Hitchcock of Amherst, Massachusetts, who, following a search in Somerset, Vermont, in 1833, concluded "that there exists a gold region in the lower part of Vermont, of considerable extent and richness."[59] In Maine Charles Hitchcock reported "an extensive tract in the north-west part of the State in which native gold has been found." He went on to report that it was only seen in alluvium, or water-deposited materials, and had been found in Madrid and on the Sandy River. He was also persuaded that it existed on the upper part of the St. John River as well.[60]

Today, western Maine still contains reminders that gold exists in the soils and rocks of New England. The Swift River in Oxford and Franklin Counties has a reputation of producing the most gold in Maine and continues to attract gold hunters to its placer (in-stream gravel) deposits. This river is a mountain stream, rising in Swift River Pond and making a turbulent journey of twenty miles to the Androscoggin River in Rumford and Mexico. Coos Canyon in Byron provides a spectacular example of the wildness and power of this river in spring. Its East Branch in Byron is regarded as one of the areas of highest gold concentration. The gold is in the stream's gravels and is extracted by a process known as panning. Charles Hitchcock gave the following early description of the operation: "A common tin pan is filled with earth, and then placed under water in a

Gold is a rarity in New England, but along western Maine's Swift River, seen here flowing through Coos Canyon in Byron, small amounts of the precious metal have been extracted by panning the river's gravel deposits.

Swift River, Maine

:ub or stream, and the whole shaken in a peculiar manner. The earth is presently washed away, leaving only gold at the bottom."[61] More than one panner working the Swift River deposits has wondered if somewhere in the surrounding hills a mother lode of gold is slowly washing into this river.

Other reminders that gold still hides beneath New England's landscape are the region's many abandoned gold mines. As late as 1861, Charles Hitchcock reported that in Maine no effort "had yet been made to mine quartz veins containing gold." He also observed that gold is found in association with iron pyrites, or fool's gold.[62]

Approximately twenty years after Hitchcock's report, the Lone Star Mine, in the Oxford County town of Wood-stock, opened for operation. Assays showed over forty ounces of gold per ton of rock, laced also with quartz and iron pyrites. The mining venture, however, was short-lived and soon went out of business.

Some years ago on a summers day, I undertook to find this mine. Aided by an old *Atlas of Oxford County* and modern-day topographic maps, I followed an abandoned wood road into a remote mountain area. The road, now only a faint trail, followed a small brook. Using the peak of a nearby mountain for a compass reading, I reached a point at the base of a steep ridge and scrambled up its thickly wooded slope to its top. According to my maps, the mine was nearby. The ridge dipped into a sag of spruces and firs where it became wet and swampy. On the other side of this low area, the ground took on a strange humpiness. Ahead I saw a long, unnaturally straight gully between long, low mounds covered with moss and large trees. I followed this ditchlike depression until it abruptly ended at a wet, mossy ledge surrounded with ferns. There, at the base of the rock face, old, decaying timbers surrounded a dark pool of water. I could see an opening in the ledge just visible above the pool's surface. I probed with a long stick and discovered that the opening extended into the mountainside beyond its reach. Without a doubt I had found the old mine shaft.

Turning my attention to the long mounds extending along both sides of the trench, I rolled back the moss between the trees, as one would roll up a carpet, and there, revealed, were the tailings of a mining operation. Stained chunks of feldspar encrusted with thousands of tiny quartz crystals and sprinkled throughout with iron pyrites crystals came to the surface as I dug into the piles. I found only fool's gold that day, but later, the small brook I had followed yielded a small trace of gold when a friend tried panning. The mountain still held a few secrets, I guessed, as does all of underground New England.

Precious Stones

Pretious stones there are too.

—John Josselyn, 1674[63]

Although prospectors have not discovered a great wealth of metallic minerals hidden beneath New England's surface, the region is recognized for producing outstanding semiprecious gemstones.[64] These include crystals of quartz, tourmaline, beryl, apatite, and topaz. They are especially associated with bodies, or pods, of pegmatite rock that occur in dikes intruded into granite rock. In fact, pegmatites are a form of granite and contain the same major minerals—quartz, feldspar, and mica. The difference is in the size of the mineral grains. In the pegmatites, they are much larger than in the granites, the result of gradual cooling, which allows time for the growth of crystals. In some instances, the pegmatite minerals grew into large and exquisite crystalline forms in rock cavities, called pockets.

Hundreds of pegmatite bodies have been discovered from Connecticut to Maine. Mining of these began in the 1800s, but most mines are now worked out and closed. A few, however, continue to yield gemstones. Among them is Mt. Mica, perhaps the most famous gem-producing mine in New England.

Mt. Mica is located in Oxford County, Maine, in the town of Paris. It was here, around 1820, that two young men discovered a green tourmaline crystal at the base of an uprooted tree—the first recorded find of this gem in North America. One of these men was Ezekiel Holmes, who was at that time a medical student—the same Ezekiel Holmes who later collaborated with Charles Hitchcock on the geological surveys of Maine. Their report in 1862

Mt. Mica, Maine

stated that "Mount Mica in Paris is the most interesting locality of minerals in the State."[65]

Mt. Mica, in Oxford County, Maine, shown being quarried in this 1895 photograph, is perhaps the most famous gem producing mine in New England. Photograph from Augustus Choate Hamlin, *The History of Mount Mica of Maine, U. S. A. and Its Wonderful Deposits of Matchless Tourmalines* (Bangor, Maine: Augustus Choate Hamlin, 1895).

During the past 175 years, the mining of Mt. Mica has produced some of New England's finest gemstones. Its tourmalines, famous for their clarity and color, reside in collections throughout the world. At this writing, mining still occurs at the Mt. Mica quarry, and it is closed to the public. But in hundreds of other places throughout New England, collectors, both professional and amateur, still search for those "pretious stones" that lie hidden.

Charles Jackson's discovery of fossils in an outcrop near Parlin Pond in west-central Maine was one of the first such discoveries in the state. Since the time of ancient Greece, fossils have been recognized as the remains of long-ago living things, and fossil shells have been seen as evidence that seas once covered the land. However, it wasn't until after the middle of the eighteenth century that fossils began to receive scientific names.

Jackson used his fossiliferous outcrop as evidence for the now outmoded theory of diluvial transportation; that is, that waters from a great flood had carried fragments of the outcrop southward to another location. Sometime during the next twenty years, fossils began to be used as

Ancient Life

I discovered a huge bed of fine grauwacke [dark gray sandstone], filled with an immense number and variety of fossil shell impressions.

—Charles T. Jackson, 1839[66]

indicators of various strata in sedimentary rocks; the science of paleontology was coming of age. In fact, in 1861, Charles Hitchcock defined this science and summarized what had been learned from fossils, concluding that those found in New England indicated that a tropical climate once prevailed here, that extinctions occurred, and that life evolved into more complex—or, in his words, "perfect"—forms.[67]

By the time of Hitchcock's report, at least thirty-five thousand fossils of plants and animals had been discovered in rocks throughout the world. Here in New England, the rocks were also giving up their secrets of ancient life. We shall look at two areas that are especially noteworthy because of their historic significance, the variety of fossils they have yielded, and the immense span of time their fossils represent. One is in northern Maine and the other is in the Connecticut Valley.

Connecticut Valley Footprints

South Hadley . . . is the most prolific locality of the tracks of this extraordinary animal.

—Edward Hitchcock, 1858[68]

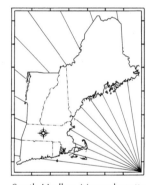

South Hadley, Massachusetts

The animal to which Professor Hitchcock referred had, in his opinion, four feet, with longer hind feet on which it walked most of the time. Further, it possibly had a tail. Although he entertained the idea that the animal could be a huge marsupial, like a kangaroo, Hitchcock assigned it to the category of a batrachian, or amphibian, naming it *Otozoum moodii*, after Pliny Moody, who had discovered its tracks. Today, we know it as a large prosauropod dinosaur with an overall length of about twenty feet.[69]

One spring day I arrived in South Hadley, Massachusetts, where in 1802 Pliny Moody made the first recorded discovery of fossil tracks in the Connecticut Valley. He was plowing his field when he uncovered a slab of rock containing the birdlike prints of an ancient animal he and his neighbors called "Noah's raven." After almost two centuries, some of the fields of Moody's day still remain. They were already well greened and dotted with dandelions when I saw them.

The field behind Moody's home slopes down to a tree-filled lowland and brook. Leaf buds were still in the process of opening. The lifeless tan of last year's cattails marked the presence of a wet depression Moody would have avoided plowing. Purportedly, the fossil tracks were found near here. These quiet and peaceful fields must have looked as innocent to him as they did to me, yet Moody's discovery that day marked the beginning in the Connecticut Valley of scientific exploration resulting in an understanding of what our world was like 190 million years ago.

Around 1835, birdlike tracks were seen again in quarried sandstone from the Turners Falls area while it was being laid for paving. The unusual tracks were examined by James Deane, a local doctor, who contacted Professor Edward Hitchcock of Amherst College. Hitchcock thus began his long involvement with the science of ichnology, or the study of fossil tracks and other indirect evidence of ancient life. He believed that many were made by birds, although he realized that this hypothesis was open to question. In 1858, after twenty-three years of trying to decipher the tracks and describe the creatures that made them, he wrote: "I feel as if I had only commenced my work. . . . how hard it has been to grope my way without guides through the thick darkness that has rested on this subject."[70]

Sometime after his examination of the fossil tracks from the Turners Falls area, Hitchcock urged one Timothy Stoughton to begin quarrying the fossil footprints for commercial sale. One quarry, leased from Roswell Field of Gill, was located at Lily Pond on the south side of Barton

An artist's rendition of the Moody Foot Mark Quarry in South Hadley, Massachusetts, the site of the discovery of the ancient tracks of an extraordinary animal named *Otozoum moodii* by Professor Edward Hitchcock, a respected scientist of the time. Illustration from Edward Hitchcock, *A Report on the Sandstone of the Connecticut Valley, Especially its Fossil Footmarks* (Boston, Mass.: William White, Printers to the State, 1858).

These fossil tracks were thought to have been made by a large bird that roamed the Connecticut Valley 190 million years ago. Local residents called it "Noah's Raven." We now know that the tracks were made by a prosauropod dinosaur that measured about twenty feet in length. Illustration from Edward Hitchcock, *A Report on the Sandstone of the Connecticut Valley, Especially its Fossil Footmarks* (Boston, Mass.: William White, Printers to the State, 1858).

Barton Cove Quarry

Layers of weathered sandstone, such as those in this outcrop at Barton Cove Quarry near the Connecticut River, have produced rock slabs containing a total of fifty-seven species of Triassic reptiles.

Cove, a backwater of the Connecticut River. During the next twenty years, the quarry produced rock slabs containing tracks of fifty-seven species of reptiles, and as its fame grew, it attracted some of the most distinguished scientists of the time, including Louis Agassiz.

Two days after my visit to South Hadley, in a brisk wind and near-freezing temperatures, I examined the dark, weathered layers of sandstone at Barton Cove Quarry, in Montague. The compressed and fused layers of sediment were laid down under much warmer conditions than I experienced that morning. Rays of sunshine streamed over the jagged top of a mossy, lichen-covered wall of a sandstone outcrop, leaving its face of well-defined strata still in the shadows. Separated sheets and chips of the bedrock surrounded the trail between the excavated outcrop and the windblown waters of the cove. Blocky, layered rock ledges poked out from last year's leaves, creating a series of shelves among the hemlocks down to the water's edge. Near the trail, a large block of sandstone stood upright and tilted back, inviting a passerby to look for tracks. I studied it intently for several minutes and saw nothing, only tiny cracks, flake marks, and small veins of minerals. My imagination took over, and the possibilities grew, but nothing emerged with certainty. It was a tantalizing experience. I learned later that there are tracks in a slab of bedrock by this trail, but not here.

After spending most of the morning in the quarry, I left, hands numb from handling freezing camera equipment—certainly not dinosaur weather. Later, as I continued my research on this fascinating subject, I came across the opening line of Hitchcock's 1858 report, in which he referred to "those remarkable footmarks in stone in the valley of the Connecticut River, which have since awakened so much interest."[71] Over a hundred years later, dinosaur tracks were still being found in the region and arousing excitement. Undoubtedly more discoveries will be made, reminding us that there is much we do not yet know about our world—a world in which we are, perhaps, making the tracks for someone else to become excited about a hundred million years from now.

Tropical Fossils of Northern Maine

Numerous fossil marine mollusca are found . . . while remains of land plants are found further north.

—Charles H. Hitchock, 1861[72]

The dark rock, almost coal-like, flaked easily—crumbling out of the ledge into the stream, now low and wadeable at the end of summer. Glossy, lined impressions of forking plant stems crisscrossed every thin leaf of the loosened shale. Many sheets had fallen out of an especially dark layer of the disintegrating rock above me. The fossils were of early plants, perhaps 390 million years old, inhabitants of Lower Devonian time. They had no leaves, for nature had not yet evolved leaves, only simple branching. The plant stems once contained green chloroplasts for capturing the sun's energy. It was here north of Katahdin in 1968 that the largest known plant of the time was discovered, *Pertica quadrifaria*, a plant that stood over six feet high—the tallest on the landscape. It's now Maine's official state fossil.

Outcrops of shale in northern Maine have yielded fossils of early plants, including this one named *Pertica quadrifaria*, thought to have been over six feet in height and the tallest plant on the landscape 390 million years ago.

When the Hitchcock party passed near those plant fossils I had investigated that summer of 1994, they were going north, up Webster Stream into Allagash country. At Telos Dam, Hitchcock reported finding fossils of ancient sea-dwelling organisms. He later wrote, "the ledges upon Telos Lake have furnished the greatest number of fossils. There are several very fine localities . . . and all sorts of marine life are preserved in the strata."[73]

New England was somewhere below the equator and some of it beneath the sea when the Allagash sediments accumulated in an ocean basin. In some areas and at various times, the seas were shallow and warm. Ancient phyla of bivalves, called brachiopods, species of gastropods and crinoids, and other organisms plied the sandy, silty bottoms for food and competed for space. Discharges of new sediment smothered them and new bottom layers were repopulated. The process of layering continued. Gradually the landmasses changed their positions, moved by tectonic forces. Collisions occurred. Continents grew in size, split apart, submerged, emerged, and erupted. Organisms trapped in the sediments mineralized, their shapes pre-

Discovered in the Telos Lake area of northern Maine, this slab of sandstone is around 395 million years old and contains the fossil shells of organisms living in a warm, shallow sea when this part of the continent was below the equator.

served in rock. The old sediments were cemented, heated, and uplifted. Sand and silt were changed to sandstone, siltstone, and slate.

Today, along the shores of Telos Lake, we can still see what Hitchcock saw—up-ended layers of dark, metamorphosed sedimentary rock of the Seboomook Formation. And squeezed between the bedding planes are the fossils of brachiopods, crinoids, gastropods, and extinct trilobites. Sheets of fossil shells are sometimes visible. And each year more fossils are uncovered by the weather and waves. I still walk those shores, head down, scanning the dark, rocky beaches and ledges. It's a different kind of shelling than one does on today's ocean beaches, but no less fascinating.

Some years ago I interviewed a well-known paleobotanist, who had spent part of his career in this section of Maine. The great mystery for him was what the forests here hide beneath their soils, where streams have not uncovered the rocks that hold the key to past life here on earth. Much is still unexplored beneath the surface of New England.

Earthquakes and Subterranean Sounds

I have something considerable awful to tell you. Earthquakes have been here . . . as has been observed for more than thirty years. . . . Whether it be fire or air distressed in subterraneous caverns of the earth, cannot be known; for there is no eruption, no explosion perceptible, but by sounds and tremors, which sometimes are very fearful and dreadful.

—Reverend Hosmer, August 13, 1729[74]

The Reverend Hosmer lived in Haddam, Connecticut, near Moodus and the mysterious Moodus noises. Tremors, quakes, various rumblings, and explosions have been recorded here since colonial times and constitute another element of New England's nature that survives to this day, reminding us that we have yet to entirely subdue a wild and unpredictable earth.

For twenty years the Reverend Hosmer heard hundreds of gunshot-like sounds. "Often times," he wrote, "I have observed them to be coming down from the north, imitating slow thunder, until the sound came near or right under, and then there seemed to be a breaking like the noise of a cannon shot, or severe thunder which shakes the houses and all that is in them."[75]

The Reverend Henry Chapman also kept a record of the Moodus noises for a period of sixteen years, beginning with one on May 16, 1791:

It began at 8 o'clock, P.M. with two very heavy shocks in quick succession. The first was most powerful; the earth appeared to undergo very violent convulsions. The stone walls were shaken down, chimnies were untopped, doors which were latched were thrown open, and a fissure in the ground several rods in extent was afterwards discovered. Thirty lighter ones [shocks] succeeded in a short time, and upwards of one hundred were counted in the course of the night.[76]

This was the worst of the Moodus quakes, although hundreds have been felt and recorded from 1702 to the present.

Earthquakes and associated sounds have been reported since 1638 in New England. The largest quake in the Northeast occurred in the St. Lawrence Valley in 1663 and was felt throughout New England, and geologists fear that if another as large should occur today in our heavily settled region, the damage could be considerable. Another occurred in Massachusetts on October 29, 1727. Later, one observer wrote: "This noise, as amazing as it was, in an instant of time, as one may say, was succeeded by a shake much more terrible. My house, which is large and well built, seemed to be squeezed or pressed uptogether. . . . 'Tis impossible to describe the terror and amazement that an earthquake carries with it."[77]

A quarter of a century later, in 1755, Massachusetts was hit by another severe quake. And in 1846, a letter to the editor in an issue of *Scientific American* reported subterranean sounds in Deerfield, New Hampshire. "During the last twelve years," according to the correspondent, "certain curious, not to say alarming phenomena in the town . . . have excited the fears of the inhabitants." The letter went on to describe explosions as loud as a cannon heard by residents year-round, with as many as twenty heard in a night. They jarred houses and overthrew stone walls.[78]

The explanations advanced for these earth movements and sounds have been many. Zadock Thompson in his *Natural History of Vermont*, published in 1853, speculated that the many earthquakes recorded in Vermont and the rest of New England since settlement may have been associated with meteors agitating the atmosphere, although he noted that it was generally supposed that earthquakes were the result of steam rushing through cavities in the earth's interior.[79] Today, we attribute earthquakes to release of stresses in rock structures and associate them with faults. We study the elastic, or seismic, waves they produce. Through a seismic study begun in 1979, for example, we know that the "Moodus noises" are caused by shallow, low-magnitude earthquakes that cause the earth's surface to act like a loudspeaker and give forth a boom.[80]

Today, our ability to predict when and where earthquakes will occur is increasing. However, there is still a mystery about them, and whenever they occur, they are still just as terrifying as they were to the early inhabitants of the New England wilderness.

THE GREAT DRIFT LANDSCAPE

Drift, the loose materials constituting the surface of the earth, sand, gravel, boulders.

—Charles T. Jackson, 1844[81]

Patches of snow and ice still covered Maine's western hills in late April and the afternoon sun was low when I hiked up an old wood road in the town of Phillips to the legendary rock. After a steep half-mile of avoiding the muddiest ruts and iciest spots, a massive, gray wall of weathered granite appeared on the hillside, partially concealed by a group of fir and hemlock trees. Viewed from the other side of the trees, the wall became a huge, rounded boulder—eight thousand tons by some estimates. Its monstrous size is so impressive that the geologist Charles Hitchcock mentioned it in his 1862 report, "A few very large boulders were noticed. . . . Another split in two."[82]

As I approached, I could see a longitudinal break separating the huge mass of rock almost evenly in half and a V-shaped break quartering the side nearest me. A trail rutted by moose tracks led to the uphill side of the rock, where snow still remained in the rock's shadow, although it had disappeared from most of the wooded slope behind.

In the mountains of western Maine, this monstrous boulder rests on a hillside, deposited there by the powerful force of the last glacier.

Snow and ice still filled much of the largest crack, suggesting the force that had split it in two. I climbed the slope above the rock so as to obtain a better view. It was only then that I gained a full appreciation of this immense erratic boulder, so out of place on this western Maine hillside—quietly testifying to the strength of the powerful force that moved it here. And, in a strange sort of way, this startling example of glacial drift is a powerful force in itself, for it has the ability to move people to contemplate, for a moment at least, the natural world around them.

Little has changed since Jackson's time in the meaning of the term *drift*, only in the theory of how these materials that bring shape and texture to the New England landscape arrived here. When Jackson conducted his early surveys, he observed the many scattered boulders and deposits of gravels, sands, and finer particles. He called these materials diluvium, based on the diluvial theory that New England once experienced a time "of great turbulence, the ocean's waters and seas of ice from the polar regions, having been hurled with violence over the surface of the northern hemisphere, breaking up and transporting masses of rocks, and driving the loose materials to the southward and depositing them, not infrequently, a hundred miles distant from their parent beds."[83] Although Jackson acknowledged a new theory in Europe, relating rock scratches and scattered boulders and gravel deposits to the action of glaciers, he dismissed it, writing that we may in this country "discover in a short time that the glacial theory of drift is absurd."[84]

By the late 1870s when Charles Hitchcock carried out his study of New Hampshire's geology and discovered that Mt. Washington was once overtopped by a glacier, the idea of an ice sheet covering the region had taken hold of the imagination. Here was a force that could account for the massive alteration of New England's surficial materials, some of which have also survived another kind of powerful force in nature—a human nature.

Striae

These smoothed and rounded ledges . . . are covered with scratches or striae, usually parallel to one another, and indicating the exact course of the drift agency.

—Charles H. Hitchcock, 1861[85]

All the geologists and naturalists commented on the grooves and scratches they saw on New England's outcrops of smoothed and polished bedrock. Hitchcock went on to note that "at several places upon the sea shore the striae have been noticed," and, he observed, "the course of the striae upon the lakes north of the Katahdin mountains have more of an easterly course."[86]

I have seen these scored lines on ledges throughout the New England region. The Wisconsin Ice Sheet was the last glacier to scour our landscape, and it left these scratchings as a lasting impression. Striae are especially noticeable when the sun is low in the sky—early morning and late afternoon—when grooves are shadowed. A compass laid beside these marks, whether on the shores of Cobscook Bay or the Allagash lakes, confirms Hitchcock's observations of an easterly direction. Our striae are perhaps one of the most permanent features of the New England wilderness and so widespread that anyone may see them just as did the first inhabitants of this region.

Low morning light on an outcrop at Cobscook Bay in eastern Maine reveals grooves and scratches, called striae, that were made when the Wisconsin Ice Sheet ground its way across the New England landscape.

The ancient river deltas found in coastal and central Maine are considered unique in the United States.[88] Maine has three that are especially good examples near the towns of Cherryfield, Columbia Falls, and Gray. They formed some twelve thousand years ago from sediments carried by glacier meltwater streams flowing out from the receding edge of the last ice sheet. "Delta" was chosen as the term to describe them because the sediments fan out at the mouths of rivers to form the triangular shape of the Greek capital letter "delta." Today, those deltas that remain undeveloped are seen as high sandy ridges and plains. One, especially, displays features little changed from the time when it was recorded in a survey notebook by Pierpont and Albee in 1792.

Ancient River Deltas

A large sandy plain— some scattering pines and birch bushes.

—Joseph Pierpont and
William Albee, 1792[87]

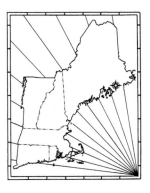

Pineo Ridge, Maine

The plain is the most remarkable in the country.

—Joseph Pierpont and William Albee, 1792[89]

On a first visit to Pineo Ridge one is little prepared for such a dramatic introduction. A narrow, almost perfectly straight gravel road, wooded to the edge on both sides, leads to it. Near its end, the road turns slightly. Abruptly the forest ends, and you are thrust out of the forest into barren, open land. The change is stunning. Immediately, the face of a steep ridge rises in front of you. The road, sandy now and rutted by erosion, goes straight up the slope, exactly where, twelve thousand years ago, waves carved their way into the front of the gigantic delta you now face.

At the top of the ridge, a flat, gently rolling plain stretches into the empty distance, given dimension by scattered solitary trees and large, gray erratic boulders. The day I was there, these lonely objects were starkly silhouetted against the swirling, fast-moving clouds of a clearing sky. "The nature of the whole is singular and different from anything I ever saw," wrote Alexander Baring after seeing it in 1796.[90] Low shrubs, mainly blueberry plants, cover the plain. Though the area was settled in the mid-eighteenth century, in fundamental ways this land has remained unchanged. A long history of burns maintains the

This slope on the seaward side of Pineo Ridge, in eastern Maine, is actually the wave-carved edge of an ancient delta formed twelve thousand years ago when the sea's edge was five and a half miles inland from where it is today. Journals of those who saw Pineo Ridge in the late 1700s reflect a stunned amazement at finding a stark, expansive plain so unlike the rest of the country they encountered.

low shrub vegetation. Some of the fires were perhaps initiated by natives before European settlement. The roads reveal a sandy, well-drained, dry soil, one that would not hinder a fire once it was started.

I followed the road westward along the top of the wave-cut slope and then turned northward. A low rise revealed the expansiveness of the plain—seventeen square miles of mostly flat, unforested land. The view is arresting. Continuing northward, the road rises and falls, moving around humps and small hills where ancient sediments mounded up along the ragged, icy edge of the receding glacier and later caved into sink holes and piled into heaps when the ice melted. Here also I saw long, sinuous depressions—channels where meltwater streamed away from the ice mass, braided out, and cut down into the accumulating sediments. The soils are coarse here where the larger, heavier particles first settled out. They were much finer at the wave-cut front of the delta. Isolated pines, an occasional boulder, and small ponds in wooded depressions become abnormally interesting in such a barren landscape. I stopped at a lone red pine. The ground was white with newly flowered bunchberries, and I lingered here for some time, perhaps because I had discovered something familiar.[91]

On my return, I found a tall, rounded knoll topped by a large, gray boulder. Here I glimpsed the corner of Maine's largest wetland, the Great Heath. The Pleasant River, which drains this four-thousand-acre undeveloped peatland, is not visible, though I looked from several locations.

I left under blue skies and bright sunshine, the remaining clouds of yesterday's storm now swept away. The plain was brilliant green—the beginning of this year's crop of blueberries. In the fall at the end of the season, the plain will turn to red, as it may have done for centuries.

Situated in swamps and other lowlands, these well-drained ridges offered natives and settlers dry pathways and thus became known as horsebacks. We now know these ridges that aroused the curiosity of our early geologists are glacially formed features. Sediments were deposited in the beds of ancient streams that flowed in channels or tunnels of ice through or beneath the glaciers. Layers of streambed sediments accumulated between the walls of ice and remained as long, sinuous ridges after the glacier melted away. Today, the scientific term for these formations is esker, from the Irish *eiscir*, meaning ridge of mountains.

Scientists in Hitchcock's time looked at eskers with interest and sought to learn about their composition, size, direction, and other characteristics. Today, scientists seek how they relate to theories of glacial processes. Eskers have helped us learn about ancient climate conditions, the direction of glacial movement (eskers are normally oriented to the direction of glacial flow), and, through the marine fossils they sometimes contain, the time and conditions of glacial recession.

But eskers have other uses of more immediate benefit to humans. They provide clean, washed, and sorted sands and gravels for construction. As of old, they are seen as

Horsebacks

Curious . . . ridges are found in great abundance in Maine, and scarcely occur out of the State, which are known by the provincial name of horsebacks. We are not ready to theorize upon their origin.

—Charles H. Hitchcock, 1861[92]

Excavation of this esker, originally called a horseback, reveals the cross-section of a riverbed of sorted sands and gravels deposited by an ancient river flowing through a tunnel of ice in the last glacier.

useful in the establishment of routes of travel, except that today we have the means to move them to where we wish to place our roads rather than simply build our roads wherever the eskers exist. As a consequence, we have excavated and removed vast numbers of them from the landscape. For example, in 1979 it was estimated that at least 25 percent had been obliterated from the face of Maine since 1935.[93] In some sections of New England they are now a rarity, and few remain relatively undisturbed.

Swamp Esker, Rhode Island

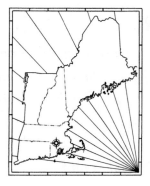

This ridge is extremely curious, and consists of sand and gravel, built up exactly like the embankments for rail-roads.

—Charles T. Jackson, in his Maine report, 1837[94]

The geologist Charles T. Jackson was curious about the horsebacks he saw and noted many of them in his reports. But he never specifically described one that a century and a half after his Rhode Island report was made would be recognized as "one of the largest and undisturbed eskers in southern New England."[95] Although on his geological map of Rhode Island he identified a swamp in the location where this esker exists, we may conclude that he never actually explored it.

When I explored this swamp esker in north-central Rhode Island, a late afternoon sun shone through pines and oaks and cast a ladderlike pattern of shadows across the sandy roadway that leads up onto its top. From the main road, little tells that this is an esker, but as I followed the road, which became more wooded with pines and oaks, it narrowed and gradually became higher. The slopes on either side dropped off more steeply, and the pathway meandered as it followed the ancient streambed. A tufted titmouse, a bird of the woodlands, sang somewhere nearby.

I left the road and bushwacked down the side of the esker to the swamp at its base. Pools of standing water filled depressions between the roots of the maples and scattered cedars. On the drier hummocks, I noticed goldthread growing profusely. Though the swamp is densely wooded, I could see into it for some distance, for it was still early spring and the leaves were not fully out. The sun was now low and silhouetted the ridge's slope. I suddenly realized I was deep into the swamp. The utility of this esker immediately impressed me, and its popularity with those who settled here became apparent.

As I returned back along the top of the ridge and neared the main road, the sounds of hammering broke the stillness. I had noticed on my way here that many homes line the road that passes by the end of this swamp and esker. How many here, I wonder, know that among them is a rare, natural feature? It has escaped the fate of so many other eskers like it that have been trucked away, to be mixed in concrete and asphalt or spread beneath our roads and highways. Ironically, this one perhaps survived because it serves as a kind of roadway—a country trail for walking and horseback riding and other recreational travel. But whatever its use, its presence preserves part of the geologic and human history of this region.

Pine River Esker, New Hampshire

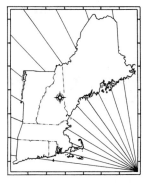

It appears east from the mouth of Poland Brook and extends in a single ridge a mile to the south, with a height 50 to 75 feet above the low modified drift on each side, or about 100 feet above the [Pine] river.

—Charles H. Hitchcock, 1878[96]

The waters of Pine River flow under Route 16 near Ossipee, New Hampshire. Here one may look eastward and several hundred feet up the stream see a high ridge rising above the river. Through openings in the dense covering of white pine, the ridge's steep slope appears. This is the segment of the Pine River Esker that Hitchcock described in 1878—a portion of one of the largest eskers in New Hampshire; seven miles long and, in places, up to 120 feet high. "South-east from Ossippee Lake," Hitchcock wrote, "a continuous belt of modified drift extends along the entire course of Pine River."[97]

A highway now follows some of this esker southward from the Pine River Bridge. I drove along the side of the esker for some distance and passed a large break where it is being commercially mined. Beyond, the esker remained undisturbed and continued to parallel the highway. Soon I came to a location where a wetland intervened between the highway and the ridge. I pulled off and walked through a fringe of woods to the edge of the bog. Directly across I could see tall white and red pines covering the esker-ridge. Here are some of New Hampshire's oldest pine trees, and the state's tallest, up to 125 feet. Many started life well back into the 1700s, and some were already over a hundred years old when Hitchcock visited this esker.

Leaving, I reflected on what I had seen. It is an extraordinary feature, but even more remarkable is that the portion I saw has survived to enrich our lives in some small but significant way.

Belgrade Esker Area, Maine

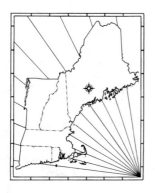

The gravel takes the form of a continuous ridge for several miles, being cut through by the Maine Central Railroad at Belgrade Station. . . . In the southeastern part of Belgrade, the system expands into a broad series of reticulated ridges inclosing numerous kettleholes and basins containing twenty lakelets.

—George H. Stone, 1899[98]

The early spring melt, I suppose, is an appropriate time to visit kettle ponds and eskers. It was April 4 when I slopped through the mud and gingerly stepped on patches of slippery ice in the wood road that leads to a kettle pond area containing one of New England's most outstanding eskers. On my way in I was continually reminded that melting ice was responsible for the rare bit of unaltered landscape I was on.

I soon found myself on a high ridge; it was the esker. Often these steep-sided ridges are sinuous, but the river that left this esker seemed to have a destination in mind, for it tracked from the north straight and true a distance of fifteen miles. A large moose had gone ahead of me, also taking the high ground. Perhaps the going was easier on the esker. A few deer tracks also rutted the mud. Soon, down through the trees, the smooth, white sheet of an ice-covered pond showed itself. I had chosen this time of year

This small kettle hole pond in the Belgrade, Maine, esker complex was formed in a depression created by the melting of a buried block of ice from the last glacier.

because later in the spring and summer when the leaves come out the unusual shape of this landscape would be difficult to discern.

The pond is the largest of the several in the area—a product of a huge block of ice, which had broken off from the melting glacier where a delta was forming. The ice chunk caused the delta to be separated into two irregular lobes. At this northern end, the old delta was fed by a river—the same river that produced the esker I was on. The result now surrounded me—a pitted, hummocky, highly scenic terrain, consisting of kettle hole ponds, kames, and esker segments. The smooth-surfaced ponds represent the only break in this chaotic topography.

As I stood looking down at the pond, imagining the events that produced it, I noticed a beaver lodge below me, snuggled up to the pond's edge. Nearby were several large trees gnawed nearly half-through.

This location is immensely attractive. A small pine-covered peninsula projects out into the pond, adding interest to the otherwise smooth shoreline. At this time of year, there is little of the recreational use that will soon come. The ground is too soft for recreational vehicles. This outstanding area is still undeveloped, surrounded as it is by residences and businesses. I heard dogs barking and a chain saw in the distance; a plane flew over, but otherwise, it was quiet and peaceful.

I left the pond and followed the esker around it. Deer-chewed shrubs, coyote scat, and a pile of blue jay feathers told of other things passing this way. The trail followed the esker's high knolls. I looked down at boggy coves of discolored, melting ice, now too dangerous to walk on. At the end of the pond, where evergreens shaded the ground, I walked through deep snow. Crossing the low land, I made my way over a ridge and through a cutting to another, smaller pond. A dense tangle of alders surrounded the snow-covered pond, but I knew that as spring wore on, an unusual ten-foot-wide bog mat around the pond's perimeter would once again bloom with sundew, pitcher plant, leatherleaf, cranberry, water willow, bog laurel, and bog rosemary. I also knew that too many visitors to this delicate fringe of bog could destroy it.[99]

I retraced my steps the mile and a half I had hiked on my way through this fascinating area of glacial deposits. Later, on the highway, I passed a concrete plant utilizing a portion of the same esker I had traversed only a short time before, and I noticed a perfect cross-section where it had been cut through. With permission, I was able to walk up to it and see firsthand its beautiful symmetrical shape and the much desired material from which it is made—a forceful example of the competitive roles aesthetic and economic values play in our land-use issues.

Boulder Fields

In almost every part of the State occur accumulations of bowlders, or large blocks of stone, with the angles more or less rounded.

—Albert D. Hager, 1861[100]

Long before the geologists began exploring New England's landscape, the settlers were aware of the rocky nature of the land. They had spent backbreaking hours clearing their fields and building stone walls, only to uncover more rocks with their plows. In some locations, the boulders were so large and numerous that it was nearly impossible to cut the trees and yard them out. These areas came to be called boulder fields.

The majority of boulders strewn over the land are chunks of granite left by the most recent episode of glaciation. Why granite? It breaks relatively easily along joints, or cracks. Blocks were commonly dislodged from our granitic mountains as the full weight of the glacier came down onto them. Granite is also very hard, and the dislodged blocks were not pulverized by the pressure and grinding that occurred while they were being dragged along beneath the ice sheet. The effect was one of breaking and rounding their sharp, angular corners.

Today, we still find a few situations where natural boulder fields exist, allowing us to study them and experience a different kind of landscape.

Ledyard Boulder Train, Connecticut

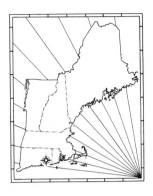

The greater part of the Diluvium was apparently deposited by a general current, traversing the surface from N.N.W. to S.S.E. This is satisfactorily indicated . . . by bowlders, scattered over the surface.

—James G. Percival, 1842[101]

When he conducted a geological survey of Connecticut over a century and a half ago, James Percival was well aware of the phenomenon of boulders on the Connecticut landscape. One especially large concentration of boulders, occurring just north of New London in a thirteen-mile belt from Ledyard Center to East Lyme, was first described in 1960 and later in 1976.[102] Scientists surveying for potential national natural landmarks wrote in 1982 that they had never seen or heard of any other boulder field in New England of this magnitude.[103] Other geologists have also acknowledged this extraordinary glacial landform.[104]

Spring was advancing rapidly in southern Connecticut when I entered the open hardwoods of Ledyard Glacial Park on a day in early May. New light-green leaves produced a gauzy effect in the forest, and the bright blossoms of wood anemone rushed to keep ahead of the leaves before they closed off the light. The trail dropped down into a hollow among black birches, oaks, red maples, and scattered boulders. Dry leaves crunched underfoot. The path now led up a rocky slope, and at the top of the rise, more large rocks appeared. Then in the distance I saw a long ridge of huge boulders interspersed with trees—a spectacular jumble of gray, lichen-covered humps.

Some of the rough, rounded blocks of granite gneiss are truly immense—twenty to thirty feet in diameter. Others are smaller. The average, I'm told, is about ten feet. The boulders are piled three and four deep, lying where they were brought to the front edge of a melting glacier and dumped some twelve thousand years ago after being dragged several miles by the ice. Meltwater from the gla-

These glacially deposited boulders are part of a thirteen-mile-long boulder train, an extraordinary landform that runs from Ledyard Center to East Lyme in Connecticut.

cier washed away the earth materials from around the rocks, leaving them exposed on the surface.

I look on this evidence of glacial force with a good deal of awe. Unlike the eskers, here is presented a landscape feature of such formidable presence that all ideas of its removal recede like the glacier that brought it here. So it is now in a park, purchased in 1979 by the town of Ledyard to be kept for our enjoyment and study.

Immense Boulders

Such huge bowlders are beginning to excite a good deal of popular interest.

—Albert D. Hager, 1861[105]

The early geologists were fascinated by the huge boulders they found on the land. We call them erratics today, partly because they occur randomly in an erratic pattern and partly because they often appear to have no logical connection to the bedrock in their immediate vicinity. The geologists weren't the first, by any means, to notice them. On January 27, 1632, Governor Winthrop and a party went up the Charles River and, exploring up a stream, came "to a great rock, upon which stood a high stone, cleft in sunder, that four men might go through, which they called Adams Chair, because the youngest of their company was Adam Winthrop."[106] Another early description came from John Josselyn who, in the 1670s, commented on the Moose Rock, discussed below. How these immense boulders got to where they were was a matter of much speculation by the early scientists, who were also interested in where they came from and their composition.

Edward Hitchcock in his 1841 report on the geology of Massachusetts reported on eleven boulders ranging in size from twenty feet to forty feet in diameter. "It seems difficult," he puzzled, "how running water should have been able to remove such enormous masses."[107] This, of course, was before the idea of glaciation had been widely accepted. In 1861, the authors of the *Report on the Geology of Vermont* discovered in Whitingham the largest rock they had seen in New England—40 feet long, 125 feet in circumference, and an average width of 32 feet. They named it the Green Mountain Giant. "Such objects," they wrote, "are beginning to be incorporated into the world's literature, and we already have at least one volume entitled 'The Bowlder,' as well as Hugh Miller's 'Autobiography of a bowlder.' "[108]

Charles Hitchcock, who identified western Maine's large rock, also surveyed New Hampshire. According to Hitchcock, when regret was expressed to that state's Governor Prescott that his state had no boulders as large as those in the other neighboring states, the governor, feeling that New Hampshire's reputation was at stake, immediately initiated a search. Subsequently, in the words of Hitchcock, the Governor "found a very formidable array of giant fragments superior to anything described elsewhere." They included rocks with names such as Churchill, Chase, Ballard, Vessel, and Elephant.[109] However, one important boulder Hitchcock missed: the Madison Boulder.

The Madison Boulder, New Hampshire

It is only quite recently that I have seen boulders in our limits [state of New Hampshire] larger than any of which mention has been made in the writings of American geologists.

—Charles H. Hitchcock, 1877[110]

The Madison Boulder holds the New England record as the largest intact boulder. In fact, it is one of the largest glacial erratics in the world. It measures eighty-three feet long, thirty-seven feet wide, and twenty feet high. However, there are some differences among estimates of its weight: a sign by the boulder claims its estimated weight as 4,662 tons while other sources claim that it weighs 7,650 tons. Whatever the case, its full significance was summed up nicely by Professor William O. Crosby, formerly head of the geology department of the Massachusetts Institute of Technology, who described the boulder as "a noble example of a glacial erratic, unequaled in size and solidity in New Hampshire, if not in New England, and of special geologic interest on account of being readily and clearly traceable to its parent ledge nearly two miles northward."[111]

It caught my attention instantly, when I drove into the parking lot—a huge, gray, granite backdrop for a grove of pruned trees. The trees imparted a dramatic sense of scale, and I found myself pondering once again the powerful force exerted by the ice sheet. Perhaps the greatest effect of these great rock hulks is a psychological one. They appear to defy a logic of situation: they don't fit what one expects to find. What must the first discoverer of this immense boulder have felt when she or he stumbled onto it?

I had a greater sense of discovery with the western Maine boulder, which is in a more remote and natural setting, but still, the Madison Boulder makes an awesome presence in these woods. In its immensity, it even overcomes the negative effect of the graffiti on its sides. The fact that such an unusual object of nature exists makes one wonder what other surprises remain that have been forgotten and are awaiting discovery by a new generation.

The Moose Rock, Maine

By Sebegug Pond . . . is a Rock of Crystal called the Moose Rock, because in shape like a Moose.

—John Josselyn, 1672[1,2]

To one who is looking for geologic remnants of the New England wilderness, John Josselyn's brief mention of the Moose Rock is an interest-provoking item. Does this rock still lie somewhere around the shoreline of Sebegug Pond, now known as Sebago Lake? In 1674, Josselyn gave a little more information in his second book:

Twelve mile from Casco-bay, and passable for men and horses, is a lake called by the Indians Sebug, *on the brink thereof at one end is the famous Rock shap'd like a* Moose-Deere *or* Helk, *Diaphanous, and called the* Moose-Rock. *Here are found stones like Crystal, and* Lapis Specularis *or* Muscovia [mica] *glass both white and purple.*[113]

It would appear that the rock was a large chunk of pegmatite with quartz and mica crystals and located near the shore at one end of the lake, perhaps at the southern end closer to Casco Bay. However, several phone calls gave me the information that the water level of the lake today may be at least ten feet higher than it was during Josselyn's time because of dams at the outlet. If a rock of the size described by Josselyn were on the brink or edge of the lake, it may well be underwater unless, of course, by brink Josselyn meant on the edge of a cliff or rock outcrop ten feet higher than the lake level of that time. There is also no way of knowing how far away from the water's edge the rock might have been. And we also don't know if Josselyn actually saw the rock or was getting his information secondhand. Calls to several local individuals who know the lake and shoreline well drew blanks in my search.

On the chance that Josselyn was referring to the southern end of the lake when he said "one end" and that the rock was either high on a ledge or far enough away from the shore to be visible today, I spent the better part of a morning exploring this part of the lake from land, stopping at several publicly owned locations. Although I was able to obtain good views of large sections of the shoreland, I saw no rock that might conceivably fit Josselyn's description. However, there were also sections that I missed because of private property restrictions, and I'm convinced that a survey of the shore by boat would be a better approach. For me, the Moose Rock still remains a tantalizing mystery.

Of all the features left on the landscape in the wake of the last glacier, none are so captivating as rocking stones. Several reports appeared in scientific and other journals in the 1820s, well before they were catalogued and described during the geological surveys. Accounts came from throughout New England, and some of these stones figured prominently in the folklore of a town or region.

A notice of two rocking stones appeared in the *American Journal of Science* in 1825—one in North Providence and the other in Smithfield, Rhode Island. The Smithfield stone weighed over eighty tons and could be moved by hand. According to the report, "when moving, the rock appears about to tumble down the declivity upon which it is situate, and very few have the resolution to stand near its north-east side while its moving."[115]

Many rocking stones have been reported in Massachusetts. Indeed, "they are common in Massachusetts," reported Edward Hitchcock. He described two in the state—one in Fall River and the other in Berlin. The Fall River rock weighed 140 tons and was of interest because

Rocking Stones

Moveable rocks, or masses of stone so nicely balanced as to be set in motion by a very small force, have excited the attention of both ancient and modern writers.

—Jacob Green, 1822[114]

the rocking stone was a different kind of rock than its base. In Hitchcock's opinion, this made the rock more interesting "because the most careless observer perceives that it is a stranger, brought thither by some powerful agency of nature."[116] Two more were reported in Roxbury in 1823 in the *American Journal of Science* and *The Boston Journal of Philosophy and the Arts*. It is difficult to tell if these are one and the same. Another in Savoy was described in 1825 in the *American Journal of Science*, and one in Chelsea in an 1837 edition of the *American Magazine of Useful and Entertaining Knowledge*.[117] It is interesting that in some cases attempts were made to dislodge the rocking stones.

In Vermont, Zadock Thompson, in 1853, described two in Greensborough.[118] But the most provocative description of a rocking stone in Vermont and the best early illustration of one was included in the *Report of the Geology of Vermont*, published in 1861. It was called the Orvis

Early geologists were captivated by rocking stones, such as the Orvis Rocking Stone in Manchester, Vermont, reported in 1861 to be so perfectly balanced that its thirty-five tons could be easily tipped by one finger. Illustration from Albert D. Hager, et al., *Report on the Geology of Vermont*, vol. 2 (Claremont, N. H.: The Claremont Manufacturing Company, 1861).

Rocking Stone, and the report described it as a "slate rock, seventeen feet in length, eight feet wide, and five feet thick, and so nicely poised upon the ledge below it as to be easily tipped with one finger, and still placed so that ten men could not throw it from its bed. . . . We regard this the best example of rocking-stones in the State, and probably the best in New England, for, were it not protected by forest trees, the winds alone would move it."[119]

New Hampshire also has its share of reports on rocking stones. Two were mentioned in separate issues of the *American Journal of Science*, one in Durham in 1822 and the other in Hanover in 1833. Charles Hitchcock, in 1877, briefly described five rocking stones in Goffstown, Mt. Pawtuckaway, Hanover, Newport, and Warren.[120]

Finally, in the 1861 report on Maine's geology and natural history, a rocking stone in Windham is described as "poised so nicely that it can be rocked by the efforts of two men." This granite stone measured 11 feet high, 18 feet long, and 19 feet wide across the middle, and Hitchcock estimated that it weighed about 230 tons.[121]

Of all the rocking stones reported in the literature, perhaps the most interesting one was reported in Rhode Island. As you will see, against great odds it still survives today. It is known as Drum Rock.

Drum Rock, Rhode Island

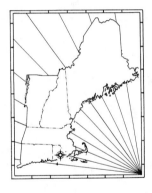

Within a mile from the village of Apponaug may be seen a huge rock, so completely balanced upon another, and its equilibrium so exact, that a boy 14 years of age may set it in such motion that the contact or collision caused thereby, produces a sound somewhat like that of a drum, but more sonorous, which in a still evening may be heard a distance of six or eight miles. Hence, from time immemorial, it has gone by the name of the Drum rock.

—John C. Rease and John M. Niles, 1819[122]

The description by Rease and Niles in 1819 is the earliest reference that I found on Drum Rock. The second appeared in the *American Journal of Science* in a letter from Steuben Taylor to Professor Silliman, dated September 20, 1823. In this account, accompanied by an engraving, the rocking stone was described as resembling a turtle and measuring about ten feet long, six feet wide, and two feet thick. It was delicately balanced on two points on a base rock of several feet in thickness. By standing on it, a child could shift his or her weight and cause it to rock back and forth. The peculiar thing was that it would make four bumps when so rocked, thus sounding like a drum. The writer also observed that the upper stone appeared to have been once a part of its base but had split off. Further, it seemed to have been shifted around from where it had been once naturally attached.[123]

My third encounter with the rock came while reading Charles Jackson's 1840 report on his geological survey of Rhode Island. He reported that "the rock is said to have served the Indians as an alarm or call, for by rocking a sound is produced audible to a great distance, and I was informed it could be heard during the stillness of night to the distance of six or eight miles. I measured the dimensions of the rocking stone, and found them to be 7½ feet in length, 5½ feet in width, and 15 inches in thickness, so it must weigh about 3½ tons."[124] Jackson also included an engraving. At this point, my interest was piqued, and I began to entertain the idea of trying to find the rock. If I could do so, I would see an example of a rocking stone that had a long oral and written history, dating back to colonial times. I made a final decision to extend my search in earnest when I came upon a 1936 publication on the history of Rhode Island that contained an old photograph of Drum Rock, showing it in a wooded area with a stone wall in the background. Attached to its base was a metal plaque.[125]

I wrote to the Rhode Island Historical Preservation Commission for information. After a follow-up phone call, I found someone who knew of the rock and provided me with a map and the name of a contact in the Rhode Island Department of Transportation. A phone call to this individual led me to a local historian and writer who had written a brief history of the rock and knew of its location.

Drum Rock in Apponaug, Rhode Island, is said to have been used by Indians to sound alarms or calls over a distance of six or so miles. Today it is found in a small protected site in the middle of housing developments.

Another telephone call and I had an appointment for a personally guided trip. To have found it alone would have been difficult, I later learned, for the field and wood lot where it resided are now a maze of roads and buildings.

One clear, cool day in early May, I met my guide, Don D'Amato, near the Apponaug City Hall. We drove through busy streets and into a residential area. After several turns, we arrived at a small wooded area. There, beyond an opening in an old stone wall, sat the rock I had so long wished to find. Through the trees all around I could see glimpses of homes. A century and three-quarters ago, Stueben Taylor had written, "This rock is surrounded with interesting scenery." He went on to describe a dark, dismal swamp to the south and the slope of a hill on the west side. I could see by the rooftops of buildings these areas were now developed. From this hill Taylor could see Narragansett Bay and several islands. To the east, he wrote, is a plain cut by a ravine containing a small stream. To the north, he saw huge gray, moss-covered rocks covering the land.[126]

Today, Stueben Taylor would find little recognizable except the rock itself. And even it is not the same, for it is now silent. It gives not the slightest hint of what we know about its noisy past in this place—a place where natives gathered and camped and possibly drummed out messages with the rock, a place frequented by early settlers of Apponaug who told stories of how in the mid-1800s those who passed it on blueberrying trips would stop and rumble the rock, a place where children of the 1920s played and made it boom. Later, the homes arrived, and when the mischievous practice of late-night drumming interrupted the peace and quiet of the neighborhood, the rock's owner had it silenced with a slight turn of its loose upper section using heavy equipment.[127]

Clues are here, however, that this gray, distinctively shaped, lichen-covered rock is valued by the community. An empty, shallow, rectangular-shaped cut gives evidence that a plaque was once attached. The understory surrounding the rock has been cleared so that the rock is now easily seen by those who pass by it. And the mere fact that this glen was spared development attests to the value some attached to the rock. Later, I learned that the rock was once considered a symbol of Apponaug.

When I left Drum Rock, I was encouraged by the signs of community concern and care I had seen. I have no doubt that sometime in the future this rock will once again produce a sound first heard when Rhode Island was still a wilderness. When it does occur, it will send a different message, a message for those who march to the drumbeat of historical and environmental preservation, for its symbolism goes far beyond the boundaries of Apponaug.

NATURAL CURIOSITIES

As I was lately travelling through the State of Connecticut, my attention was excited by a curious, and to me a novel phenomenon.

—Anonymous, 1822[128]

The phenomenon reported by the anonymous letter writer to the *American Journal of Science* in 1822 concerned the movement of rocks without apparent cause. The place this occurred was in Salisbury, Connecticut, where rocks in a pond were observed gradually moving towards the shore. Measurements indicated that a rock moved over three rods between September 1819 and February 1821. Another letter to the editor by the same individual, who then revealed his identity, reported on a number of observations and measurements to test the hypothesis that the rocks were being moved by the expansion of ice during the freezing months of winter. This was shown to be the case, and the mystery was solved.[129]

Our history contains many examples of how our country has mystified us and piqued our curiosity. Reports have been made of perpetually frozen wells and grotesquely shaped masses of a calcareous substance buried in the sand. In some cases, people were quick to accept the supernatural as a cause for the curiosities. In others, such as the case of the moving rocks of Salisbury, careful experimentation and observation usually provided an explanation. This is one of the aspects of the New England wilderness that has remained unchanged: its capacity to intrigue.

Devil's Foot Rock, Rhode Island

On the post road, between the village of Wickford and East Greenwich, there is a cleft of a rock, in which there are several holes, in the shape of the human foot; one of which is called the "Devil's foot," and is twenty inches in length.

—John C. Pease and John M. Miles, 1819[130]

I first came across this 1819 account of the Devil's Foot Rock in an old gazetteer, and although I was interested in natural features that played a role in our early history with the land, this phenomenon appeared to be too obscure and the chances of finding it too remote, considering that 175 years of development had occurred in the area. However, as I continued my research for this book, it cropped up again in Charles T. Jackson's report of the geology of Rhode Island, published in 1840. The story, according to Jackson, is that Satan carried off a sinful person, making a gigantic bound into purgatory.[131] Jackson also included an engraving of footmarks in a ledge.

Intrigued by the reports of this rock formation, I decided to search for it. After consulting with the state geologist and the Rhode Island Historical Preservation Commission, I was led to the Rhode Island Department of Transportation and from there to Nathan Fuller, who has had a long direct and indirect association with the rock. It was he who guided me there.

We arrived in North Kingston at the roadside site of the Devil's Foot Rock on a clear, spring day. It is thought that the large indentation I saw in the granite ledge is the

According to legend, this rock formation in North Kingston, Rhode Island, known as the Devil's Run, contains the footprints of the devil, made when he leaped into purgatory. References to the rock have been found in deeds dating back to 1659.

result of glacial scouring. But it is a strange sort of scouring, indeed. The footprint is long and narrow, about seventy inches by four inches and eleven inches deep. It is close to a highway at the bottom of an embankment. A rock wall several feet high with an opening at one end surrounds it. I learned from Fuller that his father worked to preserve this landmark when it was threatened many years ago by the building of a railroad through the ledge. Today, the son is carrying on the father's preservation activities by working with the Department of Transportation and the Historic Preservation Commission to protect the rock from proposed new highway construction.

There is a long oral and written history in North Kingston connected with the Devil's Foot Rock. Early deeds, dating back to 1659, are said to have included reference to the rock. The earliest published reference was apparently in 1809. These references are taken as evidence that the legend of the rock has been circulating during much of the time since European settlement.[132]

With Nathan Fuller, I explored other unusual features of this site. He showed me a series of striations in a ledge that have been interpreted as picturing a knight with a shield. I saw a feature identified as the Devil's Chair. But what interested me in particular was the Devil's Run, a series of depressions in a smoothed, lichen-covered ledge that I first saw pictured in Charles Jackson's report. I was informed that these are footprints made by the devil when he made his leap into purgatory.

Undoubtedly hundreds of formations are found throughout New England that have been identified with the devil. The legends associated with these features are examples of oral traditions that play an important role in society. In the words of one researcher who made a thorough study of Devil's Foot Rock and its meaning, these kinds of features link "people to other people; a community to its landscape; one community to other communities; a present generation to past generations; folk and religious beliefs to their ancient form; two different cultures [Native American and Euro-American] to one another."[133]

Titan's Piazza, Massachusetts

*Less than half a mile south of the point where the road . . .
on Holyoke strikes against the steep part of the mountain
. . . may be found an interesting and unique example of
greenstone columns.*

—Edward Hitchcock, 1841[134]

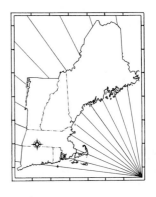

One day in mid-May I searched for Titan's Piazza, which
was first described by Edward Hitchcock in his report on
the geology of Massachusetts. I looked in South Hadley in
the vicinity of Mt. Holyoke. Hitchcock described the formation as "a projecting mass of columns." He spoke of
the columns as being in rows and hexagonal in shape with
their ends overhead. When he saw them, many had fallen
in a jumble at the base of the columnar mass.

On a map, I found a reference to Titan's Piazza, and
during my search, I came to a road sign on which is the
name Titans Pier. Hitchcock had also described this similarly shaped feature, which borders the Connecticut River.
Between the two locations, I discovered near a road an
outcrop of a rock formation that displayed the vertical
fracturing resembling the engraving I had seen. The rock
looked gray-green in the afternoon sun shining on the
south-facing ledge outcrop. I could see why the eminent
geologist was taken by this curious formation and spent
some time examining it. Later in the season when the
trees and understory shrubbery of this roadside glen are in

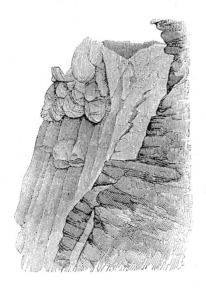

Titan's Piazza, an unusual rock
formation of hexagonally shaped
columns located in the vicinity
of Mt. Holyoke, Massachusetts,
was first described and named
by the geologist Edward Hitchcock. Illustration from Edward
Hitchcock, *Final Report on the
Geology of Massachusetts*
(Amherst, Mass.: J. S. & C.
Adams, 1841).

full leaf, this unusual ledge outcrop will be passed unnoticed and with it the opportunity to share a moment of interest with those intrigued by it centuries before.

Meteoric Stones

After the last explosion, a rending noise, like that of a whirlwind, passed along to the east of his house. . . . At the same instant a streak of light passed over the orchard in a large curve, and seemed to pierce the ground. A shock was felt, and a report heard like that of a heavy body falling to the earth.

—Benjamin Silliman and James L. Kingsley, 1808[135]

I conclude this chapter with a phenomenon that has occurred throughout the history of our planet. For a moment in this survey of our New England country, it allows for a broader perspective of our relationship with the rest of nature. I refer to the bombardment of the countryside by meteorites.

The quotation above relates to one of the early and famous meteoritic events, which the historian Zadock Thompson called in his 1853 *Natural History of Vermont* "that most remarkable meteor which passed over New England in a southerly direction in the morning of the 14th of December, 1807, and from which fell large quantities of meteoric stones in Weston, Connecticut."[136] Reports of these stones were widely circulated in the scientific community during the early 1800s. A meteorite, or aerolite as it was called, fell at Nobleboro, Maine, on August 7, 1823. It landed among some sheep with a loud explosion, and a strong, sulfurous odor surrounded the place where it struck.[137] On June 10, 1837, another meteorite fell at East Bridgewater, Massachusetts. That same year, the *New England Farmer* published an account of one falling in New Hampshire. Another fell at Concord, New Hampshire, in October 1846. One, which was later analyzed to be entirely of iron and nickel, fell at Castine, Maine, on May 20, 1848. It, like many of the others, was reported in the *American Journal of Science*.

When Silliman and Kingsley reported on the meteorite that fell on Weston, Connecticut, in 1807, scientists were only beginning to theorize that these stones had an extraterrestrial source. And although the two scientists mentioned several theories, including one where meteorites were projected from the moon—an origin they considered still more extraordinary—they concluded "till we are possessed of more facts and better observations [the subject] must be considered inexplicable."[138]

We know today that thousands of tons of meteoric material penetrate our atmosphere yearly. Some individual meteorites may reach a ton or more in weight but most of the material is dust size. Ninety percent are composed of stone or mixtures of stone and iron. Meteorites are now seen as remnants of the formation of our solar system 4.6 billion years ago. We think they originate from the asteroid belt orbiting between Mars and Jupiter and from comets.

The periodic impacts of massive objects from outer space, which many believe have caused widespread destruction and mass extinctions, are of such magnitude as to render the changes we humans have made on the New England landscape minute by comparison. The contemplation of events of such magnitude often causes us to step back and take a larger view of ourselves. We obtain a perspective on the opportunities we have to improve the quality of life in the short span of time each of us occupies. Humbled by such a view, perhaps we will be encouraged to steer in the direction of working together to respect the integrity of this New England country upon which so many now depend and upon which so many will in the future.

Chapter 4
Of the Waters

New England is a well-watered country. Its rivers and streams provided access to many areas of the interior for natives and, later, for explorers, settlers, trappers, surveyors, and others. Early settlements grew up around these avenues of transportation and sources of power. Logs were floated to mills on them. Later, roads followed their courses. Lakes and ponds provided fish and fur-bearing animals, holding areas and transportation routes for logs, and opportunities for exploration and shoreland settlement. Springs provided pure, fresh drinking water and were extolled for their healthful waters. An aesthetic attraction was also in these features, and many became well known for their beauty and appearance, their peaceful settings, and their awesome power. Today, scattered over the New England countryside, we can still find some of these features relatively untouched, just as the natives and European inhabitants discovered them.

Locating sources of good drinking water was a priority among all who visited or settled an area. Consequently, early journals, reports, and other writings of travelers and settlers contain many references to springs. For example, records suggest that sometime after their landing at the outer end of Cape Cod in 1620, the Mayflower Pilgrims drank from a spring located at North Truro—reputed to be the first one they found. The next summer, on a cross-country journey to present-day Rhode Island, Edward Winslow of the Plymouth Colony commented in his journal of "the Country so well watered that a man could scarce be drie, but he should have a spring at hand to coole his thirst, beside smal Rivers in abundance."[3] Francis Higginson in his book published in 1630 also noted that "as for fresh water the Countrey is full of daintee Springs."[4]

As you might suspect, many statements about the number of springs, their purity, and their healthful qualities were often exaggerated so as to put forth the best

Within . . . valleys are spacious lakes or ponds well stored with Fish and Beavers, the original of all the great Rivers in the Countrie, of which there are many with lesser streams.

—John Josselyn, 1674[1]

SPRINGS

The whole Countrie produceth springs in abundance replenished with excellent waters, having all the properties ascribed to the best in the world.

—John Josselyn, 1674[2]

197

image of the country and attract additional settlers and investors. As settlement progressed, many springs became well known for their supposed healthful and healing qualities. These were commonly called mineral springs. According to an early Maine report on mineral springs, when ground water dissolves earthy salts to such an extent that one can readily taste them, the water is called "mineral." The report also added that:

From the earliest time, [mineral] springs . . . have attained different degrees of celebrity as remedial agents. The use of such water has produced, in many cases, considerable relief in some diseases, and cures have been thought attributable alone to the medicinal spring. In many instances, however, the relief experienced was due more to the change in scenery, air and occupation than to the employment of the water either as a beverage or for baths.[5]

Reports of such springs were common throughout New England. A few years before the Maine report, Zadock Thompson, in his 1853 *Natural History of Vermont*, devoted a section to medicinal springs in which he discussed two of the most famous at the time, the springs of Clarendon and Alburgh. "They have at length become a place of considerable resort for the afflicted from various parts of the country," he wrote, and are "highly efficacious" in treating a number of ailments, including those of the liver, dyspepsia, urinary and all cutaneous complaints, rheumatism, and so on.[6]

As early as 1795, a mineral spring in Suffield, Connecticut, was reported to invigorate the stomach and increase the appetite as well as have medicinal qualities.[7] Another in Litchfield, Connecticut, was described in 1821. It emitted a sulfurlike odor and was reputed to be capable of medicinal cures.[8] Throughout the years, reports of springs have continued, some extolling their medicinal benefits, others their purity, their flow, or their location. One of the most remarkable, however, still remains relatively unknown and undisturbed.

Mountain Spring, Vermont

One of the most curious and important operations which nature carries on in the mountains [of Vermont], is the formation of springs and rivers.

—Samuel Williams, 1809[9]

The decade-old report I had read said that it "is the largest and most amazing undisturbed natural spring in New England." The woman at the house in Bennington County where I inquired said that I would hear it before I saw it.[10]

I followed an old road through a field on the side of the mountain. It was only June 2, but already the grass was knee-high. The road entered the woods and climbed upward, becoming washed and eroded in places. It cut across the steep side of a hill. To my right the slope fell sharply away, and I looked down through hardwood trees, fully leafed out. I moved steadily upward in a hillside corridor encased in spring green. The light rain I felt while crossing the field had stopped. I began to listen. The road continued its ascent. Then I heard a waterfall ahead, off the right side of the road. Reaching a place in the road opposite the sound, I looked down over a steep embankment. There below, surrounded by a "garden" of bright green moss, a sizable stream gushed out of the mountainside.

The waterfall I heard was the outpouring of water, gushing over and around moss-covered logs. I learned later that the estimate of this flow is fifty liters (thirteen gallons) per second. The point where the stream suddenly emerges from the hillside is a steep-sided, bowl-like depression. Trees and shrubs grow on the slopes of the basin; I saw white maple, American beech, yellow birch, black cherry, and striped maple. Farther down the slope, Christmas ferns grow profusely and foam flowers bloom.

Where the stream bubbles out of the ground, I recognized the moss-covered rocks as marble. Back under the mountainside, the stream feeding the spring is thought to flow through an underground cavern of marble rock, for several sinkholes have been observed on the hillside above the spring. The water flows year-round, I also learned

On a southern Vermont hillside, a sizable stream gushes from a spring that has been described as "the largest and most amazing undisturbed natural spring in New England."

from the landowner, and it maintains a temperature of about forty-four degrees. As soon as it comes out of the ground, the stream rushes down the mountain in a gully that it continues to widen and deepen.

I spent an hour at the spring, alone. There was no recent sign of visitors. This is without a doubt one of my most unforgettable encounters with a piece of New England's forgotten nature.

RIVERS AND STREAMS

[T]he Connecticut River has its source in that grand ridge of mountains which divides the waters of New-England and Canada. . . . it disembogues its waters into Long-Island sound between Saybrook and Old Lime. . . . A small distance from its mouth is a bar of sand, apparently formed by the conflux of the river and tide. Upon this there is but ten feet of water, at full tide. The bar is at such a distance from the mouth of the river, that the greatest floods do not increase the depth of the water.

—Benjamin Trumbull, 1797[11]

A matter of a day or two, by routine transportation, separate a tiny pond secluded in a forest of dark spruce near the Canada–New Hampshire border and a long, low bar of sand in Long Island Sound along the busy Connecticut coastline. Representing the beginning and end of the Connecticut River, more than four-hundred miles separates the two places. They are connected not only by a river but by actions of concern that have preserved them. Today, these two disparate features of the Connecticut River may still exhibit some of the undeveloped characteristics they had at the time they were described by the historian Benjamin Trumbull nearly two centuries ago.

The Connecticut River is the largest and longest body of flowing water within the borders of New England. Parts of four states are included in its watershed. Trumbull noted that none of the continent's first explorers "made any discovery of the river." Today, of course, it is well-known that the Native Americans discovered it first, and by the time the Europeans arrived on New England's shores, the natives were cultivating the low, fertile land surrounding sections of the river. Trumbull recounted that "the Indians . . . burned the country to take deer and wild game . . . [and] so thinned the groves, that they were able to plant their corn and obtain a crop."[12]

From the 1600s, when the English settlers were first attracted to its meadows, rich soils, and its large populations of fish, the Connecticut River and its basin have undergone extensive development. Yet, surprisingly, the very beginning and end of this river contain tiny fragments of its original natural features.

I first saw the mile-long, low, sandspit of Griswold Point from the shore of a marshy lagoon known as Great

Island Marsh. The spit reached westward to the mouth of the Connecticut River. Regarded as the best remaining example of a bay mouth bar along the Connecticut coast, this remarkable feature is only minutes away from a densely populated, bustling urban complex. Yet, the setting immediately behind the spit and along the shorelands that encircle the sheltered marsh presents a quiet, pastoral scene of fields, hedgerows, and scattered trees. Darkened by an overcast sky and muted by shades of browns and yellows, the early spring vegetation combines with the landscape's shapes and patterns to produce an artist's painting of an old English countryside. One grasps a strong sense of history here, perhaps because a single family name has been attached to this point of land since 1640 and its use from that time to the present has been primarily agricultural.

It was early morning and, although the sand bar is best reached by water, no boats were on its sandy beach at that hour, nor would I have expected to see many at that time of year. A light rain dimpled the waters of the lagoon, and low clouds swirled silently over the bar of sand that rises but a few feet above the high tidal waters. Farther away from the point, the bay waters had breached the spit, now requiring boat access for exploration of its outer reaches. Over the top of the bar, I could see the broad bay-mouth of the Connecticut River and the distant shoreline of the southern Connecticut coast.

The long, thin, dune-covered point of land narrows at the breach, then broadens out to perhaps four hundred feet, covering about twenty-one acres. It ends near Great Island Wildlife Refuge. For the infrequent visitor and casual observer, there is little to suggest this sandy point's dynamic history. However, within the memory of some still living, there remain graphic images of its changing size and shape—enlargement by glacial sands carried westerly by the longshore currents of Long Island Sound, breaching by the storms of 1954 and 1979, and retreat due to sea-level rise.

This natural history was not apparent to me that May day, nor were the historic effects of humans, such as the changes that have occurred in the bar's shape as a result of shifts in currents from jetties constructed at the mouth of

the river to improve navigation. Impacts from the first settlers and the Pequot Indians who once occupied this shoreland during summer seasons have long disappeared. No,
what I saw was a beautiful remnant of a sandspit beach
and dunes covered with beach grass, beach pea, and other
plants and backed by tidal marsh. Nearby, a pair of ospreys were busily building a nest. Soon the point and marsh
would again host families of piping plovers, least terns, red-
winged blackbirds, yellow-throated warblers, mallards,
black ducks, and tens of other species whose ancestors,
hundreds of generations removed, also might have returned
to this point.[13]

Later that spring, in an area more suited to Canada
jays than least terns, I visited the northern mountains of
New Hampshire. Here, observed the historian Jeremy
Belknap in 1792, "the Connecticut river rises in a ridge of
mountains, which extends northeasterly, to the Gulf of St.
Lawrence."[14] I followed the track of a moose along a
steep, mountainous path, separating the United States
from Canada. The trail and tracks led down a steep slope
through a dark forest of red spruce and balsam fir. Near
the bottom of a heavily wooded basin, patches of the
bright blue waters of the Fourth Connecticut Lake glistened through the trees. The rocky, conifer-shaded hillside
leveled off to moist, swampy ground where a profusion of
plants and shrubs circled the lake's shore. In a sheltered
pocket of young fir, three white moccasin flower blossoms
dangled from long stems over broad, parallel-veined, basal
leaves. Nearby, closer to the damp ground, green blossoms
of bunchberry, still early in their development, would soon
become as pure white as the taller orchids. Farther along
the shore, the yellow flowers of clintonia colored the lowland.

Cautiously, I peered through the dense ring of black
spruce and fir that surrounded the lake. It looked moosey,
but I saw no moose. An old beaver lodge on the far shore
was the only evidence of life. The lake is actually a small
pond surrounded by wetland—a northern tarn, such as
one might find in the northern taiga, or swampy coniferous forest to the north at the edge of the Arctic tundra.
Two acres of open water and another four of wetland
comprise this beginning of the Connecticut River and the

The Connecticut River begins at Fourth Connecticut Lake, a small pond surrounded by wetland in northern New Hampshire near the Canadian border.

chain of lakes in its headwaters. The open, acid waters are surrounded by a floating mat of mosses, sedges, and the bog-building heath plant, leatherleaf. On the mat grow carnivorous pitcher plants, sundews, and bladderworts, each with its own way of capturing and digesting insects to augment the meager nutrient supply available from the boggy soil.[15]

For a long time I watched this secluded "lake" from my enclosure of dense conifers, immersed in an absolute silence. The contrast with the flat, open, salty-aired, urban-surrounded environment of Griswold Point could not have been stronger. Yet, these two ends of the Connecticut River, one of twenty-one acres and the other of seventy-eight acres, are both owned and protected by their respective state chapters of The Nature Conservancy, and each area represents in its own way the diversity of our New England landscape.

Rivers play a critical role in the myriad of ecological relationships vital to the health of New England's environment. These relationships involve natural processes that affect humans as well as other forms of life, but Timothy Dwight alluded to other connections we have with rivers when he described the scenic effect created by the Connecticut River on the landscape between New Hampshire and Vermont at Newbury and Haverhill. He saw not only the economic value of the river and its intervale lands, but he saw a river with aesthetic value:

As we cast our eyes up and down the river, itself an object extremely beautiful, and with its romantic meanders extensively in view; a chain of intervals ... spread before us, like

a new Eden, covered with the richest verdure, and display-
ing a thousand proofs of exuberant fertility.[16]

By the time Dwight saw this river, it had lured settlers to the land along its edge over much of its length. Eventually this came to be true for most of New England's rivers. However, as we have seen, even in the case of the Connecticut River, patches of wild land still remain in the headwaters of some. And many rivers also retain other features that have escaped development. These include gorges and ravines, waterfalls, and rock-sculpted attractions like potholes and natural bridges.

Headwaters

The sources of the streams that flow from this ridge [Allegheny Ridge] in opposite directions, take their rise near each other in the same vallies . . . and in some instances they proceed from the same swamps.

—Moses Greenleaf, 1829[17]

Something is fascinating about where rivers rise. We tend to think of such places as wild, and sometimes engage in a flirtation with our curious mind by contemplating thoughts of trying to find these headwaters. Perhaps our curiosity about them relates to our need to find the roots of things, to know where and how they begin. Or perhaps we unconsciously associate them with the flow of everlasting youth or perpetual life. But these are only musings, for our history shows that the remote reaches of our rivers drew people to them for more concrete reasons.

The Native Americans were familiar with the headwaters of our rivers, for they were often places of portage between watersheds. With the expansion of European settlement, others, such as the surveyor and mapmaker Moses Greenleaf, saw rivers as helping to "diversify the face of the country," and influencing "its climate, agriculture, [and] natural value of its productions."[18] For these reasons, Greenleaf sought to map them to their sources. Such information aided timber harvesters who sought to dam the headwaters of streams and rivers and control the flow of water farther downstream for log drives. Thus, many of these remote regions have a long history of human involvement. Despite this, some of the wildest land remaining in New England lies along its northern border in the headwaters of its largest rivers. We look at two of the wildest.

Headwaters of the Penobscot and the St. John, Maine

It also appears, from the reports both of the British and American surveyors, that the source of the main branch of the St. John is on the same level with, and within a very short distance of, one of the most elevated sources of the Penobscot.

—Moses Greenleaf, 1829[19]

In 1982, Maine completed a study of its rivers. The report said the St. John River is "the largest, least developed, longest free flowing river system in one of the most remote and primitive regions east of the Mississippi River." The North Branch of the Penobscot River from Seboomook Lake to its headwaters "is one of the least developed rivers in this region of the state."[20]

Going overland past the south end of Fifth St. John Pond, which looked a brilliant blue under a bright sunny sky, two of us put a canoe into the shallow, late-summer headwaters of the North Branch of the Penobscot River. The river was rocky, and soon we were out of the canoe, wading downstream. Below the rapids the waters became deeper and canoeable once again. High banks and tall marsh grasses had compressed the sides of the river to a narrow, meandering stream. I stood up in the canoe and looked over the top of the wall of mud and grass and saw nothing but a flat marshy plain stretching more than two miles towards the southeast and a rapidly setting sun, which was somewhat worrisome. The campsite was supposed to be at the far end of the marsh at its outlet. How many meanders would double the distance I couldn't tell, nor was I certain that we would arrive before sunset. We had no alternative but to keep going. You can imagine our chagrin when, coming around the next corner, we discovered a bull moose blocking the narrow stream.

The vast wetland I saw is known as Big Bog. It is located in the region described by Moses Greenleaf, where the divide between the St. John and the Penobscot is narrow and nearly the same level. In the spring of 1861, a party of scientists and guides on Maine's second geological and natural history survey arrived at this wetland.

Wrote George Goodale, the party's botanist, "During the 23rd of May we were so fortunate as to reach what our guides supposed to be lake Abacotnetic. It was said to be much like a submerged marsh, but this lake was more like an inundated alder swamp."

This was what I saw a century and a quarter later, although I, too, expected to see more water. The moose we saw that evening, blocking our paddle through Big Bog, moved when he saw the canoe. It was dark when we pulled up onto the shore at an old dam by the outlet. Here the North Branch once again flowed swiftly, disappearing beneath a canopy of trees. This is remote, quiet country, seldom visited. In the middle of the night, I heard a deer eating grass near the tent. When I rolled over to get a look, the noise from my sleeping bag frightened the deer, and it galloped off towards the river. I heard a loud bang when the deer accidentally hit the canoe. To this day, a hoofprint is stamped in the side of the canoe.

Goodale, along with the geologist Charles Hitchcock and other members of the party, started their journey up the Penobscot from Northwest Carry, where they put in their birch bark canoes. At the Forks, the confluence of the South and North Branches, they continued up the North Branch, carrying around a falls and passing a mountain on the west side of the river and flat pine country on the northeast side. Even then, wood roads were so numerous that Goodale and Hitchcock got temporarily lost on them while out for a walk one evening. Near Big Bog, a day-long portage was completed into St. John waters, and the party paddled along a crooked stream lined with cedars and black spruces to a "beautiful lake," probably Fifth St. John Pond. Goodale described the land as low and flat, covered with pines and spruces, which mingle with beech and birch on higher areas. The next day, the party canoed to Baker Lake, their way often lined with northern white cedar. He commented on the lake's "beautiful shores" and a fine stand of pines to the east. Here, Goodale made a point to note the "characteristic plants of the St. John district."

Down the river at the confluence of the Southwest Branch, Goodale found the rare *Primula mistassinica*, or Mistassini primrose. "The shores in some places are high banks of gravel, probably terraces; in other parts of the river they are low and rocky, covered with small trees of second growth. The water washes along the shallow shore most of the way. . . . Huron tansy, Tofieldia, Oxytropis and Astragalus, are plentiful along the banks and in the woods immediately back from the river."[21] Today, botanists have found a significant number of plants along the upper St. John River that are considered rare and threatened or endangered.

As the Goodale-Hitchcock party continued down river, they encountered more roads and found them no less confusing. They saw more people and heard more sounds. But, today, these headwaters still remain relatively wild and remote. Here is possibly the last major territory of the lynx. Reports of wolves and mountain lions still come from this region. Though its future is uncertain, one can find satisfaction for now in knowing that there is a place where one can capture a sense of New England's wild headwaters of the past.

Samuel Williams, like those before and after him, was intrigued by gorges and other erosive effects of rivers and streams on solid rock. Confronted with the hardness of some rocks, it is difficult to imagine that the agency for the excavation and sculpting is running water. In his history, Williamson proposed an experiment so that future generations would have some idea of the time involved. He suggested that "if the philosophers of the present age will make accurate observations of the altitude and situations of such rocks . . . they will enable posterity to solve a problem, which we can hardly expect to determine in our day."[23] We now know that some gorges were formed directly by glacial action, either by ice cutting through the bedrock or by the erosiveness of glacial meltwater streams. Other gorges resulted from post-glacial erosion by streams acting on breaks in the rocks, such as faults and areas of weakness.

Many gorges have been discovered throughout New England, especially in mountainous regions. Maine, for example, has identified as many as twenty that possess outstanding qualities of interest to scientists and visitors.

Gorges and Ravines

It is not only in the channels and intervales, which the rivers have formed, that their effects are to be seen; but their operations are also visible, upon the stones and rocks. . . . the rocks in many places, are not only smooth and slippery, but they are much worn away by the constant running of the water.

—Samuel Williams, 1809[22]

There are many gorges, too, that remain in a condition quite unchanged from the time of their first discovery.

The Wild Mt. Riga Plateau Ravine, Massachusetts and Connecticut

Most rock ravines have remained practically unaltered since glacial times; they represent very ancient plant habitats.

—George E. Nichols, 1916[24]

The stream crosses the road quietly enough, but back up in the confines of steep, hemlock-covered slopes, it becomes a savage torrent, as if trying to escape from something evil. No signs mark the location of this ravine, which carries the stream that drains the Mt. Riga Plateau, and

This secluded ravine on the boundary between western Massachusetts and Connecticut appears to have escaped logging and contains one old hemlock tree that was aged at two hundred years.

one doesn't expect to enter a place as secluded and wild on the Massachusetts-Connecticut border.[25] Yet, within minutes of leaving the road, I found myself standing on smooth, water-worn ledges in a streambed surrounded by steep rock walls and deep shadows cast by large, old hemlocks.

The light is dim in the ravine, and I was immersed in an unceasing din of rushing water. Here in 1802, drenched in the acrid smells and blue haze of iron mining and smelting, the area experienced a mysterious bombardment. It is said that chunks of a peculiar mortar hurtled through windows on a succession of clear, quiet, moonlit nights. Later in the century, an unexplained flooding of the mines rendered them useless.[26]

Farther up the ravine grow dense stands of mountain laurel. The slopes become steeper and higher and the jumble of boulders in the bed of the ravine, larger. The stream falls and cascades over the huge blocks of rock more than 500 million years old. Almost every waterfall I encountered was clogged with the broken parts of dead trees. I tried walking the slopes above the chaotic streambed, but was forced to move down deeper into the narrow slot. The hemlocks create a dense wall of vegetation; they and yellow birches dominate the ravine. Even less light reaches the bottom of the deep trench. Ferns, mosses, and liverworts thrive in a cool, moist environment where both sun and wind are excluded. High up on the slopes, sphagnum mosses cling to the rocks and grow in crevices.

It is postulated that the northernlike vegetation seen in ravines such as this may be a remnant of that which once covered much of the landscape here during a time when the climate was much cooler. Less conjectural is the idea that the vegetation I saw here is untouched, protected by the inaccessible terrain. There is no evidence of any logging in this ravine: a hemlock found in 1972 was dated at two hundred years.

Far up in the ravine, completely surrounded by the sights and sounds of uninhibited nature, I stopped to photograph a small falls. Less than an hour away from any human-associated object or event, I was nonetheless overpowered by the feeling of wilderness.

Hemlock Gorge; Charles River, Massachusetts

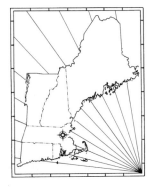

We . . . went up Charles River, until the river grew narrow and shallow, and there we landed our goods with much labor and toil, the bank being steep; and night coming on, we were informed that there were hard upon us three hundred Indians.

—Roger Clap, May 1630[27]

Several miles upstream from Roger Clap's landing in the area of present-day Watertown, the Charles River narrows into a steep, rocky gorge where, even today, one may obtain a sense of the wildness that once surrounded this

Hemlock Gorge, through which the Charles River flows in the Boston area of Massachusetts, provides a sense of wildness despite a long history of human use.

river. I arrived there on a day in May as did Roger Clap. It was a cloudy, rainy afternoon, and the river had a misty, old look to it. From beneath tall, old hemlocks on a rocky knoll, I saw the quietly swirling river tucked among soft red, yellow, and green hues of new leaves, catkins, and emerging herbaceous plants. Shrubs blossomed behind gray outcrops bordering the river. Behind, tall hemlocks on a steep embankment towered over the gorge. The damp, sweet smell of spring refreshed me.

As Roger Clap's memoir suggests, this river has had a long human history, commencing well before European settlement. Champlain in 1605 was perhaps the first European to note it: "There is, beside this bay [Massachusetts Bay] a very large river, which I named Rive du Gas."[28] A few years later, Captain John Smith wrote, "the River doth pearce many dais journeis the intralles of that Countrey."[29] Today this gorge still retains a bit of the river's historic, natural setting, and its existence is a credit to the original members of Boston's Metropolitan Park Commission who recognized its value.

Old City Falls Ravine, Vermont

The rivers and streams lying within the state of Vermont are very numerous, but small. They, in most cases, originate among the Green Mountains, and their courses are short and generally rapid.

—Zadock Thompson, 1853[30]

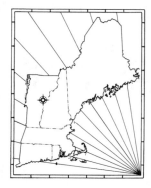

One early June morning I sought out one of Vermont's many small streams, Old City Brook, in Strafford near the New Hampshire border in Central Vermont. The brook

flows inconspicuously into a tributary of the Ompom-
panoosuc River, which flows into the Connecticut River. I
arrived just as the gate was being opened to the commu-
nity-owned area in which the brook's ravine is located. A
very steep trail, with switchbacks and some stone steps,
led down through hardwoods into the forested canyon.
The ravine is deep, about a hundred feet, and when I
reached its bottom, boulders filled the shallow flowing
brook.

The sun had yet to touch the dark, steep, ledgy, north-
facing slope on the other side of the ravine. I looked across
to huge virgin hemlocks a hundred feet in height, rising to
the top of the ravine. This is why I came: in this ravine one
can be submerged in the past, completely surrounded by
the sights and sounds of an original landscape.

Ahead at the northeast end of the ravine, I could hear
Old City Falls. A footpath along the edge of the brook led
me to it. The falls has two drops. Above me the brook
gushed out from beneath a forest of hemlocks, now silhouetted in the early sunlight, and made a beautiful, high
drop over dark ledges, stepping down to curve gracefully
over low rock shelves before dropping again to the
ravine's bottom. The scene was made even more picturesque by the variety of ferns growing out of the still-
shaded crevices in the rocks surrounding the falls. The
undisturbed setting in dim light took on an enchanting
quality and I lingered alone there for a time.[31]

I had come to the ravine with only one early report,
an 1871 comment in which the writer dismissed Old City
Falls as "frequented by those who do not find an opportunity to visit waterfalls of greater dignity."[32] When I
left, just as rays of sunlight began to dissolve the shadows to reveal the full beauty of the falls and the ravine
and its giant hemlocks, which are a living historical
record of the New England wilderness, Old City Falls
Ravine held for me a dignity well worth frequenting.

Old City Brook, in Vermont near
the New Hampshire border, falls
into a hundred-foot-deep ravine
on the slopes of which grow
large virgin hemlocks.

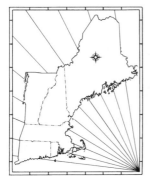

Gulf Hagas, Maine

The Gulf, which is about five miles long, is between steep often perpendicular and sometimes overhanging walls of dark slate, from 100 to 300 feet in height, and frequently separated from each other but a few rods. Between these cliffs the river is very swift, and its current, being frequently obstructed, abounds in eddies and waterfalls.

—John C. Houghton, 1861[33]

The trail to the head of Gulf Hagas follows the course of the West Branch of the Pleasant River, located in the geographic center of Maine. It's a good two-mile hike from this west end of the Gulf to its rim. For some of the way, I followed a moose track, but the animal veered off the trail, diminishing my expectation of seeing it. It was July 4 and the flowers of lady's slippers and clintonias, or bead lilies, had gone by. In their place, bunchberries, wood sorrels, and twin flowers were in bloom. The trail turned out to be fairly level and easy walking. Soon I heard the sound of rushing water, and it wasn't long before I came out on a high precipice overlooking the river.

Though Gulf Hagas has been called the Grand Canyon of Maine, it's really only a miniature. Nevertheless, it's an impressive feature—so much so that it carries a National Natural Landmark designation. For over three miles, the gorge cuts through the wilderness, dropping as much as five hundred feet in elevation. Its walls are made up of layers of slate, shale, and schist. These nearly vertical rocks rise in places up to 125 feet above the river, enclosing continuous rapids and five major falls.

This is remote country. The trail I was on follows the rim to the east end of the gorge where one may take the Appalachian Trail northward to Katahdin. This is the Hundred Mile Wilderness, the longest, most undeveloped section of the trail. I'm sure that even John Houghton would still find it little changed.[34]

Gulf Hagas Gorge, in the geographic center of Maine, contains five major waterfalls along its length and cuts down through nearly vertical layers of old sedimentary rock to a depth of 125 feet.

Upper Seboeis River Gorge, Maine

Reached Godfrey's falls, which are produced by a fall of the Seboois over high ledges of slate rocks. The banks rise perpendicularly on each side to the height of 200 feet, and we have to carry all our effects and the boats up a ledge, at an angle of 45°, and then through the burnt forest for the distance of four miles before we again reach the river. By the aid of our Indian party we shall be able to effect this in two days.

—Charles T. Jackson, 1838[35]

It was along the route of Jackson's portage on the high west bank of this gorge that I hiked on a clear August day. Tall white pines once again graced the gorge's rim where Jackson's party encountered a large burned-over area. When the naturalist Ezekiel Holmes followed here in Jackson's footsteps twenty-four years later, he reported that "this place was once covered with a heavy growth of enormous pines, but these have long since been destroyed by fires, and a stinted and scattering growth of birches, poplars and blueberry bushes, taken their place."[36]

This is an uninhabited, wild area. I had driven several miles on unimproved roads, finally being stopped by a treacherous-looking sinkhole where a brook crossed under the road. A half-mile hike through thick woods followed before I heard the sound of falls and rapids far below. I was near a section of this seven-mile-long gorge called Godfrey Pitch.[37] My first attempt down the steep, wooded slope into the 150-foot-deep gorge was stopped by a sheer drop of 50 feet or more. Through the trees back down the river, I could see a more gentle approach where the river made a bend. I retraced my steps and made my way through blowdowns and down a small eroded cut in the steep ledges to the shore.

Before me was a large pool below a small waterfall. A gravel island, built up by a deposit of gravel, lay at the foot of the pool. On it grew profuse stands of beautiful, deep-red cardinal flower, pink Joe-Pye-weed, and white Queen Anne's lace. Large boulders ringed the pool, backed by steep walls of slate interspersed with trees, shrubs, ferns, and other plants able to gain a foothold and find growing space.

In a remote section of northern Maine, the upper Seboeis River flows through a gorge seven miles long and up to 150 feet deep.

No other sound penetrates here except for the sound of the waterfall. There is no road access to this isolated area. Here one can be truly alone. With little imaginative effort I could hear the sounds of the Jackson party struggling along the rim high above me, intent on reaching the Aroostook River before a snowfall or an ice freeze trapped them. Three days after he passed here, on October 15, 1838, with an estimated 175 miles of river still ahead of him, Jackson's worst fears were realized. He recorded: "Last night was very uncomfortable, and the snow driving into our tent kept us wet and cold. . . . On reaching La Pompique [stream], we found it frozen, and the ice being one inch and a half thick it was exceedingly laborious to break our way through it with the batteau."[38] But he was driven onward and made it into the Aroostook River, thence to the St. John River, and down to Woodstock, New Brunswick, Canada, where he boarded a stage to Bangor. On November 9, he took passage to Boston.

Waterfalls

It would be endless to describe, particularly, the numerous falls, which in the mountainous parts of the country, exhibit a great variety of curious appearances, many of which have been represented in the language of fiction and romance.

—Jeremy Belknap, 1792[39]

Not unexpectedly, most of New England's notable and picturesque falls are found in mountainous areas. Measured in geologic time, they are but transitory phenomena—a part of ongoing processes that level the land. But unlike gorges that form when rivers and streams cut down into the bedrock, falls occur when the flowing waters encounter resistant rock.

The character of our waterfalls has suffered. Too often roads, trails, and walkways that allow visitors to view our scenic falls take away from the very beauty of the natural setting people come to enjoy. And our history is full of examples where falls were built upon to provide power or were blasted away to make them more amenable to log driving.

Not all waterfalls have been changed or removed. Many still remain that exhibit their original qualities, as the following examples show.

Bash Bish Falls, Massachusetts

The most remarkable and interesting gorge and cascade in Massachusetts.

—Edward Hitchcock, 1841[40]

Spring is usually the best time to visit a waterfall, so it was no accident that on a day in mid-May I could be found hiking along a gradually inclined trail to Bash Bish Falls. I was in a remote section of the Taconic Mountains in the southwestern corner of Massachusetts near the Connecticut and New York borders. The early morning air was cool in the small, steep-sided valley of Bashbish Brook, which flowed below me towards the Hudson River. The brook has its rise somewhere in a seep on Massachusetts' Mt. Washington to my southeast.

I heard the falls before I saw it and then came upon it at a point slightly above and several hundred feet distant. The view was spectacular. Before me was the largest waterfall in the Taconic region and called, by some, the most spectacular in Massachusetts. Here Bashbish Brook flows out from between a deep gorge that was cut through metamorphic schist and cascades in a winding course down Bashbish Mountain, dropping two hundred feet.[41] A description today of its major drop would still match that given by the geologist Edward Hitchcock in 1841: "The water which is divided into two parts by an enormous bowlder poised upon the brink, here falls over a nearly straight and perpendicular precipice of about 60 feet, into a deep basin, two or three rods across."[42]

Geologist Edward Hitchcock included a drawing of Bash Bish Falls in an 1841 report. The setting looks much the same today. Illustration from Edward Hitchcock, *Final Report on the Geology of Massachusetts* (Amherst, Mass.: J. S. & C. Adams, 1841).

I moved down to the edge of the pool, and for a few moments, I'm sure that I shared the exhilarating wildness that Hitchcock felt when he stood close to this high, plunging falls and the tremendous energy it contains. Its work on the mountain was well underway. Above me the deep, sharp gorge provided only a narrow "window" for the morning sunlight to penetrate. Shadows still enveloped the place where I stood, but part of the mountain above was brightly lit.

I left the falls and took a trail up to the top of the mountain. Old, large hemlocks shaded the steep slope. Many of them are more than three hundred years old.[43]

The trail was wet from seeps and rills. A darkly colored vole scurried in front of me, disappearing into the rocks. The trail became rockier as I neared the top, and I remembered a warning that rattlesnakes seek out ledges for sunning on warm spring days. I finally reached a high crag on the side of the gorge, and through the narrow V-shaped notch, I was provided a spectacular vista of the Hudson Valley and the Catskill Mountains. In the distance, I could also see fields and houses; for a moment I felt I was on the edge of civilization.

Moss Glen Falls; Stowe, Vermont

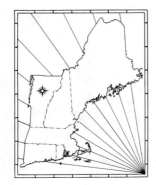

It rushes over a broad, dark-colored, solid body of rock, spreading itself into a rich, silvery cascade, and falling sixty feet.

—C. Allen Browne, 1860[44]

"A lovely little gem" is what Browne called this falls in Stowe, Vermont. Here a long, delicate, white thread of flowing water cascades between high walls of rock, dropping over a hundred feet—one of Vermont's highest falls. Few signs gave any hint of this beautiful natural feature as I followed a well-worn path through alders past a wet area to a hillside covered with hemlock. I first heard the falls when I began the climb upwards. Though I had seen an old engraving of the falls, I was not prepared for the abrupt, dramatic view that I received when I came over the top of the ridge. You see it straight on, coming directly towards you. It starts as a tiny thread in the distance, then it begins to unravel and spreads outward, forming several strands before it piles up in a pool, hidden below a steep precipice at your feet.

Moss Glen Falls, pictured here as it looked in 1861. Illustration from Albert D. Hager, et al., *Report on the Geology of Vermont*, vol. 2 (Claremont, N. H.: The Claremont Manufacturing Company, 1861).

I climbed along the edge of a high ledge wall that borders the north side of the falls. No accessible views into the gorge presented themselves as I climbed. At the top a deep, narrow, meandering, hemlock-edged gorge cuts through the rock. Far below I caught glimpses of Moss Glen Brook moving quietly along, giving little suggestion of the plunge it was about to take. Farther back, the stream assumed a lowland attitude, flowing gently between banks lined with alders. In the short distance of a few hundred yards, I had seen all the moods of a free flowing stream.

Little has changed at Moss Glen Falls in a century and a half.

Angel Falls, Maine

The country around consists of high mountains and rounded hills.

—Charles T. Jackson, 1839[45]

Charles Jackson was on a hill above Andover, Maine, when he surveyed the mountains containing Maine's highest waterfall, Angel Falls. When I first saw this falls, I found that it does, indeed, possess the delicacy that I imagine in an angel's wing. I saw a finely netted veil of pure, translucent white, fluttering lightly against a mountain headwall. For me, this waterfall was almost as elusive to see as an angel.

Angel Falls, in Maine's western mountains, is reputed to be Maine's highest waterfall and among its most beautiful.

Angel Falls is located in an isolated and remote region of Maine's western mountains. No signs lead the way to it, and after leaving a paved road, one must drive three miles on a badly rutted and washed-out road along an old railroad bed. A trail then requires that one wade a stream and climb over and around slippery rocks for another mile or so before reaching the most beautiful upper drop of the falls. I made three attempts before I saw the falls. The first was too early in the season, and the gravel road was still wet and muddy, unable to hold the weight of my vehicle. On my second attempt, I mistakenly followed the wrong trail, spending a pleasant afternoon exploring a beautiful stream, but one without the falls.

My third attempt led me up a trail through mature hardwoods. I forded a brook then continued to cross and recross it for some distance upstream before the trail led into the rocky hillside. Coming over a small knoll by immense boulders, the falls appeared before me with unexpected suddenness. I stood near the base of the falls in a jumble of rocks. A cold mist wafted around me. A hundred feet above, backlighted by the sun, the falls emerged from a small, spruce-choked notch. It cascaded down the mountainside, broadening into a wide sheet of tucks and ruffles where it caught on small ledges of gray phyllite rock jutting from the sheer face of the mountain.[46] These are thought to be hanging falls—where a stream enters the side of a deep, glaciated valley.

A little later that morning, I bushwacked up the mountainside and viewed the falls from above through a stand of beautiful red spruce. It was steep and treacherous where I set up my tripod, and I dallied little there. Exploring farther above the falls, a thick jumble of wind-thrown trees turned me back, and I retraced my steps back down the mountain.

No record shows that Charles Jackson ever saw this outstanding waterfall. None of the state's early geologists and naturalists gave any account of it that I have found. If they had seen it, I have no doubt that it would have received more than a brief mention. One wonders what other natural treasures lie hidden in the New England countryside that history failed to record.

The erosive effects of flowing, sediment-laden water on our rocks often produce the most interesting forms. Smoothed and polished shapes are one of the attractions of our gorges and falls. Among them are potholes—circular depressions ground out of the rock by slurries of abrasive materials swirling round and round in eddies. Like grindstones, they slowly remove minute particles of rock. Other interesting sculpted works are also associated with moving water. Among the most interesting are natural bridges, where streams pass through tunnels or under arches that are produced when the rock has succumbed to the grinding and dissolving action of water. We look at two examples, one still relatively unknown and the other a popular attraction.

The Giant Pothole, Maine

The existence of pot-holes in ledges of rock we have always regarded as proof that a cataract once existed at the spot, for in no other way can their formation be explained.

—Albert D. Hager, 1861[48]

A friend showed me this monster pothole several years ago. It lies in a notch in western Maine beside a small river—the river that once ran through it. One explanation of its formation suggests that for a long time the notch experienced a torrential outpouring of sediment-laden, glacial meltwater after a large lake at the head of the notch burst through a dam of glacial deposits. But whatever the explanation, the result is mind-boggling. This scoured granite basin is estimated to be thirty to forty feet in diameter and fifteen to twenty feet deep. Trees, eight to ten inches in diameter, now grow in the soil accumulated on its floor.

Recently, I visited this giant pothole again, late in the month of April. Snow filled its bottom, in some places up to twenty inches deep. Spray from the river, which passes by the outside of one wall of the pothole, drifted across an opening where the river had once made its exit. Lichens and mosses now cover the circular, undercut walls. Trees grow out of crevices along its rim. It was strange to contemplate this huge bowl as a product of the river.

Potholes and Other Sculpted Works

The rocks in many places . . . are much worn away by the constant running of water.

—Samuel Williams, 1809[47]

Most who travel through Grafton Notch are unaware that they pass only a few feet from the edge of this immense pothole, scoured out of granite by sediment-laden glacial meltwater thousands of years ago.

The day before I had visited the immense granite boulder on a hillside in western Maine, which I previously described, and had walked around its circular shape. The situation inside the pothole was the inverse; I was enclosed by the granite. While their differences are striking, they both owe their existence to temperature, water, gravity, and time. Because of the granite, both have endured to connect us to New England's natural history.

The Natural Bridge, Massachusetts

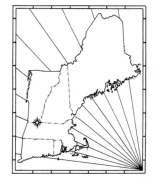

It has worn a fissure from 30 to 60 feet deep, and 30 rods long, in this limestone, and left two masses of rock connecting the sides and forming natural bridges.

—Edward Hitchcock, 1841[49]

When Edward Hitchcock last saw the Natural Bridge on Hudsons Brook in North Adams, the area was being actively quarried. He left worried that the next advance of the quarry would remove it entirely, so he made a sketch to ensure that some image of it would remain.

One spring evening I walked up the hill to the old quarry and saw the bridge for the first time. It was crisscrossed with boardwalks, stairs, and chain-link fencing—the price of providing safe public access. I searched at length for an opportunity to photograph the bridge without these intrusions before I captured part of it as it might have appeared to Edward Hitchcock.

Around 1840, when geologist Edward Hitchcock sketched the Natural Bridge in North Adams, Massachusetts, he worried that it would be demolished in the expansion of a nearby quarry. Fortunately, the bridge was saved. Illustration from Edward Hitchcock, *Final Report on the Geology of Massachusetts* (Amherst, Mass.: J. S. & C. Adams, 1841).

Born of the shells of organisms deposited over 500 million years ago and acted on by heat and pressure from geologic forces, the white, crystalline marble of the bridge has long been valued for tombstones, building materials, and other stone products. From glacial times, running water has worked this outcrop, producing a sinuous, sculpted gorge. At one point the brook runs in a deep, undercut chasm beneath an arch of solid marble. Broken pieces of the marble lie in its bottom. I wandered over and around this wildly shaped rock formation, thankful that, despite the measures to protect it and the safety of those who visit it, Hitchcock's worries were for naught.

A brook-sculpted tunnel through white, crystalline marble forms the Natural Bridge in northwestern Massachusetts.

The province Josselyn spoke of is Maine, which has within its borders approximately five thousand lakes and ponds. These bodies of water total in the thousands for the six New England states. Their presence owes much to the work of the last glacier, which scooped out basins and left depressions when ice blocks buried in glacial debris melted.

Although our lakes and ponds change naturally, generally becoming shallower, warmer, and more nutrient rich, they are especially vulnerable to human-induced changes. For example, shorelines become crowded with buildings, pollutants enter through contaminated surface and ground waters and from atmospheric fallout, populations of aquatic organisms proliferate uncontrollably, and siltation

LAKES AND PONDS

The ponds and lakes in this province are very large and many, out of which the great Rivers have their origin[s].

—John Josselyn, 1674[50]

and sediment build up at increasingly rapid rates. Few lakes and ponds have controls that completely protect their purity and aesthetic qualities against these and other assaults. Allagash Lake in northern Maine is an example of one where many protective measures are in place, including controls on the use of motor-operated boats in summer and snowmobiles in winter and the removal of all road access.

The original natural character of our lakes and ponds is in danger of being lost and forgotten. We look at two large, historically well-known lakes and then at two ponds that are remote, relatively inaccessible and, therefore, unfamiliar to most of the public.

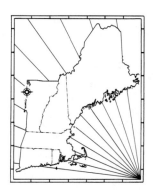

Lake Champlain, Vermont

Westwards from the Massachusetts Bay . . . is scituated a very spacious Lake . . . wherein are very many faire Islands.

—Thomas Morton, 1637[51]

Lake Champlain was discovered by the Europeans early in the exploration of the region and has held the attention of New Englanders ever since. Almost thirty years passed between the time Samuel de Champlain first set eyes on the lake and by the time Thomas Morton reported on it. Champlain entered the lake by the way of the Richelieu River from the St. Lawrence and immediately encountered the islands at the north end of the lake. He noted that "there are also several rivers which flow into the lake that are bordered by many fine trees . . . with a quantity of vines more beautiful than any I had seen in any other place."[52] The 1861 report by Albert Hager and other scientists on the geology of Vermont credited this lake as "one of the most interesting and attractive bodies of water in the State . . . on account of its size, its unsurpassed beauty, the great diversity of sublime scenery, and the historical incidents connected therewith."[53]

One spring day I sought to see the lake and its shores from several vantage points along the chain of islands that make up Grand Isle in the center of the northern half of this lake. I discovered it is possible to receive an impression similar to what others so many years ago recorded.

Roughly a hundred miles long on its Vermont shore and up to thirteen or fourteen miles wide, the lake presents expansive views. However, when one looks more closely along the Vermont shore for protected elements of New England's natural heritage, they are few and far between.

At the north end, one early June day, I roamed the swampland and marshy areas of Missisquoi National Wildlife Refuge. Later I visited Little Otter Creek Marsh, which lies farther south. Both of these preserve natural elements of the shoreline. There are also a number of small state parks and other areas, but overall, there is relatively little of the lake's natural shoreline left. It is good to know that a number of agencies and citizen groups are actively working in this direction.

Moosehead Lake, Maine

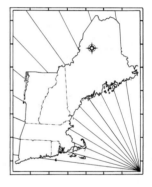

The plantation at the foot of Moose Head Lake, is called Greenville, and is yet almost an unbroken wilderness.

—Charles T. Jackson, 1839[54]

When the geologist Charles Jackson traveled to Moosehead Lake in the summer of 1838, it was still a number of years before Henry David Thoreau would praise its beauty. The road was only passable on foot or on horseback in summer, but, on seeing the lake, Jackson accurately predicted that it wouldn't be long before it became a "favorite place of resort."

I remember looking down at the lake from a high point on the Lily Bay road along the west shore. It's an immense body of water—the largest lake encompassed by a single state in New England. Yet it's small by comparison to Lake Champlain: Moosehead is about 76,000 acres to Lake Champlain's 200,000 acres. I looked over a small bay that day to Burnt Jacket Mountain, which makes up most of a large peninsula. Jackson rowed to a ledge on this point of land where he made numerous sketches and took his bearings. "The shores of the lake, far as we could see," he later wrote, "were covered with a dense forest of spruce, pine, maple and birch trees, the black growth, as it is called, being most abundant. The scenery is picturesque, but an *amateur* of fine views would find it yet too wild,

This view across Moosehead Lake from Burnt Jacket Ledge to Squaw Mountain was drawn by geologist Charles T. Jackson when he rowed to the ledge in the late 1830s. Illustration from Charles T. Jackson, *Third Annual Report on the Geology of the State of Maine* (Augusta, Maine: Smith & Robinson, 1839).

and not relieved by the habitations of man; an evil which time will remedy."[55]

Ironically, many who visit this lake and its vicinity come to be relieved from the habitations of humans and regard wildness not as an evil, but as an opportunity to escape. Fortunately, today, concern is being expressed and acted upon to preserve portions of the historically wild shoreline of this north-woods lake.

North Woods Wilderness Pond, Maine

Millinocket is a large sheet of water, surrounded on all sides by ridges and swells of land which are covered with a mixed growth of hard and soft wood.

—Ezekiel Holmes, 1838[56]

During the spring of 1838, the naturalist Ezekiel Holmes explored and surveyed the territory of the Aroostook River. To reach the river's headwaters, he went up the East Branch of the Penobscot River, across Matagamon Lake to Hay Brook, and upstream to a point where a portage of less than a mile was made into the Aroostook watershed. At Millinocket Lake, he made his observation of the surrounding country in which, some eight miles away from his route, a small pond nestles among low hills from which part of the Aroostook River begins. Isolated and not particularly distinctive, the pond remained unnoticed. In fact, the first maps of the region published in the 1840s omitted the pond. Because its outlet stream was too small for log driving and the lack of nearby roads made it out of easy reach for horse hauling, the land surrounding the pond was not cut during the early logging of the region. Today, thanks to policies of its former and present owners, the land around the pond is covered by undisturbed virgin forest and will remain so. No roads penetrate to the pond's shore.

I visited this pond in early summer, and because it's best not to go alone in these trackless woods, I had a guide. We bushwacked nearly a mile through northern hardwoods, spruce, fir, and cedar to reach the shore of the pond. It is a primitive-looking shoreline—steeply sloped and lined mostly with conifers. The spruce, pine, and cedar not only come right to the shore, but they overhang it, producing a dark shadow line along its edge. The pond is ninety acres—deep, cold, and spring-fed. So clear is the water along its shore that it magnifies the rocky bottom with the clarity of a polished lens. Beneath the pond's surface swims a relict population of the state-endangered blueback char, a fish of northern waters trapped here when the last glacier receded. This subspecies of fish inhabits only a few such ponds in the world.

I lingered at the pond's edge for some time on a tiny, rocky peninsula beside a northern white cedar. The pond can be found on present-day maps, if one knows where to look, but that it nestles within a protected, virgin forest is not shown. Perhaps that's best, for there is some satisfaction in knowing that there is still a pond with a future that preserves the past.[57]

Ell Pond, Rhode Island

Ell Pond still remains for me a wilderness unknown.

—Dean Bennett, 1994

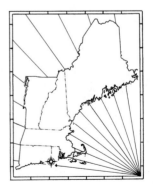

It was once described as one of the few places where one may obtain a feeling of wilderness and "such a feeling can be considered a resource in such a crowded state as Rhode Island."[58] For this reason, I set out to visit this roadless pond. I knew also from my research that it is considered to be one of the more remote, unspoiled natural areas in Rhode Island. A kettle hole pond, 102 acres in size, its edge is graced by a beautiful floating bog mat, which is backed on three sides by a swamp of Atlantic white cedar and swamp laurel. Granite cliffs rise above its eastern shore. Some trees surrounding it date back to the late 1700s. Here also prowl bobcats, one of the few areas in southern New England where they still occur.[59]

Both of my maps indicated an old trail that leads directly to the south end of the pond. I found the beginnings of the trail one day around noon. Though the trail had been obviously unused for some time, I was, nevertheless, able to discern its route. Many downed trees lay across it, and dense patches of rhododendron grew into it. When it became increasingly difficult to follow, I turned back. By the time I had found the trail that currently provides access, it was too late in the day to try again. Another appointment precluded further tries at that time, and Ell Pond remains, for me, unknown to this day. What does remain is the possibility of a future visit, for it is now protected by the state of Rhode Island, the Audubon Society of Rhode Island, and The Nature Conservancy.

Chapter 5
Of the Woods and Herbs

The map identified it as NS-6. Now I stand beside it with my hand on it. The furrows between the plates of rough bark are so wide and deep that the side of my palm fits between them. NS-6 designates one of six well-studied trees of the species *Nyssa sylvatica*, or tupelo or black gum.[2] Part of what is so utterly fascinating to me this day is the age of this tree. When John Josselyn published his remarks in 1674, NS-6 was four years old. This is not in any way a record age, for there are many tupelos in New England that far exceed the age of NS-6. No, what captures my attention about the age of this tree is its location. It grows on an island in a small pond in Plymouth, Massachusetts—the first permanent colony in New England. Remarkably, despite this town's continuous expansion and development since 1622 and the voracious appetite of its early settlers for wood, NS-6 still stands here alive and well, providing the opportunity for me to commune with a living contemporary of the Pilgrims.

Why did this old tupelo escape harvesting? Apparently, it wasn't considered valuable. The fibers of its wood are cross-woven, making it difficult to split and imparting a tendency towards warping. Not so with the mast pine that were selectively cut here centuries ago during the Plymouth ship-building era. According to the historian James Thatcher, this island "formerly furnished a large supply of masts [possibly during the late 1700s] and the road to it is still called Mast Road."[3]

My trip to NS-6 had taken me through a large, dry, sandy region—a countryside of pitch pine and scrub oak. It was pollen time, and clouds of it drifted over and around the trees like a fine, dry snow. When I at last arrived at the pond, I looked across its yellow, pollen-covered waters to the island. Immediately, I saw a different kind of forest

The plants in New England *for the variety, number, beauty, and vertues, may stand in competition with the plants of any Countrey in Europe.*

—*John Josselyn 1674*[1]

Amazingly, this large tupelo tree, known to scientists as NS-6, began its life in 1670 in Plymouth, Massachusetts, a time when some of the original European settlers in this first permanent New England colony may have been still living.

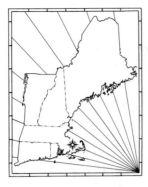

from that which I had passed through. The scraggly crowns of large white pines towered over a high canopy of hardwood trees. Though I was some distance away, I could readily tell that an assortment of trees and shrubs grew there, quite unlike the surrounding landscape.

Studies of the sediments in two nearby ponds show that centuries before the Europeans came, the surrounding forest had been dominated by white pine and oak, with some beech and hemlock.[4] But intensive clearing, grazing, and burning altered the ecology of the forests. Pitch pine, scrub oak, and other plants of pine barrens took over the land. It appears, however, that the forest on this low, damp island has been protected from wild fires and from the burning by natives and settlers. It also escaped the clearing and grazing. Thus, it now exhibits a vegetative cover similar to the original forest. Yet, as I saw on my exploration of the island, it is not an undisturbed old-growth forest, though most trees are 150 to 200 years old.

I rowed to the island with a gentlemen who has known it intimately for many years, since he was a boy. Before we started our trip across the pond, he had shown me a cross-section of a huge, old beech salvaged from the destruction of the 1938 hurricane. A ring count showed that it had begun growing in the early 1700s. Thus began my introduction to this unusual island.

We tied the skiff to a tree at a secluded site on the east shore of the boot-shaped island. It is small, fifteen acres, and can be easily covered on foot. The ground is humpy where trees, like the old beech, had been uprooted long ago by winds of hurricane force. The size of some of the tip-up mounds suggests that the trees were large. Though the island is heavily forested, walking is easy through the mostly open understory. My guide pointed out a champion American holly tree, which began its life in 1840. We headed to the north end of the island, passing yellow birch, pepperbush and, on the forest floor, spotted wintergreen. We walked through a beautiful, shaded grove of large hemlock trees and into an opening carpeted with Canada mayflower. An agitated goshawk swooped down from a tree. Soon, I saw the old tupelo, NS-6.

After spending some time with this relict of New England history, we left NS-6 and returned to our boat. I

rowed through pond lilies and pollen to the south end of
the island, and after a caution about the presence of poison sumac, we landed near a sand and gravel ridge that
crosses that end of the island. Here I found QUA-1 and
QUA-2, two old white oaks growing on the dry sands of
the ridge. These trees began their lives in 1720 and 1802,
respectively. Long, dead limbs splayed grotesquely out of
gnarled trunks and hung awkwardly in the air. We spent
some time examining these longtime residents before departing that side of the island. Rowing along its west
shoreline, we continued our circle around the island.
Large white pines lined the shore on that side. Near the
north end of the island, we went ashore again to look at a
sassafras tree. Its trunk, covered by deeply furrowed bark,
easily distinguished it from other species in the vicinity. Its
date of germination was before 1850. Nearly two and a
half centuries earlier, in this town of Plymouth, the explorer Martin Pring and his men dug up and gathered the
roots of the sassafras tree, which was valued for its curative powers. In the words of Pring: "As for trees the
Country yeeldeth Sassafras a plant of sovereigne vertue
for the French Poxe [syphilis]; and as some of late have
learnedly written good against the Plague and many other
Maladies."[5]

A short time later we launched our boat, and as I
rowed back, watching the island recede in the distance, I
was struck with how much like an oasis it is in the midst
of these Plymouth barrens—not only in the common perception of the term's literal meaning, but also in the sense
that it is a refuge in a landscape of change.

Change provides a theme for the introduction of this
chapter on the remnant plant communities of the New
England wilderness. In a peculiarly dual sort of way, our
changing understanding of the landscape led to the view
that the early New England landscape, itself, was changing. Our growing knowledge cleared away misconceptions
of a static vegetative cover—notions that the land had
reached a stable pattern of plant communities to be predictably and forever populated with climax species. We
now see that the landscape encountered by the Europeans
was a dynamic one with a long history of changing patterns before it came under human influence.

Through the centuries, we have acquired an increasingly accurate and detailed record of the plant life of the New England wilderness. Our information comes from research among several disciplines of inquiry. Through the social sciences we now have a detailed historical record. For example, from *Purchas his Pilgrimes*, a book printed in 1625, we have Martin Pring's account of his voyage of 1603 in employment of Bristol merchants to gather sassafras in the Massachusetts region. He gave us an early listing of the vegetation: "Vines, Cedars, Okes, Ashes, Beeches, Birch trees, Cherie trees bearing fruit whereof wee did eate, Hasels, Wich-hasels, the best wood of all other to make Sope-ashes withall, Walnut-trees, Maples, holy to make Bird-lime with, and a kinde of tree bearing a fruit like a small red Peare-plum."[6] In 1614, Captain John Smith expanded on Pring's list, adding: "alkermes [dwarf oak?], currans [American black currant], or a fruit like currans, mulberries [red mulberry], vines [fox grape], respices [red raspberry], goosberries, plummes, walnuts, chesnuts [chestnut], small nuts [butternut?], &c, pumpions, gourds, strawberries, beans, pease, and mayze [corn]; a kind or two of flax . . . oke [white oak?] . . . firre [eastern hemlock?], pyne [white pine?] . . . birch [American white birch?], ash [white ash], elme [American elm], cypresse [tamarack?], cedar [Atlantic white cedar], mulberrie, plum-tree, hazell, saxefrage, and many other sorts."[7]

It wasn't until 1672 that John Josselyn provided us with the earliest, most complete list of plant species in New England. In his book *New-Englands Rarities Discovered*, he catalogued a hundred species common to the region, thirty-six that were unknown elsewhere, ten that were unnamed, twenty-two that were exotics, or brought over by the English, and fifty-eight that were garden herbs.[8]

Through the years, historical records documented our expanding knowledge of plant species and the communities in which they reside. Gradually an increasingly detailed picture has emerged of a landscape with a varied pattern of ecosystems, including forests, swamps, marshes, meadows, bogs, barrens, and "mossy" alpine areas. They were described not only in the works of Josselyn and other early observers, but appeared in reports by geologists and naturalists, land surveyors, and timber cruisers. In the case of

This drawing of a bunchberry appeared in a book by John Josselyn, published in 1672, in which he provided the most complete list of plant species in New England at the time. Illustration from John Josselyn, *New-Englands Rarities Discovered* (London: G. Widdowes, 1672).

our forests, we have learned much from town property as-
sessments, real estate transfers, and business records, such
as manufacturing and shipping. In addition, those who
surveyed in the field frequently recorded the effects of natural catastrophes from hurricanes, wild fires, and insects
and disease.

The process of documentation did not occur quickly.
The northern areas were the last explored, surveyed, and
settled. As late as 1829, Moses Greenleaf wrote in his
Survey of the State of Maine that "the extensive field of
natural history has been as yet but very imperfectly explored in this state."[9] In fact, George Goodale, a botanist
with the state's 1861 geological and natural history survey
team, reported finding sixty-four species of plants heretofore unlisted in *Gray's Manual*.[10] Today, we are still un-
covering information on New England's flora. In 1994, for
example, a patch of undisturbed old-growth spruce forest
was discovered in the northern part of Maine's Baxter
State Park.

Another source of evidence relating to New England's
historic plant cover comes from the natural sciences. One
especially revealing line of research is the analysis of
pollen grains, or the science of palynology. Each species
of flowering plant produces a unique form of pollen
grain, which is resistant to decay. Over time, dispersed
pollen grains are trapped in layers of pond-bottom sediments, wetland peats, and upland soils. When a core of
the sediment is taken, its layers may be dated by analyzing
carbon-14 and the kinds and relative abundance of plants
present at the time identified by the pollen grains. Sediment layers have been dated as far back as 14,000 years,
at the time of deglaciation. When wide-ranging samples
are compared for the species of plants present during various time periods, the change in the composition of forests
can be detected. Furthermore, knowing what climatic conditions a particular species prefers allows climate change
to be inferred.

Pollen studies show that our New England forests
changed many times during the past 14,000 years in response to periods of climatic warming and cooling. Thus,
we know that a spruce-dominated boreal, or northern,
forest had become established soon after the glacier left. In

northern Maine this occurred between 10,000 and 11,000 years ago. A major warming period began around 8,000 years ago and ended around 5,000 years ago with minor increases in temperature at other times. This resulted in the northward expansion of pine, birch, and oak forests, followed by hemlock and beech. Hemlock declined rapidly beginning 5,000 years ago and recovered 1,000 to 1,500 years ago. In southern New England since 7,000 years ago, the forests have been dominated by oak in association with beech, hickory, and, until this century, chestnut. Over the past 4,000 years, the climate has been cooling, with regional increases of spruce and, more recently, a decline in hemlock and beech in many locations.[11]

Pollen analysis is also used to document the vegetative history of specific sites. For example, a black gum swamp in the central uplands of Massachusetts was sampled for pollen dispersed into the swamp from upland species of trees and other plants in the surrounding region. Analysis of pollen percentages revealed that before 1650 the surrounding upland forest was a mixed hardwood-conifer forest composed of beech, birch, oak, red maple, American chestnut, American ash, white pine, and eastern hemlock.[12]

Other approaches utilize old-growth forests to reconstruct forest history. The past is revealed through the study of live and dead plant material on undisturbed forest floors. In one forest in southwestern New Hampshire, an undisturbed plot containing much rotting material was studied and analyzed. The researchers examined every living tree in the plot, all dead and unburied trees, and all buried fallen trees and their fragments. Using techniques for dating and identifying the live and dead trees and materials, they were able to reveal the forest's history, dating back more than three hundred years. The researchers discovered that it was destroyed by fire in about 1665 and by a hurricane in 1938. They learned that before 1665 the forest consisted mainly of coniferous trees dominated by the white pine, but also present were white oak, eastern hemlock, spruces, red maple, and species of poplar.[13]

Another avenue of research in old-growth forests involves the analysis of tree rings to determine age and effects of weather, fire, and pathogens on growth patterns. Using

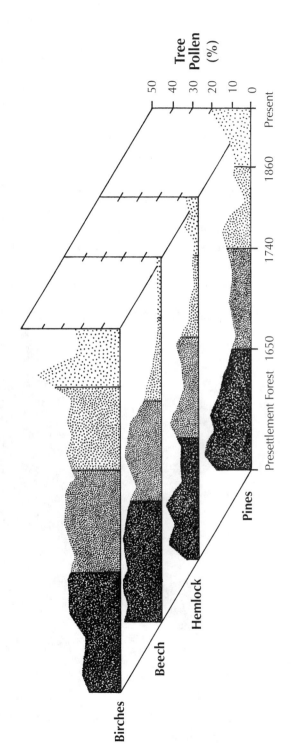

Changes in forest trees in north central Massachusetts interpreted from pollen studies of Black Gum Swamp, Harvard Forest. Redrawn and reprinted by permission, from D. R. Foster, et al., "Post-settlement History of Human Land-use and Vegetation Dynamics of a *Tsuga canadensis* (Hemlock) Woodlot in Central New England," *Journal of Ecology* 80 (1992).

an increment borer, a long, straw-sized, cylindrical core is extracted from a tree, and the number of annual rings are counted and the distances between them noted. In a good growing season, during spring and summer, a thicker layer of new wood forms, and in fall and winter, the tree grows more slowly, forming a thinner, denser layer of wood cells. The result can be seen as a series of bands indicating the number of years of growth. Cores can also reveal and date fire scars, damage from insects and disease, and increases in growth caused when light is made available by the removal of surrounding trees during hurricanes or severe storms.

From historic records and scientific studies, we have been able to construct maps showing the general nature and extent of New England's original forest before European settlement. For example, in 1956 the New England Section of the Society of American Foresters published a

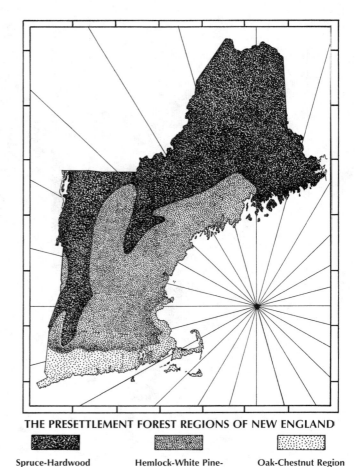

THE PRESETTLEMENT FOREST REGIONS OF NEW ENGLAND

| Spruce-Hardwood Region | Hemlock-White Pine-Hardwood Region | Oak-Chestnut Region (Pitch Pines on Sandy Soils) |

The presettlement forest regions of New England. Redrawn from Charles F. Carroll, *The Timber Economy of Puritan New England* (Providence, R. I.: Brown University Press, 1973). Reprinted by permission from Brown University.[14]

map showing the kind of forests that originally existed over the whole of New England. The map showed the location and extent of climax forests based on an analysis of present forest types and their topographic position, soils, and plant associations.[15] In 1973 Charles Carroll produced a map from data compiled from both historical and scientific information.[16] These generalized maps simplify the complex mosaic of New England's pre-European-settlement forest into three zones.

The forest of the northern zone consists of the spruces, balsam fir, and northern hardwoods. In southern New England, the forest is characterized by the oaks, pitch pine, and American chestnut. Between is a transition zone of eastern hemlock, white pine, and hardwoods. These maps, it must be remembered, show only forest types and do not depict the diversity of plant communities that actually exist on the ground, some of which are not heavily forested, that is, trees are not the dominant form of vegetation. These include alpine areas, sand plains, meadows, marshes, and bogs. Our interest here is in those vestiges of undisturbed forests and other plant communities that still remain on the New England landscape.

We now know that the remnant plant communities of the early New England wilderness are, in reality, somewhat different from those of earlier times and may be uncharacteristic of those that generally prevailed. In the case of forests, those left undisturbed are generally on steep slopes or in rocky areas that are difficult to access and therefore are uncharacteristic of much of the original forest that covered the land. Also, because most old-growth, or ancient, forests are patches surrounded by human activity and its effects, they are subjected to alteration by people, domestic animals, pollution, pathogens, insects, and seeds from exotic plants. Suitable buffer zones are effective against some of these threats but may be of little protection against those that are airborne and can travel great distances.

One ecologist noted "dramatic changes in species composition as a result of introduced pathogens or predators: American chestnut and American elm have already suffered significant declines; beech and hemlock are also declining rapidly in certain areas."[17] And in the case of exotic, or introduced, species of plants, we have already seen

The American chestnut suffered serious declines in the early years of the twentieth century due to the unintentional introduction of a fungal blight from Asia. Illustration from George B. Emerson, *A Report on the Trees and Shrubs Growing Naturally in the Forests of Massachusetts*, vol. 1 (Boston, Mass.: Little, Brown, and Company, 1875).

where John Josselyn documented the presence of alien plants. Asa Gray, the well-known and highly respected botanist, noted in 1880 that "the influx of European weeds was prompt and rapid from the first; and has not ceased to flow; for hardly a year passes in which new comers are not noticed in some parts of the country."[18]

While we have seen our relict plant communities gain non-native species, we know also that they have lost populations of some others. One report identified 101 plants as New England's rarest. It included species that appear to be in decline and noted that "residential, industrial and recreational developments and their ancillary demands on a finite land base by an ever increasing population have been and continue to be major influences on the existence and character of New England's flora."[19] Interestingly, possibly two plants listed in the report that are now extremely limited in New England and the United States were also among the plants listed by John Josselyn in 1672. They are the sedge hedgehog grass, *Carex flava*, var. gaspensis, and male fern, *Dryopteris filix-mas*. Josselyn also identified the American chestnut, *Castanea dentata*, which is now almost nonexistent compared to its previous abundance.

The changes in our plant communities led one forest researcher to state that "no examples of unaltered forests exist for comparison due to the long and pervasive impact of altered disturbance regimes, introduced pathogens, modified animal populations, and changed atmospheric conditions."[20] Still, change is a matter of degree, and within this context representative remnants of a variety of plant communities are less disturbed than others, and some remarkably undisturbed.

Some communities, as we shall see, escaped human exploitation completely; others were partially altered and have since returned to a semblance of their pre-European-settlement condition. Some are several thousand acres in size, and others provide space for a single specimen. They provide opportunities to make ecological comparisons with communities that are far more disturbed and manipulated. Their existence allows us to explore unique associations between flora and fauna that may still be relatively unaffected by human disturbance. Psychologically, their presence puts us in touch with not only their past but ours as well. We might also argue that these plant communities serve to remind us of our ethical responsibility to exercise restraint when altering our environment. These are considerations to keep in mind as we explore representatives of New England's relict plant communities of the past.

Timothy Dwight was not the first to describe the sand plains of the North Haven–Wallingford, Connecticut, area. The historian Benjamin Trumbull, who lived in their vicinity, commented that "the Indians so often burned the country . . . that in many of the plain, dry parts of it, there was but little small timber . . . [and] there grew bent grass, or as some called it, thatch, two, three and four feet high."[22] Early records suggest that in 1638, the time of English settlement in the region, these plains were covered by grassland vegetation and large scattered oaks.[23]

When the last glacier receded from the southern Connecticut region 12,000 years ago, meltwater streams carried siliceous sands from the western highlands into the Quinnipiac River Valley. Over the years, grasses, scrub oak, and pitch pine came to populate the dry, nutrient-poor soils. For centuries the delicate ecosystem survived. When the colonial settlements arrived, the fragile, impoverished soils were unable to withstand the agricultural efforts of the pioneer farmers, and by the early 1800s, the farmland was abandoned. Since that time, railroads, highways, industrial complexes, and housing developments have erased much of that early landscape. It was, therefore, a surprise when one last remnant tract of that old pine barren was reported in the New Haven area in 1982—sixteen acres of desertlike plain with patches of open and bare sand, grassy areas, and scattered, scrubby trees and other vegetation able to survive in conditions inhospitable to most plants.[24]

Pine barrens are found primarily along the northeastern coastal plain where glacial sands were deposited. The soils derived from these deposits are porous, allowing water to pass through them and creating droughty conditions. The sands and plant litter are often acidic, limiting microbes and, therefore, the decomposition of dead plant material. A layer of dry organic matter, or duff, accumulates on the

SAND PLAINS AND PINE BARRENS

Near the northern limit of the township [the soil] is so light, as in two or three places, of small extent, to be blown in drifts. In these places it is absolutely barren.

—Timothy Dwight, 1821[21]

soils and produces fire-prone conditions when combined with an understory of flammable, waxy-leaved heath plants. Thus, New England's pine barrens have a long history of fire.

The porous, dry soils of barrens also make them desirable for many human uses, such as sites for housing and industrial developments, roads, and mining operations for sand and gravel. They are popular sites for the use of off-road vehicles and, unfortunately, are also used for illegal dumping. One study included an evaluation of twenty-five pine barren sites in New England and found that, of the seventeen sites for which the historic acreage is known, almost two-thirds of their total land area is now lost. Further, it found that only five, or one-fifth, of the sites at the time of the study were fully protected. In the words of the study's author, they are "among the most threatened natural communities in the northeast."[25]

A more recent report noted that "pitch pine/scrub oak barrens once covered tens of thousands of acres in New Jersey, New York, Pennsylvania, and New England, [but] they have been so drastically reduced and fragmented by clearing, excavation, development, and fire suppression that fewer than 20 major pine barrens remain . . . and are second only to old-growth forests as a rare forest community type in the northeast."[26] In Maine, however, an impressive remnant exists of this single-most threatened forest ecosystem. It is known as the Waterboro Barrens, now protected by the Maine Chapter of The Nature Conservancy.

The Waterboro Barrens, Maine

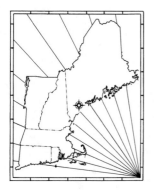

Our Sandy *plains, the natural growth of which is pitch and white pine, are sometimes large. . . . but to the extent, the writer has not satisfactory information—except that he is told there are no less than 6,000 acres of pitch-pine plains in the single town of Shapleigh.*

—William D. Williamson, 1832[27]

I sensed something peculiarly different here—a primitive kind of feeling, which fanned a flicker of excitement, and lured me on at a faster pace. The narrow road was sandy, dished by erosion from many wheels, and thoroughly dry, though it was only mid-April. Elsewhere in Maine, it was still mud season. Tall pitch pine lined the road, trunks dark, coarse, clumpy-barked. Overarching branches twisted out from the trunks, bowing and murmuring in the wind. A tangle of wiry scrub oak trunks and limbs crowded the gaps between the pines. Beneath, the ground already crackled with the litter of dead, dry leaves. No lingering of dampness from the spring season stayed here.

The four-wheel-drive vehicle came up behind me noiselessly in the soft sand. It jumped me, and I stepped aside to let it pass. A family outing, I guessed. For a few moments, I watched it go out of sight. I walked on, as intrigued by the land as I was when I first saw the dunes of outer Cape Cod. I saw no fences, no stone walls, no cellar holes—no evidence of farming. Only thin, starved topsoil.

The road joined another. I met a second family—this one on all-terrain vehicles. Again, I stepped off the road to let them pass, then took the right fork towards my first destination. The oak and pines grow more densely in this section. "Thickly set with pitch pine and scrub oak" was the description given of this place in 1800. The area was not settled until the mid-to-late 1700s. With the clearing of the land, oak increased dramatically, and so did the heath shrubs and the fires. Periodic fires were probably always a part of this land's experience. Charcoal in sediments suggests the area was burned during the 1300s or 1400s, and historic records after settlement show major fires in 1760, 1854, and 1947. The forest, both before settlement and after, has been far from static.

To what extent have the present communities of plants always been here? We have yet to know for sure. The oldest cored and aged pitch pine is 125 years old. Pitch pine is adapted to fire with its thick bark, long tap root, and sprouting capability. And scrub oak also is able to sprout quickly and produce acorns at the early age of three to four years. In a word, fire probably controlled the vegetation here. Pollen studies indicate that pitch pine and oak have been here for thousands of years. Perhaps at times in the past the forest closely resembled what we see today.

I arrived at my first destination, Buff Brook, to find the vehicle that passed me parked there. The land has taken on a new interest in the form of sand hills. Near the brook, where an old dam is now breached, the soil is sand,

Bluff Brook continues to erode a ninety-foot-high sandy bluff in Maine's Waterboro Barrens.

and I was reminded again of the dunes of Cape Cod's Province Lands. The brook is quick here, and I followed it downstream a short distance to where it slowed and curved beneath a huge sand bluff, ninety feet high. It is here that one appreciates the most interesting feature of these barrens—their topography. Sand hills, eskers, kettles, bluffs—they are all here. Beneath them is a large aquifer, fed by the rainwater that so easily percolates through their soils. The varied terrain creates microclimates that in turn influence the vegetation and, ultimately, the niches available for animal life. I climbed up the hillside through scrub oak and pitch pine and came out at the top of the bluff. Far below, sheltered by the bluff and beside the wide sandy edge of the brook, the family that passed me was enjoying a preview of summer.

Leaving the old dam-site, I explored another road that would take me near a wetland. Soon, through the trees, I saw the opening where it lay. At its edge, surrounding an area of open water, were hummocks of heath plants, especially the ubiquitous leatherleaf. Alders, aspens, gray birches, and white and pitch pines lay farther back. The bog vegetation was still brown from winter. The shock of winter was still wearing off. Later in the season, this wetland is alive with insects, birds, and other animal life.

I returned to the road. Small patches of ice still smoothed the bottoms of the ruts. In the woods, vernal pools reflected the blue sky, adding a bit of color to the brown understory. In places scrub oaks were thick between the pitch pines, and in other areas the woods were more open. I heard an all-terrain vehicle in the distance. The road forked, and I turned onto another road, heading northward, and searched the woods along its edge. In summer the edges of these pathways are likely homes for two rare plants: rattlesnake weed, endangered in Maine, and fern-leaved false foxglove.

The road entered the other prevalent plant community of these barrens, the pitch pine heath. Here one can see through open woods of almost pure pitch pine. Their dark trunks are spaced out over a low knoll surrounded by a lawnlike ground cover of sheep laurel and other heath plants, grasses, and mosses—all resting on a thick layer of pine needles and bits of broken branches. I left the road and followed a trail, probably made by white-tailed deer, for they are widespread here. I stopped to photograph a reflection of the forest in a vernal pool—a wet depression, which, during its temporary life, is valuable to species of amphibians and reptiles. Moving on, I flushed an American woodcock, another sign of spring. It was still early for the explosion of insects that will occur here. Eleven rare moths, whose life cycles are tied entirely to specific species of barren's vegetation, are known to inhabit this area, as do numerous, equally rare, leaf and plant bugs. It was a place about to experience a rejuvenation of life.

In some ways the pitch pine heath community had a manicured look about it, suggesting a human presence. I realized this was its normal appearance, but I also knew that some areas of these barrens are probably greatly altered from their pre-colonial character. Yet, once one leaves the well-used network of roads, there is a remote, even primitive feeling here. And another feeling is also here—a feeling that one has time to enjoy these unusual woodlands, that there is some stability and permanency. Much of the Waterboro Barrens is now protected, ironically, by an attitude of unfitness that is quite the opposite of that which first protected them. The old settlers left the barrens undeveloped because they saw them "unfit for settlement." Today we leave some undeveloped because their settlement is unfit for a world that needs to preserve biodiversity.[28]

Dark, rough-barked trunks of pitch pine rise above a lawnlike ground cover of sheep laurel and pine needles in this open forest in Maine's Waterboro Barrens.

NATURAL MEADOWS

There be likewise in divers places neare the plantations great broad Medowes, wherein grow neither shrub nor Tree.

—William Wood, 1634[29]

High among the first needs of the colonists were fertile, hay-producing meadows, and in the opinion of many historians and naturalists, the settlers owe much in this regard to the beaver. This unusual animal engineered dams and created ponds in valleys throughout New England. The rising waters behind the dams drowned the roots of trees and shrubs and slowly killed them. Over time the ponds filled with sediments brought in by the brooks and streams, and the dead trees fell into the accumulating muck and decayed. Inevitably, the dams were breached, or if the beaver were trapped or left because of exhausted food supplies, the dams were abandoned and slowly eroded away. As a result, the ponds drained and left behind a flat land of rich, mucky soil in which grasses took root.

"Many of the richest tillable lands of New England were formed by the artificial works of the beaver," observed the naturalist Enos Mills in 1913.[30] Others agreed.

Early farmers owed much to the beaver for the natural hay-producing meadows they needed. The "beaver meadow" pictured here is in its early stages of development.

The geologist Charles Hitchcock, surveying New Hampshire in 1878, noted that "the name 'beaver meadow' is frequently heard throughout the state." He mentioned a large meadow nearly a mile in length in Weare that was used for grass. Upon investigating it, he found the soft, muddy soil to be several feet deep.[31] Stanley Bromley, in his paper *The Original Forest Types of Southern New England*, also suggested that "many natural wet meadows may have originated as beaver meadows."[32] More recently, the scholar Carolyn Merchant wrote, "Over thousands of years, all over New England rich meadows with fertile soils had been created by beavers. Both Indians and whites recognized the beaver as an active agent in nature."[33]

However, another source of natural grasslands existed for the early New England farmers. "The best were river meadows," observed Betty Flanders Thompson in her book *The Changing Face of New England*.[34] These low-lying lands are kept fertile by seasonal flooding and fresh deposits of silt and mud. Due to the periodic disruption and constantly changing soil conditions, shallow-rooted, quick-growing grasses are favored on these intervale lands.

Through the centuries, the beaver disappeared in some sections of New England, although it has since made a comeback. Agriculture changed, and developments replaced many of the old meadow lands. In the words of Enos Mills, "A populous village stands upon the seat of a primitive and forgotten [beaver] colony."[35] The natural grasslands of river bottomlands changed, too, and were often turned to other forms of agriculture than hay production, or they were drained and developed to other uses. Still, remnants of these natural meadows are waiting to be rediscovered by one who perseveres.

Hay Brook Meadow, Maine

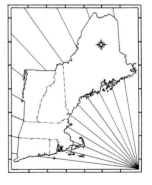

We found Hay Brook to be a crooked stream, at first skirted by larches, or hacmatacks, as this growth is commonly called. After leaving this growth, you find the course of the stream lies through a tract of "Brook Interval," forming a natural meadow, from which hay is annually taken to supply the teams of the lumberman.

—Ezekiel Holmes, 1839[36]

In my search for remnants of the early New England landscape, I came across the above description of a natural meadow in northern Maine. Ezekiel Holmes, on a state-sponsored survey, was in the process of leading his party of explorers from the Penobscot River watershed to that of the Aroostook River. Some twenty years later, reporting on another survey, he again described this meadow: "[It is] a large interval in the bend of the Nutupsenuc stream, commonly called 'Hay brook'. . . . It is frequently overflowed, and too low for cultivating, but very productive in grass."[37]

One late afternoon in the fall of 1994, I retraced Ezekiel Holmes's route in search of that meadow and farm, the buildings of which have long since gone. Six miles of narrow gravel road led me through remote, densely wooded land to Hay Brook. An old road, reduced now to a narrow path, provided access to the old farm site, still a mile away when I left my vehicle. The sunlit woods that afternoon were densely populated with red spruce, hung thickly with long strands of old man's beard lichen. Low, mossy swamps bordered sections of the trail. Moose tracks and the scat of bear and coyote frequently appeared along my route. It is always somewhat amazing to learn that in these deep woods so far from human habitation, homes and businesses once existed, bustling with activity.

At last I came to a slight rise in the otherwise flat lowland, and the dense forest gave way to a more open land of grasses and other herbaceous plants growing among scattered alders and firs. Here at the junction of two brooks, I found the remnants of the natural meadow described by Holmes over a century and a half ago. Betty Flanders Thompson couldn't have described it more perfectly: "Other little pockets of rich, grassy bottomland, even intervales tucked away far from the main body of settlement, had their small hamlets or isolated farms when the nearby upland was still a silent, empty wilderness."[38] Today, at Hay Brook Meadow, the silence has returned and the old meadow is once again empty of the scythes, rakes, and wagons that once worked over its surface. In the distance, I could see Hay Brook Mountain, and for a moment, I wished I could have stood on its top and looked down at this place from time to time over the past two centuries. What changes I would have seen.

The early settlers called them mires, swamps, and boggy lands and often regarded them as useless and the cause of putrid fevers and sickness. As late as 1853, the Vermont naturalist Zadock Thompson stated that "these are hardly of sufficient importance to deserve a separate notice [in his book]." Further, he claimed that the marshes in stagnant coves around Lake Champlain "during the hotter parts of the summer generated intermittent and bilious fevers."[40]

As a result of these attitudes, marshes and bogs have a history of human alteration and abuse. They have been drained, filled, and dumped upon. For many, they are still regarded as wastelands. In recent years, we have come to recognize that they are ecologically valuable for aquifer recharge, critical habitat for many plants and animals, and water run-off control. Additionally, scientists have found that their sediments hold information about thousands of years of environmental change.

Many kinds and variations of these wetlands abound, and scientists in the twentieth century busily studied those differences and wrestled with classifying them. We consider here two categories: freshwater marshes and peatlands, or bogs. Marshes, for our purposes, develop along the shores of lakes and streams in shallow, moving waters where emergent plants like cattails, grasses, sedges, and rushes can obtain a foothold. Peatlands develop in low-flowing or standing waters that are oxygen-starved and nutrient-poor. These are favorable to sphagnum mosses and heath plants such as leatherleaf. Peatlands are often grouped as bogs or fens. Bogs have low-flowing, acidic waters with nutrients obtained primarily from the atmosphere. Bogs are further divided into those that are level and those that are raised. Fens have less acidic waters more enriched by minerals and thus support a greater diversity of plant species. Maine has the greatest number and variety of peatlands in New England, with some 10,000 over one acre in size, covering an estimated 750,000 acres.

Today, many acres of Maine's peatlands remain relatively unaltered. Two alone account for over 5,500 acres. One is Number Five Bog. A few years ago I paddled completely around the forested boundaries of this little-disturbed bog, located in a remote area in the northern

MARSHES AND BOGGY LANDS

It is true that in a territory where there are no very high mountains which give rise to streams, the waters must collect in what are called bogs, and many of the streams take their rise in such places.

—Ezekiel Holmes, 1839[39]

part of the state. The secluded nature of this bog gives it an aura of mystery. It is now a National Natural Landmark, so designated in recognition of its unusual pattern of long string ponds, which are interspersed with narrow ridges of bog vegetation; an uncommon stand of jack pine; a broad diversity of plants; and outstanding scenic views.[41]

The other bog I saw more recently. The Great Heath is Maine's largest peatland. A 4,000-acre raised bog, it is located next to Pleasant River and the ancient river delta known as Pineo Ridge in Washington County.[42] The isolation, vastness, and undisturbed qualities of this bog give an impression of primitiveness. Here, one can easily imagine being the first to see it. Other bogs and marshes in New England also retain the primitive qualities one would associate with the early New England wilderness, and we will visit a few of them in the following pages.

Missisquoi Marsh, Vermont

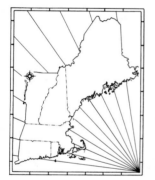

There is a considerable tract of swampy land. . . . about the mouth of Missisco River.

—Zadock Thompson, 1853[43]

Michiscoui, according to the historian Samuel Williams, is the Indian name of the most northerly river in the state of Vermont.[44] Rising in the north-central part of the state, the seventy-five-mile-long river flows in and out of Canada before arriving at the shore of Lake Champlain. There it forms a huge delta and separates into several channels. If the Native Americans who named this river could return to its delta-land today, they would see many changes, but if they explored its marshes and swamps, they would see familiar sights as well, for parts of it have remained relatively free of long-term human alteration.

In early times, the marshes here were viewed as useless to human enterprise. This was expressed by Ira Allen in a letter dated February 8, 1786, to James Whitelaw: "The lake is over it [the marsh] great part of the year & cannot be fit for any use or Produce."[45] A century and a half later, the marshes and swamps were viewed with a new eye: in 1943 the area was declared a national wildlife refuge. Today, 95 percent of the delta is within the 5,839-acre refuge, of which 500 acres are natural marsh and 1,800 acres are managed wetlands.

While development has occurred outside the refuge, subtle, natural changes have gone on inside as well. These processes are continuous. Noticeable over time is the shifting number and pattern of channels made by the Missisquoi River as it makes its way over and through the delta to the lake. This kind of change influences both the nature of vegetation present and the wildlife dependent upon it. A report in 1861 mentioned that "besides the six present channels of egress for the river there were once two others, which are called Charcoal Creek and Dead Creek."[46] Indeed, an atlas printed in the latter half of the 1800s doesn't show either of those two creeks. Current maps show even fewer channels: Dead Creek, entering Goose Bay on the northern side of the delta, and, depending upon which map one looks at, only three other direct channels to the lake.

On the first of June, Black Creek was full. Low, muddy banks, ordinarily beyond the reach of the stream, felt its soft, silty caress. The water looked green, mirroring the curving archway of maples and other overhanging

Black Creek in Vermont's Missisquoi National Wildlife Refuge flows through a lush wetland to Lake Champlain's Maquam Bay.

swamp trees fully adorned with the fresh leaves of spring. On the banks above the stream, bright green, newly formed fronds of sensitive ferns covered the rich, dark silt. The quiet waters of the creek flowed almost imperceptibly through the lush wetland towards Maquam Bay nearly a mile away. Ahead, the creek covered the wet trail, so I turned back to try the trail along Maquam Creek. It, too, was high, threatening the trail along the top edge of its bank. Vernal pools created a beautiful, complicated world of reflections in the swamp bordering the trail. A beaver cutting raised my expectations of an encounter. I stopped to photograph the tall, as yet unfurled fronds of a fern before the sun's rays abandoned it for another subject. Moving on, I found the stream had also claimed this trail. In the meantime, the trail and swamp have captured my imagination, and I hope to return someday.

Later, in another location, I found the Missisquoi River. It was also full, and its swampy banks were dark, too, with fresh silt. Great willow trees lined the river where I walked. The swamps here are thick with silver maples. The rich soils also find favor with swamp white oak, white and black ashes, black alder, and, in the openings, buttonbush. At ground level, sensitive ferns luxuriate in the damp earth, shaded by the trees and shrubs. They are joined occasionally by royal ferns and marsh ferns. At the water's edge, a swimming muskrat rose over a submerged branch and settled again into a low wake on the river's surface. A great blue heron stood motionless in a shallow cove. Overhead, a sharp cheeping drew my attention to three ospreys circling high above as they searched the shallow waters for fish. The heron and osprey are among eighty-three bird species that nest near or on the refuge, and well over a hundred others stop here for food and rest, many in large migrating flocks.

The river leaves the swamp and meanders through large, dense stands of great bulrush. In shallows, pickerel weed grows. Arrowhead, water smartweed, marsh fern, and various sedges, rushes, and grasses, including wild rice, grow where flats are exposed intermittently by the rise and fall of the river and lake. Cattails, swamp milkweed, and many other wetland plants fit in where they are adapted. In open waters are white water lilies, eel grass, and bladderworts. Many of these plants have a historic association with this marsh and contribute to those qualities reminiscent of a past when it was called *Michiscoui* by a people who saw it first.[47]

Little Otter Creek Marsh, Vermont

Well within my memory, the west banks of both were clad with primeval forest whose border of great trees, fallen and bending streamward in every degree of incline, like an immense chevaux de frise, still held for one shore the wildness and gave one an idea of the appearance of all the shores in the days of the pioneers.

—Rowland E. Robinson, 1894[48]

The west banks of the two streams Rowland Robinson described are the South and East "slangs," tributaries of Little Otter Creek. Robinson suggested that the word "slang" came from a corruption of "slank," meaning a small, sluggish, marshy stream. That's exactly what I saw one spring day when I stopped to explore the west bank of the South Slang. The stream here is only a mile and a half from Lake Champlain in Ferrisburg. Looking northward, I saw in the distance Little Otter Creek and its marshland. The view southward looked along a wooded shoreline with a marshy border. Little development intruded here. The marsh near the mouth of this creek has been described as "an outstanding unspoiled example of a shallow water marsh. . . . [and] the best large expanse of marshland in Vermont."

The beauty of a marsh coming to life in spring is rejuvenating to the spirit. I had stood quietly for several minutes, totally immersed in the scene along the South Slang, when I saw something swimming. It rose up slightly. Could it be? Did I see an otter? Whatever it was, it quickly disappeared into the marsh grasses. I suppose it was perfectly logical to see such an animal in a stream emptying into Little Otter Creek, though it has been a long time since the Abenakis gave it the name Wonakaketuk, or River of Otters.[49] Back in the 1800s the otters had all but disappeared here. Rowland Robinson recalled that the last otter in the South Slang was killed in the 1840s.

Robinson was well acquainted with the waterfowl attracted to these marshes: "One who knows these marshes only in the almost lifeless desolation that now pervades them can hardly imagine how they swarmed with feathered life in autumn, from the falls to the lake and throughout

The South Slang in Ferrisburg, Vermont, flows gently on its way to Little Otter Creek and its expansive marsh.

the length and breadth of both slangs, in flocks of countless wood ducks, teal, dusky ducks, and divers other sorts that came thronging down from the northward."[50] Today, the 735-acre marsh abounds once again with many species of waterfowl and other birds, such as the black tern, attracted by its extensive, rich, and varied marsh vegetation. Here aquatic plants grow in profusion, including wild rice, bulrush, bur reed, and cattail. Along the densely wooded banks are shrubs like buttonbush and red-osier dogwood, and the lowland trees, red maple and willows.[51]

The first settlers arrived in the vicinity of this marsh in 1769. Yet, despite more than two hundred years of development, the marsh still remains unspoiled, and even I sensed the wildness Rowland Robinson felt a century ago.

Black Spruce Bog, New Hampshire

Although the ascent was difficult, we were amply repaid by the magnificent extent of the view which was displayed before us, as the veil of clouds gradually rolled away before the wind. . . . and to the west lay the lakes and tributary streams of the Connecticut.

—Messrs. Whitney and Williams, 1844[52]

When Whitney and Williams, assistants to the geologist Charles T. Jackson, ascended Rump Mountain on the Maine–New Hampshire border, their trip took them through relatively unexplored wilderness. Even today pockets of this country are still wild and unspoiled. If you were to explore up one of those tributaries of the Connecticut River that the geologists saw from the summit of the mountain, you would come to the edge of a magnificent wetland and, adjacent to it, a virgin forest of red spruce and balsam fir.

A brisk wind blew through the narrow valley and pushed the canoe up the long pond, which is really a dead water created by the dam I had left only a few moments before. The paddle served best as a rudder during much of the mile-long trip. I steered the canoe into a small cove out of the wind and into an open sphagnum bog. Emergent reeds, sedges, and grasses gave the edge of the bog mat a soft, green fringe. But the real supporting framework of this bog, like all of its kind, lies hidden—a maze of inter-locking roots from the heath plants, penetrating deep into the sphagnum.

The heath family of woody shrubs was well repre-sented—Labrador tea, rhodora, sheep laurel, bog laurel, bog rosemary, leatherleaf, and small cranberry. Near the

Remote and wild, this black spruce bog in northern New Hampshire lies beneath Rump Mountain on the Maine–New Hampshire border.

water's edge, the herbaceous round-leaved sundew and horned bladderwort would soon color the edge of the mat. Behind the expansive, greening mat, a long, dense band of sharply pointed black spruce and the less spirelike tama-rack breaks the scene's foreground of open wetland from the distant view of Rump Mountain. In the shade of the thickly growing spruce grow mountain holly, witherod, black chokeberry, and, on the sphagnum floor, bunchberry and creeping snowberry.[53]

As I moved my canoe to leave, a green heron took flight. I watched it out of sight. It's uncommon in these parts, yet so is a bog as splendid as this. I left reluctantly, wishing for the next half hour that I could move as easily against the wind as the heron.

A Bog Pond, New Hampshire

The great Ossapy . . . comes from a large pond, under a high mountain . . . which bear[s] the same name.

—Jeremy Belknap, 1792[54]

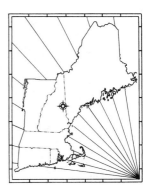

A short distance from Jeremy Belknap's "large pond" near the Maine–New Hampshire border, now known as Os-sipee Lake, lies a tiny, unobtrusive pond. Although it is within sight of a busy highway, it is safe to say that few notice its presence and fewer still are aware of its significance. Juxtaposed to an increasingly bigger transportation corridor, the bog and pond remain "entirely natural and unspoiled." According to those who have studied it, the bog surrounding the pond contains "the greatest variety of plant species of any peat bog in the state."

In mid-April, the wood road, still thawing out from winter, was soft and spongy and forced me to walk along its drier edge. The road traversed the top of a low ridge of hardwoods and pines and took me away from the sounds of traffic. I saw the pond's surface-glare first, shining through the large pines growing on the hillside below. The afternoon sun warmed the south-facing slope as I came down off the ridge, a welcome and pleasant feeling for one who came from the north where snow still covered woodland floors.

At the bottom of the slope, the land was wet and hummocky. Standing water filled the spaces between the mounds. A dense ring of black spruce, tamarack, numerous shrubs, and occasional pines surrounds the outer edge of the bog. Beyond, the encircling swamp gives way to a ten-foot-wide floating mat of sphagnum mosses, sedges, and heath shrubs. "A classic example of bog succession" is how scientists see it. But what struck me about this bog was not its variety of plants—it was the color. Some of the peat moss was strikingly red, and, against it, I had never seen evergreens looking greener. I expected such color later in the season, not then.[55]

Year by year the bog mat builds towards the center of the pond, now only five acres in size, and the swamp follows. Someday the pond will be gone, its unique bog community replaced by the swamp with its own specialized species. As I left, I looked over to the bog from the highway and wished it could have stayed more secluded and buffered from the encroachment of busy human activities. Yet the very fact that this small, wild area is here is a source of satisfaction in itself and shows that some cared about it.

Saco Heath, Maine

Some ⅔ of the area . . . consists of this mossy or open heath; the remainder is firm land but nearly level & but little elevated above the elevation of the mossy heath & is quite thickly covered with young growth. The mossy heath is not . . . altogether "open," but is covered to a considerable extent with small trees, in some portions these trees being mostly scrubby cedars.

—Isaac Boothby, 1899[56]

The winter's snow was barely gone and the hum of insects still a month away—a window of time to enjoy a bog or a swamp. The Saco Heath is both, but also more: "an undeveloped wild land in the heart of southern Maine," according to my guidebook. A boardwalk trail to the heath enters a swamp at the edge of a neighborhood. It's not unusual for human settlement to occur close to this heath, for English dwellings were first put up in this area in 1623—some of the earliest in Maine. People were slow to come at first, but after 1763 when hostilities with the French and Indians came to an end, development rapidly surrounded this "unsuitable" piece of land. By the time Isaac Boothby had this wetland surveyed in 1899, both logging and agriculture had peaked and manufacturing was rising in economic importance.

The boardwalk draws you away from the signs of human history, although a few stumps in the swamp are reminders. A large tupelo beside the trail is another kind of reminder—that this is a place of limits, for the tree is near the northern limit of its range. So is the Atlantic white cedar, which, by its presence this far north, imparts a special value to this wetland. Saco Heath enjoys a certain distinctiveness, being the southernmost of its kind in Maine, perhaps even in North America: a raised bog of sphagnum mosses and heath plants, which has built up over time, raising the water table and pioneering a new community. From the boardwalk, you don't see how the heath has changed from a lake to a marsh to a wooded fen to a bog and, finally, to a raised bog. You don't see the increase in Atlantic white cedar since settlement, probably caused by a combination of climatic warming and,

The Saco Heath is called an "undeveloped wildland in the heart of southern Maine."

possibly, the addition of nutrients from nearby human activity. Nor do you see the decrease in sphagnum mosses, probably attributable to the same nutrients.

As I walked along, the staccato drumroll of a hairy or downy woodpecker and the syncopated, jazzed-up rhythm of a yellow-bellied sapsucker competed with the sounds of a plane and the distant rumbling of some industrial operation. Here in the swamp the balance tipped towards the birds. The boardwalk wound on through the wet lowland and abruptly out onto the heath. Strangely, I felt a strong sense of loneliness, more so than in the swamp. The comparative emptiness and absence of signs of human presence, except for the boardwalk, strengthened the impression of isolation and remoteness. A wildness is found in a world of heath plants and sedges, of mosses and peat, of clumps of black spruce and dark trunks of solitary pitch pine. Such a place reinforces an image of the past. And it will remain this way until something unforeseen occurs.

No longer is this wild area threatened by mining, ditching, harvesting, or other activities that might irreversibly alter its qualities. Over eight hundred acres are now protected by The Nature Conservancy, and over time, most of the traces of human activity, like the old tracks of an all terrain vehicle crossing beneath the boardwalk, will fade away. Species other than humans now have some guarantee of a future. Here the palm warbler finds its southernmost breeding site on the Atlantic coast. This is also home to the globally threatened Hessel's hairstreak butterfly, which feeds only on Atlantic white cedar.

Later that day I entered the heath from another side, only a little over a mile north of the boardwalk. An old road leads to the site of a former peat mining operation, an area now protected. A large, flat section is barren and littered with the spoils of dredging. It serves as a graphic reminder of an alternative future this wetland could have met had it not been protected. Nearby, I found a large, boggy area, untouched and crowded with young Atlantic white cedars. On the far side, I saw a forest of pine and black spruce. I sensed that beyond those trees were opportunities for exploration where few have gone. I was reminded of my first trip to this heath at a time when no boardwalk nor trail existed. It was then that I discovered my first Atlantic white cedar. When we protect places such as this, we also protect an opportunity for discovery—a chance to explore the unknown and know a little of what those first settlers experienced here in 1623.[57]

Bog of the Old Green-Woods, Connecticut

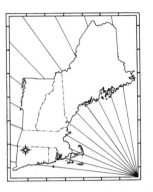

The Green-Woods derive their name from a vast forest of stately pines, which cover the face of this part of the country. . . . The scene is now and then varied as we reach the summit of the mountain: here a distant prospect of an immense succession of hills, gently swelling into form, and everywhere covered with trees, breaks upon the eye.

—James Trenchard, 1789[58]

The Green-Woods was a name given to a region in northwestern Connecticut that extended from Canaan Mountain eastward to the Farmington River Valley. In the late 1700s, the road from Hartford to Norfolk came to be known as the Greenwoods Turnpike. Today, it's Route 44.

One evening in mid-May, I drove east from the village of Norfolk on the old Greenwoods Turnpike. I turned onto a gravel road into a long, beautiful, wooded valley. The road soon narrowed to the width of my vehicle and

Evidence of beaver abounds around the shore of this pond where one of Connecticut's finest examples of a northern bog exists.

deteriorated into a roughly cut terrace in the side of a steeply sloped hill covered with hardwoods. Below, I could see a pond—a small body of water, seven acres in size. A turnout provided room to park, and as soon as I had gotten out of the car, I heard the honking of Canada geese.

The slope leading to the pond was steep and covered with dense stands of mountain laurel and old, fallen trees. In a round-about way, I reached the shore of the pond where a small seepage trickled into it. Here, I saw much past evidence of beaver—old cuttings and four abandoned houses in the pond. Many standing dead trees stood along the boggy margin of the opposite shore. The geese kept up their incessant honking; I counted a total of six swimming about the pond. Except for their sounds, it was completely quiet. The sun was now beginning to set, and shadows were creeping over the slopes of the surrounding hills. It felt remote and peaceful. If not for the black flies that had discovered a warm-blooded creature standing in their territory, the tranquillity would have been complete.

One of Connecticut's finest northern, or boreal, quaking bogs occupies a portion of the shore of this small pond—a floating mat of heath plants and sphagnum mosses, slowly edging its way into the open water. Though typical of such bogs in northern New England, it is rare to find one this far south. Plants that I once found in a remote bog in Maine's Allagash wilderness are here: the insectivorous sundews, pitcher plants, and bladderworts; the delicate orchids—grass pink, rose pogonia, white-fringed orchid; and the characteristic trees, shrubs, mosses, sedges, rushes, and grasses, even the rare bog clubmoss. Scattered tamarack and black spruce become more dominant as one moves away from the edge of the mat toward the uplands. The bog has been building here undisturbed for many years; one researcher measured the depth of peat to be fifty-one feet.[59]

On my return, after the last rays of sunshine had penetrated the valley, I stopped to investigate the northern end of the bog. From the edge of an old beaver flowage near a decaying mound of sticks that was once the home for a thriving colony of beavers, the silhouetted hills of the steep-sided valley reflected in the calm pool. It was at that moment, in that rapidly fading scene, that I caught the full magnificence of this remote and undisturbed bit of Trenchard's wild Green-Woods.

As John Josselyn pointed out early in the settlement of the country, swamps are low wetlands, overgrown with trees and shrubs. The English used the term "swamp" to describe wooded bogs. It is thought that the early English inhabitants of New England were unfamiliar with swamplands, since these wetlands had long ago disappeared from their native England.[61]

The vegetation in our pre-European-settlement swamps, like those today, varied, depending on their location. In northern New England, the swamps were dominated by northern white cedar, spruce, and fir. In central New England, pine and hemlock were frequent inhabitants, but Atlantic white cedar was also common in the more southerly swamps of Massachusetts, Rhode Island, and Connecticut. The Atlantic white cedar is now scarce in these swamps because of heavy clearcutting, after which it rarely returns. Of the early swamps in southern New England, the researcher Stanley Bromely reported, they "were largely red maple, elm, pin oak. . . . Swamp white oak was a component here also, while black gum occurred in most of the swamps of the entire oak region."[62]

Swamps were not favorite places of the settlers, as in the following 1600s description of a swamp near Ipswich, Massachusetts: "[Ipswich is] situated by a fair River, whose rise is from a Lake or Pond twenty mile up, betaking its course through a hideous *Swamp* for many miles, a Harbour for Bears."[63] Others, such as the Vermont naturalist Zadock Thompson, believed that swamps were sources of sickness and disease and wastelands which were "to a great extent incapable of settlement."[64] It is no wonder then that many swamps have since disappeared. Thompson, for example, reported that in Vermont by the 1850s many had been drained and converted to other uses.

While many of New England's swamps remain today, most of those that are relatively undisturbed are found in northern areas. Two of large size remain in southern New England with, perhaps, still relatively unaltered sections that typify the kinds of swamps that once covered large areas of the region—the hardwood swamp and the Atlantic white cedar swamp.

SWAMPS

The valleys and swamps . . . are low grounds and bottoms infinitely thick set with Trees and Bushes of all sorts for the most part.

—John Josselyn, 1674[60]

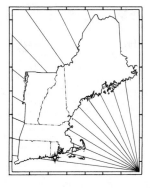

Great Swamp, Rhode Island

There is no underwood saving in the swamps, and low grounds that are wet. . . . Of these swamps, some be ten, some twenty, some thirty miles long, being preserved by the wetnesse of the soile wherein they grow.

—William Wood, 1634[65]

Great Swamp is said to be the largest swamp in New England, covering three thousand acres only five miles from the Atlantic Ocean in southeastern Rhode Island. The area is dominated by dense red maple swampland with some areas of Atlantic white cedar. Its vastness, thick cover of vegetation, wetness, and lack of roads all help to maintain the deep interior of this swamp in a relatively wild condition visited by few people.[66] Here one can find isolation and seclusion. These were, perhaps, exactly the reasons why a band of Narraganset Indians was living here in a winter camp on a fateful day in December 1675—a day when they suffered defeat in a decisive battle of the Indian Colonial wars in southern New England.

Along a swampy trail into the interior of Great Swamp, swollen buds of maples had burst and their red flowers opened. Pools of water filled and coalesced, forming quiet, watery trails into the dense tangle of undergrowth. Overhead a pair of osprey carried twigs and small limbs to a nearby nest under construction. They paused for a moment in their work, cheeping loudly at the disturbance caused by the passing hikers below.

A side trail led through dense woods over a cool, damp ground. The forest floor was a carpet of green with the emergence of herbaceous plants. Ferns, wildflowers, shrubs, and trees—spring aroused all of them. Coyote scat in the trail made me wonder what other life forms haunted the swamp. It is believed that Rhode Island's largest populations of mink, snowshoe hare, and otter live here. Other animals live here as well: white-tailed deer, ruffed grouse, wild turkey, woodcock, ducks, and geese. We hope still others might survive here from earlier times.

The ground became wetter, and the forest opened to an expansive "lawn" of sedges and standing pools of water, covering layers and centuries of sphagnum mosses.

A secluded bog surrounded by Atlantic white cedars provides an opening in Rhode Island's Great Swamp.

Gray-green Atlantic white cedars surrounded the irregular perimeter of the bog and were scattered over its surface. The swamp enclosed and isolated the bog; it was intimate, mysterious, and seemingly impenetrable beyond the wall of evergreens at its edges, unlike the more prevalent, open, and colorful maple-wooded wetlands found in other parts of this swamp.

On another roadway, passing between hardwood swamplands, the high waters of the wet season came to the shoulders of the road. An eastern painted turtle sunned itself on a log, one of many fallen trees in the jumble of deadwood scattered in the swamp. In the distance, a power line intruded on the setting. The road rose slightly to drier land, perhaps only a few inches in elevation but enough to cause a change in the surrounding vegetation. American holly appeared, adding the only bright green to the early awakening of the hardwoods here. In a few weeks it will lose its prominence, becoming only one of many trees in a sea of green. But this evergreen, unlike its hardwood neighbors, is a rarity in Rhode Island and will retain some distinctiveness despite the eventual greening of the swamp around it.

The evergreen leaves of an American holly in Rhode Island's Great Swamp give it a noticeable presence before the surrounding hardwoods leaf out.

Soon the road dipped to a lower elevation, and, not unexpectedly, wet swampland once again bordered the roadside, for two-thirds of Great Swamp is wet land. This is the secret of why such a large piece of wild land still exists in the midst of such a densely populated state, a secret not unnoticed by William Wood over three and a-half centuries ago when he observed that the swamps are "preserved by the wetness of the soil."

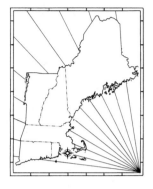

Acushnet Cedar Swamp, Massachusetts

The 3d month 23d day 1789 Laid out half an acre of Land to James Hathway on the N.E. Side of Accushnet Great Cedar swamp.

—Samuel Smith, 1789[67]

It is likely that the surveyor Samuel Smith was intimately aware of the untamed, densely wooded character of Acushnet Cedar Swamp at the edge of New Bedford. It is also safe to say he never imagined that two hundred years after he surveyed this swamp, it would be protected and given National Natural Landmark status as "one of Massachusetts' largest, wildest and most impenetrable swamps."[68] A recent study of Atlantic white cedar wetlands in Massachusetts reported that this swamp "has long been recognized as one of the best remaining examples of the extensive cedar wetlands of southeastern Massachusetts. . . . [and] The interior of the swamp is largely undisturbed."[69] This was the relict of Atlantic white cedar swamp that I had hoped to find.

Dark, acid waters sloshed within inches of the top of my hip boots. The corduroy tote road was dry when we started out, but it had become a long, straight corridor of water, narrowed to a few feet wide by thick, overhanging limbs. My guide, a Massachusetts forester, was ahead, testing the depth of the water with every step. As I wrote this, Thomas Morton's words, written in 1637, came to mind: "If any man be desirous to finde out in what part of the Country the best cedars are, he must get into the bottom grounds, and in vallies that are wet at the spring of the yeare."[70] He couldn't have said it better.

We still had almost a mile to go, and the water remained consistently deep. I remember that Samuel Smith's survey notation was written in March when the ground was probably still frozen, and for good reason. We slogged on. Somewhere in this swamp, perhaps at our destination, we would find a contemporary of Samuel Williams—an old cedar that some believe dates back to the 1770s, one that the surveyor might even have seen. One grove of Atlantic white cedars was discovered here with trees over eighty feet high, measuring twelve to twenty-six inches in diameter and dating back to the late 1700s. The original cedars are now likely gone. Many were cut when the nearby Turner Pond Dam was put in sometime before 1794. When the pond was drained in the 1970s to dredge out accumulated sediments, primeval stumps were discovered. One dated back to 1509. A red maple stump measured over five feet in diameter. Stumps were also discovered in another place where a brook had cut a channel down into the peat. One stump there had 276 annual rings, yet it was but thirteen inches in diameter.

The water became shallower, and I sensed that we were, at last, nearing the "island," one of two rises of land deep within the swamp. Within minutes we reached the dry land of Holly Island, so named because of the abundance of American holly there. Trees of this species are up to eight inches in diameter and twenty-five feet tall. The island is small—one and a half to two acres. It's also populated with large hemlock, black gum (or tupelo), yellow birch, red maple, beech, sassafras, and sweet pepper. At least seventy-eight species of plants have been identified on this small piece of dry land, along with signs of white-tailed deer, snowshoe hare, red fox, great horned owl, and, perhaps, bobcat. Over twenty years ago, the naturalist John Richardson, who had explored throughout this swamp and island, expressed my own feelings as I stood on the island alone for a moment while my companion searched the surrounding swamp for the largest cedars: "The water is high, the going rough and wet but the unspoiled beauty, the subtle changes of light and shadow, the color, the odors, the songs of birds and the mental knowledge of your isolation is a supreme natural experience."[71]

My guide called to me from the other side of the island. We called back and forth to give me direction. The going was wet through a profusion of royal and cinnamon ferns and dense growths of sweet pepper and other shrubs. I crossed a small, wet opening covered with deep beds of sphagnum mosses and bordered by clumps of colorful blue flag. At the edge of another small rise in the swamp, we found our old cedars. Some were nearly a foot and a half in diameter. Surrounded by pools of water and mossy, fern-covered hummocks, they rose sixty, seventy, perhaps,

Deep within Acushnet Cedar Swamp State Reservation near New Bedford, Massachusetts, Austin Mason of the state's Division of Forests and Parks examines an old Atlantic white cedar.

eighty feet above the floor of the swamp. Their trunks, covered with long strands of green-gray bark, stood tall and graceful beneath short, conically shaped, symmetrical crowns. Below, I stood deep in water in a jungle of green vegetation.

We found our way back to the old tote road by following our footprints in the deep moss. Some time later, we stopped by the High Hill Road Bridge that passes over Turner Pond. "The vista north over the pond and bog to the big cedars and beyond," wrote John Richardson in his report to the National Park Service on the potential of the swamp as a national landmark, "imparts a true feeling of wilderness. The view is spacious, emotional and wild—full of beauty, interest and meaning." He spoke for all of us who have seen this swamp or who will be merely satisfied in just knowing that it exists.

FORESTS

The Firre and Pine bee trees that grow in many places, shooting up exceeding high, especially the pine. . . . I have seene of these stately highgrowne trees, ten miles together close by the River side.

—William Wood, 1634[72]

The forests dominated the early New England landscape and the eyes and minds of the European settlers and visitors. We were left with many descriptions and impressions of the early forests and have since tried to confirm them through scientific means. We know that the forests were extensive and that some of the trees were extremely large and had other unique and desirable qualities. We also know that the forests varied in their composition from north to south and from the ocean to inland. The forests were dynamic and subject to changes in climate in the long term and by wind, fire, and disease in the short term. Thus, the forests changed through the centuries. We know that as they changed during the past four hundred years, so did our attitudes towards them. In recent times, we have come to value the relics of the forests that once existed. We are learning how to locate, identify, protect, and learn from them. Such is our relationship with New England's forests.

Our first descriptions of New England's forests came early, when exploration and settlement had just begun. In southern New England, an account of a trip by the Puritans from Plymouth to Rhode Island in 1621 and published in 1622 described a region of "much good Timber both Oake, Waltnut-tree, Firre, Beech, and exceeding great

Chessnut-trees. . . . And . . . wilde and over-growne with woods."[73] In northern New England, where settlement didn't occur until the late 1700s and early 1800s, reliable descriptions of the unharvested forests came from land surveyors and timber cruisers. For example, the original land surveys of township lines in northern Vermont, as well as surveys of lots within townships of Chittenden County in that state, tell us the composition of the forests and their distribution. From them we learn what tree species existed along lot boundaries, their sizes, and other information describing the forests. Beech, it was found, comprised more than 40 percent of the original forest in that area.[74]

In northern Maine, government land surveys conducted between 1793 and 1827 provided sufficient data for an estimation of the composition of the presettlement forest in that region. Thus, we know that for a large section of northern Maine a fairly stable virgin forest existed. At least 50 percent of it consisted of roughly equal amounts of spruce species, balsam fir, American beech, northern white cedar, and yellow birch. Approximately 10 percent was burned land of birch-aspen forest, and almost 3 percent was windblown.[75] In western Maine, one timber cruiser exploring a township in 1851 reported that "this town is watered by a stream which takes its rise in the southwest quarter. . . . The soil is about half second quality, the other half third quality. . . . The south half . . . contains a number of high mountains. . . . The growth is spruce, fir, birch, beech. . . . The quantity of pine timber is estimated at 600,000, which is all on the east half."[76]

In New Hampshire, as late as 1874, the geologist Charles Hitchcock mapped the uncut forests in and around that state. He found that they occupied "most of Essex County, Vt., the adjacent townships of Quebec, and nearly twenty townships" in northern New Hampshire, with smaller patches scattered throughout the state.[77]

The early, firsthand reports not only inform us of the expanse of the "original" forest covering New England and its geographic differences, but they tell us about the many large and old trees that it contained. In 1857, Henry David Thoreau measured a white birch at Pine Stream

Location of beech trees from land surveys, 1763–1802, in Chittenden County, Vermont. Beech was one of the species used as bearing and witness trees by surveyors running original lot lines. Town-line surveyors marked trees every mile on the township lines and at each township corner. Trees marked directly on the line were called bearing trees. If a suitable tree was not on the line at the mile point or corner, a stake was used and a nearby tree, called a witness tree, was marked. Because beech trees were plentiful in the early forest of Chittenden County, there was a greater probability that they would be selected as bearing and witness trees. Large gaps in the distribution of beech trees on the map are due to absence of survey records for some areas. Redrawn and reprinted, by permission, from Thomas G. Siccama, "Presettlement and Present Forest Vegetation in Northern Vermont with Special Reference to Chittenden County," *The American Midland Naturalist* 85 (1) (1971).

This 1855 drawing of a giant white oak, called the Charter Oak, in Hartford, Connecticut, is an example of our fascination with large old trees. Illustration from George B. Emerson, *A Report on the Trees and Shrubs Growing Naturally in the Forests of Massachusetts*, vol. 1 (Boston, Mass.: Little, Brown, and Company, 1875).

Falls on the West Branch of the Penobscot in northern Maine; it was over four and a half feet in diameter.[78] Charles Hitchcock gave dimensions for a number of large trees, including a chestnut tree in Amherst, Massachusetts, measuring 7 feet in diameter where it was cut at the butt; an elm in Greenland, New Hampshire, 8½ feet in diameter at 6 feet above the ground; a hemlock in Moultonborough, New Hampshire, 90 feet in length and over 290 years old; a red oak in West Concord, New Hampshire, 5 feet in diameter at the butt; a maple in Peterborough, New Hampshire, 3 feet in diameter with 370 annual rings; and a spruce tree in Littleton, New Hampshire, 130 feet tall and 16 inches in diameter at 65 feet above the ground.[79] The most majestic tree, however, towering over all others in the forest, was the white pine. Yale president Timothy Dwight, during his travels through New England in the late 1700s and early 1800s, was told of a white pine 264 feet in height in Lancaster, New Hampshire.[80]

The old forests of New England also impressed its early inhabitants with other qualities. Jeremy Belknap, commenting in 1792 on the pleasing nature of the American forest, remarked on "the silence that reigns through it. In a calm day, no sound is heard but that of running water, or perhaps the chirping of a squirrel, or the squalling of a jay."[81] Edward Hitchcock, who roamed the New England countryside in his career as a geologist in the 1800s, wrote that "perhaps no country in the world exhibits in its autumnal scenery, so rich a variety of colors in the foliage of trees, as our own. But it is particularly beautiful in the more mountainous parts of the land."[82]

Snapshots of our forests from these first-recorded observations, however, do not give us a complete picture of their character and changing nature. We have already seen from our studies of pollen, climate, and historic records that they were dynamic. And we have learned that, in the long term, climate probably has had the greatest effect since the last period of glaciation. Over shorter time periods, wind, storms, fire, disease, and animals, such as grazing insects and pond-building beavers, took their toll. We know, for example, that major hurricanes likely occurred every fifty to one hundred years and were more severe in southeastern sections of New England and less so in northeastern areas.

Especially damaging hurricanes are known to have swept across New England in 1400, 1635, 1815, and 1938. The 1938 hurricane leveled several old-growth forests, including a highly valued primeval forest in southwestern New Hampshire that contained trees up to 150 feet tall, 4 feet in diameter, and more than 300 years old.[83]

Fire also has had a long history of widespread impact on New England's forests. Sediment studies of charcoal, surveyors' records, and historic accounts have all helped document major fires in the region. For example, surveyors' records for northern Maine show two large fires in 1825—one burning twelve thousand acres along the Seboeis River and another of four thousand acres along the Penobscot River.[84] Of particular interest is the extent of burning by Native Peoples. Historic accounts, analysis of fire scars in tree-ring studies, pollen studies, and charcoal counts have been used, along with archaeological research, in efforts to show a link between fires and natives. Studies of native population density, for example, appear to show a parallel with fire frequency in some locations. We now know with a fair degree of certainty that burning was carried out by Indian populations, but studies are not conclusive in showing the extent of burning.[85]

Pathogens have had infrequent effects, but when they occurred, they were devastating. Prior to European settlement, the major event involving disease happened in the hemlock population about 4,800 years ago. The species was reduced to a low level, from which it recovered in 1,000 to 1,500 years. Currently, the tree is declining again due to the eastern hemlock looper, an insect. Two species to suffer greatly since European settlement are the American chestnut and the American elm. The chestnut was almost completely obliterated around the turn of the twentieth century.

With the arrival of the Europeans, widespread removal of the New England forests began. We have already learned that, as early as 1603, Martin Pring and his crew began harvesting sassafras around Plymouth Harbor.[86] When settlement began and spread across New England, the clearing and harvesting increased with a fierce intensity. Not only was the wood used domestically, but great quantities were exported to Europe, the West Indies, Nova Scotia, and Africa. In a two-year period, from October 1, 1789, to October 1, 1791, almost three-hundred-thousand dollars worth of pine boards, oak planking, staves, clapboards, shingles, hoops, oak rafters, pine and oak timber frames for houses, pine masts, spruce spars, wooden wagons, cart wheels, yokes and bows, and wooden boats were shipped out of the New Hampshire port of Pascataqua.[87] By 1874 even the New Hampshire state geological report warned that "the destruction of the forests by the ax and by fire is becoming a matter of serious consideration."[88] By 1880 all of the New England states except Maine had lost half or more of their forest cover.[89] In Vermont in 1853, Zadock Thompson discussed in detail the effects of this cutting on flooding: "It is a well known fact that the freshets in Vermont are more sudden and violent than when the country was new."[90]

Today, the forests of New England have rebounded and cover a large portion of the countryside with new generations of growth, but the amount of uncut, old-growth forest that still survives is only a tiny fraction of the region's forest cover. For the northeast, it is estimated to be less than a tenth of one percent.[91] One forest ecologist estimates that only six-tenths of one percent of the northern forest escaped cutting.[92]

How does one identify an untouched forest—an old-growth forest? What characteristics does it exhibit? Ecologists and researchers of such forests have identified a number of criteria. Among the more important are the following: (1) no evidence of human disturbance exists on the site or in archival records, (2) uneven-aged trees are present but dominant, late-successional species have reached at least half their maximum age, (3) a high density of species exists at all levels, (4) gaps in the forest exist because of blowdowns, (5) downed logs and standing dead trees are conspicuous, (6) soils are undisturbed, and (7) the floor of the forest displays a rolling topography of pits and mounds produced by decaying wind-thrown trees. The forest ecologist Charles Cogbill reminds us, however, that these remnant forests—ancestral forests as he prefers to call them—are generally unrepresentative of the original forests. They were often left uncut because they were unproductive, inaccessible, or contained uneconomical species. In addition, today they are likely to have been affected by air pollution, pathogens, exotic species, changes in fire frequency, and the absence of influential native species.[93]

Nevertheless, the remnants of our original forest possess a number of values. Much has been written of their scientific worth. They serve as a baseline against which studies of ecological processes can be compared, such as the recycling of nutrients and flow of energy. They provide opportunities to reconstruct forest history. They make possible studies to identify species uniquely associated with them. They serve as experimental controls for forest management practices. There are other values as well. The remnants of our ancestral forest are part of our heritage, our history. They are vestiges of the forest in which Native Americans lived and which the first Europeans explored and settled. The historian Frederick Jackson Turner contended that our forests made a significant impact on America's culture and institutions.[94]

Our old forests also have an ethical dimension. By preserving them, we demonstrate a respect for their uniqueness as natural communities and their right to exist relatively free of human interference. Psychologically, our ancient forests provide a kind of stability—a connection in space and time with a place that seems unchanging. They provide a place for us to slow our thinking and reflect on our lives and the world around us.[95]

What remnants of New England's forests exist today that demonstrate our will to set them aside for their tangible and intangible values? The following represent some of the diversity of what remains.

Big Reed Forest Reserve, Maine

The part of the township East of a line drawn from the N.E. corner to the 2 mile tree in the south line is covered with a dense growth of spruce, fir, cedar, larch, alder, birch & pine.

—Zebulon Brodley and Edwin Rose, 1833[96]

The way in is by map and compass; no roads go into this nearly five-thousand-acre tract of old-growth forest. It is the way Brodley and Rose went in, and if they could go into this forest today, it is quite possible they would see little change. In the opinion of forest ecologist Charles Cogbill, who has studied old-growth forests throughout northern New England, "The nature of the original landscape can perhaps best be seen in the . . . Big Reed Forest Preserve in northern Maine." He further noted that its forest "communities, as well as the dominance of spruce and sugar maple, are amazingly similar to presettlement description of the same region."[97]

The hillside is steep here near one of the knobs of Reed Mountain, and the group I was with made its way slowly down the slope. Sunshine streamed in through the tall hardwoods in this forest community. The Big Reed tract has other communities not dominated by forest but with wetlands, streams, and ponds. Variety is one of the valued characteristics of this reserve. In the forest community, beech, yellow birch, and sugar maple are most prevalent. One sugar maple somewhere in this reserve began its life before 1770, sixty-plus years before Brodley and Rose made their survey.

A blowdown impeded our downhill progress. A large, arching root framed a view of the massive, downed tree and the others it took with it. A strong smell of damp earth permeated the air as I stopped for a moment to inspect its roots and the huge hole it produced. It was not the first downed tree we would encounter before reaching the pond. The lumpy surface of the hillside suggests a long history of such disturbances. "Old growth mostly fallen down," noted Brodley and Rose. Records show that a hurricane had swept through in 1815, eighteen years before they surveyed the area, and a fire in 1816. Before those catastrophes, a serious spruce budworm infestation hit the area and since then, two more. Disturbance is a regular occurrence here as it was in the original forest that blanketed the north woods before the surveyors and lumbermen arrived. For this reason, the average age of the old trees in the reserve is about 180 years.

Lower down on the slope the vegetation became

denser. It being the end of June, the trees and shrubs were nearly leafed out. Finding our direction became more difficult. We took another compass reading before moving on. A giant yellow birch appeared ahead—tall and straight, reaching into the canopy. Its rough and platy bark showed the rigors of age. A large, double-topped red spruce came next. The top of a moss-covered dead cedar lay in the fork of a spruce where it fell years ago. The spruce had now grown around it, clenching it in a death-vise. Many dead trees were standing, leaning, and down.

The cedar signaled a change in the forest. The land became swampy, and northern white cedars became more prevalent. The forest floor was covered with mossy logs. The beautiful, rare orchid fairy slipper, or calypso, lives in this cedar swamp. Two deteriorating stumps covered with fallen branches and green with moss provided the first evidence of cutting we'd seen. Historic records indicate little cutting or evidence of roads in this reserve. It was passed over during the initial cuts of the mid-1800s. There was little white pine, that much sought-after "gold nugget" of the forest, and no nearby stream presented an opportunity to float logs. For more than a century, the logging roads skirted or stopped short of the core of this tract. The extent to which incursions were made is not completely known, but ground observation also suggests that little cutting occurred here.

The cedars were thick in the lowland near the stumps, but none of us were prepared for the breathtaking encounter that soon occurred. A gigantic cedar—over four feet in diameter (fifty-two inches to be exact) at the base—filled an opening in the forest. The tree's bark was long and stringy and spiraled up the trunk. On one side, a long strand had sprung away from the tree and bowed outward. I imagine few have seen a cedar of these proportions.

A brook flowed through the swamp. The land was level and wet. The woods seemed brighter ahead. A ledge led to a rocky point, covered with cedars, and to the edge of Big Reed Pond. The view here encompassed almost the entire watershed of the pond, now completely protected. A dense ring of vegetation, mostly conifers, crowded the steep-sided shoreline.

A member of a guided field trip party visiting Big Reed Forest Reserve in northern Maine photographs a gigantic northern white cedar measuring over four feet in diameter at breast height.

To the west, the view across the pond centered on Reed Mountain, over 850 feet higher than the pond. It's part of the rugged terrain for which this reserve is known. From this location on the pond, we could pick out different forest communities—softwoods, hardwoods, mixed softwoods and hardwoods. I saw only conifers on an exposed ridge. On the slope below, primarily hardwoods. Back from the pond's edge, the tops of cedars. It's difficult to imagine that so large an area is uncut wilderness. Thoreau might have seen it like this in 1857 when he canoed through this region only eleven miles to the south. Yet, this pond is in the middle of the largest tract of virgin forest left in New England. It is unlike so many of our old-growth forests that escaped the ax because they were different in some way from the norm. "The rarity of the area," points out Charles Cogbill, "is that it is a typical piece of northern Maine, which does not share the common regional history."

We left the point and followed the ledge back into the woods, away from the shore and towards the road, nearly a mile away. The route passed over the end of a ridge populated by large red spruce and hardwoods. The spruce were magnificent specimens. I have heard that one old spruce in this reserve began its life around 1700 and today is two feet in diameter. We passed other large, old trees covered with mosses and lichens. One researcher reported finding 180 species of lichens in this forest, an unparalleled richness when compared to the surrounding managed forests.[98]

This mature forest is also home to pine martens. Boreal woodpeckers are here, too, the black-backed three-toed and the northern three-toed, both attracted by the many standing dead trees, common to old forests like this. The trek out led through dense and open woods, over and around downed trees, and through openings, some crowded with the shoots of poplars and birches to be nibbled by moose, deer, and snowshoe hares this winter, others filled with raspberries, which, come August, might also attract a bear or two.

Frequent compass checks were required, but soon we climbed the hillside below the road. I understand why unguided visitation is discouraged here: it's easy to become lost. But there is another reason: if we are to retain the wildness of places like this and protect their integrity, then we must protect them from ourselves and tread lightly when we are here.[99]

Old Forests of the Green-Woods, Connecticut

Here the trees are superb. They are hemlocks, and they are so large, so straight, and so tall that I do not believe their equals can be found in all North America.

—Francois Jean, Marquis de Chastellux, 1786[100]

It was actually on January 4, 1781, when Francois Jean, a French writer and veteran of the Seven Years War, discovered the impressive hemlocks that so enthused him. He was on a three-year tour of the United States when he passed through the Green-Woods, a name given in the mid-1700s to the forested region between Canaan Mountain in northwestern Connecticut and the Farmington River.

Timber drew the settlers into this high, hilly country of northern Litchfield County. From early descriptions by travelers and from the records of surveyors, the forest found by the settlers was composed of stands of hemlock and beech and of oak, chestnut, and hickory. From settlement time to the present, the forests have been extensively harvested. It was, therefore, something short of astonishing when my inquiries revealed the possibility that two small relicts of that ancient forest of the Green-Woods might still exist near its western edge on the Canaan Mountain plateau.

We left the truck at the end of the road and entered a swamp. I followed a forester who worked in this country. The dark evergreens and the overcast sky created a pall over the swamp. We crossed a brook. A dwarf ginseng plant caught my eye as we passed by. Gradually the land got higher, and soon we came up onto a knoll and into a stand of huge hemlock trees. A scattering of beech and striped maple struggled for light beneath them. One old yellow birch and a few beech had successfully made it through the canopy. Large boulders lay on a bed of dead needles and twigs beneath the trees. A bright opening on

The author stands beside an immense hemlock located in a three-acre stand of virgin trees at the edge of an old beaver flowage in northwestern Connecticut.

the other side of the knoll drew me through the grove by a large clump of mountain laurel and down onto the decaying dam of an old beaver flowage. Already, reclamation by the forest was well underway.

We explored the forest. It is small; only three acres escaped cutting. One hemlock, especially, caught our attention, growing between moss-covered boulders on the bank overlooking the beaver meadow. It is a superlative specimen, perhaps forty inches in diameter and eighty feet high. A close examination revealed evidence that it had been cored. I had already learned that cores had been extracted from trees here and age determinations made. A tree that died here in 1935 had begun growing in 1638. Some of these hemlocks are believed to have originated in the seventeenth and eighteenth centuries. I counted at least a dozen of these denizens.

Later in the day in a hilly area three miles north of the swamp and its secluded knoll of hemlock, we entered a steep hillside ravine. Our destination was another relict forest three times as large—nine acres. The ravine was bordered on one side by a high ledge. Large white maple, red oak, and black cherry trees grew on the steep slope. Beneath the trees on the floor of the ravine rested large boulders. Everywhere between the rocks and trees grew a lush carpet of ferns.

At the bottom of the ravine, the going became easier. We crossed a well wooded swampy area and came to a small knoll near the edge of a pond. Large hemlocks covered the knoll to the water's edge. Behind the knoll on a hillside, we came to a gigantic red oak, at least four feet in diameter. Penetrating the forest farther along the side of the hill, we saw below a grove of immense hemlock trees. The trees rose to heights exceeding 110 feet. Some trees were over three feet in diameter. Studies have shown that some trees here began growing in the 1600s. One hemlock that blew down in 1950 was 335 years old.

The canopy in some places is 80 percent closed, "giving the stands a grand gloomy aspect," wrote one visitor. In these places the understory is open, thinly populated with striped maple, hobblebush, and maple-leaved viburnum. On the humpy, needle-covered ground, a sparse growth of herbaceous plants includes lily-of-the-valley, shining club moss, princess pine, and a smattering of ferns.

We paused awhile among the hemlocks. Rays of sunlight penetrated the canopy and dappled the tree trunks and the forest floor, flickering here and there as a light breeze rustled the branches above. A large downed hem-

These giant hemlocks in northwestern Connecticut are in a nine-acre virgin forest harboring trees that began growing in the 1600s.

lock behind us was a reminder that the wind is not always as gentle nor the forest as peaceful. One wonders why this remnant forest remains. The surrounding forests have been cut repeatedly from the mid-1800s. Was it because of the quality of the wood or logging difficulties? Was it an appreciation of its beauty and majestic nature? For whatever reason, this old stand and its isolated counterpart on the undisturbed knoll a few miles south allow us the opportunity to capture the flavor of the Green-Woods extracted by those who first visited here.[101]

The Berkshire Wilderness, Massachusetts

We set out from thence toward Albany the nearest way through ye woods. . . . Ye greatest part of our road this day was a hideous howling wilderness.

—Rev. Benjamin Wadsworth, August 1694[102]

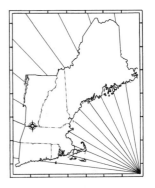

Wild and forbidding, pastoral and inviting—two views of the Berkshire Hills in western Massachusetts call attention to a three-hundred-year change in land and mind. But even today traces of earlier attitudes and physical realities still linger within the hidden recesses of this country's sharply dissected topography. Forests of trees are still living from that time when the Reverend Wadsworth accompanied a group of Massachusetts commissioners to a conference of the colonies in Albany. When one comes into these original woods, the mind forms a vivid image of the high, rough, pathless wilderness that halted the frontier here until the mid-1700s.

Change is not new to these hilly uplands carved from the eroded roots of ancient Taconic mountains. From that once high, craggy range and its progressive reformation into flat plains, uplifted plateaus, and glaciated, deeply incised highlands, the Berkshires, as we know them today, emerged as distinctive features of the New England landscape.

For the past eight thousand years, a mixed northern hardwood-coniferous forest has clothed the northern region of these hills. Beech, sugar maple, yellow and white birch, white pine, hemlock, and other species still nestle in the valleys and cling to the steep hillsides. And, amazingly, despite the rigors of fires, hurricanes, disease, and 250 years of clearing the land, pockets still remain of pristine forest untouched by human hands.

I remember my anticipation on the way to one of these secluded places—a cove, as it is called, containing the headwaters of Fife Brook. Indeed, it looked like a cove when my companions and I gazed into it from a back-country road. And I was struck at that moment by the aptness of the term "cove": here I saw a safe haven for a forest.

Steep slopes surrounded the basin and dropped sharply to a narrow V. Below me, beneath a crush of fallen boulders and a tangle of vegetation, earthy-hued from the November frosts, the brook rushed noisily. To my right, the sun cast its low, morning light on the south-facing slope. Somewhere on that hillside, near its top, our ancient forest stood—the remnant of a "hideous howling wilderness."

Slashwise, across the "close" contours of our map, we struggled up the steeply inclined slope. Newly fallen leaves, as frictionless as an ice-glazed walkway, forced a hand-holding intimacy with every limb and trunk within reach. We rested briefly, finding secure footing in a large pit where the roots of a gigantic tree had been torn from the ground when it toppled. Now, only a long mound of earth showed where it had fallen.

The November sun shone warmly on the steep slope, angled perpendicularly to the rays of incoming light. Here the warm soil was favorable to a deciduous forest and, to our surprise, to a plant in flower. On a brightly lit, sheltered ledge among protruding garnets, a pale corydalis still bloomed. Its delicate pink and yellow blossoms were as unexpected as the forest that was discovered here.

The hemlock grove we entered leaned against the sharp incline of the hill. The trees stood tall and stately, but one caught my eye. Its girth was immense—over ten feet around. Since the late 1500s, it had stood in this place, each year strengthening its grip on the uneasy hillside. I wondered what it had witnessed during those four hundred years.

We walked on, in and out of groves of conifers and stands of hardwoods—a few very old, others young, and some dead, still standing upright or lying where they had fallen. We paused at a 1700s sugar maple, its yellowing crown towering more than one hundred feet above the forest floor. Beneath, clumps of maidenhair ferns added patches of bright green to the muted hues of fallen leaves. We passed another maple, alive during Reverend Wadsworth's trip; an old, black cherry more than two feet in diameter; a grove of ancient oak high up on the hillside; huge birches; and an aged hornbeam. A hemlock log lay wedged between boulders and trees, stretching a hundred feet across the side of the hill. We counted more than 250 rings. Here was an old-growth forest of magnificent diversity—one of the finest examples in Massachusetts, I was told.

Robert T. Leverett, an old-growth forest sleuth, examines a large hemlock tree over four hundred years old in the headwaters of Fife Brook located in the Berkshire Hills of western Massachusetts.

The sun settled quickly over the hill, and with the enveloping shadows came an instant chill. We headed back, dropping down toward the bottom of the cove and closer to the sound of the flume below. The ruts of an old wood road showed faintly between mature trees; the forest's reclamation was nearly finished. The road had stopped here, the loggers unable to continue beyond the barrier of slope and ledge. Clearly, all who value those old trees on the hillside above us owe a debt to terrain.

Later I learned that one of the region's first settlers, Mrs. Jonathan Taylor, used to converse with contemporaries of the old Fife Brook trees. It was said that she worried she would lose her power of conversation to the effects of isolation. Two hundred and fifty years later, four of us sought the isolation of that old Berkshire forest so that the trees of Mrs. Taylor's time might talk to us. And they did. Those trees—those original inhabitants of a wilderness barrier once called hideous and howling— helped us to see even more clearly the need to overcome the cultural barriers that separate us from nature.

Gifford Woods, Vermont

The sun arose, and soon the clouds dispersed, and we beheld immediately around us an unbroken wilderness.

—Albert D. Hager, 1861[103]

In the shadow of Killington Peak, where Albert Hager and his party stood, lies a tiny, fragile pocket of that unbroken wilderness they saw in 1861—a fragment that to this day remains essentially undisturbed. "One of the few remaining virgin sugar maple-beech climax forests in Northeastern United States," reported one botanist who visited it.[104] And at the conclusion of a seven-year study, two other researchers were also taken by this small stand of primeval woods: "The grandeur of its trees and general impressiveness of the forest make it a unique and interesting forest remnant characteristic of much of the original forest cover of the state."[105]

One often thinks of virgin woods as remote and isolated, to be entered with compass and map and prepared for emergency. I found, instead, an eight-and-a-half-acre strip of old forest squeezed between a busy highway and a pond. But I soon found that what it lacked in size it more than made up for in the enormity of its trees.

I came into this trailless woods from the south end on a very showery day in early June. The woods were dull and wet, but when the sun poked through, as it did occasionally, the forest radiated phosphorescent hues of green. Inside, one is immediately aware of the trees. The force of their presence comes from their size, dominating all aspects of the forest. Most are maples, up to a hundred feet tall, and many are over three feet through. I measured one, which turned out to be ten feet around. Most of the giants

Two aged white maples (sugar maples), over three feet through, grow in Gifford Woods, a tiny fragment of Vermont's original unbroken wilderness. Maidenhair ferns flank the base of one of them.

are over two hundred years old. A beech here was aged at 241 years. And a hemlock, almost three feet in diameter, began its life almost four and a half centuries ago in the mid-1500s when the first Europeans were exploring the New England coast.

Although the sugar maples make up 87 percent of this forest, many American beech and yellow birch are here as well. I also saw large white ash, black cherry, and other hardwood species. Hobblebush, beaked hazel, and striped maple grow in the understory with young hardwoods. Interestingly, in the deep shade beneath some of these trees, many of the saplings only an inch in diameter are thirty to fifty years old.

I wandered on through the forest. On one side through the trees I caught glimpses of the pond; on the other I could hear the nearby sounds of traffic. A blow-down lay in my path, and in the opening created by its death, the understory had come to life, crowding the opening with persistent opportunism. Farther along, I stopped to admire two large maples. Their bark no longer displayed the large, rough, defined scales of younger trees. Now the scales were smaller, smoother, and flakier. Mosses crept up their trunks. Maidenhair ferns clustered delicately around their bases. There are seventeen species of ferns and club mosses on this forest floor and sixty-four flowering plants, including lily-of-the-valley, Indian cucumber root, jack-in-the-pulpit, blue cohosh, and several species of violets. The soil in which they sink their roots is moist and black and teeming with earthworms. As I walked, I felt its softness. I came to a wet seep, a brooklet, hardly discernible beneath the ferns and flowering plants. Above me the highway seemed busier. I checked my watch. The commuter traffic was homeward bound. Time had slipped away while the woods turned it back. But that is why I came here—for a kind of time warp.[106]

Wilderness Forest of the Upper Connecticut Lakes, New Hampshire

The view from the summit is extensive. . . . To the west . . . there is a succession of undulating ridges and hills, which, with their shadows and ever-changing color, give a peculiar charm to the scene;—then, in the midst of the forests, those sheets of water that we can see are the Connecticut lakes. . . . the whole country, is one vast wilderness.

—Charles H. Hitchcock, 1874[107]

Deep within the "vast wilderness" Charles Hitchcock saw from the top of Rump Mountain in the headwaters of the Connecticut Lakes, at least one tract of virgin forest remains. A small, alder-choked stream flows quietly along the edge of this 146-acre magnificent spruce-fir forest located only a few miles from the Canadian border.

This is not an easy forest to find, much less to enter. It requires a measure of the persistence demonstrated by those early geologists, surveyors, and wood cruisers who first penetrated this wild country. Yesterday, I wrote about another virgin forest, Gifford Woods, which I had visited in Vermont. I found the forest without trouble beside a paved, well-traveled road. I easily traversed its eight and a half acres through open hardwoods. Today, I write about a piece of primeval forest of more northerly country.

To reach it I first acquired maps and detailed information about road gates, road conditions, distances, and parking. Fortunately I own a four-wheel-drive vehicle, otherwise I could never have driven over the washed-out culverts and deeply eroded gullies on the unimproved road that leads to the trail that would take me to the forest. I clocked mileages carefully to identify the location where I should park. Once on foot, alders almost obliterated the old logging road I followed, and I soon found that "on foot" meant crawling on hands and knees beneath a morass of bent shrubs and crisscrossed limbs for a good portion of the quarter-mile to the stream. At that point, I balanced with my tripod and backpack on the remaining timbers of an old, washed-out bridge and crossed it in a swarm of black flies and mosquitoes. At last I came to a well-marked boundary line and entered the forest, only to find a chaotic jumble of blowdowns packed with impenetrable young firs with deep holes beneath them, camouflaged by layers of moss.

At last I came to a section of large, old balsam firs. Firs dominate this forest, and specimens measure up to two feet in diameter and seventy to eighty feet tall. The going was easier here through the understory of small firs. Fewer recent blowdowns made progress easier, but I knew by the unevenness of the thick mosses on the forest floor that

The headwaters of the Connecticut Lakes in northern New Hampshire rise deep in the mountains, where a 146-acre virgin spruce-fir forest is now protected from human disturbance.

buried beneath me were generations of trees that didn't survive the winds and competition. The blanket of mosses was spongy, and I sank deeply into it with every noiseless step. The base of every large, standing tree was surrounded by a mound of mosses and liverworts.

I stopped to photograph a deep carpet of sphagnum moss covered with common wood sorrel, perhaps the most abundant herbaceous plant in this forest. There are other flowering herbs that I saw—clintonia, bunchberry, goldthread, and Canada mayflower. A few ferns, including the shield fern, sprouted from the forest floor. The plants here are those that can survive in cold weather, short growing seasons, and deep snows of winter. Though there are fewer red spruce than fir in this forest, the mature spruce are impressive, reaching ninety feet in height. Both black and white spruce are present but in lesser numbers. Paper birch and yellow birch also grow here. The shrub layer is sparse, limited mainly to scattered mountain ash, mountain maple, bristly black currant, red osier dogwood, speckled alder, and raspberry.[108]

I saw no wildlife that day, but as a consolation I'm now reminded of Charles Hitchcock's thoughts when he, too, experienced a day in this forest without the pleasure of a wildlife encounter:

To-day we see no sign of animal life, and the songs of birds, even, break not the stillness of these deep solitudes, to-morrow we may be carried away in ecstacies of delight as the song of the hermit thrush greets the ear, or we wonder at the extraordinary volume of song that the little winter wren puts forth; and as we see its diminutive size, we mark the force of the comparison of the Indian who said that, if he had strength in proportion as this bird has power to sing, he could move the world.[109]

Later, as I gain the high ground where my truck is parked and look over the spires of firs in the forest below, I think of Hitchcock's faith in tomorrow. This is the value of this remnant woodland: it will remain undisturbed by human hands and so can evolve as it will.

Crawford Notch Virgin Forest, New Hampshire

My father and I made a foot path from the Notch out through the woods.

—Ethan Allen Crawford, May 1819[110]

I came into the ravine in late afternoon. It was early June, and Gibbs Brook still retained some of its spring high, making it known who controls this steep-walled cut in the mountainside. I heard its noisy cascades long before I arrived here. On my way, the trail had taken me through a forest of previously cut red spruce, but here in the ravine, I knew the forest was virgin. It survived the extensive logging that removed most of the original forests below four thousand feet.

I began my hike in the ravine at about two thousand feet up the Crawford Path out of Crawford Notch. Mt. Washington is six air-miles away. The path follows the brook along the side of the ravine. Many others have come this way, for it is said to be the oldest continuously used hiking path in New England.[111] The path is steep and rocky, surrounded by many large red spruce and yellow birch. Some spruces are two and a half feet in diameter and grow to eighty feet high. There are also large hemlocks; one of New England's oldest hemlocks, dating to the 1400s, supposedly survives here. This is not an easy accomplishment, for storms rip with devastating fury up this ravine. I saw dead wood, standing and down, throughout this forest. Snags with broken tops were common.

Understandably, many openings are in the canopy. Here grow mountain ash, hobblebush, and mountain maple. In one such opening on a knoll next to a storm-flattened tree, I stopped to admire and photograph a clump of white moccasin flowers, painted trilliums, and star flowers. Though it's not unusual to see them by themselves, here these flowers made a rare and beautiful display of togetherness.

The path continued by a small falls. When it reaches twenty-five hundred feet, the vegetation begins to take on a subalpine character. The hemlocks are left behind, and the trees become progressively shorter. Patches of virgin spruce have been discovered at this elevation, some with trees over two hundred years old. They escaped the ax when this path was made. So when you pass through here, be reminded that you touch the entire history of hiking in these mountains.[112]

An assemblage of flowering starflowers, white moccasin flowers, and painted trilliums huddle next to a fallen tree in Gibbs Brook old-growth forest in New Hampshire's Crawford Notch. Large red spruce, hemlocks, and yellow birch grow here.

A Chestnut Forest from the Past, Maine

Chestnutt: of this sorte there is very greate plenty.

—Thomas Morton, 1837[113]

The American chestnut was a major component of the southern New England forest when Thomas Morton noted it in his book, and its presence was mentioned in many early accounts. Even Champlain, entering Lake Champlain in 1609, reported "many chestnut trees . . . on the shores of the lake."[114]

The chestnut became perhaps the most valued tree in the eastern forest. A vast market grew for its decay-

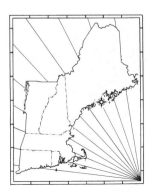

resistant nature of its wood and flavorful nuts. As early as 1672, John Josselyn noted that its nuts are "very sweet in taste and may be (as they usually are) eaten raw; the *Indians* sell them to the *English* for twelve Pence the bushel."[115] The tree also grew to enormous size. In 1848, the Maine botanist Aaron Young mentioned that "there are many . . . in Massachusetts from five to seven feet [in diameter], and a few have attained a diameter of ten feet."[116] By 1920, despite its ubiquitous nature, the American chestnut had almost disappeared from New England's forests, the result of a fungal blight unintentionally brought here in the late 1800s from Asia, most likely on imported plant materials.

Strangely, on a tiny five-acre site in midcoast Maine exists a stand of forty of these trees. Although they are not old, some are relatively large and produce a good crop of seeds. Unfortunately, at this writing, about two-thirds are now infected with the fungus, eroding the hope that they represent a disease-resistant strain. It was the opportunity to experience a reminder of our American chestnut forests of long ago that prompted my visit one spring to this small preserve.

I parked on the street of a residential neighborhood almost within sight of Penobscot Bay. A path led into the woods, and directly ahead a tall American chestnut stood illuminated in an opening. It grew on a low rise of land and beneath were strewn the prickly husks of last year's seed crop. At this time of year it was still too early for the trees' leaves to emerge. Around the small knoll the ground is swampy. Standing pools of water mirrored the surrounding trees. I saw a large hemlock and several pine, red spruce, and fir that cut off the views of nearby homes.

Deeper inside the preserve, I came to a shallow gully and an intermittent stream still being fed by a few patches of melting snow. The ground is humpy, such as one might expect in older forests, though this forest is not exceptionally old. A few old stumps indicate that cutting has occurred, but I have learned that for the past twenty-five years this patch of woods has been largely undisturbed. I encountered a stone wall and moved back into the woods. Here I found more chestnuts, distinctive with their shiny, ridged, dark bark. The dead leaves on the ground beneath

In spring, beneath a rare stand of American chestnuts located in midcoast Maine, the ground is strewn with the prickly husks of the previous year's seed crop.

them are large, narrow, and coarse-toothed. Under some of the trees, I saw spiny, chestnut-colored open husks where seeds had been housed. Other hardwoods live here, too—oaks, maples, and aspen.

It was still too early for most of the herbaceous flowering plants and ferns that would be coming up shortly. I saw no wildlife, but neighbors have reported seeing deer and even a moose. Only the wind brought life to the forest that day. Over its sound, I heard the noise of nearby traffic. When the reigning chestnuts of New England were removed from their position of dominance on the landscape, the sounds of the internal combustion engine had barely begun their assault on our ears. But seeing the chestnuts here brings the mind back to the reality of that time and to an awareness of the changes we've made in our environment.[117]

Big trees to the botanists were of the same interest as immense boulders to the geologists. We still have not lost this fascination with large trees. We are awed when we encounter huge trees, and their age stimulates our imagination of the past. They arouse our aesthetic sensitivities and, for many, encourage calculations of monetary value.

One spring, I stood beside the centerpiece of Pequot Indian councils that were held before New England was settled. It was a white oak, and it had been dead a quarter of a century when I visited in 1994. When Captain John Smith explored the region's coastline, it was forty-five years old. I knew it as the Ledyard Oak, but it has been known also as the Great Oak, the Larabee Oak, the Graves Oak, and the Lester Oak. Every new generation, it seems, needed to give it a new name. I suspect that if we lived that long, we would appreciate a new name occasionally.

The trunk had long shed its bark, and the tree stood there riddled with the scars of time. Its gigantic limbs, once supporting a crown that spread 105 feet, were now pruned to short, gray stubs. Today, they offer support for a few vines that in summer provide a pitiful amount of greenery and shade compared to the tree's once massive crown. Yet, it still retains one awesome dimension—

BIG TREES

A white oak standing . . . in Bolton [Massachusetts], measured, in 1840, nineteen feet just above the roots and fourteen feet at three feet from the ground.

—George B. Emerson, 1875[118]

The awesome hulk of the long-dead Ledyard Oak in Ledyard, Connecticut, stands in a clearing where Pequot Indian councils were held beneath its spreading crown of over one hundred feet.

twenty-one feet of circumference around its trunk—over six and a half feet in diameter. It appears an anomaly today, but when this oak was young, such sizes were common among individuals of its species.

In 1809, the Vermont naturalist Samuel Williams gave some insight into the dimensions of trees that were "esteemed large ones of their kind in this part of America: Maple, 5'-9" [diameter]; elm, 5'-9"; hemlock, 4'-9"; oak, 4'-0"; ash, 4'-0"; and birch, 3'-0"." He also listed a pine (presumably a white pine) at six feet in diameter and 247 feet tall. Williams included a footnote referring to a white pine at Dunstable, New Hampshire, measured in 1736, that had a diameter of seven feet eight inches.[119]

A temptation is to equate size with age, and although it generally holds true that exceptionally large trees are old, small trees growing under poor conditions, such as in deeply shaded understories and in areas of high elevation where soils are thin and conditions are harsh, may be of great age. The question often arises as to what the maximum life expectancies of different tree species are. The following ages in years are given for selected species: black spruce, 250; red pine, 350; white pine, 450; hemlock, 600; sugar maple, 300; northern red oak, 200; beech, 350; red spruce, 400; white spruce, 250; northern white cedar, 400; and pitch pine, 200.[120]

Of all of New England's trees, the white pine is the most impressive. In Maine, which calls itself the Pine Tree State, a number of large, old, pine trees have been discovered during surveys dating back into the 1970s. One of the oldest was discovered near Chesuncook Lake in northern Maine in 1980. At that time, the pine was estimated to be 406 years old and measured 32 inches in diameter at breast height.[121] The largest Maine pine, however, was discovered in the 1970s south of Moosehead Lake. The tree is 18 feet and 2 inches in circumference, or about 5 feet and 9 inches in diameter, and is 147 feet high. In 1988 it was co-champion for the largest white pine in the United States.[122]

New England's white pine tree figured prominently in the region's history in one very special way; it was highly sought after for masts for ships. We now look at one living pine that some believe was once a candidate for a place in the King of England's fleet of tall-masted ships.

The King's Pine, Maine

Ride into a swamp to see a mast drawn of about twenty-six inches or twenty-eight. . . . 'Twas a noble sight.

—Samuel Sewall, September 1687[123]

When Samuel Sewall rode into that swamp in Salmon Falls, Maine, to watch a mast pine being pulled out by teams of oxen, another pine was already being groomed for masthood twenty-five miles away. It grew in a small ravine in the headwaters of the Saco River. Here in the shelter of a steep slope on one side and a small stream on the other, the pine lived through the events that shaped the

A nineteenth-century drawing depicts how trees were once cut and pulled out of the woods by teams of oxen. Illustration from John S. Springer, *Forest Life and Forest Trees* (New York: Harper and Brothers, 1851).

settlement and growth of New England and, of greater relevance to this tree, the colonial interest in mast pines. These pines became so much a part of the economy and so impressed the early settlers that the term "mast pine" presented an image of a certain kind of tree. In 1792, the historian Jeremy Belknap observed that of all the aged and majestic trees, "the most noble is the mast pine. This tree often grows to the height of one hundred and fifty, and sometimes two hundred feet. It is straight as an arrow, and has no branches but very near the top. It is from twenty to forty inches in diameter at its base, and appears like a stately pillar."[124]

In the headwaters of the Saco River in Maine stands an impressive white pine, more than 300 years old and 125 feet high. Some believe that this tree may have been a Broad Arrow Pine, marked in colonial times to become a mast on a ship in England's Royal Navy.

This is what I saw when I entered that ravine one April morning. Belknap's adjectives were all beautifully expressed. The pine stood by itself, emphasizing its distinctiveness. Patches of snow still covered the sunny bottom of the large gully, and the brook rushed through it, full to its banks with the spring runoff. What one notices first is the perfection of the tree, true and straight to its first limbs, tens of feet above the needle-covered floor beneath it. It towers 120 feet high. Its top was broken off at 110 feet, and a limb has now turned upward and replaced it. If the original top still existed, it might, today, reach 140 feet. At breast height, it measures almost forty-nine inches in diameter and seven feet at the butt.

The King's Pine started its life at a time when England was turning to the colonies for a supply of the gigantic masts required by the Royal Navy for its ships. When shiploads of masts began arriving on British shores in the mid-1600s, sources of these wooden masts in the British Isles were depleted. "The very good newes comes of four New England ships come home safe to Falmouth with masts for the King," wrote Samuel Pepys in his diary on December 3, 1666.[125] In 1691, the Crown placed a restriction in a new charter of Massachusetts that reserved for the King all white pine within three miles of water and having a diameter of at least twenty-four inches a foot above the ground and which stood on land not previously granted to private individuals. The position of surveyor general was also established to blaze the trees. A marking hatchet was used to make three cuts through the bark in the shape of the head of an arrow—the sign for Royal Navy property. This came to be known as the King's Broad Arrow.

I looked hopefully, as have countless others, for any sign of this mark on the great pine, knowing full well that any blaze mark would by now be covered with new bark. There are those who believe, despite the absence of any visible sign, that the tree could be a Broad Arrow Pine for several reasons: it was a hundred years old before the King of England lost his claim to the mast pine with the defeat of the British during the American Revolution; it is of exceptional size and form; and it is near the Saco River where it could have been floated to a yard for processing.

If it qualified as a mast, why does it still survive today, one might ask. Perhaps its location in the bottom of the ravine made it difficult to remove it without damage, or perhaps the outcome of the American Revolution saved it. Also, it has for generations remained in the ownership of one family, undoubtedly aware of the connection it makes between the family and the past. Perhaps we should also acknowledge the ravine for nurturing and protecting the pine.

Sometime in the future, the pine will come to the end of its natural life, and perhaps after it falls we will be able to look beneath the bark for the old scar of a King's Broad Arrow. Then we will know for sure. But between now and then, it commands those who see it to remember our history and our heritage.[126]

The plant John Josselyn found was white lettuce, or rattlesnake-root, found in rich woods and thickets throughout New England. He included it in a list of native plants for which no name had been given. Josselyn recorded several observations about this plant, including the nature of its habitat and the fact that it was "somewhat scarce."

People have always been curious and interested in unknown, unusual, and rare objects, and Josselyn was no different. He was an inquisitive botanist who roamed the New England countryside in search of plants. In his book *New-Englands Rarities Discovered*, he listed and described over two hundred species, often mentioning their medicinal qualities, where they were found, and, on rare occasions, other plants growing near them.

Early on, naturalists were quick to notice unusual assemblages of plants, and many of these historic communities survive today. Some are well known, while others have been forgotten. Some, perhaps, still remain to be discovered. Some are readily accessible and others are located in remote or difficult areas to reach. Some have been protected by conservation efforts, while some are now threatened. We now look at three of New England's fascinating plant communities of historic character.

UNUSUAL COMMUNITIES

This Plant I found in a gloomy dry Wood under an Oak, 1670. The 18th of August. Afterwards I found it in open Champain grounds, but yet somewhat scarce

—John Josselyn, 1672[127]

Bartholomew's Cobble, Massachusetts

*If we were required to know the position of the fruit dots
or the character of the indusium, nothing could be easier
than to ascertain it; but if it is required that you be affected
by ferns, that they amount to anything, signify anything to
you, that they be another sacred scripture and revelation to
you, help to redeem you, this end is not so easily accomplished.*

—Henry David Thoreau, 1800s

We do not know if Thoreau was aware that the greatest
natural concentration of ferns in the United States occurred in his state. It may have been that during Thoreau's
time it didn't hold that distinction, but today, in the corner
of southeastern Massachusetts, is a natural area where
forty-three species of ferns now grow. Its name is
Bartholomew's Cobble.

Habitat conditions change, and we do know that in
the 1800s this area near the Housatonic River was used as
a cow pasture. However, before farming took place in the
early- to mid-1700s, it might have resembled more closely
what we see here today. And among the plant life we now
see here are trees that put us in touch with those early days
of settlement, for some old red cedars have been estimated
to be 150 to 200 years old.

Underfoot the needles were brown and soft. They
pulsed with light flickering through the hemlocks and
pines lining the trail. Overhead the needles were green,
crisp, and sharply silhouetted against the bright sky. On
one side of the trail, beneath the tree-lined bank, the bright
blue waters of the Housatonic River lazed pleasantly by.
On the other side, gray, rough, knotty ledges of a rocky
knoll stand firm and severe. This knoll is what attracted
my attention—my reason for coming. Two such knolls are
here—two bubbles of 500-million-year-old dolomite marble and quartzite. These two cobbles, so named because of
their humpy, rounded, cobblelike appearance, leach out
lime and "sweeten" the soil, causing the release of nutrients and spurring a lush growth of plants, including
species that prefer such limey soils. The quartzite creates
more acidic soil conditions, favored by other plants. The
result: over eight hundred species of plants, including

nearly five hundred wildflowers and one hundred trees, shrubs, and vines. The plant life in turn draws animals, especially birds—240 species, to be exact. But my objective the day I was there was to see the spectacular array of ferns and to visit the old cedars.

Dark, solemn patches of moss sprawled over a lumpy, cracked, ledgy slope. Lichens filled in between the mosses, but everywhere splashes of gray-and-white rock appeared. And sprouting from this chaotic hillside were the ferns. I saw their backlighted, finely etched fronds display varied shapes and sizes and hues of green. Back from the trail in a secluded cut in the ledge, tiny walking ferns found a foothold on its vertical face. When the tips of their leaflike fronds become embedded in the sparse soil, they sprout new plants and so, generation by generation, move, or "walk," across the ledge. This uncommon evergreen fern favors soils that are enriched by the dissolving marble. But the presence of the ferns and the rocky nubble they are on depend somewhat on the quartzite that also makes up a part of these cobbles: its hardness may have slowed the erosion of the knolls so that we are still able to see a remnant of them today.

The trail brought me down to the river past thick stands of graceful ostrich ferns. The trail then turned away from the water, passing by the deeply lobed leaves and white flowers of the bloodroot plant. Higher up beside

These tiny walking ferns are among the more than eight hundred species of plants that inhabit Massachusetts' Bartholomew's Cobble.

Old red cedar trees at Bartholomew's Cobble survive from the early days of settlement in southwestern Massachusetts.

a steep-walled ledge, I saw the Housatonic below, framed by a gauzy, yellow-green scrim of spring leaves. Farther along, I followed a trail leading up onto the cobble into a stand of the old red cedar trees, their fine, flaking reddish bark complementing the emerging bright-green vegetation in an open glen. Near a cedar grew a beautiful columbine in full bloom with drooping red bells and long curved spurs above. I moved off the cobble and followed a dark, hemlock-shaded trail back to my point of entrance.[128]

As I write this, I have just come upon the following passage from the *History of New-Hampshire* by Jeremy Belknap, written at the end of the eighteenth century and so descriptive of what I saw: "Amidst these wild and rugged scenes, it is amusing to observe the luxuriant sportings of nature. Trees are seen growing on a naked rock; their roots either penetrate some of its crevices, or run over its surface, and shoot into the ground. When a tree is contiguous to a small rock, it will frequently inclose and cover it."[129] By the middle of that century, Henry Thoreau was expressing his sentiments about the "sportings of nature." If he had seen Bartholomew's Cobble, as I did, he would have readily seen that this is the place to be affected by ferns.

Jack Pine Island, Maine

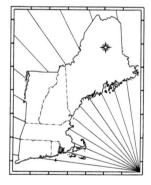

We stopped to dine on an interesting high rocky island, soon after entering . . . [the] Lake, securing our canoe to the cliffy shore. . . . A peculiar evergreen overhung our fire. . . . a new tree to us.

—Henry David Thoreau, July 30, 1857[130]

Thoreau and companion Edward Hoar identified their new tree as *Pinus banksiana*, the jack pine. It was known by them and others of the time as gray pine, scrub pine, and Labrador pine. Thoreau reported that several on the island were thirty or thirty-five feet tall. He and Hoar collected specimens, which were deposited in the collections of the New England Botanical Club Herbarium in Cambridge, Massachusetts. Today, this stand of jack pine, still appearing undisturbed, is perhaps the northernmost stand of this tree in New England.[131]

One August day, two of us paddled down a tiny stream to the lake Thoreau passed through in 1857. Our destination was the island and the stand of jack pine he described. I had found another confirmation in an 1861 report by a team of geologists who saw the pine on the same island and reported the following: "Here we found it was abundant, and was informed by an experienced lumberman, attached to our party, that this 'Shore pine' or 'Rock pine' occurs very rarely in the forests of the State."[132]

Near the lake, the morning sun shined on banks of wool grass on the south side of the stream, while on the other side, ledge outcrops reflected crisply in the quiet water. High in a tree on the left bank, an osprey sat motionless in the sunshine as we passed. On the opposite shore was its nest in a tall, dead pine. Beyond the pine, a large backwater extended far into a cove in which there sat a perfect reflection of a mountain. On the far shore, the red coat of a deer shined brightly in the sun. We swung the canoe into the cove a short distance, and a loud honking of geese commenced. Several took flight and flew out of the backwater. I looked up at two heads peering out of the osprey nest, curiously seeking the cause of the commotion below.

At the mouth of the stream we paddled by the geese, now resting on a low marshy island. Ahead, the hazy outline of Thoreau's island appeared in the distance. It was difficult paddling against the stiff breeze. Coming around in the lee of the island, I saw the jack pine. A little cove out of the wind provided a quiet but rocky place to land. I discovered little opportunity to tie up anywhere without encountering Thoreau's "cliffy" shore.

The island is well wooded with much jack pine, red pine, white pine, and red oak. I expected the island to be somewhat level but discovered that a high ridge runs down its length, peaking in the center. There are many vertical outcrops, and the topography is irregular, up and down and, for me, interesting. Thoreau said, "I saw where the Indians had made canoes in a little secluded hollow in the woods, on the top of the rock, where they were out of the wind, and large piles of whittlings remained. This must have been a favorite resort of their ancestors."[133]

I climbed the ridge where Thoreau saw "a fine view hence over the sparkling lake, which looked pure and deep, and had two or three, in all, rocky islands in it."[134]

My view was equally as fine and still retained a certain wildness about it, framed as it was by the jack pine with their seemingly unkempt limbs in disarray and irregular clumps of needles. Reaching the other end of the island, I saw another nearby island. Wedged between it and the island I was on, was a solid mass of dri ki—a graveyard of bleached trunks and limbs shoved into the shallows by the wind. I returned along the other side of the island, passing fresh beaver cuttings among northern white cedar. This side of the island is sheltered and quiet. Here I found the largest jack pines.

I left the island believing Thoreau would find it much the same if he returned. Little differs from the description he gave. But I would like to have seen the pile of whittlings he saw. Sometimes I wish I were not held to a place in time.

The Highlands of Katahdin, Maine

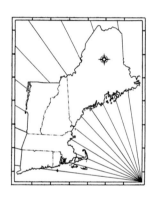

To the eye of those unacquainted with botany, the mere summit of Katahdin would possess very little of interest; but the botanist sees these shattered rocks, and bleak regions, everywhere covered with attractive vegetation of some sort,—something which possesses even in its self, a peculiar interest.

—J. K. Laski, 1847[135]

The mountaintops of the Katahdin Range have attracted botanists since the 1800s. Here still live Maine's richest diversity of Arctic alpine plants assembled into six communities. They are nearly as undisturbed as when they were found by Aaron Young, Maine's state botanist. He saw them in 1847 on an official state botanical survey, which also had in the party the writer J. K. Laski. A few years later, in 1856, the Reverend Joseph Blake made a botanical discovery on the mountain of importance to this day. After exploring the top of Katahdin, he began his descent of the mountain, which he described as follows:

I made a discovery of great interest to me; I found a little plant not new indeed to science, but one that has a place in our flora only in consequence of my detecting it that day on the side of that towering mass of rocks. It was a species of Saxifrage, a name derived from saxum, *a rock, and* frango, *to break, and is given to many plants that grow in the clefts of rocks. The scientific name of the plant I found is Sax-ifraga stellaris var comosa. It was never found before, I be-lieve, south of Labrador.*[136]

The botanist Donald Hudson wrote in 1988 that this plant, the star-saxifrage, now named *Saxifrage foliolosa*, "is one of the rarest plants on the mountain, and is found nowhere else in the eastern United States."[137] It grows in mossy, wet habitats in the high Arctic.

I crossed the Tableland and the Northwest Plateau on a clear July day in 1978. This huge, flat, rocky land is a land of another place and another time. I was transported to remote lands in the north and at the same time carried back thousands of years ago to a land abandoned by the

The Tableland and Northwest Plateau of Mt. Katahdin, on which grow Maine's richest diversity of Arctic alpine plants, have attracted botanists since the 1800s.

ice sheet, where lichens pioneered the regeneration of vegetation. This was a land of caribou, and so they remained until my grandfather's youth, during the 1890s, a time when this native animal's life on this mountain was drawing to a close. That day, however, when I crossed the Tableland, I was surrounded by other species clinging to a fragile life on the mountain. Thirty-one alpine species of Maine's plants only grow on Katahdin.[138] The Reverend Blake's saxifrage is not alone in its claim to rarity. Here also I photographed the rare Katahdin Arctic butterfly, found nowhere else in the world but in the Arctic-alpine zone of Katahdin.[139]

I chose to conclude this chapter with the treeless top of one of New England's least disturbed mountains. It overlooks our region's largest wilderness, where nearly 175,000 acres of plant communities will be allowed to live and evolve "forever wild." As such, it stands unique in "the variety, number, beauty, and vertues" (to borrow from John Josselyn's opening quotation) of the New England plants that we pass on to future generations.

Chapter 6

Of the Beasts, Feathered Fowls, and Fishes

Sometime between a thousand years ago and before European settlement, a Wabanaki Indian bent over a ledge of metamorphosed slate on the banks of the Kennebec River in central Maine. The Indian was a shaman, possessed of magical powers and holding a special relationship with a world of spirits. With light blows on a hard, sharply pointed stone, an image of an animal began to emerge in the softer rock of the ledge. Here on the west bank of the river, the rock carving would receive the first rays of the morning sun—a place suited to the ancient Indian ritual of meeting the rising sun to receive its energy. The process of pecking the rock, or dinting, was slow and painstaking. The Indian carefully formed the stylistic and delicate image—a representation of an animal which was likely grounded in observation of the region's early fauna. Thus, the petroglyph left by the shaman and the rock carvings created by others like him are perceptions of animal life that was a part of the early New England wilderness.

Petroglyph. Drawn from a photograph of a Wabanaki shaman's rock carving of a wild animal, possibly a moose.

One early morning I set out for the ledge where that ancient shaman greeted the rising sun on the bank of the Kennebec River and began work on that carving. The well-worn trail led down to the river through open, mature woods of white pine, northern white cedar, hemlock, and various species of hardwoods. It was a short walk from the road, and I soon came to the ledge outcrop jutting northerly into the river. The brightly lit east side of the outcrop angled directly toward the still-low sun. Here were numerous pictures "dinted" into the rock. Situated on the downstream side, they have been protected from the erosive effects of the river. I saw what I interpreted as moose, deer, a canine (a wolf?), a catlike animal, and a bird, although these petroglyphs likely connote more than what I may see in them, for they are concepts of an ancient mind—a mind that perhaps saw a different reality than we.

Behind the ledge, by the path that I had followed, archaeologists have found evidence of a small native campsite with artifacts dating back to the late 1600s or early 1700s. And directly across the river, where I could see another wooded shore, ancient campsites have been discovered that were occupied six thousand years or more ago.[1] These and other prehistoric sites were likely used in summer and perhaps in fall by the early Native Peoples, while during the remainder of the year, they lived closer to the coast.[2] It is in their coastal sites that we find more direct evidence of New England's fauna before European observations were recorded. There, in shell heaps where the refuse of countless meals was left by generations of Native Peoples, we have found the bones of moose, deer, beaver, black bear, raccoon, red fox, harbor seal, mink, and the extinct sea mink. Identified from among the bones are also birds: the extinct great auk, goose, scaup, loon, black duck, black-backed gull, and greater yellowlegs. Fish include sturgeon, alewife, and bass.[3]

Among the earliest European records of New England's animal life is Martin Pring's account of his 1603 voyage to Plymouth Harbor. In his report, printed in 1625, Pring included the following list:

The Beasts here are Stags, fallow Deere [white-tailed deer] in abundance, Beares, Wolves, Foxes, Lusernes, and (some say) Tygres, Porcupines, and Dogges with sharpe and long noses [foxes], with many other sorts of wild beasts. . . . The most usuall Fowles are Eagles, Vultures, Hawkes, Cranes, Herons, Crowes, Gulls, and great store of other River and Sea-fowles. And as the Land is full of Gods good blessings, so is the Sea replenished with great abundance of excellent fish, as Cods sufficient to lade many ships, which we found upon the Coast in the month of June, Seales to make Oile withall, Mullets, Turbuts [flounder], Mackerels, Herrings, Crabs, Lobsters, Creuises and Muscles with ragged Pearles in them.[4]

Captain John Smith, in a report of his exploration of the New England coast about a decade later, expanded on

Pring's list, including among the mammals: red deer (wapiti, or elk), beaver, gray and red fox, raccoon, bobcat, river otter, marten, striped skunk, muskrat, whales, dolphins, and porpoises. His list of birds added brant, cormorant, whistling swan, merganser, marsh duck, mew gull, and turkey. He also included a much longer list of fish than Pring, including hake, haddock, cusk, shark, cunner, perch, eel, whelk, clam, and periwinkle.[5]

Once settlement occurred, documentation of New England's wildlife increased dramatically. Descriptions took on more detail, including observations of behavior and habitat. A body of folklore also grew in proportion to published material, clouding the accuracy of information but probably influencing attitudes and increasing interest in the animal life in the colonies and surrounding country. William Wood, for example, wrote that "concerning Lyons, I will not say that I ever saw any my selfe, but some affirme that they have seene a Lyon at *Cape Anne* which is not above six leagues from *Boston*; some likewise being lost in woods, have heard such terrible roarings, as have made them much agast; which must eyther be Devills or Lyons."[6]

Other settlers, travelers, and visitors added to the accumulating information and misinformation. Thomas Morton's book, *New English Canaan*, published in 1637, contained many references to animals, including even the hummingbird, which he said is "no bigger than a great Beatle; that out of question lives upon the Bee, which he eateth and catcheth amongst Flowers: For it is his Custome to frequent those places."[7]

Perhaps the most thorough cataloguing of species in the seventeenth century is found in John Josselyn's book *New-Englands Rarities Discovered*, published in 1672. He began to correct some misconceptions but added his own. He also wrote of hummingbirds, noting that "they feed upon Honey, which they suck out of Blossoms and Flowers with their long Needle-like Bills," but, he added, "they sleep all Winter and are not to be seen till the Spring."[8] Two years later, Josselyn published a second book in which he expanded on some of his earlier descriptions with more folklore of the day about everything from wasps to salamanders, and "flitter mice" (bats) to eels. Being a physician, Josselyn also gave many medicinal uses for animals.

Something of greater import, however, was going on in the expanding immigrant community. It was the introduction into this "new world" of a different attitude towards nature. It would not bode well for wild things in that early wilderness. For thousands of years the creatures had shared the land and water with humans who viewed them as equal, who saw their world and that of other animals as one, both connected and a part of a natural fabric in which they were embedded. They believed in a symbiotic relationship with nature and showed a life-giving reciprocity. Indeed, the legends of these Native Americans related stories of ancestors who were, themselves, animals, and families took the names of animals. Their legends taught them to conserve animal populations for future generations of Native Peoples. During the hunts, they respected the creatures that had given up their lives so others could survive. The land these people hunted upon could not be owned. When animals were scarce and hunting was poor, they turned to their shamans—men and women who could transform themselves into animals with which they had once had a powerful experience. The shamans had the ability to guide the hunts and bring about their success. This was the prevailing view of the human population of New England when Verrazzano made his historic exploration along the coast in 1524.

A commodity-driven conscience colored much of the behavior of the new arrivals to New England. "Let me leade you to the Sea," wrote William Wood, "to view what commodities may come from thence; there is no countrey knowne, that yeelds more variety of fish winter and summer: and that not onely for the present spending and sustentation of the plantations, but likewise for trade into other countries."[9] Thomas Morton began each of his chapters on animal life with a description of the animal he considered of greatest value in a commodity sense: "Of the Beasts of the forrest. . . . I begin with the most usefull and most beneficiall beast which is bredd in those parts, which is the Deare." And of geese, he wrote, "I have had often 1000. before the mouth of my gunne. . . . the fethers of the

Geese, that I have killed in a short time, have paid for all the powther and shott I have spent in a yeare, and I have fed my doggs with as fatt Geese there as I have ever fed my selfe in England."[10]

It is true that the growing colonial society, trying to carve an existence out of the wilderness, needed the country's natural resources for survival. But the abundance of animals they observed suggested that there was no limit to their numbers, just as in my lifetime we once believed that our atmosphere and our oceans were so vast that it was inconceivable that they could be dangerously polluted. Little constrained the settlers from taking more than they needed. There was also the motivation for economic gain, of which the explorers and settlers were ever mindful. A furious trade of bartering and selling animal meat, feathers, and furs quickly entered the new economy.

The killing of animals was reinforced by the cultural values of the time. The European society was intent on becoming civilized and distancing itself from those aspects of nature it considered wild and animal-like. Wilderness, of which wild animals are a part, was seen as a threat to the human soul. Furthermore, Christian religion had given the Puritans the concept of dominion over animal life and instructed them to void the waste and remove the "hideous wilderness." Wild things became objects of unrestrained exploitation. Some animals were seen as beneficial, such as deer, geese, and fish, while others were considered threatening, such as wolves. Bounties on wolves, for example, were enacted, and the inhabitants were even required by law to rid the towns of this hated and feared predator.

Native Peoples were widely seen as associated with beasts and representative of a lower level of humanity in need of civilizing and redemption to save their souls. This superior attitude towards the Indian rationalized in the collective colonial mind the taking of the land. Thus, they superimposed the European belief, indeed the practice, that land could be privately owned. Maps, fences, and stonewalls were used to transform this concept into direct management and control for individual wealth. The Indians were taken advantage of by a people who were guided by a different set of values. The Native People's numbers were diminished by disease, their way of life became dependent on trade with the colonies, and the Indians lost their rights to the land. More devastating for the future of New England's wild creatures was the loss of the human conscience that had given the animal-life equality and had held a reverence for the land that provided for their needs.

The unfortunate effects of this change in attitude have been well documented. Exotic animals were introduced, intentionally and unintentionally. Critical habitat was lost, either removed outright or altered to the extent that some species had to move or became rare and endangered. Overharvesting went unchecked. In a few cases, extinction occurred. Gradually the realization grew that wildlife was disappearing, and a faint stirring of concern crept into the public's mind. It began first with laws to control the harvesting of species of economic value. It evolved into the concerns expressed today for the health of ecosystems, the preservation of evolutionary processes, and the rights of other species to share the earth with us.

In 1973, the United States Congress enacted the Endangered Species Act, recognizing that endangered species of fish, wildlife, and plants "are of esthetic, ecological, educational, historical, recreational, and scientific value to the Nation and its people." By 1991, a committee of program coordinators from thirteen northeastern states had compiled a list of all fish and wildlife species legally recognized as rare and endangered. Eleven mammals, twenty-one birds, ten reptiles, one amphibian, five fish, and twenty-five species of invertebrates were identified as endangered in one or more of the six New England states.[11]

Some species are on our endangered lists about which we have good historical records. Unfortunately, some don't show up on these lists because they no longer exist. In some cases, these existed in large numbers; in others, their populations already may have been reduced or declining when European settlement occurred. But in all cases the demise of the extinct species discussed below involved human actions. In all cases their loss means we will never be able to capture, no matter how much we try, the fullness of the wilderness that once existed. We can, however, appreciate a knowledge of these extinct species and perhaps learn lessons from their loss that we can apply to those species that are close to following them into oblivion. We look at those species now extinct and a few examples of those that are now endangered—species once enmeshed in the fabric of New England's early wilderness.

The Reverend Francis Higginson's life in the colonies was brief. He arrived in Salem, Massachusetts, from England on June 29, 1629, with his wife and eight children. The next winter he was stricken by sickness, as were so many others, which, unfortunately, led to his death on August 6, 1630. He did, however, in this short time produce a small book describing the "commodities and discommodities" of the country, including its wildlife.

Today, some of the "beasts" Reverend Higginson listed are no longer in Salem, or even in New England. The wolf and the lion, if he meant the mountain lion, are both now extirpated, or removed, from the region, although reports of sightings still persist. It is also unlikely that molke (moose), wild cat (bobcat), marten, and black bear are in Salem. By 1800 the white-tailed deer was almost nonexistent in Massachusetts.[13] It has since returned. The otter was reported in 1880 as nearly extinct.[14]

In those early years of exploration and settlement, a number of other creatures were seen that are no longer present in New England today. In the sixteenth century at least one polar bear was seen on an ice flow off Cape Cod.[15] Several sources attest to the presence of elk, or wapiti. The Vermont naturalist Zadock Thompson wrote in 1853 that "the horns of the elk have been often found in Vermont, which may be regarded as sufficient proof of the former existence of that animal within the state."[16] In 1880, Joel Allen of the Museum of Comparative Zoology at Harvard University, added that although "there appears to be no evidence of the presence of elk in eastern Massachusetts within historic times . . . it occupied the country not far to the westward."[17] Three years later, the historian Charles Francis Adams, Jr., cited a corroborative report that early in the 1700s sixteen elk were seen west of Boston in South Lancaster. One was killed and its antlers preserved.[18] That the elk in the wild is now gone from New England (except where introduced in private pre-

BEASTS OF THE LAND

For Beasts there are some Beares, and they say some Lyons. . . . also here are severall sorts of Deere. . . . Also Wolves, Foxes, Beavers, Otters, Martins, great wild Cats, & a great Beast called a Molke as bigge as an Oxe.

—Francis Higginson, 1630[12]

Beaver. Redrawn from *A Mapp of New England*, circa 1676, by John Seller, Hydrographer to the King.

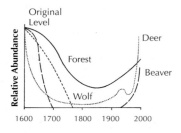

Relative changes among selected wildlife populations in Massachusetts. Habitat alteration, including the loss of forest, and unregulated harvesting of wildlife resulted in a severe decline in animal populations in Massachusetts and other New England states during the seventeenth and eighteenth centuries. Regeneration of forest cover on abandoned farm land, enforcement of new laws and regulations, and application of scientific management practices during the nineteenth and twentieth centuries contributed to an extraordinary resurgence of the abundance of many wildlife species. Redrawn and reprinted, by permission, from Walter E. Bickford and Ute Janik Dymon, *An Atlas of Massachusetts River Systems: Environmental Designs for the Future* (Amherst, Mass.: Univ. of Massachusetts Press, 1990).

serves) is undisputed, but exactly when it disappeared from the region is subject to opinion.

The beaver is one mammal that completely disappeared from parts of New England but has since made a vigorous comeback. Its story illustrates the powerful influence humans can have on their wild neighbors. The beaver had the misfortune of sporting a fur coat from which could be made a fur-napped felt hat—a hat that held popular from the 1600s to the 1800s. Martin Pring reported that he was informed that "the *Frenchmen* brought from *Canada* the value of thirtie thousand Crownes in the yeare 1604. Almost in Bevers and Otter skinnes only."[19] John Smith, a decade later, noted in the account of his voyage to New England that "ranging the coast in a small boat, wee got for trifles neer 1100 Bever skinnes, 100 Martins, and neer as many Otters; and the most of them within the distance of twenty leagues."[20]

Through the centuries, the fate of the beaver has been well documented. For example, John Josselyn remarked in 1674 that "their skins are highly valued."[21] By 1809 the Vermont historian Samuel Williams noted that "the beaver has deserted all the southern parts of Vermont, and is now to be found only in the most northern, and uncultivated parts of the state."[22] And in New Hampshire in 1792, Jeremy Belknap gave a similar assessment: "It is now become scarce in New-Hampshire."[23] At the midpoint of the century, Zadock Thompson confirmed the worst in Vermont. It is, he wrote, "probably now nearly or quite exterminated, none of them having been killed within the state, to my knowledge, for several years."[24] A report published in Maine in 1862 noted that the beaver are "fast dying out" and will soon become extinct.

In the year 1745, nearly 150,000 skins were imported into London and Rouchelle. By 1827, the importation had fallen away to about 50,000. The writer of the report also observed that in Maine "beaver now choose very small streams in the deepest recesses of the wilderness to build their dams and houses, since they have been so often disturbed."[25] Not surprising, in Massachusetts a zoologist at Harvard University confirmed that the animal had entirely disappeared from the eastern section of that state in 1880.[26] Five years later, Maine passed a law protecting the beaver.

At one time, overtrapping completely removed the beaver from parts of New England, but today it has recovered and once again beaver flowages are seen throughout the region.

Today, the beaver has recovered in New England. Only recently, I saw a large beaver flowage in western Connecticut, and throughout the New England region northward on my travels, I have seen its dams and houses. While the market still exerts an influence on the beaver's population, laws and regulations now maintain safe levels, and we are still able to marvel at the seemingly humanlike behavior that produces its intricate works of engineering.

The beaver was fortunate that a combination of factors—human intervention, an adaptive capacity, and available habitat—conjoined to prevent its complete disappearance from New England. Others were not so fortunate: gone forever is the sea mink and driven out are the wolf, mountain lion, wolverine, and the caribou. The lynx and timber rattlesnake, among others, are now hanging on. We look now at these animals of a wilder New England.

Sea Mink

This heap is distinct from any of the others in several features, but especially in having large numbers of mink bones in it.

—F. B. Loomis, 1911[27]

Eight years after the bones of a giant sea mink were first discovered in an Indian shell heap on the coast of Maine by Blue Hill Bay, a biological expedition in 1911 discovered more bones of the unusual mammal on an island in Casco Bay. Reporting on the expedition, F. B. Loomis wrote that the mink was "larger than any species now liv-

Sea mink. Drawn from a photograph of the only known mounted specimen published in Donald F. Mairs and Richard B. Parks, "Once Common . . . Now Gone," *Maine Fish and Game* (Spring 1964). Original photograph courtesy of the Portland Society of Natural History.

ing in New England and markedly different from any that are known."[28] Further, because the scientists guessed that the heaps took hundreds of years to accumulate and they found no items of European origin in them, they believed that the mink bones dated well before European contact. A total of forty-five individual mink were identified. The condition of the bones indicated that the animal served as food for the Indians. Based on the recovery of its remains in New England's coastal Indian middens, the sea mink, as it came to be called, may have ranged from southwestern Nova Scotia to the coast of Connecticut.[29]

In 1903, a well-known Maine hunter and naturalist, Manly Hardy, who also traded in furs, described the sea mink as having coarse, reddish fur and a fishy odor about it.[30] Manly was also familiar with the methods used by hunters to kill the sea mink, which he described as follows:

They carried their dogs with them, and besides guns, shovels, pickaxes, and crowbars, took a good supply of pepper and brimstone. If they [the mink] took refuge in holes or cracks of the ledges, they were usually dislodged by working with shovels or crowbars, and the dogs caught them when they came out. If they were in the crevices of the rocks where they could not be got at, and their eyes could be seen to shine, they were shot and pulled out by means of an iron rod with a screw at the end. If they could not be seen, they were usually driven out by firing in charges of pepper. If this failed, then they were smoked with brimstone, in which case, they either came out or were suffocated in their holes. Thus, in a short time, they were nearly or quite exterminated.[31]

Sometime in the last half of the nineteenth century the sea mink became extinct. Today, only one mounted specimen possibly exists. The mink was reportedly taken near the Bay of Fundy in 1874. Its total length measured twenty-eight and a half inches and its tail, a little over eight inches. This is all we have left.

Wolf

Another thing did very much terrifie them, they heard as they thought two Lyons roaring exceedingly for a long time together, and a third, that they thought was very nere them.

—William Bradford, 1621[32]

It was only a month after the Pilgrims landed at Plymouth Rock that two members of the plantation heard what they thought were lions roaring, but more likely it was wolves. The two were lost in the woods after pursu-

Wolf. Illustration from John S. Springer, *Forest Life and Forest Trees* (New York: Harper and Brothers, 1851).

ing a deer and were so frightened by the sound that they walked up and down under a tree all night.

I have never heard a wolf, but I hope I do. In my mind, to have never heard a wolf is to never have fully experienced wildness. A dozen years or so ago, while canoeing in a remote section of northern Maine, I met a forester who had. It was a howling sound one night in the middle of winter, he said, and I could tell by the way he spoke that it was something he would never forget. Others have felt similarly. "It tingles in the spine of all who hear wolves by night," wrote Aldo Leopold."[33]

To the early settlers, the howl of a wolf soon became a reminder that this "ravenous ranger," as one colonial

writer called it, must be exterminated, for it quickly became a threat to the farmers' swine, goats, and livestock.
Within a decade of the Pilgrims' arrival in Plymouth, "the
Court of Massachusetts ordered rewards for their [the
wolves'] destruction."[34] By the mid-1630s, William Wood
described them as "the greatest inconveniency the Countrey hath, both for matter of dammage to private men in
particular, and the whole Countrey in generall." They
have a bounty on their head, he wrote, and are being killed
daily.[35]

Society turned against the wolf and resolved that it
should be removed by whatever means at hand. In this
context, John Josselyn's reaction to meeting up with a wolf
during his first visit to Scarborough, Maine, in 1638 is understandable: "I heard a hollow thumping noise upon the
Rocks approaching towards me, which made me presently
recover my piece [gun], which I had no sooner cock'd than
a great and grim over-grown she-Wolf appears, at whom I
shot."[36]

The colonists also had other justifications for killing
wolves. Thomas Morton reported in his book, published
in 1637, that "the Salvages will willingly give 40. beaver
skinnes for the purchase of one of these black wolfe
skinnes. . . . which is esteemed a present for a prince."[37]
And in keeping with the popular belief that the characteristics of natural objects suggest their curative powers,
called the doctrine of signatures, John Josselyn advanced
the idea that "the Fangs of a *Wolf* hung about childrens
necks keep them from frightening, and are very good to
rub their gums with them when they are breeding of Teeth,
the gall of a *wolf* is soveraign for swelling of the sinews;
the frants or dung of a *wolf* drunk with white-wine
helpeth the *Collick*."[38]

The wolf is an intelligent animal and "so cunning,"
commented Josselyn, "that seldome any are kill'd with
Guns or Traps." He then went on to describe how the
colonists tried to destroy them, by "binding four Maycril
Hooks a cross with a brown thread, and then wrapping
some Wool about them, they dip them in melted Tallow
till it be as round and big as an Egg; these (when any
Beast hath been kill'd by the *Wolves*) they scatter by the
dead Carkase, after they have beaten off the *Wolves*."[39]

Presumably a wolf that ate the hooks would suffer fatal injury to its internal organs.

For three centuries, bounties on the wolf continued throughout New England, spurring its destruction. Providence, Rhode Island, established a bounty in 1659.[40] In 1698, the town of Lynn, Massachusetts, voted a bounty of twenty shillings for every wolf killed in town.[41] In 1738, Falmouth and North Yarmouth, in Maine, offered six pounds for each grown wolf killed in addition to that already paid by the province.[42] In New Hampshire a bounty of twenty dollars was in place when Jeremy Belknap advocated that "if it were doubled, the breed of sheep would be augmented sufficiently to make up the difference."[43] Vermont, in 1853, still paid twenty dollars for each grown wolf and ten dollars for each "sucking whelp of a wolf."[44]

Gradually, the killing took its toll, and the wolf began to disappear, first in southern New England and later in western Massachusetts and the northern three states. In 1809, the Vermont historian Samuel Williams reported that, although wolves were still numerous, they "are gradually decreasing, as our settlements increase and extend."[45] Two decades later, it was acknowledged that in Berkshire County in western Massachusetts the wolf had "long since disappeared."[46]

Through the 1800s, encounters with wolves became fewer and, as they did, the public's interest in such occurrences increased as well as their newsworthiness. A geologist in the area of Rump Mountain near the New Hampshire border in western Maine reported in 1839 that "wolves are abundant in this section; And on one occasion . . . I was serenaded all night by the unceasing music of one of those animals, which, probably, for a want of taste for music, on my part, I was rendered rather uncomfortable through the night."[47]

Unfortunately, while that wolf pack on Rump Mountain was doing its serenading, the final destruction of the wolf in New England was taking place. Right around that time the last wolf in Portland, Maine, was trapped and killed.[48] Nearer still, in Farmington, Maine, during that same time period, the last wolf recorded in that town met its end.[49] And in 1887, the last wolf purportedly in New Hampshire's White Mountains was killed.[50] In the same decade, a few wolves were reported seen in northern Maine.[51] Gradually, however, the reports became sporadic, isolated events and then only rumors, fulfilling what the early settlers desired but did not believe possible, a belief expressed by William Wood a dozen years after the Pilgrims landed: "there is little hope of their [the wolves'] utter destruction the Countrey being so spacious, and they so numerous."[52]

But is the wolf really gone? Throughout the twentieth century, the rumors persisted. Then on August 31, 1993, a black, wolflike animal was killed by a bear hunter in western Maine. Laboratory examination later confirmed that it was, indeed, a purebred timber wolf. Once again, another generation of New Englanders reexamined the issues raised by the presence of this predator. The early attitudes toward the wolf are understandable when viewed in the context of their time, but what should our attitude be today?

Aldo Leopold, one of our country's most eloquent advocates for wilderness and for a land ethic, shot a wolf when he was a young man. He later wrote:

We reached the old wolf in time to watch a fierce green fire dying in her eyes. I realized then, and have known ever since, that there was something new to me in those eyes— something known only to her and to the mountain. I was young then, and full of trigger-itch; I thought that because fewer wolves meant more deer, that no wolves would mean hunters' paradise. But after seeing the green fire die, I sensed that neither the wolf nor the mountain agreed with such a view.[53]

He never shot another.

Catamount

There are those that are yet living in the Countrey, that do constantly affirm, that about six or seven and thirty years since an Indian shot a young lion, *sleeping upon the body of an Oak blown up by the roots, with an Arrow, not far from Cape* Anne, *and sold the Skin to the English.*

—John Josselyn, 1672[54]

There is little, if any, dispute that the lion John Josselyn mentioned in his *New-England Rarities Discovered* was a

Mountain lion, or catamount. Illustration from Zadock Thompson, *Natural History of Vermont* (n.p.: Zadock Thompson, 1853).

mountain lion.[55] This animal was reported from throughout New England, although records are few in Rhode Island. In Connecticut it is thought to have been more prevalent in the northern mountainous country of Litchfield County.[56]

In scientific terminology, the mountain lion is *Felis concolor*, but among New Englanders it has carried many names: cougar, catamount, panther, painter, and puma. There is one name, however, given to it by the Wabanakis, that perhaps most accurately depicts the early attitude toward it. According to the Maine historian William Williamson, the Indians called it *lunkson*, or evil devil. "The Catamount," he wrote, "is a most ferocious and violent creature, more to be feared by the hunters and Indians, than any other one in our woods."[57]

The mountain lion is an animal of secretive ways — and of formidable physical size, strength, and appearance. In 1853, one was killed in New Hampshire that measured over eight feet long and weighed 198 pounds. Another taken in Vermont in 1875 was over seven feet long and weighed 100 pounds.[58] Its scream was said to be dreadful. After finding a deer bitten through the back one night, Henry Clapp, an experienced hunter and guide from Brownsville, Maine, related the following in 1868: "I heard a shrill screech, like that of a woman in distress. I heard the same screech and saw the same track again not far off. I think the animal was a catamount."[59] It is easy to see why early New Englanders were fearful of this great cat.

Not surprisingly the colonists turned to bounties as a way of ridding the country of this worrisome creature. Bounties were established in Connecticut as early as 1694 and were in effect until 1769. Massachusetts enacted a bounty in 1742.[60] Vermont, in the mid-1800s, still offered a bounty of twenty dollars for each animal killed in the state.[61]

Although the mountain lion was declared extinct in Maine in 1899, one was reported to have been trapped sometime between 1935 and 1938 in the state east of Little St. John Lake in Somerset County.[62] Many believe that the cat still frequents New England, for reports of sightings still continue to this day. One researcher compiled fourteen reports from Maine between 1897 and 1965, four reports from New Hampshire in 1948, three reports from Vermont between 1948 and 1963, five reports from Massachusetts between 1953 and 1969, and two from Connecticut in 1967.[63] A compilation by the Eastern Puma Research Network of sightings between 1983 and 1993 gives the following: Maine, 69; New Hampshire, 31; Vermont, 29; Massachusetts, 23; Connecticut, 5; and Rhode Island, 0.[64] Hard evidence is scarce, however, and the question of a viable breeding population remains.

Setting aside the debate as to whether or not the eastern mountain lion still roams New England, we can take heart that a growing number in our society are actively concerned about its future. What that future will turn out to be, we are unable to say. At least we have declared it an endangered species and so protect it. And if there is still the possibility of an encounter with this beast of the early wilderness, perhaps those who enter New England's wild, remote country can experience a twinge of the apprehension felt by those who first ventured into the region's unexplored wilderness.

Devil-Bear, or Wolverine

This animal is of a very fierce, carnivorous dispostion.

—Samuel Williams, 1809[65]

Wolverine, or devil-bear. Although the wolverine was probably not ever very plentiful in New England, it is now considered extirpated from the region.

In the human mind, the wolverine is something of an enigma. It has been called fierce, gluttonous, mischievous, playful, curious, intelligent, and elusive. It has been given the names skunk-bear and devil-bear. John Josselyn may have described it in 1674 when he wrote of the Mattrise—

"a Creature whose head and fore parts is shaped somewhat like a Lyons, not altogether so big as a house-cat,
they are innumberable up in the Countrey, and are esteemed good furr."[66]

John Josselyn probably never saw the wolverine because it may have never been numerous in the areas he
frequented. According to one zoologist, writing in the late
1800s, it "seems to have been formerly of frequent occurrence in the northern parts of Vermont, New Hampshire,
and Maine and once probably inhabited the highlands of
western Massachusetts."[67] Timothy Dwight confirmed in
1803 that it was still in northern New Hampshire. In a letter from Colebrook, he wrote: "The wolverin is found
here. This animal is of the size of a small dog; and is
striped perpendicularly, like a raccoon, from the back to
the belly: it is fierce, and voracious; and frequently de-
stroys sheep."[68] As for its early existence in Maine, Ernest
Thompson Seton expressed the opinion that it lived in the
northern two-thirds of the state.[69]

Hunted and trapped and pushed by civilization, the
wolverine retreated farther north. By 1809 it was reported
scarce in Vermont and was only found "in the northern
most uncultivated parts of the state."[70] A half-century
later, its status in that state was again assessed by Zadock
Thompson who judged it as "extremely rare, none having
been met with to my knowledge for several years."[71] In
Maine, one was reported taken near Houlton in 1844.[72]
By 1876, however, the animal was so scarce one expert
wrote it is "now rarely recognized as an animal that was
ever found in New England."[73]

Although a few reports from northern areas of New
England continued into the 1900s, the wolverine had by
the twentieth century moved to the far north. There it is
still trapped, but as one naturalist noted, it is "still feared
and greatly respected by the native people of the north
country."[74]

Maccarib, or Caribou

The Maccarib, Caribo, *or* Pohano, *a kind of Deer, as big as a Stag, round hooved, smooth hair'd and soft as silk; their horns grow backwards a long their backs to their rumps, and turn again a handful beyond their Nose, having another Horn in the middle of their Forehead.*

—John Josselyn, 1672[75]

By the time John Josselyn came to the colonies, the eastern woodland caribou had long ago disappeared from most of New England. It had been fifteen hundred years since native peoples had thrown the bones of caribou into a shell

Caribou herd on ice. Illustration by A. B. Frost from Henry P. Wells, *City Boys in the Woods or A Trapping Venture in Maine* (New York: Harper & Brothers, Franklin Square, 1890).

heap in the Plymouth area.[76] But the caribou has had a far longer history in New England. Archaeologists have found bones in New Hampshire and possibly in Massachusetts from Paleo-Indian sites, suggesting that the caribou was hunted in the region soon after the last glacier retreated, between 12,000 and 10,000 years ago.[77]

When Josselyn first came to New England in 1638, the caribou was a permanent resident only in northern Maine and probably only a visitor in northern New Hampshire. Because northern New England was the last to be settled, there are fewer reports of caribou sightings before the late 1700s and early 1800s. The Maine historian William Williamson wrote in 1832 that "it is seen about the upper branches of the river St. John, and in many other parts of the State."[78]

A number of sightings through the 1800s were documented in various reports, books, and articles. Charles

Jackson in 1838 reported seeing one on the shore of Ambajejus Lake near Mt. Katahdin: "A noble looking carriboo suddenly started from the woods, and trotted quietly along the shores of the lake, quite near us, but we were not prepared to take him, and he presently darted into the forest and disappeared."[79]

A true feeling of being in a wilderness of which the caribou was a part comes from the accounts of two hunters and trappers who spent a fall and winter in the late 1870s in the region of the upper Magalloway River in western Maine:

While we were standing there deciding which side of the brook to go up, we heard a tremendous splashing in the stream above. We dropped every thing but the rifle and ax and crept along back of the alders in the spruce growth for several rods. But soon the splashing ceased. We listened, holding our breaths, but could hear nothing. Then we crept along several rods further, and all at once we heard a bush break near the alders. We now laid flat down on the snow, and hardly breathed. Soon we heard a step, then another and another, then the bushes began to move. One of us was lying on his side, rifle cocked and ready; the other lying in the same way, a few feet distant and nearer the alders with the ax. In an instant more the head and shoulders of a bull caribou came out of the alders not more than ten feet from us.[80]

Up until the late 1800s there was little regulation of caribou hunting in Maine. Before 1895 a person could kill two caribou and hunt summer and winter. It wasn't until 1886 that the Maine Commissioners of Inland Fisheries and Game began reporting on the status of the animal. From that time until the early 1900s, the reports documented the caribou's disappearance from New England. Beginning in 1886, the Commissioners reported that caribou "are of plenty in all sections. We have heard of many being killed, but of all our game animals the caribou is the most capable of taking care of itself." Almost a decade later, in 1895, the Commissioners noted that 105 caribou were shipped by hunters, double that of 1894 and concluded that "the indications therefore, seem to be in favor of an increase in caribou, but no definite rule can be applied to these animals as to increase or decrease in any given territory as they are migratory and range large stretches of the country."

The next year the commissioners' attitude had drastically changed, and with a sense of urgency, the following warning and appeal was issued: "From the best information obtainable, from the most reliable sources, the caribou is fast disappearing, and will very soon be practically extinct, unless a close time, for a series of years, is put on them or more stringent laws enacted for their protection. Summer and winter killing has accomplished this. Every effort should be made to preserve this species of our big game, because of its vast importance to our citizens." In 1898, the commissioners wrote, "There are but few caribou in Maine compared with a few years ago." The report of 1900 began, "By the provisions of section 19, of Chapter 42, of the Public Laws of 1899, it is unlawful to hunt or kill caribou before October 15, 1905. It appears to be certain that there are practically no caribou in the State." And in 1904, "There is no indication that the caribou are returning or will ever return."[81]

The Katahdin area seems to have been the last outpost for the caribou. In 1905, a party making a winter ascent of Mt. Katahdin encountered seven caribou on the Tableland. Several were photographed.[82] The last sighting of caribou reportedly occurred in 1908.[83] Years later, when the possibility of reintroducing caribou to Maine excited the public's imagination, the Katahdin area was chosen as the site.

Two reintroduction efforts were made, both in the last half of the twentieth century, and reflect the public's fascination with this animal. The first occurred in early December of 1963. Twenty-four caribou were released on the Tableland and at the base of Mt. Katahdin in Baxter State Park. They were monitored for the next year by airflights. Although cows with calves were sighted in northern Maine the following spring and summer and a cow and calf in 1965, they disappeared. The second attempt began in 1986. Twenty-two caribou were captured in Newfoundland and brought to pens in Orono, Maine, where young were born, reared, and prepared for release. But in the end, this effort, too, failed.

We are led to ask why the caribou no longer roams northern New England. What answers are suggested from our research of its history and our efforts at its reintroduction? Although we will never know the exact causes for the decline and eventual loss of the caribou in the early twentieth century, historic evidence points to over-hunting as a major factor, with the possible added factor of disease. A fatal infection by the parasitic meningeal worm *Parelaphostrongylus tenuis* (commonly known as brain worm) is carried by white-tailed deer, a species that extended its range into interior northern Maine in the mid-1800s.

Conclusions from the last reintroduction effort indicate that infection by brain worm and predation by black bear were major factors for the reintroduction project's failure. However, the project was terminated prematurely due to lack of funds and was unable to test conclusively the hypothesis that the woodland caribou cannot be successfully restored to parts of its former range. We do know from this experience that any future efforts will be very costly and the probability of failure will be high. Only time will tell if we have the will to embark on another attempt to realize the dream of those who originally conceived the Maine Caribou Project: "to restore a vestige of our natural heritage."[84]

Lynx

The Lynx was never very greatly multiplied in Vermont, but when the country was new, it was frequently met with, and individuals have been taken occasionally down to the present time.

—Zadock Thompson, 1853[85]

It was in Allagash country in northern Maine where my wife and I saw what we now believe was a lynx. The day was overcast and rainy. Ahead of us an animal jumped into the gravel road and crossed it. We expected it to disappear quickly, but it stopped by the tall, mud-splashed grasses on the other side. As we drew close, we could see that it was a cat. Its wet fur was grayish, rather unmarked, and its legs appeared to be long. In one leap, it was gone.

Lynx. Illustration from Zadock Thompson, *Natural History of Vermont* (n.p.: Zadock Thompson, 1853).

We thought, at first, we had seen a bobcat, but later, after consulting our field guides, we decided we had seen a lynx.

For many reasons, it is unusual to have such an experience. One of our least known larger predators, the lynx is uncommon. It is shy and secretive and prowls mainly at night. It stays to the remotest and deepest woods away from humans, and its major range is thought to have shrunk to a narrow belt of remote country extending from northwestern Maine into northern New Hampshire and Vermont. It is also known to live in a lakes area in Maine's Down East Washington County.

Early reports and bounty records indicate that at one time, the lynx may have ranged throughout New England in all six states.[86] John Josselyn mentioned a wildcat, which could have referred to the lynx.[87] An 1862 account of the lynx noted that "when the country was first settled, the animal was quite troublesome among the sheep and lambs. They went in droves and were more bold than when single." At that time the author noted that New Hampshire paid a bounty of one dollar for each lynx killed.[88] Other states paid bounties as well.

Encouraged to kill the lynx because of its perceived nuisance behavior and because of the value of its pelt, hunters and trappers reduced its numbers. These factors in combination with loss of habitat by the expanding settlements so affected the population that in 1967 Maine gave the animal complete protection by law. Today, the lynx is considered endangered by several New England states. But this cat still remains something of a mystery, and in that respect, the mere knowledge that we still have this wild predator lurking in our deep woods connects us to that wilderness of long ago.

Rattlesnake

This Countrey being very full of Woods and Wildernesses, doth also much abound with Snakes and Serpents of strange colours, and huge greatnesse: yea there are some Serpents called Rattle-snakes, that have Rattles in their Tayles.

—Francis Higginson, 1630[89]

Francis Higginson's description of the timber rattlesnake may well be the earliest published account from the colonies. His account included above reflects a rather neu-

The timber rattlesnake still survives along seven miles of ledges and rocky terrain in the Blue Hills within the Boston area. Illustration from Zadock Thompson, *Natural History of Vermont* (n.p: Zadock Thompson, 1853).

tral attitude, but, in fact, great fear and hatred was felt for snakes in general and especially for *Crotalus horridus*, the rattlesnake. Unfortunately for the snakes, that attitude continues to the present.

Most of the early writers primed our distaste for the rattlesnake and fueled our repulsion of it. The second half of Reverend Higginson's description undoubtedly struck fear in the hearts of most who read it. He wrote that the rattlesnake "will not flye from a man as others will, but will flye upon him and sting him so mortally, that hee will dye within a quarter of an houre after, except the partie stinged have about him some of the root of an Hearbe called Snake weed to bite on, and then hee shall receive no harme."[90]

Four years later, William Wood gave a more complete description of the rattlesnake but left no doubt about its wickedness:

Of the evills. . . . that which is most injurious to the person and life of man is a rattle snake which is generally a yard and a halfe long, as thicke in the middle as the small of a mans legge, she hath a yellow belly, her backe being spotted with blacke, russet, yellow, and greene colours, placed like scales; at her taile is a rattle, with which she makes a noyse when she is molested, or when she seeth any approach neere her, her neck seems to be no thicker than a mans thumbe yet can she swallow a Squerill, having a great wide mouth, with teeth as sharpe as needles, wherewith she biteth such as tread upon her: her poyson lyeth in her teeth, for she hath no sting.[91]

As one might imagine, a considerable amount of folklore surrounded the rattlesnake. Wood related the belief that "if the party live that is bitten, the snake will dye, and if the partie die, the snake will live."[92] John Josselyn wrote that swallowing the snake's heart when it is fresh is a good antidote against its venom.[93] It was also a common belief that its age could be determined by counting its rattles— one rattle for each year. Many also wrote about the snake's ability to charm birds, squirrels, and other prey right into its mouth.

The Vermont historian Samuel Williams included many accounts of this "power of fascination" of the rattlesnake, including the following: "The snake lies stretched out his full length, in some open place; his head raised eight or ten inches from the ground; his colors glow with their greatest brightness; his eyes play with an uncommon brilliancy, and fire, and are steadily fixed on the enchanted animal." When the animal is drawn close enough to it, he wrote, the snake will seize it with its "voracious jaws."[94] From Maine came the report a few years later that the oil or grease from the rattlesnake "when put into the ear will make the head and hearing extremely clear."[95]

It is likely that the timber rattlesnake once lived over a wide area of New England, favoring south-facing slopes in rocky, wooded areas. Its range extended southward from the southern parts of the three northern states. In winter, it survived by retreating into rocky caves, crevices, and underground areas, where many congregated and to which they returned year after year.

The rattlesnake's habit of denning led to large numbers being killed. An early account of such exterminations comes from a letter written in 1712 by Cotton Mather of Massachusetts to England's Royal Society: "The Rattlesnakes havd their Winter-habitations on our Hills, in hideous Caves, and Clefts of Inaccessible Rocks. In the Spring they come forth, and ly a Sunning themselves, but still in pretty feeble circumstances. Our Trained Bands in some of our Countrey towns, take this time, to carry on a War with the *Snakes*, and make the killing of them, a part of their Discipline."[96] At the end of that century, Jeremy Belknap of New Hampshire recounted how "during their torpid state, some persons make a practice of drawing them from their dens, with hooks, and destroying them."[97] And in that same state around the same time, Jacob Bigelow, writing of his travels in the White Mountains, reported that "twenty of these reptiles had been killed in a day" in the vicinity of Bartlett and Conway.[98] In the early 1800s, the historian Williamson wrote that a "great number of the Rattlesnake have been taken on a hill of that name in Raymond, and in some other places in Maine."[99]

By the mid-1800s, signs of the rattlesnake's diminishing numbers began to be acknowledged. Zadock Thompson reported that it had at that time nearly disappeared. Belknap in New Hampshire had already noted that "as the countrey is settled, the number decreases." A Maine report in 1862 noted that it is "rare [and] in the southwest parts of the State only." Joel Allen in 1880 also reported that in eastern Massachusetts it is "found now only at a few localities." An attempt to confirm its presence in Maine between 1909 and 1924 met without success.[100]

Today, the timber rattlesnake has been extirpated from much of its former range. It is still known to occur in four or five of the New England states, but not in Maine. The species is rare, however, and its numbers are probably continuing to decline. As of 1991, three states listed it as endangered—New Hampshire, Vermont, and

Massachusetts. One habitat close to the early settlements and within the urban area of Boston, the Blue Hills, surprisingly still supports a population of timber rattlesnakes.

The Blue Hills were recognized as rattlesnake habitat early in the colonial period. As early as 1634, William Wood noted that "up into the Countrey westward from the plantations is a high hill, which is called rattlesnake hill, where there is great store of these poysonous creatures."[101] Jeremy Belknap in 1792 compared the color of New Hampshire's rattlesnake to "that which is found about the blue-hills in Suffolk county, Massachusetts."[102] At the time Belknap was working on his history, most of the towns surrounding these hills were paying bounties for the snake, and it was being killed in great numbers. Today, the timber rattlesnake still survives here along seven miles of south-facing slopes of ledges and talus. But in the opinion of one naturalist, who has studied this reptile, "He is quietly making his exit."[103] Whether this is good or bad provokes as much controversy as preserving wilderness areas, themselves. One thing remains unarguable: if this creature disappears, another irretrievable piece of our original wilderness will be lost.

BIRDS AND FEATHERED FOWLS

Of Birds there are not many more than 120 kinds as our Naturalists have conjectured, but I think they are deceived; they are divided into land-birds and water-birds, the land-birds again into birds of prey, birds of meat, singing birds and others.

—John Josselyn, 1674[104]

If there is any one thing that distinguishes New England's bird-life at the time of European settlement from today's, it is the astounding flocks that darkened the skies and covered feeding and nesting grounds. Accounts in the early 1600s are filled with estimates of their numbers. William Wood said of the migrations of white geese, or snow geese, "sometimes there will be two or three thousand in a flocke."[105] Thomas Morton wrote that "Cranes are in great store," probably referring to the sandhill crane, in the opinion of one historian. And of the quail, or common bobwhite, Morton wrote, "I have numbered 60. upon a tree at a time."[106] Small shorebirds, such as sanderlings, were in such numbers, wrote Wood, that "I my selfe have killed twelve score at two shoots."[107] John Josselyn recalled that he had seen "threescore broods of young Turkies on the side of a Marsh sunning of themselves in a morning."[108]

Beyond the amazingly large flocks, New England's early bird-life also differed from today's by the presence of species now extinct. Four that frequented colonial New England are now gone forever: passenger pigeon, heath hen, great auk, and Labrador duck. Several factors undoubtedly had roles in bringing about their demise. Specialized adaptations and behavior can make animals vulnerable to changes in food supply, habitat alteration, and predation. Bird species that have small populations to begin with are less likely to survive large reductions in numbers. And uncontrolled alteration of habitat, removal of food supply, and killing can have devastating effects. Commented James C. Greenway, Jr., in his book *Extinct and Vanishing Birds of the World*: "The history of the recent extinction of birds on the North American Continent is so closely related in time to the penetration of the continent by Europeans and their civilization that it is impossible not to believe that the one is the result of the other."[109]

Very early in the colonies wild birds were killed and sold for meat. William Wood gave the prices paid for a number of birds: swans—6 shillings each, brant—6 pence, snow geese—8 pence, Canada goose—18 pence, duck—6 pence, and teal—3 pence. "If I should tell you," he wrote, "how some have killed a hundred geese in a week, fifty ducks at a shot, forty teals at another, it may be counted impossible through nothing more certain."[110]

While some birds encountered by the colonists are now rarely, if ever, seen in New England, such as the whistling swan and the sandhill crane, the wild turkey is one that has returned after being nearly eliminated. Turkeys were plentiful in the early days of settlement. Wood wrote, "of these sometimes there will be forty, threescore, and a hundred of a flocke." Large numbers may be easily killed, he noted, especially when tracked on snow. "Some have killed ten or a dozen in halfe a day; if they can be found towards an evening and watched where they peirch, if one came about ten or eleaven of the clocke he may shoot as often as he will."[111]

By 1672, however, it was a different story, and Josselyn remarked about "the *English* and the Indians having now destroyed the breed, so that 'tis very rare to meet with a wild *Turkie* in the Woods."[112] In addition to hunting, the clearing and loss of beech, oak, hickory, and chestnut

Wild turkey. Redrawn from *A Mapp of New England*, circa 1676, by John Seller, Hydrographer to the King.

trees, which supplied food in the form of nuts, also contributed to the turkey's decline. Writing in 1880 about the turkey in eastern Massachusetts, Joel Allen confirmed that "the complete extirpation of the wild stock appears to have occurred at an early date."[113] This was true for other states as well. In 1853, Zadock Thompson mentioned that a few still could be "found in southern Vermont." Jeremy Belknap, at the end of the previous century in New Hampshire, reported that they were formerly plentiful but "are now retired to the inland mountainous country." In Maine they were probably never numerous and were confined to the southern counties. In Connecticut, the turkey disappeared sometime before 1813.[114] Today, however, thanks to careful management, the turkey has now recovered to a level where it is once again hunted in some areas.

A number of other birds present during European exploration and settlement also had a hard time surviving. The bald eagle, though removed from federally endangered status in the mid-1990s, still does not fare well in the

Bald eagle. Illustration from Zadock Thompson, *Natural History of Vermont* (n.p.: Zadock Thompson, 1853), 59.

east due to the presence of a variety of toxic substances in the environment. It is most abundant in eastern Maine. Golden eagles are very rare in the east. Another raptor, the peregrine falcon, is officially endangered, but it is now returning, thanks to the success of reintroduction efforts. In 1994 a number of eyries were reoccupied. Ten to eleven pairs nested in Vermont that year.[115] Other birds receiving federally endangered designation include the piping plover, Eskimo curlew, and roseate tern.

Though we can't capture directly the full flavor of the New England wilderness with its early bird-life intact, we may at least better imagine it by taking a moment to consider the contributions of the four extinct species.

Passenger Pigeon

Upon the 8th of March, from after it was fair daylight until about eight of the clock in the forenoon, there flew over all the towns in our plantations so many flocks of doves, each flock containing many thousands, and some so many that they obscured the light.

—Thomas Dudley, 1630[116]

Smugglers Notch in Vermont is one of the state's successful nesting sites in a peregrine reintroduction effort.

Of all the sights contributed by wildlife to the early New England wilderness, none is more remarkable than the immense congregations of passenger pigeons. It was described in words of amazement by all early writers who saw them. William Wood, asking to be believed of an account that was not so strange as it was true, told of seeing "them fly as if the Ayerie regiment had beene Pigeons; seeing neyther beginning nor ending, length, or breadth of these Millions of Millions. . . . Many of them build amongst the Pine-trees, thirty miles to the North-east of our plantations; joyning nest to nest, and tree to tree by their nests, so that the Sunne never sees the ground in that place, from whence the *Indians* fetch whole loades of them."[117] Thomas Morton also remarked about discovering "millions of Turtledoves one [on] the greene boughes, which sate pecking of the full ripe pleasant grapes."[118] One researcher, studying historic records, estimated the total population of the passenger pigeon at three billion birds.[119]

The pigeons, when nesting, also added sounds to the wilderness that impressed those who heard them. William Brewster described the pigeons as "very noisey when building. They make a sound resembling the croaking of wood-frogs. Their combined clamor can be heard four or five miles away when atmospheric conditions are favorable."[120]

The value of passenger pigeons as a food source was recognized early by the Europeans. Samuel de Champlain, exploring the Maine coast in 1605, reached some islands in the vicinity of Kennebunkport, Maine, on July 12 and reported that "there are an infinite number of pigeons, of which we caught a good many."[121] In the middle of the century after settlement had occurred and a scarcity of food threatened the colonists, Governor Winthrop wrote that the pigeons "proved a great blessing, it being incredible what multitudes of them were killed daily. It was ordinary for one man to kill eight or ten dozen in half a day, yea five or six dozen at one shoot, and some seven or eight."[122]

Through the next two and a half centuries, the passenger pigeon was killed in unbelievable numbers, both privately for sport and food and commercially for the food market. Especially desirable were the squabs, or young pigeons, and for these the hunters turned to the huge nesting sites where thousands were killed at a time. A feeling for the attitude towards the pigeon is found in a letter published in 1857 by a resident of Connecticut, recalling a pigeon hunt he made as a boy a half-century before:

I can recollect no sports of my youth which equaled in excitement our pigeon hunts. We usully started on horseback before daylight, and made a rapid progress to some stubble-field on West Mountain. . . . on every side the ear was saluted by the mocking screams of the red-headed woodpecker, the cawing of congresses of crows . . . and finally the rushing sound of the pigeons, pouring like a tide over the tops of the trees. By this time of course our nets were ready, and our flyers and stool-birds on the alert. What moments of ecstasy were these, and especially when the head of the flock—some red-breasted old father or grandfather— caught the site of our pigeons, and turning at the call, drew the whole train down into our net-bed. I have often seen a hundred, or two hundred of these splendid birds, come upon us, with a noise absolutely deafening, and sweeping the air with a sudden gust, like the breath of a thundercloud. Sometimes our bush-hut, where we lay concealed, was covered all over with pigeons, and we dared not move a finger, as their red, piercing eyes were upon us. When at

Netting passenger pigeons in Connecticut during the mid-1800s. Illustration from S. G. Goodrich, *Recollections of a Lifetime, or Men and Things I have seen in a Series of Familiar Letters to a Friend*, vol. 1 (New York: Miller, Orton and Mulligan, 1857), 100a.

last, with a sudden pull of the rope, the net was sprung, and we went out to secure our booty—often fifty, and sometimes even a hundred birds—I felt a fullness of triumph, which words are wholly inadequate to express![123]

The slaughter for sport and financial gain continued to increase into the 1800s. Despite the killing on historic nesting grounds, pigeons returned again and again only to be repeatedly attacked and driven away. Unable to sustain their rate of reproduction and faced with a decreasing supply of nuts and seeds as the deciduous forests were cleared, their number began to slowly decline. Yet, when voices of alarm and concern were raised, few believed that such numbers could ever be exterminated.

In New England, it was near the end of the 1800s when the last encounters with the passenger pigeon in the wild were recorded. In Maine, one of the last, perhaps the final one, came on August 16, 1896, when a passenger pigeon was shot in Dexter.[124] Several pigeons were seen feeding in a tree in Greenfield, New Hampshire, in the fall of 1891.[125] The last sighting in Vermont was possibly around 1900.[126] In Massachusetts, the last pigeon was taken at Melrose on April 12, 1894.[127] A flock of eight was seen in August 1893 in Rhode Island.[128] And in Connecticut, a young male was shot at Portland on October 1, 1889.[129]

The year 1900 is considered to mark the end of the passenger pigeon in the wild in the United States. The last one died on September 1, 1914, at the Cincinnati Zoo.

Heath Hen

Heathcockes and Partridges be common; he that is a husband, and will be stirring betime, may kill halfe a dozen in a morning.

—William Wood, 1634[130]

From the sandy scrub oak plains of Massachusetts and Connecticut, the early morning calls of the heath hen, or heathcocke, were well known to those who lived in their vicinity. Whether or not their calls were heard in southern New Hampshire and Maine is a question still not totally resolved, although one researcher recently concluded that

Heath hen. The heathcocke, as it was once called, is now extinct, the last one having died on Martha's Vineyard off the coast of Massachusetts in 1932.

the heath hen probably did occur in Maine on some of the
sandy plains in southern sections of the state.[131]

Heath hens were edible and easy to kill, and the
colonists, according to William Wood, were willing to pay
four pence per bird. Although hunting was a factor in the
initial process of the bird's extinction, it was probably the
loss of its habitat that in the end was more responsible. It
was a habitat that depended upon periodic burning to
maintain the scrub-plainlike conditions that the bird required.[132] The small acorn of the scrub oak was a prime
source of food, although the heath hen was adaptable,
eating a variety of berries and tender herbaceous plants.
The increasing control of wild fires and encroachment by
settlements reduced its living space considerably. Another
factor may have been predation, especially by the
goshawk, which is known to be particularly effective on
the grouse.

Soon after 1840, the heath hen is thought to have been
eliminated from the mainland, and by 1870, it was only
on Martha's Vineyard off the coast of Massachusetts. An
1880 report confirmed that a few still remained on that island, but the writer doubted that they were original stock
"by the fact that birds introduced from the West have been
at different times turned out on this and neighboring islands."[133] Here they continued to decline in number until
1908, when, with only fifty birds remaining, a refuge was
established. By 1915, their number had grown to two
thousand. But then a series of unfortunate events occurred
during the next decade that resulted in the eventual extinction of the bird. A fire, which destroyed much of the
breeding area, was followed by a hard winter and heavy
predation by goshawks. Inbreeding and an unbalanced
male-to-female ratio resulted in fewer births. A poultry
disease infected the population. By 1927, only eleven
males and two females were left, and the next year only
one bird remained. It was last seen in 1932.

Scientist David Raup viewed the extinction of the
heath hen as a two-stage process—the first occurring during the initial decline up to 1870 and the second during its
last stand on Martha's Vineyard. He concluded that the
heath hen would have survived unfortunate events like

those that occurred on Martha's Vineyard had its range remained large and not limited to the island.[134]

One thing is certain: another voice has been lost from the early New England wilderness. We will never be able to hear or see again what Arthur Cleveland Bent did on Martha's Vineyard on April 11, 1923: "At 4.21 [A.M.] the first 'toot' of the heath hen was heard, a note that has often been mistaken for a muffled blast of a tug boat or a fog horn. . . . At 4.27 a heath hen appeared from the scrub oaks on the south side of the meadow."[135]

Wobble, or Great Auk

The Wobble *an ill shaped Fowl, having no long Feathers in their Pinions, which is the reason they cannot fly, not much unlike the Penguin; they are in the Spring very fat, or rather oyly.*

—John Josselyn, 1672[136]

Great auk. Illustration from Justin Winsor, ed., *The Memorial History of Boston*, vol. 1 (Boston, Mass.: J. R. Osgood and Co., 1880), 12.

Did he see the wobble here? I asked myself, as I climbed over the rocks at Prouts Neck in Scarborough, Maine. It was low tide, and I imagined John Josselyn exploring this same section of the coast. This is where he lived during visits in the 1600s, and it was here that he might have seen the great auk, or "wobble," as he called it, presumably after its side-to-side, rocking gait when walking. It would have been an impressive sight, seeing this two-foot-tall black-and-white bird on the rocks here. I was also at Prouts Neck during April, the season when the great auk migration would have been underway. The weather that day was still cold and raw, but I was sure the auk wouldn't have minded. It migrated by swimming through the frigid Atlantic waters, for it could not fly. Instead, its small wings, powered by strong pectoral muscles, were used to propel it through the water.

Spring was when the Indians captured and roasted the great auk, so conclude archaeologists who have determined that its bones, found in shell heaps along the coast in Massachusetts and Maine, were deposited during the months of March and April. These scraps of evidence have been found, among other places, in Maine at Mount Desert Island, Winter Harbor, and islands in Casco Bay, and in Massachusetts at Plum Island, Ipswich, Marble-head, and Cape Cod.

Centuries later, after those ancient refuse piles had long been abandoned, the great auk was reported along the New Hampshire and Massachusetts coasts by Gabriel Archer. Chronicling Bartholomew Gosnold's voyage of 1602, Archer wrote that around latitude 43 degrees "penguins" were seen, and farther south "by the ships side we there killed Penguins."[137] These are thought to be the earliest written references to the great auk on the New England coast. During that time, the population of the great auk is estimated to have run into the millions, and it was frequently encountered by coastal voyagers during its migrations.

Through the years of early exploration and settlement into the early 1800s, the great auk was killed in great numbers for its meat, oil-producing fat, and feathers. Its eggs, which were five inches long, were also highly desired for food. After its largest breeding colony was discovered on Funk Island, a small rocky island off the east coast of Newfoundland, the auk, which was docile and defenseless on land, was slaughtered mercilessly by fishermen and others for food and for feathers for pillows and mattresses. It was reported that hundreds at a time could be driven on boards directly into boats. During the second half of the 1700s, crews lived on the island during summers for the purpose of killing them for their feathers. They would be herded into stone pounds and clubbed to death.[138]

As with the passenger pigeon, the great auk appeared to be so plentiful that it was inconceivable to many that it could be ever completely annihilated. This view was often capitalized upon by those who profited in the short term by the harvesting of wildlife. Unfortunately, the great auk's extermination reflected a pattern that happened time and time again in human history and still occurs today.

Pied Duck, or Labrador Duck

Ducks there are of three kindes, pide Ducks, gray Ducks, and black Ducks.

—Thomas Morton, 1637[139]

According to Charles Francis Adams, Jr., who edited Thomas Morton's *New English Canaan*, the mention of "pide Duck" may have referred to the Labrador duck. This sea, or diving, duck was a relative of the scoters and frequented the New England coast. During winters, the black-and-white males and brown, white-breasted females were seen feeding in sandy bays and estuaries. The bird's range and breeding grounds are unknown. Although it appeared in markets in cities along the east coast, it was apparently never plentiful. It was also wary and difficult to shoot.

Labrador duck. This sea duck, which frequented the New England coast, is now extinct.

Sometime between 1850 and 1875, the Labrador duck disappeared. It is generally accepted that the last one was shot in 1875 on Long Island, New York. Four years before that, one was taken near Canada's Grand Manan Island, which can be seen off the eastern end of the Maine coast.

The reasons for the extinction of the Labrador duck are not precisely known. Some have suggested that its peculiar bill, which seemed to be equipped to sift sandy and muddy sediments in shallow waters for shellfish, might have made the bird vulnerable to changes in food supply or habitat conditions. Perhaps the duck may have been adapted to specialized habitats or sites. Detrimental circumstances related to either of these two conditions might have posed great danger to a bird that already existed in small numbers. We will probably never know.[140]

FISHES AND OTHER CREATURES OF THE WATERS

*We had pestered our
ship so with Cod fish,
that we threw numbers
of them over-boord
againe . . . for the sculls
of Mackerell, herrings,
Cod, and other fish,
that we dayly saw . . .
were wonderfull.*

—John Brereton, 1602[141]

In the mid-1990s, almost four centuries after John Brereton's account of the great abundance of codfish off Cape Cod, that fish and others, including haddock and yellowtail flounder, were at historic lows on Georges Bank east of the Cape. In an effort to restore the depleted stocks, the United States government issued an emergency order in 1994 that placed a temporary ban on most fishing in an area 6,600 square miles in size. For years, the catch of groundfish and flounder had been declining. A combined index of principal groundfish and flounders caught in the Atlantic waters of the northeastern United States showed a decrease of about 80 percent between 1962 and 1991.[142]

Of all the things one learns from the early records of our aquatic creatures, two observations appear over and over: the great diversity of species and the large numbers of them. The clear coastal waters held great numbers of groundfish. These included the Atlantic cod, haddock, pollock, and the flat yellowtail flounder, a strange looking fish with both of its eyes on one side of its head. Swimming in the water column above the groundfish, Atlantic herring, Atlantic mackerel, and skates plied the waters. Lobsters and crabs traveled the bottoms. Near the shores, clams and mussels buried themselves in the flats. Great quantities of oysters also inhabited the estuaries. Seasonally, the alewife, American shad, striped bass, Atlantic salmon, and sturgeon entered the rivers to spawn.

James Rosier, with the Waymouth expedition exploring the mouth of the St. George River in 1605, wrote: "This day our boat went out about a mile from our ship, and in small time with two or three hooks was fished sufficiently for our whole Company three dayes, with great Cod, Haddocke, and Thornebacke."[143]

In 1609, Henry Hudson, approaching the Maine coast, had a similar experience: "After supper we tryed for fish, and I caught fifteene cods, some the greatest that I have seene."[144]

One of the most complete accounts came from Captain John Smith: "Cod, Cuske, Hollybut, Mackerell, Scate, or such like, a man may take with a hooke or line what he will. And, in diverse sandy baies, a man may draw with a great store of Mullets, Bases, and diverse other sorts of such excellent fish, as many as his Net can drawe on shore: no River where there is not plentie of Sturgion, or Salmon, or both; all which are to be had in abundance observing but their seasons."[145]

Later during settlement, William Wood gave us a feeling for the tremendous runs of anadromous fish up the rivers: "Alewives . . . in the latter end of Aprill come up to the fresh Rivers to spawne, in such multitudes as is allmost incredible, pressing up in such shallow waters as will scarce permit them to swimme."[146]

On the flats of estuaries and inlets at the mouths of rivers and streams and out in the bays, the explorers and settlers found unbelievable populations of shellfish. Wrote John Smith, recalling his 1614 voyage: "You shall scarce finde any bay, shallow shore or Cove of sand, where you may not take many Clampes, or Lobsters, or both at your pleasure, and in many places lode your Boat if you please; Nor Isles where you find not . . . Crabs, and Muskels, or all of them, for taking, at a lowe water."[147] Others commented on the abundance of mussels, clams, and the huge beds of oysters. Morton observed that "there are great store of oysters in the entrance of all Rivers. . . . I have seen an Oyster banke a mile in length."[148] "Some be a foote long," wrote Wood.[149]

The ocean also harbored seals and the fishlike whales, dolphins, and porpoises, among other marine mammals, and early reports described both their variety and abundance. "I saw great store of Whales, and Grampusse [a species of dolphin] . . . that it would astonish one to behold," wrote Francis Higginson in 1630.[150] John Josselyn wrote of the sperm whale: "I shall begin first with the Whale a regal fish, as all fishes of extraordinary size are accounted, of these there are . . . seven kinds, the Amber-greese-*Whale* [sperm whale] the chiefest. *Anno Dom.* 1668 the 17 of *July* there was one of them thrown up on the shore between *Winter-harbour* and *Cape-porpus*, about eight mile from the place where I lived, that was five and fifty foot long."[151]

A far different creature was the sea turtle. Again, Josselyn documented its existence, even commenting on its usefulness: "Of Sea-*Turtles* there are five sorts . . . . The ashes of a Sea-*Turtle* mixt with oyl or *Bears*-grease causeth hair to grow."[152] It is possible that these were the leatherback, loggerhead, Atlantic green, Atlantic Ridley, and hawksbill turtles. All are, today, rare along the New England coast.

These and the many other historic accounts and early records show how the presence of these creatures influenced the perception of a wilderness richly endowed with an abundance of fascinating animals. John Smith wrote that "all these and divers other good things do heere, for want of use, still increase, and decrease with little diminution, whereby they growe to that abundance."[153]

Smith didn't forsee what effects our "want of use" of our ocean and coastal resources would have on these animals. Not only were increasingly sophisticated harvesting methods and equipment used to feed the rapidly growing human population, but coastal development heavily impacted the fisheries and coastal wildlife resources. Expanding towns and cities introduced human effluent directly into the waters, and dumps were created on wetlands. Harbor and port facilities produced dredging, accidental oil spills, and shipboard discharge of human wastes. Power plants, roadways, and other developments introduced many forms of pollution. Recreational development modified beaches, wetlands, and other ecosystems. Dams on our rivers prevented fish from reaching spawning grounds.[154] The end result was and still is the decline of our coastal and marine animal life.

The effects on animals that depend upon clean waters and access to spawning habitats have been devastating. By the early 1800s, declines were already being noticed. William Williamson noted in 1832 that, in Maine, oysters "are quite scarce at the present period."[155] Anadromous fish, prevented from spawning, began to decline. The hundreds of thousands of Atlantic salmon and American shad that once came to Vermont and New Hampshire by way of the Connecticut River disappeared—stopped by dams, pollution, and nets. Almost every river on the New England coast supported shad migrations. Today, they are at very low levels in Maine.[156] Landings from the Gulf of Maine and middle Atlantic are down from an average of over two metric tons in 1963 to only one in 1991.[157] The shortnose sturgeon is now listed as federally endangered, and twelve other fish from coastal and inland waters have classifications ranging from special concern to endangered in various New England states.[158] All the large whales are now protected in United States waters by the Endangered Species Act of 1973.

We here examine a few creatures from the sea and our rivers that have survived from when they were freer to go about their lives. Today, they challenge us to act on a concern for their future.

Sturgeon

East-ward is Kenebeck-*river fifty leagues off of* New Plymouth *Eastward, and* Pechipscut *[Androscoggin River] famous for multitudes of mighty large* Sturgeon.

—John Josselyn, 1674[159]

Two cormorants floated by on a piece of driftwood—an easy way to relax, dry out, and travel to another fishing location, all at the same time. Between the islands and the edge at Chopps Point, where I stood, the current quickened and gripped the driftwood. The Kennebec River here

Atlantic sturgeon. Illustration from Zadock Thompson, *Natural History of Vermont* (n.p.: Zadock Thompson, 1853).

was a small rapid now that the tide was going out. It was quiet that sunny September afternoon. The only sounds were of acorns dropping from the large red oaks on the shore behind me and the gush of water flowing over the ledge. A warm breeze rippled the bay. Across from me, far in the distance, the Androscoggin entered—one of the six rivers that meet here at Merrymeeting Bay.

Beneath the bright surface, I imagined giant, armor-plated fish grubbing in the bottom sediments for worms and shellfish. It would be a thrill to see one of these monster sturgeon leap above the surface as they have for centuries here. When members of the Popham expedition sailed up this river in 1607, they saw around their ship

Merrymeeting Bay, seen here from Chopps Point, continues to attract sturgeon, although in much smaller numbers than historically reported.

an abundance of these "greatt fyshe in ytt Leaping above the Watter on eatch syd."[160] Later in the same century, Josselyn, writing on the sturgeon, mentioned this area specifically: "This Fish is here in great plenty, and in some Rivers so numerous, that it is hazardous for Canoes and the like small Vessels to pass to and again, as in Pechips-cut River [Androscoggin River] to the Eastward."[161]

Two species of sturgeon are in New England's coastal region. The Atlantic sturgeon reaches gigantic proportions, and though average size ranges from 6 to 10 feet in length and 60 to 250 pounds in weight, it has been known to reach 14 feet in length and 850 pounds in weight. The shortnose sturgeon is much smaller, perhaps reaching 40 pounds and something over 3 feet. Both are bottom feeders that suck up their food from the bottom sediments and, consequently, have no teeth.

All of the early seventeenth-century writers commented on the sturgeon. William Wood wrote that "the Sturgeons be all over the countrey, but the best catching of them be upon the shoals of *Cape Codde*, and in the River of *Merrimacke*, where much is taken pickled and brought to *England*."[162] Thomas Morton observed that "there are multitudes of them, and they are much fatter than those that are brought into England from other parts."[163]

These fish have long been valued for their roe, known also as caviar, and for their oil and flesh. Josselyn called it a regal fish, perhaps in recognition that in England it was a royal fish: the king had a right to all sturgeons, except in cases where others had been granted that right. Because of the sturgeon's value, it supported a large commercial fishery in the early years. Even in the early 1800s, it was still doing well. The historian Williamson wrote in 1832 that in Maine the Atlantic sturgeon migrates "into almost all of our rivers and returns in Autumn."[164] In the Kennebec River, 160 tons were caught in 1849.[165] But this river, like so many of New England's rivers, lost its fishery before the 1900s due to dams, industrial pollution, and overfishing. In 1890, seven million pounds of sturgeon were landed on the east coast. A hundred years later in 1990, only 152,000 pounds were caught.[166]

Today, only a few rivers support populations of sturgeons—the Connecticut, Merrimack, and the Kennebec-Androscoggin system, which also includes the Sheepscot and Montsweag Bay area. A 1994 survey found none in the Penobscot River.[167] And by comparison with their former abundance, only remnant populations of the Atlantic and shortnose sturgeons survive, and unsuitable habitat and dams continue to stand in the way of re-establishing these fish in any large numbers. Still, as I stood on the ledge at Chopps Point that fall day, there was a twinge of excitement knowing that a sturgeon just might, just might, show itself.

Salmon

Here we saw great store of fish, some great, leaping above water, which we judges to be salmons.

—James Rosier, 1605[168]

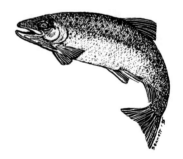

Atlantic Salmon. In pre-colonial times, an estimated 300,000 salmon migrated up New England's rivers to spawn. In 1993, only about 3,500 were reported.

When the European explorers and settlers arrived on New England's shores and explored up its rivers, they saw many Atlantic salmon, as did James Rosier accompanying Captain George Waymouth up the St. George River. The abundance of this fish was documented in many early reports and records. William Wood reported in 1634 that "the Sammon is as good as it is in *England* and in great plenty."[169] In his time, at least twenty-eight major rivers contained large populations.[170] More than 300,000 adult salmon may have migrated each year into these rivers. Those accounting for the greatest numbers of salmon were the Connecticut, Merrimack, Androscoggin, Kennebec, and Penobscot Rivers. Thousands of boatloads, for exam-

Although the Penobscot River in Maine, seen here in South Orrington below Bangor, experiences the largest runs of Atlantic salmon in New England, the numbers are pitifully small compared to colonial times.

ple, were shipped from the Kennebec to east coast markets. They were so plentiful that farmers used the fish for fertilizer.[171] Even at the beginning of the eighteenth century reports said that the rivers were still well populated by salmon. In Vermont, Samuel Williams wrote in 1809 that "in the spring, about the 25th of April, these fish begin to pass up Connecticut river, and proceed to the highest branches. About the same time, or a little later, they are found in Lake Champlain, and the large streams which fall into it. . . . Some of these salmon in the spring, will weight thirty five or forty pounds."[172]

In New Hampshire, however, near the end of the eighteenth century, Jeremy Belknap noted that, though salmon once frequented the Piscataqua River, "the numerous dams built across its branches, have obstructed the course of this valuable fish, and it has, for many years, totally forsaken the river. It still ascends the Saco, Merrimack and Connecticut."[173] The salmon in the Connecticut soon experienced the same fate as those in the Piscataqua, for Zadock Thompson unhappily reported that in Vermont by mid-century "the Salmon, formerly very plentiful in nearly all the large streams in this state, is now so exceedingly rare a visitant that I have not been able to obtain a specimen taken in our waters."[174] By 1865, the dams, overfishing, and pollution had eliminated the salmon runs in southern New England.

Today, the salmon enters about sixteen river systems in New England. About 3,000 to 7,000 salmon run up these rivers, and of that number, only 1,500 to 2,500 are wild stock. In 1993, an estimated 3,433 returned to spawn in New England's rivers, and of these, 3,123 were in Maine's rivers. This is a far cry from the estimated 300,000 pre-colonial number. The only wild salmon runs now occur in eight Maine rivers. Restoration efforts are underway in the St. Croix, Penobscot, Saco, Aroostook, and Union Rivers in Maine; the Merrimack River in Massachusetts; the Pawcatuck River between Rhode Island and Connecticut, the Connecticut River, and the Lamprey and Cocheco Rivers in New Hampshire.

New England's largest runs of salmon occur in the Penobscot River. The river is undammed below Bangor, and I visited this area on a day in early fall. The weather was cloudy and a sprinkle dampened the grassy point I stood on at the edge of the river. The well-wooded shoreline might have passed for one of an earlier day when thousands of salmon ran up the river by that point to spawn. The difference today is in the number and origin of salmon that migrate here. Only 6.8 percent of the run in 1993 contained salmon of wild origin. The remainder was stocked fish and reflected the long restoration effort here. And though this was the largest salmon run in New England, the returning adult salmon numbered only 1,769. Anglers caught 574 of them.[175]

As I write this, the future of the Atlantic salmon is uncertain. There is no uncertainty, however, about the loss in numbers of New England's wild spawning salmon. We are fortunate that a population still remains, but how it will fare in the future is a question still to be answered.

Seals

I manned my Boat and went on shoare, where I found great store of Seales: And I killed three Seales with my hanger. This Iland is not halfe a mile about, nothing but a Rocke, which seemed to be very rich Marble stone.

—Samuel Argall, 1610[176]

Exactly what species of seal Captain Argall encountered in the outer Penobscot Bay area is not certain. If we go by the range habits of known seals today, they were likely harbor or gray seals. Harp and hooded seals are rare visitors south of eastern Canada.

Today, harbor seals breed as far south as New Hampshire, but until 1994, no breeding colony of gray seals along the New England coast had been documented. In that year during the winter, thirty-nine gray seal pups were spotted on an island in mid-coast Maine.[177] Why a colony has now appeared this far south is not known, although it was reported in 1983 that Canadian stocks were expanding.[178] Whether or not this seal formerly bred along the New England coast is not known. It does, however, have an ancient history in New England because its remains have been found in Indian middens at Mt. Desert Island, Cape Cod, Martha's Vineyard, Nantucket Island, and Block Island.[179]

From the time of European contact, New England's seals were hunted. As early as 1603, Martin Pring, while in the area of Plymouth Harbor, reported that he found "Seales to make Oile withall."[180] But it was the fear of competition for fish that spurred much of their killing through the centuries and even the payment of bounties by Maine and Massachusetts. By the early part of the twentieth century, seals were eliminated from much of the coast. In Maine, a statewide bounty was established in 1895, but in 1905 it was recalled because of fraudulent claims. Since then the seals have made a slow recovery. Massachusetts recalled its bounty in 1962.

In 1967, after an absence of years, three gray seals were discovered on Green Island Seal Ledges in Penobscot Bay. In 1972, the gray and other seals received protection from passage of the United States Marine Mammal Protection Act. By 1973, an estimated one hundred gray seals lived along the Maine coast and a dozen or more on Massachusetts islands during the summer dispersal from northern breeding grounds.[181] In 1976, the gray seal was a known summer resident on fifteen of Maine's coastal islands.

It was on one of those islands that I saw my first gray seal. I was on a whale watch excursion, which was aborted because of fog. On the way, however, the captain took us by an island. Through the heavy mist, we saw a group of harbor seals on dark, rocky ledges at the edge of the water, and in their midst, a large gray seal. It was unmistakable with its lighter color, patterned coat, large size, and heavier muzzled head. The great seal looked at us disinterestedly, unafraid. Only a few of us on that boat knew that the reception it and its neighbors got that day was not one they would have received during most of the four centuries since Captain Argall had discovered their kind on another island not too far distant. No, the reception the seals got the day I saw them was one of welcome.

Whales

Now we saw . . . a great store of great whales puffing up water as they go; some of them came near our ship. Their greatness did astonish us that saw them not before; their backs appeared like a little island.

—Francis Higginson, June 25, 1629[182]

We end this chapter of early New England wildlife with whales. Those who see these great creatures today still share the same reaction Francis Higginson recorded in his journal of his early voyage to New England. Of all the creatures once common in those early years of exploration and settlement, when the wild, unspoiled character of the land extended to the sea, none has captivated and thrilled us more over the centuries than the whales. Perhaps in no other creature do we have a greater poetic expression of wildness.

When the Pilgrims arrived in Cape Cod Bay, William Bradford wrote: "Every day we saw Whales playing hard by us, of which in that place, if we had instruments & meanes to take them, we might have made a very richy returne, which to our great griefe we wanted. Our master and his mate, and others experienced in fishing, professed, we might have made three or foure thousand pounds worth of Oyle."[183]

Whales appeared to be plentiful then, but from the first, as we see from the early reports, they were looked on with more than astonishment, for they represented valued products. Long before the Mayflower, Captain John Smith had arrived at Monhegan Island off the Maine coast intent on taking whales. "We saw many," he wrote later, "and spent much time chasing them, but could not kill any."[184] This was, however, not to be the case in many of the hunts to come, for as methods and equipment improved so did the success rate of killing. A little more than two centuries later, the Maine historian William Williamson wrote that "*Whales*, two centuries ago, were common in our waters, when Capt. Smith fished for them about our great bays. Such as we now see, are the *Humpback*, which are the most common."[185]

Williamson was writing his history during what we now call the "golden age of whaling," a period between 1825 and 1860. After that, whaling declined due to both lack of demand for whale products and decreasing numbers of animals. Little hunting has occurred in the Gulf of Maine in the twentieth century. With the passage of the Marine Mammal Protection Act of 1972, whaling ceased in the United States, and with enactment of the Endangered Species Act of 1973, six species of whales in or near New England waters are now listed as federally endangered. Two of the most common whales are the finback, second only in size to the blue whale, and the humpback. The other endangered species of whale are rarely seen.

Today, concern continues over the future of these marine mammals. Though protected in United States waters, they are still vulnerable to fateful entanglements in fishing gear, injury from ships, pollution, illegal killing, and effects of other human activities. We must still continue to educate ourselves about these creatures and the requirements for their long-term survival. But as with all the remnants of the early New England wilderness discussed in this book, we must have the concern and motivation that will lead to efforts on their behalf. Perhaps we should take a lesson from the journal of the Reverend Francis Higginson; if we could all have the kind of firsthand experience he had on that windy Thursday off Cape Anne in 1629, perhaps that is the secret.

Chapter 7

Of Values and Hope

One warm summer day while completing this book, I sat at the edge of the field on the hill behind my home and watched a hawk riding the thermals high in the sky. It was a northern harrier, or marsh hawk, that I had seen hunting the bog in front of my house, and it caught my attention because this species seldom soars so high except during courtship. It dipped and swayed from side to side with fully expanded wings, adjusting itself to the rising air currents. Its slow, circular, uplifting pattern reminded me of a theory about learning: we can develop deeper levels of understanding if we keep returning to a concept as we gain experience and maturity—a kind of learning spiral, if you will. I believe that this applies also to ideas that are carried through time, to be revisited and examined by succeeding generations. Like a hawk widening its view as it circles, soaring higher and higher, we must expand our perspective on our role in the natural world, especially as it relates to wilderness.

The concept of wilderness has evolved through several value-laden meanings since John Josselyn's day, when wilderness was commonly viewed by Europeans as a fearsome condition, an obstacle to civilization, and a wasteland to be removed. Two centuries after John Josselyn's first visit to Maine, Henry David Thoreau saw in wildness "the preservation of the world."[1] In Thoreau's time, new views on wilderness were emerging as people began to recognize our need for wild nature. But another century of thinking, debate, and political action would pass before the idea of wilderness preservation became public law. That act of law, the Wilderness Act of 1964, and others that followed were giant strides toward the recognition that we humans share our planet with millions of other species that are important in their own right and to which we are connected.

A mossy trail on an island off the coast of Maine leads one into a dense, untouched forest of spruce and fir. Protecting wild places, such as this, preserves ecological and psychological values and gives hope for the future of the planet and its life.

Our connections in nature are more than physical; they are also emotional and spiritual. The hawk provoked my interest, and in the moment I watched it soar out of sight, I was connected to it by my thoughts and emotions. The many wild places I visited in the course of working on this book affected me similarly, but they also raise an important question: what special values does nature hold for us? (Or, more specifically, what are the values represented most strongly by wild places and less by tamer animals and more disturbed habitats?) I've read extensively and talked with many who share my passion for wilderness, but what insights and feelings I've acquired have come mainly from personal experience of wild things and wild places. The values I see most clearly are those I group as ecologial and psychological.

My sense of the ecological value of wild land was acquired initially from lengthy excursions into the Allagash Wilderness Waterway and Baxter State Park in northern Maine. At the same time, I observed the effects of human activities on the lands surrounding these protected areas. I returned each year to these two state parks, where the protection of wilderness character is a strong management objective, and found mountains, valleys, and shorelines that appeared unchanged and waters that remained pure. I became aware that within the borders of these protected areas are many undisturbed ecosystems that offer us opportunities to learn firsthand about the progression of natural processes. At the same time, however, I worried about the disappearing pockets of unaltered land outside their boundaries. It is gratifying to know that, through the efforts of public and private organizations and supportive landowners, some places are now being preserved and protected.

In the 1980s I learned about the existence of the Big Reed Forest Reserve, five thousand acres of pristine woodland in northern Maine. When I was guided into this pathless forest one early summer day a decade later, I saw a place that we have chosen to let alone, leaving its natural processes to work without direct human interventions. I also saw a place where, if we could do so without disturbing those processes, our best scientists might design studies that would compare an untouched forest with those affected by logging and other uses. Such studies could produce information that would result in our taking better care of the land. Fundamentally, however, I saw in Big Reed that day a representation of an ecological value in wild land preservation.

There are other values inherent in wild places that relate directly to our psychological, or emotional, well-being. When we reached Big Reed Pond, following compass readings through a roadless and trailless forest, I pulled away from the group and sat by the water's edge on a ledge outcrop. No evidence of human intrusion appeared anywhere. I was strongly aware of the vivid contrast between that lonely peninsula on Big Reed Pond and the developed areas we had driven through to get there. As I reflected on the differences between the two worlds, I developed a fresh perspective on the changes we are making on the land. I did not conclude that what I had seen was all bad; rather, I came to question why certain decisions had been made. For example, part of our trip had followed a major highway across a large wetland; why was it built there? Visits to wild places give us a means of comparison—the opportunity to step back and view our activities more critically. We find that they are valuable for the perspective they can give us on our ethical responsibility to the land.

The preservation of wild lands provides other psychological values as well. Later that summer, my wife and I made our annual canoe trip to the Allagash Wilderness Waterway. The Allagash region has a rich and long history of logging, and on our trips we are reminded of its role in shaping the culture of northern New England when we notice the remains of an old trestle slowly sinking into the upper end of Chamberlain Lake, or two giant steam locomotives rusting away in the middle of the forest. Old cogged wheels rising above the alders on the lake shore show where a turn-of-the-century tramway once carried logs on an endless cable between two lakes. A lone building, squeezed between the shore and the advancing forest behind, marks the location of the six-hundred-acre Chamberlain Farm, developed in 1846 to meet the growing logging industry's need for food, fodder, and a supply depot.

The farm was a stopping point in the 1800s for wilderness romantics like Henry Thoreau and sportsmen like Lucius Hubbard and Thomas Steele, all of whom wrote about their travels in this country. Today one of the farm buildings and remnants of old fields are preserved within the waterway, giving us the opportunity to encounter reminders of a time when the taming of the wilderness laid one cornerstone of Maine's identity. Wilderness areas in this respect are living museums that give us a firsthand impression of the conditions indigenous peoples and European settlers faced.

Still later that summer, we hiked into the northern part of Baxter State Park, another wilderness area that will be here for future generations to experience. It doesn't

A lone hiker pauses to view Mt. Katahdin's Chimney Basin and the Knife Edge. We must be touched directly by the objects of the natural world and experience intimately the natural events around us to care deeply about them.

matter whether or not they avail themselves of this spectacular preserve, but it does matter that they have the opportunity to do so. I know that someday I will be unable to traverse the trails of this park, but I will have the satisfaction of knowing that it will continue to be there. In this sense, a wild area is like an heirloom, and one might argue that an area representing untarnished nature expresses this value more strongly than one that is more altered.

My trips throughout New England to visit our remaining unspoiled natural areas and features were efforts to identify how each uniquely represents the ecological and psychological values I have described in this final chapter. Most, if not all, of the sites I visited have been threatened by economic pressures. For example, New England's most recently designated wilderness—the 12,000-acre Caribou–Speckled Mountain Wilderness in Maine's section of the White Mountain National Forest—required an intensive eight-year effort to become a reality. Even after wild lands are set aside, they must be diligently safeguarded. This was impressed upon me time and time again as I observed the encroachments on the wild and scenic character of the Allagash Wilderness Waterway. And I still marvel at how much of the natural setting and integrity of Drum Rock, in Rhode Island, still survives.

Inevitably the question arises of how much wilderness is enough. At this writing, there are several proposals for protecting large areas of relatively undeveloped wild lands in northern New England, proposals that would allow human uses but would favor protection of natural processes. These proposals are aimed at preventing the detrimental and often irreversible effects of development. All recognize the need for study, citizen support, and planning for long-range protection through a variety of means. The window of opportunity for setting aside areas large enough to fully protect and restore the region's diversity of ecological systems closes a little more with each development. Can we afford to ignore the opportunity?

Neither can we afford to be complacent about those wilderness areas which now appear to be protected, for even they can be degraded by air pollution, uncontrolled access (particularly by motorized vehicles and boats), and encroaching development. Underlying these problems are the extremely difficult and complex issues of controlling our numbers and limiting our use of natural resources. These give rise to serious questions. Do we have the moral capacity and intellectual will to solve these problems for the future of all species? As a symbol of the restraint that we must exercise, can we not protect a few remnants of New England's wild nature? What makes it so difficult to answer these questions in the affirmative and follow through with appropriate actions is that, having tamed John Josselyn's colonial wilderness, we now find ourselves so removed from the rest of nature that we are in danger not only of losing our sense of connectedness to the natural world but of substituting a disregard for it.

Could it be that in the very remnants of the wilderness we are in danger of losing we have one of our best hopes of regaining our sense of connection to the planet? In a world where we encounter so many objects and events indirectly through electronic media, it's easy to miss or underestimate the powerful effects of firsthand experiences. During my odyssey through New England, I had the experience of standing on a narrow stretch of lonely beach between the sea and Block Island's towering Mohegan Bluffs as evening shadows enveloped me. Another time I sat in the close dampness of Connecticut's historic Moodus Cave, straining to hear the rumblings of the legendary Moodus noises. By the time I had completed my journeys, I had felt the touch of more than a hundred remnants of an earlier time. From them I not only gained a sense of connectedness with the rest of nature, I experienced a deep sense of moral responsibility for safeguarding what is left of our original landscape. It was a lesson I learned over and over again: we must be touched directly by the objects of the natural world and experience intimately the natural events around us to care deeply about them.

As I watched the hawk spiral up over my old farm, becoming a mere speck in the sky and finally vanishing from sight, I hoped it would return so that I might again benefit by its presence, just as I hope that future generations might benefit by the presence of New England's natural heritage. Hope is the human emotion behind the theme of this book. It was written with the hope that the nature of the New England wilderness will not be forgotten, that its remnants will be preserved and protected, and that all those who visit these remaining traces of wilderness, or simply know about them, will be more caring of this planet and the future of all species.

Notes

CHAPTER 1: OF THE WILDERNESS

1. Edward Gaylord Bourne, ed., *The Voyages and Explorations of Samuel de Champlain: 1604–1616, Narrated by Himself*, Trans. Annie Nettleton Bourne, vol. 1 (1904; reprint, New York: Allerton Book Co., 1922), 124

2. Some of the description of the Monomoy National Wildlife Refuge is from *Environmental Assessment: Master Plan Monomoy National Wildlife Refuge* (Chatham, Mass.: U.S. Fish and Wildlife Service, Department of the Interior, 1988), 39–62; *Morris Island Trail Guide: Monomoy National Wildlife Refuge* (Chatham, Mass.: U.S. Fish and Wildlife Service, Department of the Interior, U.S. Fish & Wildlife Service, 1993).

3. John Josselyn, *An Account of Two Voyages to New-England*, 2d ed. (1675; reprint, Boston, Mass.: William Veazie, 1865), 20.

4. Lawrence C. Wroth, *The Voyages of Giovanni da Verrazzano: 1524–1528* (New Haven, Conn.: The Pierpont Morgan Library, Yale University Press, 1970), 11.

5. Giovanni da Verrazzano, *To the Most Christian King of France, Francis the First: The Relation of John de Varazzano, a Florentine, of the Land by Him Discovered in the Name of His Magestie*, in *Collections of the New-York Historical Society for the Year 1809*, vol. 1 (New York: I. Riley, 1811), 58.

6. John Brereton, *A Briefe and True Relation of the Discoverie of the North Part of Virginia*, in *Sailors Narratives of Voyages along the New England Coast: 1524–1624*, ed. George Parker Winship (1905; reprint, New York: Burt Franklin, n.d.), 34.

7. Quoted in David B. Quinn, ed., *North American Discovery: Circa 1000–1612* (Columbia: S.C.: University of South Carolina Press, 1971), 261.

8. Martin Pring, *A Voyage set out from the Citie of Bristoll*, in *Sailors Narratives*, 54–55.

9. For a discussion of the style and significance of Champlain's and Smith's maps, see Douglas R. McManis, *European Impressions of the New England Coast: 1497–1620*, research paper No. 139 (Chicago: The Department of Geography, The University of Chicago, 1972), 40–48.

10. Samuel Eliot Morison, *Samuel de Champlain: Father of France* (Boston: Little, Brown and Company, 1972), xi, 22.

11. Regarding the length of a league, Ganong noted that it had several values. In English miles, the common league of France was 2.76 miles; the legal league, 2.42 miles; and the marine league, 3.45 miles. See William F. Ganong, *Denys: Description & Natural History of the Coasts of North America (Acadia)* (1908; reprint, New York: Greenwood Press, Publishers, 1968), 106.

12. Bourne, *Champlain*, 95–96.

13. James Rosier, *A True Relation of the Most Prosperous Voyage made this present yeere 1605, by Captaine George Waymouth*, in *Sailors Narratives*, 116.

14. [James Davies?], *The Relation of a Voyage unto New England*, in *Sailors Narratives*, 171–72.

15. John Smith, *A Description of New England*, in *Sailors Narratives*, 243.

16. Three sources of bibliographic information pertaining to early accounts that include reference to New England's wilderness are the following: Edward G. Cox, "The New World," in *Reference Guide to Literature of Travel*, vol. 3 (Seattle, Wash.: n.p., 1938); Harriette Merrifield Forbes, comp., *New England Diaries, 1602–1800: A Descriptive Catalogue of Diaries, Orderly Books and Sea Journals* (New York: Russell & Russell, 1967); Justin Winsor, *The Earliest Printed Sources of New England History, 1602–1629* (Cambridge, Mass.: John Wilson and Son, University Press, 1894).

17. John Josselyn, *New-Englands Rarities Discovered* (1672; reprint, Chester, Conn.: Applewood Books, n.d.), 4.

18. William Bradford, *Of Plymouth Plantation: 1620–1647*, ed. Samuel Eliot Morrison (New York: Alfred A. Knopf, 1959), 62.

19. William Wood, *New England's Prospect* (1634; reprint, New York: Burt Franklin, 1967), 17.

20. Josselyn, *Two Voyages*, 155.

21. Thomas Morton, *New English Canaan*, ed. Charles Francis Adams, Jr. (1637; reprint, New York: Burt Franklin, 1967), 180.

22. William Bradford and Edward Winslow, *Mourt's Relation*, in *The Journal of the Pilgrims at Plymouth: in New England in 1620*, ed. George Barrell Cheever (New York: John Wiley, 1848), 57.

23. Wood, *Prospect*, 16.

24. Francis Higginson, *New England's Plantation* (1630; reprint, New York: The New England Society in the City of New York, 1930), B.

25. Smith, *Description of New England*, 239.

26. Josselyn, *Rarities*, 4.

27. Increase Mather, *The Day of Trouble is Near* (Boston, Mass.: J. Foster, 1677), 3.

28. John White, *The Planter's Plea or the Grounds of Plantations Examined and Usual Objections Answered* (1630; reprint, New York: Da Capo Press, 1968), 28.

29. Thomas Shepard, Jr., *Eye-Salve; or, a Watch-Word From our Lord Jesus Christ unto his Churches* (Cambridge, Mass.: n.p., 1673). 3–4.

30. White, *Planter's Plea*, 9–10.

31. William Hubbard, "Hubbard's Narrative," in *Chronicles of the First Planters of the Colony of Massachusetts Bay, from 1623 to 1636*, ed. Alexander Young (1846; reprint, Williamstown, Mass.: Corner House Publishers, 1978), 29.

32. Roger Clap, "Captain Roger Clap's Memoirs," in *Chronicles*, 348.

33. R. S. Kellogg (1909), quoted in Roland M.

Harper, "Changes in the Forest Area of New England in Three Centuries," *Journal of Forestry* (1918): 442.

34. The limitation of government land surveys in determining the early character of southern New England's original landscape is pointed out by Richard B. Brugam, "Pollen Indicators of Land-Use Change in Southern Connecticut," *Quaternary Research* 9 (1978): 351.

35. See D. Foster and E. Boose, "Patterns of Forest Damage Resulting from Catastrophic Wind in Central New England, USA," *Journal of Ecology* 80 (1992): 79–98.

36. For a summary of the extent of Indian burning, see David Foster, "Land-Use History and Four Hundred Years of Vegetation Change in New England," in *Global Land Use Change: a Perspective from the Columbian Encounter*, ed. A. Gomez Sal (n.p.: Scientific Research Council of Spain, 1995).

37. For a brief overview of the state of science of geology in the late 1700s, see Kenneth L. Taylor, "Geology in 1776: Some Notes on the Character of an Incipient Science," in *Two Hundred Years of Geology in America: Proceedings of the New Hampshire Bicentennial Conference on the History of Geology*, ed. Cecil J. Schneer (Hanover, N.H.: University Press of New England, 1979), 76–90.

38. For an analysis of the social and scientific setting which contributed to the initiation of state geological surveys, see Michele L. Aldrich, "American State Geological Surveys, 1820–1845," in *Two Hundred Years of Geology in America: Proceedings*, 133–43; Dick J. Struck, *Yankee Science in the Making* (Boston, Mass.: Little, Brown and Company, 1948), 181–201.

39. See M. J. S. Radwick, *The Great Devonian Controversy* (Chicago: University of Chicago Press, 1985).

40. Ezekiel Holmes and Charles H. Hitchcock, "General Reports upon the Natural History and Geology of Maine," in *Sixth Annual Report of the Secretary of the Maine Board of Agriculture: 1861* (Augusta, Maine: Stevens & Sayward, 1861), 152–54.

41. For a brief biographical examination of Charles T. Jackson, an assessment of his contributions, and the scientific context in which he worked, see Mark Hineline, "Charles Thomas Jackson and the First Geological Survey of Maine, 1836–1838," *Studies in Maine Geology: Structure and Stratigraphy*, ed. Robert D. Tucker and Robert G. Marvinney, vol. 1 (Augusta, Maine: Maine Geological Survey, Department of Conservation, 1988), 1–16.

42. Charles T. Jackson, *Second Annual Report on the Geology of the Public Lands Belonging to the Two States of Massachusetts and Maine* (Boston, Mass.: Dutton and Wentworth, 1838), 21.

43. Ezekiel Holmes, *Report of an Exploration and Survey of the Territory on the Aroostook River During the Spring and Autumn of 1838* (Augusta, Maine: Smith & Robinson, 1839), 50.

44. Edward Hitchcock, *Final Report on the Geology of Massachusetts* (Amherst, Mass.: J. S. & C. Adams, 1841), 227.

45. James G. Percival, *Report on the Geology of the State of Connecticut* (New Haven, Conn.: Osborn & Baldwin, Printers, 1842), 478.

46. Holmes and Hitchcock, "General Reports," 99.

47. Holmes and Hitchcock, "General Reports," 346.

48. Ezekiel Holmes and Charles H. Hitchcock, "Second Annual Report upon the Natural History and Geology of the State of Maine: 1862," in *Seventh Annual Report of the Secretary of the Maine Board of Agriculture: 1862* (Augusta, Maine: Stevens & Sayward, 1862), 296.

49. Albert D. Hager, et al., *Report on the Geology of Vermont: Descriptive, Theoretical, Economical, and Scenographical*, vol. 2 (Claremont, N.H.: The Claremont Manufacturing Company, 1861), 904.

50. Charles H. Hitchcock, *The Geology of New Hampshire*, vol. 1 (Concord, N.H.: Edward A. Jenks, 1874), 216–18.

51. For an overview of evidence of Maine's extinct and extirpated animal life from shell middens and other archaeological sites, see Arthur Spiess, "Comings and Goings: Maine's Prehistoric Wildlife," *Habitat: Journal of the Maine Audubon Society*, 5 (1) (January 1988): 30–33.

52. Michael J. Heckenberger, et al., "Early Woodland Period Mortuary Ceremonialism in the Far Northeast: A View from the Boucher Cemetery," *Archaeology of Eastern North America*, 18 (Fall 1990): 109–144.

53. For a general description of Maine petroglyphs and their role in Native culture, see Mark H. Hedden, "Prehistoric Maine Petroglyphs (A Videoscript)," *The Maine Archaeological Society, Inc., Bulletin*, 28 (1) (Spring 1988): 3–27.

54. For a brief discussion of the meaning and role of Native American legends, see Maine Indian Program, *The Wabanakis of Maine and the Maritimes* (Bath, Maine: Maine Indian Program of the New England Regional Office of the American Friends Service Committee, 1989), B-67, B-68.

55. Rosier, "*A True Relation*," 150.

56. Wood, *Prospect*, 25–26.

57. Jeremy Belknap, *The History of New-Hampshire*, vol. 1 (Dover, N.H.: S. C. Stevens and Ela & Wadleigh, 1831), 424.

58. Samuel Williams, *The Natural and Civil History of Vermont*, vol. 1 (Burlington, Vt.: Samuel Mills, 1809), 137.

59. T. D. Seymour Basset, ed., *Natural History of Vermont*, by Zadock Thompson (1853; reprint, Rutland, Vt.: Charles E. Tuttle Company, Inc., 1971), viii.

60. Benjamin Trumbull, *A Complete History of Connecticut, Civil and Ecclesiastical from the Emigration of its First Planters from England*, vol. 1 (Hartford, Conn.: Hudson & Godwin, 1797), 15.

61. William D. Williamson, *The History of the State of Maine from Its First Discovery, A. D. 1602, to the Separation, A. D. 1820, Inclusive*, vol. 1 (Hallowell, Maine: Glazier Masters & Co., 1832), 2.

62. See Moses Greenleaf, *A Survey of the State of Maine in Reference to its Geographical Features, Statistics and Political Economy* (Portland, Maine: Shirley and Hyde, 1829).

63. For a discussion of the role of mapmakers and a review of New England maps, see McManis, *European Impressions*. Also see John Goss, *The Mapping of North America: Three Centuries of Map-Making 1500–1860* (Secaucus, N. J.: The Wellfleet Press, 1990).

64. The possible influence of geology on the work of Thomas Cole is discussed by Ellwood C. Parry, III, "Acts of God, Acts of Man: Geological Ideas and the Imaginary

Landscapes of Thomas Cole," in *Two Hundred Years of Geology in America: Proceedings of the New Hampshire Bicentennial Conference on the History of Geology*, ed. Cecil J. Schneer (Hanover, N.H.: University Press of New England, 1979), 53–71.

65. David Foster, "Land-use History and Forest Transformations in Central New England," in *Humans as Components of Ecosystems: Subtle Human Effects and the Ecology of Populated Areas*, ed. M. McDonnell and S. T. A. Pickett (New York: Springer-Verlag, 1993), 10–13.

66. Graph for loss of original forest land in Maine is based on data from Philip T. Coolidge, *History of the Maine Woods* (Bangor, Maine: Furbush-Roberts Printing Company, Inc., 1963). Data for the graph for the other New England States used, by permission, from David Foster, "Land-Use History and Four Hundred Years of Vegetation Change in New England," in *Global Land Use Change: a Perspective from the Columbian Encounter*, ed. A. Gomez Sal (n.p.: Scientific Research Council of Spain, 1995), Fig. 8. The presettlement forest map is redrawn from Charles F. Carroll, *The Timber Economy of Puritan New England* (Providence, R.I.: Brown University Press, 1973). Reprinted by permission from Brown University. Map based on the following sources: David M. Smith, "The Forests of the United States," in John W. Barrett, ed., *Regional Silviculture of the United States* (New York, 1962); John W. Barrett, "The Northeastern Region," in John W. Barrett, ed., *Regional Silviculture of the United States*; Stanley W. Bromley, "The Original Forest Types of Southern New England," *Ecological Monographs* 5 (1935); Betty Flanders Thomson, *The Changing Face of New England* (New York, 1958). Settlement maps for 1660 and 1760 redrawn and reprinted, by permission, from Stanley D. Dodge, "The Frontier of New England in the Seventeenth and Eighteenth Centuries and its Significance in American History," in *Papers of the Michigan Academy of Sciences, Arts, and Letters*, 18 (Ann Arbor, Mich.: The University of Michigan Press, 1942, 1971). Settlement map for 1860 is from *Growth Management in Maine* (Augusta, Maine: Maine State Planning Office, n.d.).

67. John W. Barrett, "The Northeastern Region," in *Regional Silviculture of the United States*, ed. John W. Barrett (New York: Wiley, 1980), 45.

68. Harper, "Changes in the Forest Areas of New England," 442–52.

69. Henry David Thoreau, *The Maine Woods*, (New York: Thomas Y. Crowell & Co., 1906), 168.

70. Charles F. Carroll, *The Timber Economy of Puritan New England* (Providence, R.I.: Brown University Press, 1973), 29.

71. Timothy Dwight, *Travels in New-England and New-York*, vol. 2 (New Haven, Conn.: Timothy Dwight, 1822), 92.

72. See Brugman, "Pollen Indicators," 349–62; Ronald B. Davis, et al., "Vegetation and Associated Environments During the Past 14,000 Years Near Moulton Pond, Maine," *Quaternary Research*, 5 (1975): 435–65.

73. G. E. Nichols, "The Vegetation of Connecticut, II, Virgin Forests," *Torreya*, 13 (9) (September 1913): 206.

74. See W. E. Bickford and U. J. Dyman, *An Atlas of Massachusetts River Systems—Environmental Designs for the Future* (Amherst, Mass.: University of Massachusetts Press, 1990), 27.

75. Roderick Nash, *Wilderness and the American Mind* (New Haven, Conn.: Yale University Press, 1982), 249.

76. Quoted in Richard S. Dunn, *Puritans and Yankees: The Winthrop Dynasty of New England, 1630–1717* (Princeton, N. J.: Princeton University Press, 1962), 108.

77. For a summary of early laws protecting natural resources, see Charles E. Clark, *The Eastern Frontier: The Settlement of Northern New England, 1610–1763* (New York: Alfred A. Knopf, 1970), 342–43.

78. George Catlin, *Letters and Notes on the Manners, Customs, and Conditions of the North American Indians*, vol. 1 (New York: Wiley and Putnam, 1841), 262.

79. Henry David Thoreau, *Excursions* (Boston, Mass.: Ticknor and Fields, 1863), 191.

80. Michael Williams, *Americans & Their Forests: A Historical Geography* (New York: Cambridge University Press, 1989), 17.

81. Alexis de Tocqueville, *Journey to America*, Trans. J. P. Mayer (London: Faber and Faber, 1960), 329.

82. George Perkins Marsh, *Man and Nature; or, Physical Geography as Modified by Human Action* (New York: Scribner, 1864), 327.

83. John Muir, *John of the Mountains: The Unpublished Journals of John Muir* (Madison, Wis.: University of Wisconsin Press, 1979), 315.

84. See Aldo Leopold, *Sand County Almanac* (New York: Ballantine Books, 1966).

85. Public Law 88–577, *The Wilderness Act*, 1964.

86. Joan S. Elbers, comp., *Changing Wilderness Values, 1930–1990: An Annotated Bibliography* (Westport, Conn.: Greenwood Press, 1991), xii.

87. Josselyn, *Two Voyages*, 36.

88. Fannie Hardy Eckstorm, "History of the Chadwick Survey From Fort Pownal in the District of Maine to the Province of Quebec in Canada in 1764," *Sprague's Journal of Maine History* (April–June 1926): 83.

89. Reverend Joseph Blake, "A Second Excursion to Mount Katahdin," *The Maine Naturalist* 6 (2) (June 1926): 79.

90. Holmes and Hitchcock, "General Reports," 396.

91. Blake, "Second Excursion," 81.

92. See Myron H. Avery, "The Monument Line Surveyors on Katahdin," *Appalachia* (June 1928): 33–43.

93. Myron H. Avery, "The Dead Water Mountains," *The Maine Naturalist* 10 (1) (April 1930): 16–17.

94. Hudson, et al., *Old-Growth Forest, Subalpine Forest, and Alpine Areas in Baxter State Park* (Augusta, Maine: Baxter State Park Authority and Critical Areas Program, Maine State Planning Office, 1985), 42.

95. Laura Waterman and Guy Waterman, *Forest and Crag: A History of Hiking, Trail Blazing, and Adventure in the Northeast Mountains* (Boston, Mass.: Appalachian Mountain Club, 1989), 56.

96. This and other information on northern New England's virgin forests and trees is from Charles Cogbill, interview with the author, Plainfield, Vt., 19 November 1992.

97. The history of Baxter State Park and the dedicated efforts of Governor Percival P. Baxter to acquire and give the park land to Maine is documented in the book by John W. Hakola, *Legacy of a Lifetime: The*

Story of Baxter State Park (Millinocket, Maine: Baxter State Park Authority, 1981).

98. Holmes and Hitchcock, "General Reports," 399.

99. See Jackson, *Second Annual Report*, 59.

100. *Fourth Report of the Forest Commissioner of the State of Maine, 1902* (Augusta, Maine: Kennebec Journal Print, 1902), 17–18.

101. Reports of the sightings of extirpated wildlife were obtained from interviews with rangers and others who worked in the waterway.

102. Holmes and Hitchcock, "Second Annual Report," 353.

103. Homes and Hitchcock, "Second Annual Report," 352–53.

104. Jackson, *Second Annual Report*, 57.

105. Jackson, *Second Annual Report*, 57–58.

106. Holmes and Hitchcock, "General Reports," 344.

107. Thoreau, *Maine Woods*, 266.

108. Thoreau, *Maine Woods*, 246–47.

109. Jackson, *Second Annual Report*, 58.

110. See Philip W. Conkling, *Old Growth White Pine (*Pinus strobus L.*) Stands in Maine and their Relevance to the Critical Areas Program*, planning report no. 61 (Augusta, Maine: Critical Areas Program, Maine State Planning Office, 1978).

111. Holmes and Hitchcock, "General Reports," 348.

112. "Maine Talgia," *The Maine Sportsman* (January 1990): 9.

113. Bourne, *Champlain*, 80–83.

114. Charles T. Jackson, *First Report on the Geology of the Public Lands in the State of Maine* (Boston, Mass.: Dutton and Wentworth, 1937), 18–19.

115. Observations on the location and character of the old-growth forest in the Baring Wilderness Area of the Moosehorn National Wildlife Refuge were supplemented by an unpublished report dated July 8, 1980, of a survey conducted by John Grena for the Maine Critical Areas Program, Maine State Planning Office.

116. An interesting history of the Wild River area, including its lumbering, settlement, businesses, and change to a national forest, is chronicled in the book by D. B. Wight, *The Wild River Wilderness* (Camden, Maine: Down East Books, 1971).

117. Evans Notch Ranger District of the White Mountain National Forest, *Caribou–Speckled Mountain Wilderness Plan* (1993), 2.

118. *Caribou–Speckled Mountain Wilderness Plan*, 2.

119. Wight, *Wild River*, 34.

120. Charles T. Jackson, *Final Report on the Geology and Mineralogy of the State of New Hampshire* (Concord, N.H.: Carroll & Baker, 1844), 137.

121. See Forest Service, U.S. Department of Agriculture, White Mountain Forest, *Sandwich Range Wilderness Management Plan* (January 1989).

122. The general description of the Sandwich Range Wilderness is from Forest Service, *Sandwich Range Wilderness*, 2–3.

123. Forest Service, *Sandwich Range Wilderness*, 3.

124. Charles J. Lyon and William A. Reiners, *Natural Areas of New Hampshire Suitable for Ecological Re-search*, no. 4 (Hanover, N.H.: Department of Biological Science, Dartmouth College, 1971), 14.

125. Information on the size of the Bowl and its maximum aged trees is from Charles Cogbill, interview with the author, Plainfield, Vt., 19 November 1992.

126. Lyon and Reiners, *Natural Areas*, 14.

127. William B. Leak, *Characteristics of Five Climax Stands in New Hampshire*, research note NE-336 (Durham, N.H.: Forest Service, Northeastern Experiment Station, U.S. Department of Agriculture, 1987), 4.

128. H. J. Oosting and W. D. Billings, "A Comparison of Virgin Spruce-Fire Forest in the Northern and Southern Appalachian System," *Ecology* 32 (1951): 102.

129. Forest Service, *Sandwich Range Wilderness*, 4.

130. The remarks by Reverend Hugh Peters during a ceremony to christen the Green Mountains are from a footnote by Basset, ed., *Natural History of Vermont*, 4.

131. Hager, et al., *Geology of Vermont*, 872.

132. Charles W. Johnson, *The Nature of Vermont* (Hanover, N.H.: The University Press of New England, 1980), 44.

133. Hubert W. Vogelmann, *Vermont Natural Areas*, report 2 (Montpelier, Vt.: Vermont Central Planning Office, 1969), 27.

134. Reference to the possibility of an old-growth forest in Downer Glen along the northern border of the Lye Brook Wilderness is from Mary Byrd Davis, *Old Growth In the East: A Survey* (Richmond, Vt.: Cenozoic Society, 1993), 49.

Chapter 2: Of the Isles, Bays, and Coastal Lands

1. Verrazzano, *The Relation of the Land*, 53.

2. While it seems logical that Block Island is the triangular-shaped island to which Verrazzano referred, questions remain. See Wroth, *Verrazzano*, 87.

3. J. B. Woodworth and Edward Wigglesworth, *Geography and Geology of the Region including Cape Cod, the Elizabeth Islands, Nantucket, Marthas Vineyard, No Mans Land and Block Island*, vol. 52, *Memoirs of the Museum of Comparative Zoology at Harvard College* (Cambridge, Mass.: Museum of Comparative Zoology, Harvard College, 1934), 211.

4. Holmes and Hitchcock, "General Reports," 210.

5. Verrazzano, *The Relation of the Land*, 58–59.

6. Champlain's observations of the coast are from Bourne, *Champlain*, 95–96; Smith's descriptions are from Smith, *Description of New England*, 237–41; some translations of place-names are from Henry F. Howe, *Prologue to New England* (New York: Farrar & Rinehard Incorporated, 1943), 253–62.

7. Morton, *Canaan*, 228–29.

8. Morton, *Canaan*, footnote no. 1, 229.

9. Verrazzano, *The Relation of the Land*, 48.

10. [Davies ?], *Relation of a Voyage*, 162.

11. Rosier, *A True Relation*, 106.

12. Bill Caldwell, *Islands of Maine: Where America really began* (Portland, Maine: Guy Gannett Publishing Co., 1981), 18.

13. Louis Clinton Hatch, ed., *Maine: A History*

(1919; reprint, Somersworth, N.H.: New Hampshire Publishing Company, 1974), 911.

14. Wroth, *Verrazzano*, 141.

15. Rosier, *A True Relation*, 106.

16. Information on the virgin characteristics of the forest on Monhegan Island is from Lowell Sumner, *Evaluation of Monhegan Island, Lincoln County, Maine, for eligibility for Registered Natural Landmark designation* (Washington, D.C.: National Park Service, U.S. Department of the Interior, 1966, photocopy). For a discussion of the character of the original forest on Monhegan, see also Philip W. Conkling, *Islands in Time: A Natural and Human History of the Islands of Maine* (Camden, Maine: Down East Books, 1981), 127–28.

17. Information on the old-growth yellow birch stands on the island in Georges Harbor is from a 1989 report to the Critical Areas Program, Maine State Planning Office, Augusta, Maine.

18. Bourne, *Champlain*, 83–84.

19. Williamson, *History of Maine*, 78.

20. Some information is from Maine Critical Areas Program, *Natural Old-Growth Forest Stands in Maine*, planning report no. 79 (Augusta, Maine: Maine State Planning Office, 1983), 90–91.

21. Some information is from Philip W. Conkling, *Old Growth White Pine (Pinus strobus L.) Stands in Maine*, planning report no. 61 (Augusta, Maine: Critical Areas Program, Maine State Planning Office, 1978), 31–32.

22. Samuel Adams Drake, *Nooks and Corners of the New England Coast* (1875; reprint, Bowie, Md.: Heritage Books, Inc., 1991), 33.

23. Samuel de Champlain, *Discovery of the Coast of the Almouchiquois*, in *Sailors Narratives*, 67.

24. Morison, *Champlain*, 56.

25. The description of Great Wass Island's natural history is augmented by information from the Maine Chapter of The Nature Conservancy, especially from Ruth Ann Hill, *Maine Forever: A Guide to Nature Conservancy Preserves in Maine*, 2d ed. (Topsham, Maine: Maine Chapter, The Nature Conservancy, 1989), 94–97.

26. Bourne, *Champlain*, 83.

27. Bourne, *Champlain*, 105.

28. Drake, *Nooks and Corners*, 161.

29. Smith, *Description of New England*, 243.

30. Christopher Levett, *My Discovery of diverse Rivers and Harbours, with their names, and which are fit for Plantations, and which not*, in *Sailors Narratives*, 261

31. Jackson, *Geology of New Hampshire*, 44.

32. Some information is from Thomas G. Siccama, et al., *Potential Ecological and Geological Natural Landmarks of the New England–Adirondack Region* (Washington, D.C.: Division of National Natural Landmarks, U.S. Department of the Interior, 1982), 214–17.

33. Drake, *Nooks and Corners*, 180.

34. Charles T. Jackson, *Report on the Geological and Agricultural Survey of the State of Rhode Island*, (Providence, R.I.: B. Cranston & Co., 1840), 114.

35. John Winthrop, *Winthrop's Journal "History of New England" 1630–1649*, ed. James Kendall Hosmer (1908; reprint, New York: Barnes & Noble, Inc., 1966), 187.

36. Peter W. Dunwiddie, "Postglacial Vegetation History of Coastal Islands in Southeastern New England," *National Geographic Research* 6 (2): 178–95.

37. Jackson, *Geological Survey of Rhode Island*, 117.

38. Information on rare species of plants and animals is from Rick Enser, *Rare Species Concerns on Block Island* (Providence, R.I.: Rhode Island Natural Heritage Program and Rhode Island Department of Environmental Management, 1993).

39. Verrazzano, *The Relation of the Land*, 58.

40. Bourne, *Champlain*, 80.

41. See Reed & D'Andrea, *Coastal Overview: Conservation Priorities Plan of the Coast of Maine*, draft (Gardiner, Maine: The Smithsonian Institution's Center for Natural Areas, 1973), III 6–III 9.

42. See Reed & D'Andrea, *Protection Priorities Plan: Conservation Priorities Plan* (Gardiner, Maine: The Smithsonian Institution's Center for Natural Areas, 1973), 1–1; Division of National Natural Landmarks, *Ecological and Geological*.

43. Levett, *My Discovery*, 262.

44. Levett, *My Discovery*, 262.

45. Belknap, *History of New-Hampshire*, vol. 3, 201.

46. Lyon and Reiners, *Natural Areas*, 24.

47. Smith, *Description of New England*, 243.

48. Rosier, *A True Relation*, 136–137.

49. Williamson, *History of Maine*, 95.

50. Smith, *Description of New England*, 238.

51. Information on the Megunticook Mountain old oak stand is from Critical Areas Program, *Natural Old-Growth Forest Stands in Maine*, planning report no. 79 (Augusta, Maine: Maine State Planning Office, 1983), 166–170.

52. Williamson, *History of Maine*, 96.

53. Belknap, *History of New-Hampshire*, vol. 3, 31.

54. Williamson, *History of Maine*, 96.

55. Williamson, *History of Maine*, 96.

56. Williamson, *History of Maine*, 96.

57. Maine Chapter, The Nature Conservancy, *Maine Legacy* (February 1991): 1.

58. Hitchcock, *Geology of Massachusetts*, 250.

59. Background information on the Blue Hills is from the following sources: Alan Fisher, *AMC Guide to Country Walks Near Boston* (Boston, Mass.: Appalachian Mountain Club, 1976); *Blue Hills Reservation Trail Map & Guide* (Boston, Mass.: Metropolitan District Commission, n.d.); Siccama, et al., *Potential Natural Landmarks*.

60. Edwin M. Bacon, *Boston: A Guide Book to the City and Vicinity*, revision by LeRoy Phillips (New York: Ginn and Company, 1922), 120.

61. Quoted from Albert K. Teele, *The History of Milton Massachusetts, 1640–1887* (Boston, Mass.: n.p., 1988), 146.

62. Hitchcock, *Geology of Massachusetts*, 251.

63. Robert Juet, *The Third Voyage of Master Henry Hudson*, in *Sailors Narratives*, 191.

64. See *Sailors Narratives*, 171, 267, 55, 208, 243.

65. Drake, *Nooks and Corners*, 50

66. Drake, *Nooks and Corners*, 50.

67. *The Heads of Inquiry, relative to the Present State and Condition of his Majesty's Colony of Connecticut,* Collections of the Massachusetts Historical Society, vol. 7 (Boston, Mass.: Massachusetts Historical Society, 1800), 234.

68. Background on Bluff Point is from the Connecticut Geological and Natural History Survey and included maps and two unpublished papers: *Bluff Point, A Connecticut State Park* (photocopy) and *Summary of Outstanding Natural Features at Bluff Point Coastal Reserve in Groton, Connecticut* (photocopy).

69. Brereton, *A Brief and True Relation,* 36.

70. Smith, *Description of New England,* 241.

71. Bourne, *Champlain,* 115.

72. Information on the geology and ecology of the Province Lands is from Cheryl A. McCaffrey, *An Ecological History of the Province Lands, Cape Cod National Seashore,* report no. 1, Dune Stabilization Study (Washington, D.C.: National Park Service, U.S. Department of the Interior, 1973); Woodsworth and Wigglesworth, *Geography and Geology,* 295–98.

73. Quoted in William Bradford and Edward Winslow, *Mourt's Relation or Journal of the Plantation at Plymouth,* ed. Henry Martyn Dexter, footnote no. 32 (1865; reprint, New York: Garrett Press, Inc, 1969), 11.

74. Bourne, *Champlain,* 115.

75. Bradford and Winslow, *Mourt's Relation,* 29.

76. McCaffrey, *Ecological History of the Province Lands,* 27.

77. Bourne, *Champlain,* 121–122.

78. Brereton, *A Brief and True Relation,* 35.

79. Information on the Barnstable Marsh and Sandy Neck is from the following sources: Carol M. Shifflett, *Potential Natural Landmarks Selected for the Geologic Themes Study on the Atlantic Coastal Plain, Florida to Cape Cod, Massachusetts* (Springfield, Va.: National Technical Information Service, 1981), 63–65; Catherine Keever, *A Study of the Mixed Mesophytic, Western Mesophytic and Oak Chestnut Regions of the Eastern Deciduous Forest Including a Review of the Vegetation and Sites Recommended as Potential Natural Landmarks* (Washington, D.C.: National Park Service, U.S. Department of the Interior, 1971), 158–160; Alfred C. Redfield, "Development of a New England Salt Marsh," *Ecological Monographs* 42 (2) (Spring, 1972): 201–37.

80. Quoted in Barbara Blair Chamberlain, *These Fragile Outposts: A Geological Look at Cape Cod, Marthas Vineyard, and Nantucket* (Garden City, N.Y.: The Natural History Press, 1964), 176.

81. Morton, *Canaan,* 185.

82. General scientific and historical information is from Glenn Motzkin, William A. Patterson III, and Natalie E. R. Drake, "Fire history and vegetation dynamics of a *Chamaecyparis thyoides* wetland on Cape Cod, Massachusetts," *Journal of Ecology* 81 (1993): 391–402.

83. Because of fires, vegetation in the Marconi Swamp before European settlement was probably patchy, and dense stands of mature Atlantic white cedar were present for short periods of time, unlike the stands of pure cedars seen today. This is discussed in Motzkin, Patterson, and Drake, "Fire History," 400–401.

84. Reported by Robert Finch, "The Woodlands, Heaths, and Grasslands," in Greg O'Brien, ed., *A Guide to Nature on Cape Cod and the Islands* (New York: The

Stephen Greene Press/ Pelham Books, 1990), 154.

85. Morton, *Canaan,* 215.

86. See Chamberlain, *Fragile Outposts,* 127–28.

87. Bourne, *Champlain,* 103–4.

88. Holmes and Hitchcock, "General Reports," 187.

89. Supplemental information on this beach located in the eastern section of the Maine coast is from a planning report published by the Critical Areas Program, Maine State Planning Office, Augusta, Maine, and a report by the Division of National Natural Landmarks, *Ecological and Geological.*

90. [Davies ?], *The Relation of a Voyage,* 168.

91. Background information on the Popham area beach system is from Bruce W. Nelson and L. Kenneth Fink, *Geological and Botanical Features of Sand Beach Systems in Maine* (Augusta, Maine: Critical Areas Program, Maine State Planning Office, 1980).

92. Wood, *Prospect,* 11.

93. Wood, *Prospect,* 11–12.

94. M. L. Fernald and K. M. Wiegand, "A Summer's Botanizing in Eastern Maine and Western New Brunswick," *Rhodora* 12: 101–46.

95. Background information on Carrying Place Cove is from Ian A. Worley, *Botanical and Ecological Aspects of Coastal Raised Peatlands in Maine,* planning report no. 69 (Augusta, Maine: Critical Areas Program, Maine State Planning Office, 1980), 123–26.

96. Drake, *Nooks and Corners,* 161.

97. Drake, *Nooks and Corners,* 46–47.

98. Holmes and Hitchcock, "General Reports," 180.

99. Jackson, *Geological Survey of Rhode Island,* 94.

100. Background on Purgatory Chasm is from Alonzo W. Quinn, *Rhode Island Geology for the Nongeologist* (n.p.: 1976), 53–57; Hitchcock, *Geology of Massachusetts,* 295–97; Drake, *Nooks and Corners,* 383.

101. Drake, *Nooks and Corners,* 56.

102. Geologic information about the caves is from Carleton A. Chapman, *The Geology of Acadia National Park* (n.p.: The Chatham Press, Inc., 1970).

103. Jackson, *First Report,* 15–16.

104. Jackson, *First Report,* 15.

105. Holmes and Hitchcock, "General Reports," 189.

106. Jasper Cates, letter to the author, 7 April 1994.

107. Information on the "Bold Coast" is, in part, from Robert Kimber, "Saving Maine's Bold Coast," *Down East: The Magazine of Maine,* reprint (April 1991); *The Geology of Maine's Coastline* (Augusta, Maine: Maine State Planning Office, 1983).

CHAPTER 3: OF THE COUNTRY AND ITS STONES

1. Josselyn, *Rarities,* 3.

2. Williams, *History of Vermont,* 26.

3. Holmes and Hitchcock, "General Reports," 105.

4. Hitchcock, *Geology of New Hampshire,* vol. 1, 636.

5. An excellent history of the New England mountains and mountain climbing, including first ascents, is given by Waterman and Waterman, *Forest and Crag.*

5. Josselyn, *Rarities*, 3.

7. Champlain, *Discovery of the Coast*, 72.

8. Smith, *Description of New England*, 243.

9. An excellent summary of available information on Darby Field and his Mt. Washington trip is in Waterman and Waterman, *Forest and Crag*, 6–14.

10. Lucy Crawford, *The History of the White Mountains from the First Settlement of Upper Coos and Pequaket* (1845; reprint, Portland, Maine: Hoyt, Fogg & Donham, 1883), 63.

11. Jeremy Belknap, "Description of the White Mountains in New-Hampshire," *Transactions of the American Philosophical Society* 2 (1786): 44.

12. Background on the Great Gulf Wilderness is from Lyon and Reiners, *Natural Areas*, 17; Forest Service United States Department of Agriculture, White Mountain Forest, *Great Gulf Wilderness Management Plan* (January 1989).

13. William Oakes, *Scenery of the White Mountains: with Sixteen Plates, from the Drawings of Isaac Sprague* (Boston, Mass.: Wm. Crosby and H. P. Nichols, 1848), Plate 16.

14. Background information on the Presidential Range alpine area is from Lyon and Reiners, *Natural Areas*, 5–6.

15. Belknap, "White Mountains," 45.

16. Jacob Bigelow, "Some Account of the White Mountains of New Hampshire," *The New-England Journal of Medicine and Surgery* V (IV) (October 1816): 333

17. Dwight, *Travels*, vol. 2, 148.

18. Carlos Wilcox, "Account of the Late Slides from the White Mountains," *The Boston News-Letter and City Record* (September 16, 1826), 125.

19. Edward Flaccus, *Vegetation Natural Areas of the Hemlock–White Pine–Northern Hardwoods Region of the Eastern Deciduous Forest*, prepared for the National Park Service (Springfield, Va.: National Technical Information Service, U.S. Department of Commerce, 1972).

20. Oakes, *Scenery*, Plate 3.

21. Charles T. Jackson, *Geology of New Hampshire*, 75.

22. Background information on Franconia Notch is from Paul G. Favour, Jr., *Evaluation of Franconia Notch, Grafton County, New Hampshire, for eligibility for Registered Natural Landmark designation* (Washington, D.C.: National Park Service, U.S. Department of the Interior, 1969).

23. Jackson, *Geology of New Hampshire*, 76.

24. Jackson, *Geology of New Hampshire*, 75.

25. Jackson, *Geology of New Hampshire*. 75.

26. Hitchcock, *Geology of New Hampshire*, vol. 1, 641.

27. Jackson, *Geology of New Hampshire*, 70.

28. Hitchcock, *Geology of New Hampshire*, vol. 1, 641–642.

29. Greenleaf, *Survey of Maine*, 45.

30. Paul Favour, Jr., 1969, quoted in Siccama, et al., *Potential Natural Landmarks*.

31. Supplemental information on the Mahoosuc Notch and Range is from: Siccama, et al., *Potential Natural Landmarks*; Donald Hudson, et al., *Old-Growth Forest, Subalpine Forest, and Alpine Areas in the Mahoosucs, Baldpates, and the Bigelow Preserve* (Augusta,

Maine: Maine Bureau of Public Lands and the Critical Areas Program, Maine State Planning Office, 1986); and Ingrid Burke, *The Mahoosuc Mountains: A Natural Areas Inventory* (Augusta, Maine: Maine Department of Conservation, 1982).

32. Charles T. Jackson, *Third Annual Report on the Geology of the State of Maine* (Augusta, Maine: Smith & Robinson, 1839), 111.

33. Some information on the Bigelow Mountain Range is from Caren Caljouw and Sarah Roeske, *A Natural Resource Inventory and Critical Areas Survey of the Bigelow Preserve* (Augusta, Maine: Maine Bureau of Public Lands and Critical Areas Program, Maine State Planning Office, 1981); Hudson, et al., *Forest and Alpine Areas*.

34. John Shay's report and background on the publicly owned Deboullie Township in northern Maine is from Mark Kern, *Natural Resources Inventory and Critical Area Survey of T. 15 R. 9* (Augusta, Maine: Bureau of Public Lands, Maine Department of Conservation, 1985).

35. Bourne, *Champlain*, 207.

36. The discussion on the possibility of snow on the Green Mountains in July drew upon Zadock Thompson, *Natural History of Vermont* (1853; reprint, Rutland, Vt.: Charles E. Tuttle Company, 1971), *vii*; Bourne, *Champlain*, 207; Charles W. Johnson, letter to the author, 8 February 1994.

37. Hager, et al., *Geology of Vermont*, vol. 2, 877.

38. Hager, et al., *Geology of Vermont*, vol. 2, 883.

39. *A History of the County of Berkshire, Massachusetts* (Pittsfield, Mass.: Samuel W. Bush, 1829), 16.

40. Background on the old-growth spruce on Mt. Greylock is from Ian A. Worley, *Evaluation of Mt. Greylock (The Hopper) Old Growth Spruce, Williamstown, Berkshire County, Massachusetts, for Eligibility for Registered Natural Landmark Designation* (Washington, D.C.: National Park Service, U.S. Department of the Interior, 1980, photocopy).

41. *A History of Berkshire County*, 17.

42. The Scout Willard's 1725 report is quoted from Hitchcock, *Geology of New Hampshire*, vol. 3, 1878, 373.

43. Quoted in Hitchcock, *Geology of New Hampshire*, vol. 3, 200.

44. Belknap, *History of New-Hampshire*, vol. 3, 188.

45. Belknap, *History of New-Hampshire*, vol. 3, 188.

46. For a discussion of New England's limestone caves and their formation see Richard F. Logan and H. Elmer Ekblaw, "The Geology of the Caves of New England," in Clay Perry, *Underground New England* (Brattleboro, Vt.: Vermont Printing Company, 1939), 228–233.

47. Quoted in Perry, *Underground New England*, 88.

48. P. J. Barosh, David London, and Jelle de Boer, "Structural Geology of the Moodus Seismic Area, South-Central Connecticut," in *New England Intercollegiate Geological Conference, 74th Annual Meeting, Guidebook for Fieldtrips* (Storrs, Conn.: The University of Connecticut, 1982), P7–1.

49. Perry, *Underground New England*, 87.

50. Background information on the Moodus Cave is from Daniel A. Huntington, ed., *The Caves of Connecticut*, second edition (Storrs, Conn.: Yale Speleological Society, 1963), 14, 26.

51. "Natural Curiosity. Description of a Newly Discovered Cavern, on the North-East End of Mount Anthony, in Bennington, Vermont," *The Nightingale, or, a Melange de Literature*, 1 (36) (1796): 424.

52. Additional information on the southern Vermont cave came from John Scott, *Caves in Vermont: A Spelunker's Guide to Their Location and Lore* (Hancock, Vt.: Killooleet, 1959), 9–10; Perry, *Underground New England*, 180–182.

53. "Natural Curiosity," 426.

54. Holmes and Hitchcock, "General Reports," 337.

55. Holmes and Hitchcock, "General Reports," 339.

56. Morton, *Canaan*, 220.

57. "Gold in New England," *The Naturalist* 1 (10) (October 1846): 456.

58. Jackson, *Geology of New Hampshire*, 228.

59. See Hager, et al., *Geology of Vermont*, vol. 2, 842–843.

60. See Holmes and Hitchcock, "General Reports," 309–310.

61. Holmes and Hitchcock, "General Reports," 310.

62. Holmes and Hitchcock, "General Reports," 310.

63. Josselyn, *Two Voyages*, 39.

64. Background information on Maine's semiprecious minerals is from Woodrow B. Thompson, *Maine Tourmaline Localities and Their Relevance to the Critical Areas Program* (Augusta, Maine: Critical Areas Program, Maine State Planning Office, 1977); Woodrow B. Thompson, *Rose Quartz Crystal Localities in Maine* (Augusta, Maine: Critical Areas Program, Maine State Planning Office, 1977); and Woodrow B. Thompson, et al., *A Collector's Guide to Maine Mineral Localities* (Augusta, Maine: Maine Geological Survey, Department of Conservation, 1988).

65. Holmes and Hitchcock, "Second Annual Report," 408.

66. Jackson, *Third Annual Report*, 46.

67. Holmes and Hitchcock, "General Reports," 148.

68. Edward Hitchcock, *A Report on the Sandstone of the Connecticut Valley, Especially its Fossil Footmarks* (1858; reprint, New York: Arno Press, 1974), 125.

69. The section on fossil tracks in the Connecticut Valley drew on Hitchcock, *Connecticut Valley Fossil Footmarks*; Richard Swann Lull, *Triassic Life of the Connecticut Valley*, (Hartford, Conn.: Connecticut State Geological and Natural History Survey, 1953); Claudia F. Sammartino, *The Northfield Mountain Interpreter* (Berlin, Conn.: Northeast Utilities, 1981); Paul Grzybowski, "Footprints in the Sands of Time, " *Northfield Mountain* (Autumn 1993): 1–2, 9; Richard D. Little, *Dinosaurs, Dunes, and Drifting Continents: The Geohistory of the Connecticut Valley* (Greenfield, Mass.: Valley Geology Publications, 1984).

70. Hitchcock, *Connecticut Valley Fossil Footprints*, 45.

71. Hitchcock, *Connecticut Valley Fossil Footprints*, 1.

72. Holmes and Hitchcock, "General Reports," 103.

73. Holmes and Hitchcock, "General Reports," 406.

74. Quoted from excerpts of a letter to Mr. Prince of Boston, published in "Earthquake in Connecticut, etc.," *American Railroad Journal and Mechanics Magazine*, 5 (1840): 251–252.

75. "Earthquake in Connecticut," 252.

76. "Earthquake in Connecticut," 250–251.

77. Paul Dudley, "An account of the earthquakes which have happened in New England, since the first settlement of the English in that country, especially of that, which happened on October 29, 1727," *The American Museum; or Universal Magazine* 5 (April 1789): 364–365.

78. "The Deerfield (N.H.) Phenomena," *Scientific American* 2 (1846): 2.

79. Thompson, *Natural History of Vermont*, 18.

80. Dick Lehr, "Seismic Detective Solves 'Moodus Noises' Mystery," *Hartford Courant*, 19 October 1981.

81. Jackson, *Geology of New Hampshire*, 366.

82. Holmes and Hitchcock, "Second Annual Report," 377.

83. Jackson, *Geology of New Hampshire*, 23.

84. Jackson, *Geology of New Hampshire*, 24.

85. Holmes and Hitchcock, "General Reports," 260.

86. Holmes and Hitchcock, "General Reports," 261.

87. Joseph Pierpont and William Albee, 1792, *A Journal of over 1,000,000 Acres of Land in the Counties of Hancock and Washington*, survey notebook in the Bingham Papers, the Historical Society of Pennsylvania.

88. Information on Maine's ancient delta is from Harold W. Borns, Jr., *Emerged Glaciomarine Deltas in Maine* (Augusta, Maine: Critical Areas Program, Maine State Planning Office, 1981).

89. Pierpont and Albee, *A Journal*.

90. Alexander Baring to Mssrs. Hope, Philadelphia, 3–28 December 1796, *Calendar of the Letters of Alexander Baring, 1795–1801*, Ruth Ann Fisher (Washington, D.C.: Manuscript Division, Library of Congress, 1954), No. 41.

91. Some background information on the ancient Pineo Ridge Delta is from Borns, *Glaciomarine Deltas*, 14–19. For an excellent study of the effect of fire on the vegetation of Pineo Ridge, see J. Chris Winne, "History of Vegetation and Fire on the Pineo Ridge Blueberry Barrens in Washington County, Maine," (Master's thesis, University of Maine, 1988).

92. Holmes and Hitchcock, "General Reports," 271.

93. Harold W. Borns, Jr., *Eskers in Maine* (Augusta, Maine: Critical Areas Program, Maine State Planning Office, 1979), 21.

94. Jackson, *First Report*, 21.

95. Siccama, et al., *Potential Natural Landmarks*, 599–601.

96. Hitchcock, *Geology of New Hampshire*, vol. 3, 147–148.

97. Hitchcock, *Geology of New Hampshire*, vol. 3, 147.

98. George H. Stone, *The Glacial Gravels of Maine and Their Associated Deposits*, prepared for the U.S. Geological Survey (Washington, D.C.: Government Printing Office, 1899), 183.

99. Information on the Belgrade esker/delta complex is from James B. Barnes, Ray B. Owen, Jr., and Malcolm W. Coulter, *Evaluation of Penney Pond–Joe Pond Complex, Belgrade and Sidney, Maine, for eligibility for Reg-*

istered *National Landmark* designation (Washington, D.C.: National Park Service, U.S. Bureau of the Interior, 1972, photocopy); Kathleen M. Kehoe, *The Belgrade Esker/Delta Complex* (Augusta, Maine: Critical Areas Program, Maine State Planning Office, 1982).

100. Hager, et al., *Geology of Vermont*, vol. 1, 56.

101. Percival, *Geology of Connecticut*, 453.

102. See Richard Goldsmith, "A Post-Harbor Hill-Charlestown Moraine in Southeastern Connecticut," *American Journal of Science*, 258 (December 1960): 740–783; Barbara M. Maire, *Ledyard Glacial Park Environmental Review Team Report*, on file at Connecticut Department of Environmental Protection.

103. Siccama, et al., *Potential Natural Landmarks*, 141–144.

104. Margaret Thomas and Nancy McHone, letter to the author, 14 April 1994.

105. Hager, et al., *Geology of Vermont*, vol. 1, 58.

106. John Winthrop, *Winthrop's Journal: History of New England, 1630–1649*, ed. James Kendall Hosmer, vol. 1 (New York: Barnes & Noble, Inc., 1966), 73.

107. Hitchcock, *Geology of Massachusetts*, 373–374.

108. Hager, et al., *Geology of Vermont*, vol. 1, 58–59.

109. Hitchcock, *Geology of New Hampshire*, vol. 3, 264–268.

110. Hitchcock, *Geology of New Hampshire*, vol. 3, 264.

111. Quoted in *Natural Landmark Brief: Madison Boulder, Carroll County, New Hampshire* (Washington, D.C.: National Park Service, U.S. Department of the Interior, 1969, photocopy). Supplementary information is also from Paul G. Favour, Jr., *Evaluation of Madison Boulder, Carroll County, New Hampshire, for eligibility for Registered Natural Landmark designation* (Washington, D.C.: National Park Service, U.S. Department of the Interior, 1969).

112. Josselyn, *Rarities*, 155.

113. Josselyn, *Two Voyages*, 155.

114. Jacob Green, "Notice of a Mineralized Tree—Rocking Stone, etc.," *American Journal of Science*, 5 (2) (1822): 252–253.

115. O. Mason, "Notice of a Rocking Stone," letter to the editor, *American Journal of Science* 10 (1) (1825): 9.

116. Hitchcock, *Geology of Massachusetts*, 374–375.

117. The Massachusetts accounts of rocking stones included reports in the following journals: Jacob G. Porter, H. U. Cambridge, and T. H. Webb, "Account of the Roxbury Rocking Stone," *American Journal of Science* 7 (1) (1823): 59–60; John White Webster, "Primitive Boulders: On Boulders from Massachusetts, and a rocking stone at Roxbury, Massachusetts," *The Boston Journal of Philosophy and the Arts* 1 (1) (1823): 91–92; Jacob G. Porter, "Notice of a rocking stone in Savoy, Massachusetts, with a drawing," *American Journal of Science* 9 (1) (1825): 27; "Immense boulder," *The American Magazine of Useful and Entertaining Knowledge* 3 (5) (1837): 184.

118. See Thompson, *Natural History of Vermont*, Appendix, 52.

119. Hager, et al., *Geology of Vermont*, vol. 2, 890.

120. Jacob Green, "Notice of a Mineralized Tree—Rocking Stone, etc.," *American Journal of Science* 5 (2) (1822): 252; Chandler Eastman Potter, "Notice of a Rocking Stone," *American Journal of Science* 24 (1) (1833): 185–186; Hitchcock, *Geology of New Hampshire*, 271.

121. Holmes and Hitchcock, "General Reports," 259–260.

122. John C. Pease and John M. Niles, *A Gazetteer of the States of Connecticut and Rhode Island* (1819; reprint, Bowie, Md.: Heritage Books, 1991), 372.

123. Steuben Taylor, "Notice of a Rocking Stone in Warwick, R.I.," *The American Journal of Science* 7 (2) (1824): 201–203.

124. Jackson, *Geological Survey of Rhode Island*, 84–85.

125. Howard Willis Preston, *Rhode Island's Historic Background* (n.p.: Rhode Island Tercentenary Commission, 1936), 8.

126. Taylor, "Rocking Stone," 202–203.

127. Much of Drum Rock's history is from Don D'Amato, *Warwick's Historic Homes, Places and Personalities, Book Two* (n.p.: Beacon Communications, 1989), 43–44.

128. Anonymous, "On certain Rocks supposed to move without any apparent cause," letter to the editor, *American Journal of Science* 5 (1822): 34–37.

129. Charles Alfred Lee, "Remarks on the moving rocks of Salisbury," letter to the editor, *American Journal of Science* 9 (2) (1825): 239–241.

130. Pease and Niles, *Gazetteer*, 385.

131. Jackson, *Geological Survey of Rhode Island*, 86–87.

132. Information on Devil's Foot Rock is from Michael E. Bell, "Devil's Foot Rock: The Folkloristic Component—Final Report" (18 February 1994, photocopy, unpublished); additional information supplied by Nathan A. Fuller.

133. Bell, "Devil's Foot Rock," 50.

134. Hitchcock, *Geology of Massachusetts*, 244.

135. Benjamin Silliman and James L. Kingsley, "Account of a Remarkable Fall of Meteoric Stones in Connecticut," *The Philadelphia Medical and Physical Journal* 3 (Part 1) (1808): 48.

136. Thompson, *Natural History of Vermont*, 16–17.

137. Parker Cleveland, "Notice of the late Meteor in Maine," *American Journal of Science* 7 (1) (1823): 170–171.

138. Silliman and Kingsley, "Account in Connecticut," 57.

CHAPTER 4: OF THE WATERS

1. Josselyn, *Two Voyages*, 37.

2. Josselyn, *Two Voyages*, 38.

3. Bradford and Winslow, *Mourt's Relation*, 70.

4. Higginson, *Plantation*, B.

5. See Holmes and Hitchcock, "General Reports," 443–444.

6. Thompson, *Natural History of Vermont*, 7–8.

7. Alexander King, "The Natural History of the

Mineral Spring in Suffield, Connecticut," *The Rural Magazine; or, Vermont Repository*, 1 (1795): 400–403.

8. James Pierce, "Chalybeate Spring at Litchfield," *American Journal of Science*, letter to the editor 3 (2) (1821): 235–236.

9. Williams, *History of Vermont*, 31.

10. To protect this sensitive area, the scientific reports and names of individuals contacted are not referenced.

11. Trumbull, *History of Connecticut*, 16–17.

12. Trumbull, *History of Connecticut*, 15–24.

13. Supplementary information on Griswold Point is from E. Griswold, et al., *An Ecological Inventory of Griswold Point Preserve, Old Lyme, Connecticut* (Middletown, Conn.: Connecticut Chapter, The Nature Conservancy, 1975, photocopy); Siccama, et al., *Potential Natural Landmarks*.

14. Belknap, *History of New-Hampshire*, vol. 3, 55.

15. Background information on the Fourth Connecticut Lake is from the New Hampshire Chapter of The Nature Conservancy.

16. Dwight, *Travels*, vol. 2, 313.

17. Greenleaf, *Survey of Maine*, 40–41.

18. Greenleaf, *Survey of Maine*, 37–38.

19. Greenleaf, *Survey of Maine*, 42.

20. Some of the description and quoted material on the St. John River and North Branch of the Penobscot River is from *Maine Rivers Study: Final Report* (Augusta, Maine: Maine Department of Conservation, 1982), 117, 141; additional information is from Siccama, et al., *Potential Natural Landmarks*, 277–280.

21. Early descriptions of the Penobscot–St. John headwaters are from Holmes and Hitchcock, "Second Annual Report," 334–339.

22. Williams, *History of Vermont*, 47.

23. Williams, *History of Vermont*, 49.

24. George E. Nichols, "The Vegetation of Connecticut: V. Plant societies along rivers and streams," *Bulletin of the Torrey Botanical Club* 43 (1916): 245.

25. To protect this fragile area from overvisitation, the name of the ravine is not given. Supplementary information on its natural character is from Siccama, et al., *Potential Natural Landmarks*; New England Natural Areas Project, *Natural Areas Reporting Form* (February 8, 1971), photocopy; Nichols, "Vegetation of Connecticut."

26. These strange events were recounted by David E. Philips, *Legendary Connecticut*, second edition (Willimantic, Conn.: Curbstone Press, 1992), 186–191.

27. Clap, "Memoirs," 349.

28. Bourne, *Champlain*, 111.

29. Smith, *Description of New England*, 241.

30. Thompson, *Natural History of Vermont*, 4.

31. Supplementary information on Old City Falls Ravine is from Hugh W. Vogelmann, *Natural Areas in Vermont*, report 1 (Montpelier, Vt.: Central Planning Office, State of Vermont, 1964), 7.

32. Quoted in Abby Maria Hemenway, *The Vermont Historical Gazetteer*, Vol. 2 (Burlington, Vt.: A. M. Hemenway, 1871), 1068.

33. Quoted in Holmes and Hitchcock, "General Reports," 430.

34. Supplementary information on Gulf Hagas

Gorge is from Thomas Brewer, *Gorges in Maine* (Augusta, Maine: Critical Areas Program, Maine State Planning Office, 1978), 17.

35. Jackson, *Second Annual Report*, 27.

36. Holmes and Hitchcock, *Second Annual Report, Geology of Maine*, 365.

37. See Brewer, *Gorges*, 15.

38. Jackson, *Second Annual Report*, 28.

39. Belknap, *History of New-Hampshire*, vol. 3, 62.

40. Hitchcock, *Geology of Massachusetts*, 288.

41. See Siccama, et al., *Potential Natural Landmarks*.

42. Hitchcock, *Geology of Massachusetts*, 291.

43. Davis, *Old Growth*, 25.

44. Quoted in Hager, et al., *Geology of Vermont*, vol. 2, 882.

45. Jackson, *Third Annual Report*, 101.

46. Supplementary information is from Alvin K. Swonger and Thomas Brewer, *Maine's Waterfalls* (Augusta, Maine: Critical Areas Program, Maine State Planning Office, 1988), 40–41.

47. Williams, *History of Vermont*, 47.

48. Hager, et al., *Geology of Vermont*, vol. 1, 216.

49. Hitchcock, *Geology of Massachusetts*, 287.

50. Josselyn, *Two Voyages*, 155.

51. Morton, *Canaan*, 234.

52. Bourne, *Champlain*, 205.

53. Hager, et al., *Geology of Vermont*, vol. 2, 898.

54. Jackson, *Third Annual Report*, 38.

55. Jackson, *Third Annual, Report*, 39–40.

56. Holmes, *Report on the Aroostook River*, 20.

57. The name of this pond and sources of information are not included here in order to help ensure its protection.

58. This quotation by Thomas Hardy, Jr., is from Terry Webster, *Evaluation of Ell Pond, Hopkinton, Rhode Island, for eligibility for Registered Natural Landmark Designation* (Washington, D.C.: National Park Service, U.S. Bureau of the Interior, 1972, photocopy). 3.

59. Information on Ell Pond is from Webster, *Evaluation of Ell Pond* and *Natural Landmark Brief* (Washington, D.C.: National Park Service, U.S. Bureau of the Interior, 1985).

Chapter 5: Of the Woods and Herbs

1. Josselyn, *Two Voyages*, 49.

2. The study referred to is Peter W. Dunwiddie, "Forest History and Composition of Halfway Pond Island, Plymouth County, Massachusetts," *Rhodora* 93 (876) (1991): 347–360. Additional information is from Thomas G. Siccama, et al., *Potential National Landmarks; Halfway Pond Island*, information sheet (Boston, Mass.: The Nature Conservancy, n.d.).

3. James Thatcher, *History of the Town of Plymouth* (1835; reprint, East Orleans, Mass.: Parnassus Imprints, 1972), 321.

4. William A Patterson, III, and Andrew E. Backman, "Fire and Disease History of Forests," in *Vegetation His-*

tory, ed. Brian J. Huntley and Thompson Webb (Boston, Mass.: Kluwer Academic Publishers, 1988), 603–632.

5. Pring, *A Voyage*, 59.

6. Pring, *A Voyage*, 59–60.

7. Captain John Smith's list of fruits and woods is from Smith, *Description of New England*, 244. Bracketed interpretations are from Dean R. Snow, *The Archaeology of New England* (New York: Academic Press, 1980), 67.

8. Josselyn, *Rarities*, 41–91.

9. Greenleaf, *Survey of Maine*, 110.

10. Holmes and Hitchcock, "General Reports," 125–129.

11. For an overview of the postglacial forest changes in Maine and a nontechnical explanation of pollen study techniques and their applications, see George L. Jacobsen, Jr., and Ronald B. Davis, "Temporary and Transitional: The Real Forest Primeval—the Evolution of Maine's Forests over 14,000 Years," *Habitat: Journal of the Maine Audubon Society* 5 (1) (January 1988): 26–29. For a summary of postglacial forest changes in New England see Foster, "Land-Use History." For technical reports on palynological studies see Theodore E. Bradstreet and Ronald B. David, "Mid-Postglacial Environments in New England with Emphasis on Maine," *Arctic Anthropology* 7 (2) (1975): 7–22; Davis, et al., "Vegetation and Environments," 435–65.

12. David R. Foster, et al., "Post-Settlement History of Human Land-Use and Vegetation Dynamics of a *Tsuga canadensis* (Hemlock) Woodlot in Central New England," *Journal of Ecology* 80 (1992): 776–77.

13. J. D. Henry and J. M. A. Swan, "Reconstructing Forest History from Live and Dead Plant Material—An Approach to Study of Forest Succession in Southwest New Hampshire," *Ecology* 55 (1974): 772–83.

14. The Presettlement Forest Regions map is based on the following sources: David M. Smith, "The Forests of the United States," in John W. Barrett, ed., *Regional Silviculture of the United States* (New York, 1962); John W. Barrett, "The Northeastern Region," in John W. Barrett, ed., *Regional Silviculture of the United States*; Stanley W. Bromley, "The Original Forest Types of Southern New England," *Ecological Monographs* 5 (1935); Betty Flanders Thomson, *The Changing Face of New England* (New York, 1958).

15. See Marinus Westveld, et al., "Natural Forest Vegetation Zones in New England," *Journal of Forestry* 54 (May 1956): 332–38.

16. See Charles F. Carroll, *The Timber Economy of Puritan New England* (Providence, R.I.: Brown University Press, 1973), 24.

17. Lesley Sneddon, letter to the author, 29 October 1992.

18. Asa Gray, "The Flora of Boston and its Vicinity, and the Changes it has Undergone," in *The Memorial History of Boston*, ed. Justin Winsor, vol. 1 (Boston, Mass.: J. R. Osgood and Co., 1880), 19.

19. See Garrett E. Crow, *New England's Rare, Threatened, and Endangered Plants* (Washington, D.C.: U.S. Government Printing Office, 1982).

20. See Foster, "Land-Use History."

21. Dwight, *Travels*, vol. 2, 50.

22. Trumbull, *History of Connecticut*, 24.

23. For a discussion of the pre-colonial vegetation of

the sand plains of North Haven and Wallingford, Connecticut, see Charles E. Olmsted, "Vegetation of Certain Sand Plains in Connecticut," *The Botanical Gazette*, vol. 99 (2) (December 1937): 266–67.

24. See Siccama, et al., *Potential Natural Landmarks*, 149–52.

25. See Lissa Widoff, *Pitch Pine/Scrub Oak Barrens in Maine*, Planning Report No. 86 (Augusta, Maine: Critical Areas Program, Maine State Planning Office, 1987), 14–16.

26. Polly Harris, *The Waterboro Barrens* (n.p.: Maine Chapter, The Nature Conservancy, 1991, photocopy), 1.

27. Williamson, *History of Maine*, 97.

28. Background information and quotations on the Waterboro Barrens is from Harris, *Waterboro Barrens*.

29. Wood, *Prospect*, 12.

30. Enos A. Mills, *In Beaver World* (1913; reprint, Lincoln, Nebr.: University of Nebraska Press, 1990), 219.

31. Hitchcock, *Geology of New Hampshire*, vol. 2, 313.

32. Stanley W. Bromley, "The Original Forest Types of Southern New England," *Ecological Monographs* 5 (1) (January 1935): 67.

33. For a discussion of the role of the beaver in creating natural meadows and the values of these fertile lands to the colonists, see Carolyn Merchant, *Ecological Revolutions: Nature, Gender, and Science in New England* (Chapel Hill, N.C.: The University of North Carolina Press, 1989), 36–38.

34. Betty Flanders Thomson, *The Changing Face of New England* (New York: The Macmillan Company, 1958), 41–42.

35. Mills, *Beaver*, 220.

36. Holmes, *Report on the Aroostook River*, 18.

37. Holmes and Hitchcock, "Second Annual Report," 366.

38. Thomson, *Changing Face*, 41.

39. Holmes, *Report on the Aroostook River*, 44.

40. Thompson, *Natural History of Vermont*, 6.

41. Information on No. 5 Bog is from Harry R. Tyler, Jr., and Christopher V. Davis, *Evaluation of No. 5 Bog and Jack Pine Stand, Somerset County, Maine, as a Potential National Natural Landmark*, prepared for the National Park Service (Augusta, Maine: Critical Areas Program, Maine State Planning Office, 1982).

42. Background on the Great Heath is from Caljouw, *A Preliminary Description of The Great Heath and Environs*.

43. Thompson, *Natural History of Vermont*, 6.

44. Williams, *Natural History of Vermont*, 41.

45. Ira Allen to James Whitelaw, 8 February 1786, *Papers of the Surveyors-General*, vol. 1, pt. 1 (Montpelier, Vt.: State Archives, n.d.), 115.

46. Hager, et al., *Geology of Vermont*, vol. 1., 145.

47. Background information on the natural history of Missisquoi Marsh and the Missisquoi National Wildlife Refuge from Vogelmann, *Vermont Natural Areas*, report 2, 8–9; brochures published by the U.S. Fish and Wildlife Service, Department of the Interior: *Missisquoi National Wildlife Refuge, Black Creek and Maquam Creek Trail, Birds: Missisquoi National*

Wildlife Refuge, and *Mammals: Missisquoi National Wildlife Refuge*.

48. Rowland E. Robinson, *Uncle Lisha's Outing: The Buttler Gals and Along Three Rivers*, ed. Llewellyn R. Perkins (1894; reprint, Rutland, Vt.: The Tuttle Company, 1934), 234.

49. Abby Maria Hemenway, *The Vermont Historical Gazetteer*, vol. 1, pt. 1 (Burlington, Vt.: A. M. Hemenway, 1859), 31–32.

50. Robinson, *Three Rivers*, 236–37.

51. Background information on Little Otter Creek Marsh is from Vogelmann, *Natural Areas of Vermont*, report 1, 13–14; *Little Otter Creek Marsh: Natural Landmark Brief* (Washington, D.C.: National Park Service, U.S. Department of the Interior, 1973).

52. See Jackson, *Geology of New Hampshire*, 69.

53. Background information for this bog is from Paul G. Favour, Jr., *Evaluation of . . . Natural Area, Coos County, New Hampshire, for eligibility for Registered Natural Landmark designation* (Washington, D.C.: National Park Service, U.S. Department of the Interior, 1969, photocopy).

54. Belknap, *History of New-Hampshire*, vol. 3, 58.

55. The quoted material on this pond bog is from Richard H. Goodwin and William A. Niering, *Inland Wetlands of the United States: Evaluated as Potential Natural Landmarks*, prepared for the National Park Service, U.S. Department of the Interior (Washington, D.C.: Government Printing Office, 1975); Lyon and Reiners, *Natural Areas*, 61.

56. York County, Maine, Registry of Deeds, Alfred, *Survey Plan of the Great Heath in Saco*, Isaac Boothby, 1899.

57. Background information on the Saco Heath is from Hill, *Maine Forever*, 22–23; "Saco Heath Preserve Expands," *Maine Legacy: The Nature Conservancy* (Winter 1994): 1–3; Timothy P. Kluge, "Changes in Vegetation of the Heath, Saco, Maine, U.S.A., since European Settlement of the Region" (Master's thesis, University of Maine, 1991); *Saco Heath Preserve Self Guiding Trail*, a brochure published by the Maine Chapter, The Nature Conservancy.

58. James Trenchard, "Description of the Green-Woods, in Connecticut," *Columbian Magazine* 3 (1789): 366, quoted in Herbert Isaac Winer, "History of the Great Mountain Forests, Litchfield County, Connecticut" (Ph.D. diss., Yale University, 1956), 73.

59. Background information on this bog is from Paul Favour, Jr., *Evaluation of . . . Bog, Norfolk, Litchfield County, Connecticut, for eligibility for Registered Natural Landmark designation* (Washington, D.C.: National Park Service, U.S. Department of the Interior, 1976, photocopy).

60. Josselyn, *Two Voyages*, 38.

61. For a discussion of swamps in early New England, see Carroll, *Timber Economy*, 32–33.

62. Bromley, *Forest Types*, 70.

63. Quoted from Josselyn, *Two Voyages*, 129, but appears to have been taken verbatim by Josselyn from Edward Johnson's *Wonder-Working Providence*, published in 1654.

64. Thompson, *Natural History of Vermont*, 6.

65. Wood, *Prospect*, 17.

66. Supplementary information on Great Swamp is

from Goodwin and Niering, *Wetlands of the U.S.*; *Great Swamp Wildlife Management Area*, Division of Fish and Wildlife, Rhode Island Department of Environmental Management (flier).

67. *The Field Notes of Benjamin Crane, Benjamin Hammond and Samuel Smith* (New Bedford, Mass.: New Bedford Free Public Library, 1910), 725.

68. Quoted from John P. Richardson, *Potential Natural Landmark Identification*, a report to the National Park Service, 23 October, 1970, and published in *National Registry of Natural Landmarks* (Washington, D.C. National Park Service, U.S. Department of the Interior, 1992), 54.

69. The quote and other information is from Glenn Motzkin, *Atlantic White Cedar Wetlands of Massachusetts* (Amherst, Mass.: Agricultural Experiment Station, University of Massachusetts, 1991), 33. Additional background information is from Paul G. Favour, Jr., *Evaluation of Acushnet Cedar Swamp, New Bedford, Massachusetts, for eligibility for Registered Natural Landmark* (Washington, D.C.: National Park Service, U.S. Department of the Interior, 1971, photocopy); John P. Richardson, *The Primeval Stumps of Turners Pond* and *How Old Are the Oldest Acushnet Swamp White Cedars?* (Boston, Mass.: Division of Forests and Parks, Massachusetts Department of Natural Resources, 1970, photocopy); Aimlee D. Laderman, *The Ecology of Atlantic White Cedar Wetlands: A Community Profile*, biological report 85 (Washington, D.C.: Fish and Wildlife Service, U.S. Department of the Interior, 1989).

70. Morton, *Canaan*, 184.

71. Quoted in Favour, *Acushnet Cedar Swamp*, 4.

72. Wood, *Prospect*, 19.

73. Bradford and Winslow, *Mourt's Relation*, 70.

74. Thomas G. Siccama, "Presettlement and Present Forest Vegetation in Northern Vermont with Special Reference to Chittenden County," *The American Midland Naturalist* 85 (1) (1971): 153–72.

75. Craig G. Lorimer, "The Presettlement Forest and Natural Disturbance Cycle of Northeastern Maine," *Ecology* 58 (1977): 139–48.

76. See Massachusetts House Document no. 105 (1851), 10.

77. Hitchcock, *Geology of New Hampshire*, vol. 1, 576.

78. Thoreau, *Maine Woods*, 214.

79. Hitchcock, *Geology of New Hampshire*, vol. 1, 579–80.

80. Dwight, *Travels*, vol. 1, 36.

81. Belknap, *History of New-Hampshire*, vol. 3, 73.

82. Hitchcock, *Geology of Massachusetts*, 297.

83. See David Foster and E. Boose, "Patterns of Forest Damage Resulting from Catastrophic Wind in Central New England, USA," *Journal of Ecology* 80 (1992): 79–98.

84. Lorimer, *Presettlement Forest*, 144.

85. Research on the extent of Indian burning was briefly summarized by Foster, *Land-Use History*, 9.

86. Pring, *A Voyage*, 59.

87. Belknap, *History of New-Hampshire*, vol. 3, 219.

88. See Hitchcock, *Geology of New Hampshire*, vol. 1, 581.

89. Barrett, "The Northeastern Region," 45.

90. Thompson, *Natural History of Vermont*, 5.

91. Robert T. Leverett, "Foreword," in *Old Growth in the East: A Survey*, Mary Byrd Davis (Richmond, Vt.: Cenozoic Society, Inc., 1993), 10.

92. Charles Cogbill, "The Ancestral Forest," *The Northern Forest Forum* (Mud Season 1993): 31.

93. For a discussion of the characteristics of old-growth forests, see Leverett, "Foreword," 8–15. See also Cogbill, "Ancestral Forest," for a discussion of the representativeness of old-growth forests.

94. Frederick Jackson Turner, "The Significance of the Frontier in American History," *Annual Report of the American Historical Association for 1893* (1894): 199–227.

95. For a discussion of the values of old-growth forests, see Leverett, "Foreword," 14–15; Peter Dunwiddie, "Reading Ancient Forests," *Sanctuary* (September 1990): 14–16; Gordon G. Whitney, "Some Reflections on the Value of Old-Growth Forests, Scientific and Otherwise," *Natural Areas Journal*, 7 (3) (1987): 92–99.

96. State Land Records, Field Notes 16:92 (Augusta, Maine: State Archives, 1833).

97. Cogbill, "Ancestral Forest," 31.

98. Steven B. Selva, *Lichens as Indicators of Old-Growth Forests: Results of First Year's Field Work* (Brunswick, Maine: Maine Chapter, The Nature Conservancy, 1986, photocopy).

99. Background information on the Big Reed Forest Reserve is from Hill, *Maine Forever*, 109–110; Charles V. Cogbill, *Evaluation of the Forest History and Old-Growth Nature of the Big Reed Pond Preserve, T8 R10 and T8 R11 W.E.L.S., Maine* (Brunswick, Maine: Maine Chapter, The Nature Conservancy, 1985, photocopy); Lissa Widoff, *The Forest Communities of Big Reed Preserve* (Brunswick, Maine: Maine Chapter, The Nature Conservancy, 1985, photocopy); John M. Kasner, "A Biogeophysical Description of a Portion of the Big Reed Pond Preserve, Northern Maine," (Master's thesis, University of Vermont, 1985); Cogbill, "Ancestral Forest."

100. Francois Jean, Marquis de Chastellux, *Travels in North America, in the years 1780, 1781, and 1782*, trans. George Grieve (London: G. G. J. and J. Robinson, 1787), 446.

101. Background information is from Winer, "History of the Great Mountain Forest," 8–132. Additional information is from an article by Herbert I. Winer and Edward C. Childs in *The Connecticut Arboretum* published by Connecticut College, New London, Connecticut.

102. Quoted in Walter Prichard Eaton, "Two Hundred and Fifty Years of History," in *The Berkshires: The Purple Hills*, ed. Roderick Peattie (New York: The Vanguard Press, Inc., 1948), 278–79.

103. Hager, et al., *Geology of Vermont*, vol. 2, 885.

104. Vogelmann, *Natural Areas in Vermont*, report 1, 10

105. F. H. Bormann and M. F. Buell, "Old-Age Stand of Hemlock-Northern Hardwood Forest in Central Vermont," *Bulletin of the Torrey Botanical Club* 91 (6) (November–December 1964): 451.

106. Background information on Gifford Woods is from Vogelmann, *Natural Areas in Vermont*, report 1; Bormann and Buell, "Old-Age Stand in Central Vermont"; Paul Favour, Jr., *Evaluation of Gifford Woods,*

Sherburne, Rutland County, Vermont, for eligibility for Registered Natural Landmark designation (Washington, D.C.: National Park Service, U.S. Department of the Interior, 1978, photocopy).

107. Hitchcock, *Geology of New Hampshire*, vol. 1, 639–40.

108. Background information on the virgin forest in the upper Connecticut Lakes region is from Paul G. Favour, Jr., *Evaluation of East Inlet Natural Area, Coos County, New Hampshire, for eligibility for Registered Natural Landmark* (Washington, D.C.: National Park Service, U.S. Department of the Interior, 1969); Lyon and Reiners, *Natural Areas of New Hampshire*, 19–20; Richard W. Rhoades, "The Distribution of White Spruce (*Picea glauca*) in New Hampshire, (Master's Thesis, University of New Hampshire, 1961).

109. Hitchcock, *Geology of New Hampshire*, vol. 1, 216–18.

110. Crawford, *History of the White Mountains*, 43.

111. Waterman and Waterman, *Forest and Crag*, 41.

112. Background information on the Gibbs Brook old-growth forest came from Lyon and Reiners, *Natural Areas of New Hampshire*, 16; Jeffrey R. Foster and William A. Reiners, "Vegetation Patterns in a Virgin Subalpine Forest at Crawford Notch, White Mountains, New Hampshire," *Bulletin of the Torrey Botanical Club* 110 (2) (April–June 1983): 141–153; Charles Cogbill, interview.

113. Morton, *Canaan*, 183.

114. Bourne, *Champlain*, 205.

115. Josselyn, *Rarities*, 51.

116. Aaron Young, "The Forests of York County," *Maine Farmer and Mechanic* (May 25, 1848).

117. Background information on the small stand of American chestnut trees is from the Maine Chapter of The Nature Conservancy.

118. George B. Emerson, *A Report on the Trees and Shrubs Growing Naturally in the Forests of Massachusetts*, vol. 1 (Boston, Mass.: Little, Brown, and Company, 1875), 149.

119. Williams, *Natural History of Vermont*, 87.

120. *Natural Old-Growth Forest Stands in Maine*, planning report no. 79 (Augusta, Maine: Critical Areas Program, Maine State Planning Office, 1983), 13.

121. *Natural Old-Growth Forest Stands in Maine*, 114.

122. Unpublished report for the Register of Critical Areas, Critical Areas Program Maine State Planning Office, February 3, 1988.

123. Quoted in William Hutchinson Rowe, *The Maritime History of Maine: Three Centuries of Shipbuilding & Seafaring* (1948; reprint, Freeport, Maine: The Bond Wheelright Company, n.d.), 37.

124. Belknap, *History of New-Hampshire*, vol. 3, 73.

125. Rowe, *Maritime History*, 33.

126. Background information on the King's Pine is from Philip W. Conkling, *Old Growth White Pine (*Pinus strobus L.*) Stands in Maine and their Relevance to the Critical Areas Program*, planning report no. 61 (Augusta, Maine: Critical Areas Program, Maine State Planning Office, 1978), 28–29; Philip W. Conkling, "Stalking the Broad Arrow Pine," *Down East Magazine* (April 1980): 45–47, 74–77.

127. Josselyn, *Rarities*, 75–77.

128. Background information on Bartholomew's Cobble is from Paul G. Favour, Jr., *Evaluation of Bartholomew's Cobble, Ashley Falls, Massachusetts for eligibility for Registered Natural Landmark* (Washington, D.C.: National Park Service, U.S. Department of the Interior, 1971); Howard T. Bain, *Ledges Interpretive Trail, Bartholomew's Cobble* (Milton, Mass.: The Trustees of Reservations, n.d.).

129. Belknap, *History of New-Hampshire*, vol. 3, 74.

130. Thoreau, *The Maine Woods*, 293–94.

131. Background information on the history and character of this island jackpine stand located in northern Maine is from a report by the Critical Areas Program, Maine State Planning Office, Augusta, Maine.

132. Holmes and Hitchcock, "General Reports," 364.

133. Thoreau, *The Maine Woods*, 294.

134. Thoreau, *The Maine Woods*, 294.

135. J. K. Laski, "Dr. Young's Botanical Expedition to Mount Katahdin," reprinted from *Bangor Courier*, September 1847, *The Maine Naturalist* 7 (2) (June 1927): 51.

136. Joseph Blake, "A Second Excursion to Mount Katahdin," *The Maine Naturalist* 6 (2) (June 1926): 81.

137. W. Donald Hudson, Jr., *A Preliminary Vascular Flora of Baxter State Park*, miscellaneous report no. 37 (Augusta, Maine: Baxter State Park Authority and Critical Areas Program, Maine State Planning Office, 1989), 1.

138. Information on the natural history of Baxter State Park and its alpine areas is from Hudson, Jr., et al., *Old-Growth Forest in Baxter State Park*.

139. A. E. Brower, *Katahdin Arctic Butterfly, Oeneis polixenes katahdin, Newc., in Maine and its Relevance to the Critical Areas Program*, planning report no. 35 (Augusta, Maine: Critical Areas Program, Maine State Planning Office, 1977).

CHAPTER 6: OF THE BEASTS, FEATHERED FOWLS, AND FISHES

1. Portions of this section on petroglyphs are drawn from the following sources of information: Hedden, "Prehistoric Maine Petroglyphs," 3–27; Garrick Mallery, *Picture-Writing of the American Indians*, vol. 1 (1893; reprint, New York: Dover Publications, Inc., 1972), 31–36, 81–82, 218; Snow, *Archaeology of New England*, 62.

2. For a discussion of Indian settlement patterns and food resources, see Snow, *Archaeology of New England*, 301–305.

3. See Bruce J. Bourque, "Aboriginal Settlement and Subsistence on the Maine Coast," *Man in the Northeast* 6: 3–20.

4. Pring, *A Voyage*, 60–61.

5. Smith, *Description of New England*, 244.

6. Wood, *Prospect*, 21.

7. Morton, *Canaan*, 199.

8. Josselyn, *Rarities*, 6–7.

9. Wood, *Prospect*, 35.

10. Morton, *Canaan*, 190, 199.

11. Northeast Nongame Technical Committee, *List of Legally Recognized Rare Species in the Northeastern States*, comp. Thomas French and Diane Pence (n.p.: Northeast Nongame Technical Committee, 1991).

12. Higginson, *Plantation*, B4.

13. See Bickford and Dyman, *An Atlas of River Systems*.

14. See Allen, "The Fauna of Eastern Massachusetts," 9–11.

15. Bill Lawrence, *The Early American Wilderness as the Explorers Saw It* (New York: Paragon House, 1991), 15.

16. Thompson, *Natural History of Vermont*, 50.

17. Allen, "Fauna of Eastern Massachusetts," 10.

18. See footnote 1 in Morton, *Canaan*, 200.

19. Pring, *A Voyage*, 60.

20. Smith, *Description of New England*, 214.

21. Josselyn, *Two Voyages*, 74.

22. Williams, *Natural History of Vermont*, 121.

23. Belknap, *The History of New-Hampshire*, vol. 3, 154.

24. Thompson, *Natural History of Vermont*, 39.

25. Holmes and Hitchcock, "Second Annual Report," 140.

26. Allen, "Fauna of Eastern Massachusetts," 11.

27. F. B. Loomis, "A New Mink from the Shell Heaps of Maine," *American Journal of Science* Ser. 4 (31) (1911): 227.

28. Loomis, "A New Mink," 227.

29. For a summary of studies relating to the distribution of the extinct sea mink, see Alfred J. Godin, *Wild Mammals of New England* (Baltimore, Md.: The Johns Hopkins University Press, 1977), 230.

30. Manly Hardy, "The Extinct Mink from the Maine Shell Heaps," *Forest and Stream* 61 (7) (1903): 125.

31. Hardy, "The Extinct Mink," 125.

32. Bradford and Winslow, *Mourt's Relation*, 53. (Also see the reprint edition of *Mourt's Relation* edited by Henry Martyn Dexter [New York: Garrett Press, 1969] fn 270, 75.)

33. Leopold, *Sand County*, 137.

34. Allen, "Fauna of Eastern Massachusetts," 10.

35. Wood, *Prospect*, 27.

36. Josselyn, *Two Voyages*, 21.

37. Morton, *Canaan*, 209.

38. Josselyn, *Two Voyages*, 61.

39. Josselyn, *Rarities*, 15.

40. John M. Cronan and Albert Brooks, *The Mammals of Rhode Island*, wildlife pamphlet 6 (Providence, R.I.: Division of Fish and Game, Rhode Island Department of Agriculture and Conservation, 1968).

41. See Godin, *Wild Mammals*, 281.

42. See Clark, *The Eastern Frontier*, 117.

43. Belknap, *History of New-Hampshire*, vol. 3, 147.

44. Thompson, *Natural History of Vermont*, 34.

45. Williams, *Natural History of Vermont*, 101.

46. *History of the County of Berkshire*, 36.

47. See Jackson, *Third Annual Report*, 205.

48. Stella M. Davis, "The Last Wolf in Portland," *The Maine Naturalist* 9 (2) (June 1929): 73.

49. See Francis Gould Butler, *A History of Farmington, Maine, 1776–1885* (Farmington, Maine: n.p., 1885).

50. See Richard Lorey Day, "The Wildlife of Maine—A Geographic Study," (Master's thesis, Clark University, 1948), 132.

51. See Glover M. Allen, "History of the Virginia Deer in New England," *New England Game Conference* (n.p.: Massachusetts Fish and Game Association, 1930), 19–41.

52. Wood, *Prospect*, 27.

53. Leopold, *Sand County*, 138–39.

54. Josselyn, *Rarities*, 21–22.

55. For example, see Allen, "The Fauna of Eastern Massachusetts," 10; Morton, *Canaan*, footnote 2, 214.

56. See Godin, *Wild Mammals*, for a summary of research on the distribution of the mountain lion in New England.

57. Williamson, *History of Maine*, 134–35.

58. Helenette Silver, *A History of New Hampshire Game and Furbearers*, survey report 6 (Concord, N.H.: New Hampshire Fish and Game Department, 1957).

59. Henry Clapp, "Notes of a Fur Hunter," *American Naturalist* 1 (1868): 652.

60. See Glover M. Allen, *Extinct and Vanishing Mammals of the Western Hemisphere, with the Marine Species of All the Oceans*, (n.p.: American Committee for International Wild Life Protection, 1942).

61. Thompson, *Natural History of Vermont*, 38.

62. Bruce S. Wright, "The Latest Specimen of the Eastern Puma," *Journal of Mammology* 42 (2) (1961): 278–79.

63. Bruce S. Wright, *The Eastern Panther: A Question of Survival* (Toronto, Canada: Clarke Irwin & Company Limited, 1972), 164–65.

64. John A. Lutz, *1993 Statistical Review of Felis concolor Sightings* (Baltimore, Md.: Eastern Puma Research Network, 1993, photocopy), 2.

65. Williams, *Natural History of Vermont*, 106.

66. Josselyn *Two Voyages*, 69. For an opinion that the animal described by Josselyn is the wolverine, see Paul J. Lindholt, ed., *John Josselyn, Colonial Traveler: A Critical Edition of Two Voyages to New England* (Hanover, N.H.: University Press of New England, 1988), footnote 114, 62.

67. Joel A. Allen, "Former Range of New England Mammals," *American Naturalist* 10 (12): 708–15.

68. Dwight, *Travels*, vol. 2, 313.

69. Ernest Thompson Seton, *Lives of the Game Animals*, vol. 2 (New York: Doubleday Doran & Co., Inc., 1929), 522.

70. Williams, *Natural History of Vermont*, 106.

71. Thompson, *Natural History of Vermont*, 30.

72. Ralph S. Palmer, "Mammals of Maine," (Bachelor of Arts thesis, University of Maine, 1937), 57.

73. Allen, "Former Range," 708–15.

74. Leonard Lee Rue, III, *Furbearing Animals of North America* (New York: Crown Publishers, Inc., 1981), 226.

75. Josselyn, *Rarities*, 20.

76. See John E. Guilday, "Archaeological Evidence of Caribou from New York and Massachusetts," *Journal*

of Mammology 49 (2): 344–45.

77. See Robson Bonnichsen, et al., *The Environmental Setting for Human Colonization of Northern New England and Adjacent Canada in Late Pleistocene Time*, special paper (n.p.: Geological Society of America, 1985), 157–58.

78. Williamson, *History of Maine*, 136.

79. Jackson, *Second Annual Report*, 11–12.

80. Capt. F. C. Barker and J. S. Danforth, *Hunting and Trapping on the Upper Magalloway River and Parmachenee Lake: First Winter in the Wilderness* (Boston, Mass.: D. Lothrop and Company, 1882), 45–46.

81. See reports of the Maine Commissioner of Inland Fisheries and Game (1886, 1895, 1896, 1898, 1900, 1904).

82. Edward S. C. Smith, "An Early Winter Trip to Katahdin," *Appalachia* (December 1926): 493–96.

83. See Annie Lorenz, "Notes on the Hepaticae of Mt. Katahdin," *Bryologist* 20: 41–46.

84. Information on the disappearance of the woodland caribou in Maine and lessons from reintroduction efforts is from Mark McCollough, *A Management and Research Plan for the Reintroduction of Woodland Caribou to Maine 1987* (Orono, Maine: Maine Caribou Reintroduction Project, n.d.); Mark McCollough, "Lessons in Reintroduction Policy from an Attempt to Restore Caribou to Maine," in *Final Report: Maine Caribou Project 1986–1990* (Portland, Maine: Maine Caribou Project, 1991); Mark A. McCollough and Bruce A. Connery, "An Attempt to Reintroduce Woodland Caribou to Maine 1986–1990," in *Final Report*.

85. Thompson, *Natural History of Vermont*, 36.

86. For a discussion of the distribution of the lynx, see Godin, *Wild Mammals*, 238–39; William J. Hamilton, Jr., *Mammals of Eastern United States* (Ithaca, N.Y.: Comstock Publishing Company, 1943), 190.

87. Josselyn, *Two Voyages*, 68.

88. Holmes and Hitchcock, "Second Annual Report," 137.

89. Higginson, *Plantation*, C3.

90. Higginson, *Plantation*, C3.

91. Wood, *Prospect*, 49–50.

92. Wood, *Prospect*, 50.

93. Josselyn, *Rarities*, 38–39.

94. Williams, *Natural History of Vermont*, 155.

95. Williamson, *History of Maine*, 170.

96. Quoted in Albert Matthews, "Rattlesnake Colonel," *New England Quarterly* 10 (June 1937): 343.

97. Belknap, *History of New-Hampshire*, vol. 3, 175.

98. Jacob Bigelow, "Some Account of the White Mountains of New Hampshire," *The New-England Journal of Medicine and Surgery* 5 (4) (October 1816): 338.

99. Williamson, *History of Maine*, 170.

100. For reports documenting the disappearance of the rattlesnake, see Thompson, *Natural History of Vermont*, 119; Belknap, *History of New-Hampshire*, vol. 3, 175; Holmes and Hitchcock, "Second Annual Report," 141; Allen, "Fauna of Eastern Massachusetts," 14; Arthur H. Norton, "The Rattlesnake in Maine," *The Maine Naturalist* 9 (1) (March 1929): 25–28.

101. Wood, *Prospect*, 51.

102. Belknap, *History of New-Hampshire*, vol. 3, 174–75.

103. For a sensitive and comprehensive history of the rattlesnake in Blue Hills of Massachusetts, see Thomas Palmer, *Landscape with Reptile: Rattlesnakes in an Urban World* (New York: Tichnor & Fields, 1992).

104. Josselyn, *Two Voyages*, 75.

105. Wood, *Prospect*, 34.

106. See Morton, *Canaan*, footnote no. 1, 192, 194–95.

107. Wood, *Prospect*, 35.

108. Josselyn, *Rarities*, 9.

109. James C. Greenway, Jr., *Extinct and Vanishing Birds of the World*, special publication 13 (New York: American Committee for International Wild Life Protection, 1958), 39.

110. Wood, *Prospect*, 34.

111. Wood, *Prospect*, 32.

112. Josselyn, *Rarities*, 9.

113. Allen, "Fauna of Eastern Massachusetts," 12.

114. The disappearance of the wild turkey was documented by Thompson, *Natural History of Vermont*, 101; Belknap, *History of New-Hampshire*, vol. 3, 170; Day, "Wildlife of Maine," 194; Arthur Cleveland Bent, *Life Histories of North American Gallinaceous Birds* (New York: Dover Publications, Inc., 1963), 327.

115. Steve Parren, letter to the author, 14 June 1994.

116. Thomas Dudley, "Letter to the Countess of Lincoln," in *Chronicles*, 320.

117. Wood, *Prospect*, 31–32.

118. Morton, *Canaan*, 180.

119. A. W. Schorger, *The Passenger Pigeon: Its Natural History and Extinction* (Norman, Okla.: University of Oklahoma Press, 1973), 205.

120. William Brewster, "The Present Status of the Wild Pigeon (*Ectopistes migratorius*) as a Bird of the United States, with Some Notes on Its Habits," *Auk* 6 (1889): 285–91.

121. Bourne, *Champlain*, 104.

122. John Winthrop, *The History of New England from 1630 to 1649*, ed. James Savage, vol. 2 (Boston, Mass.: n.p., 1843), 404–405.

123. S. G. Goodrich, *Recollections of a Lifetime, or Men and Things I have seen in a Series of Familiar Letters to a Friend*, vol. 1 (New York: Miller, Orton and Mulligan, 1857), 99–101.

124. Ora W. Knight in *Maine Sportsman* 4 (November 1896): 8.

125. "Swain," *Shooting and Fishing* 10 (October 1, 1891): 10.

126. George H. Perkins and Clifton D. Howe, "A Preliminary List of the Birds Found in Vermont," *21st Annual Report of the Vermont State Board of agriculture* (n.p.: 1901), 101.

127. Edward H. Forbush, *Game Birds, Wild-Fowle and Shore Birds*, 2d ed. (Boston, Mass.: n.p., 1916), 461.

128. Reginald H. Howe and Edward Sturtevant, *The Birds of Rhode Island* (Middletown, R.I.: n.p., 1899), 88.

129. J. H. Sage, L. B. Bishop, and W. P. Bliss, *The Birds of Connecticut*, Bull. 20 (Hartford, Conn.: Connecticut State Geological and Natural History Survey, 1913), 69.

130. Wood, *Prospect*, 32.

131. For a discussion of the original range of the heath hen, see Greenway, *Extinct and Vanishing Birds*, 188–93; Roger D. Applegate, "Did the Heath Hen Occur in Maine?" *Maine Naturalist* 1 (2) (1993): 1–4.

132. See Applegate, "Heath Hen in Maine," 1–4.

133. Allen, "Fauna of Eastern Massachusetts," 12.

134. A summary of the extinction of the heath hen is given by David M. Raup, *Extinction: Bad Genes or Bad Luck* (New York: W. W. Norton & Company, 1991), 121–23.

135. Bent, *Life Histories*, 269–70.

136. Josselyn, *Rarities*, 11.

137. Quoted in Allen, "Fauna of Eastern Massachusetts," 13.

138. For background on the great auk, see Allen, "Fauna of Eastern Massachusetts," 12–13; Greenway, *Extinct and Vanishing Birds*, 271–304; Snow, *Archaeology of New England*, 301–303.

139. Morton, *Canaan*, 190.

140. A review and analysis of literature on the Labrador duck is found in Greenway, *Extinct and Vanishing Birds*, 173–75.

141. Brereton, *A Brief and True Relation*, 36.

142. Information on the status of fish associated with the New England coast is from *Status of Fishery Resources off the Northeastern United States for 1992*, NOAA Technical Memorandum NMFS-FINEC-95 (Woods Hole, Mass.: Northeast Fisheries Science Center, U.S. Department of Commerce, 1992).

143. Rosier, *A True Relation*, 110.

144. Juet, *The Third Voyage of Master Henry Hudson*, 181.

145. Kupperman, *Captain John Smith*, 237–38.

146. Wood, *Prospect*, 38.

147. Smith, *Description of New England*, 245.

148. Morton, *Canaan*, 227.

149. Wood, *Prospect*, 39.

150. See Higginson, *Plantation*.

151. Josselyn, *Two Voyages*, 82.

152. Josselyn, *Two Voyages*, 86.

153. Smith, *Description of New England*, 245.

154. For a review of the impact of development on marine ecosystems, see John B. Pearce, "Collective Effects of Development on the Marine Environment," *Oceanologica Acta*, vol. sp (11) (March 1991): 287–298.

155. Williamson, *History of Maine*, 166.

156. The report on shad migration levels in Maine is from Thomas Squiers, telephone conversation with the author, 13 June 1994.

157. *Status of Fishery Resources*, 124–25.

158. Northeast Nongame Committee, *Legally Recognized Rare Species*, 10–12.

159. Josselyn, *Two Voyages*, 156.

160. [Davies ?], *Relation of a Voyage*, 169.

161. Josselyn, *Rarities*, 32.

162. Wood, *Prospect*, 37.

163. Morton, *Canaan*, 223.

164. Williamson, *History of Maine*, 162.

165. Background information on sturgeon in the Kennebec River, Maine, is from Kennebec River Council,

The Fishery Resources of the Kennebec River: Discover the Kennebec (n.p.: Kennebec River Council, n.d.), 21–22.

166. *Status of Fishery Resources*, 130–31.

167. The report on the Penobscot River survey is from Thomas Squiers, telephone conversation with the author, 13 June 1994.

168. Rosier, *A True Relation*, 140.

169. Wood, *Prospect*, 37.

170. Information on the history of the Atlantic salmon in New England is from *Final Environmental Impact Statement: Restoration of Atlantic Salmon to New England Rivers* (Newton Corner, Mass.: Fish and Wildlife Service, U.S. Department of the Interior, 1989).

171. *The Fishery Resources of the Kennebec River*, 10.

172. Williams, *Natural History of Vermont*, 147.

173. Belknap, *History of New-Hampshire*, vol. 3, 179.

174. Thompson, *Natural History of Vermont*, 140.

175. Figures for the 1993 salmon populations in New England rivers came from *Annual Report of the U.S. Atlantic Salmon Assessment Committee*, report 6—1993 activities (Turners Falls, Mass.: U.S. Atlantic Salmon Assessment Committee, 1994).

176. Samuel Argall, *The Voyage of Captaine Samuel Argal . . . Begun the nineteenth of June, 1610*, in *Sailors Narratives*, 206.

177. "Maine's 1st Gray Seal Colony Found," *Kennebec Journal*, 10 March 1994.

178. See Steven K. Katona, Valerie Rough, and David T. Richardson, *A Field Guide to the Whales, Porpoises, and Seals of the Gulf of Maine and Eastern Canada, Cape Cod to Newfoundland*, 3rd ed. (New York: Charles Scribner's Sons, 1983), 186–90.

179. See Valerie Rough, "Gray Seals in New England," *Massachusetts Audubon Society* 3 (1968): 20–27.

180. Pring, *A Voyage*, 60.

181. See Anne LaBastille, *Rare, Endangered, Threatened Vertebrate Species of the Atlantic Coastal Plain and Maine Coast* (Washington, D.C.: Center for Natural Areas, Smithsonian Institution, 1973), 127.

182. Higginson, "Higginson's Journal of His Voyage," *Chronicles*, 232.

183. Bradford and Winslow, *Mourt's Relation*, 30.

184. Kupperman, *Captain John Smith*, 220.

185. Williamson, *History of Maine*, 164.

CHAPTER 7: OF VALUES AND HOPE

1. Henry David Thoreau, "Walking," in *Henry David Thoreau: The Natural History Essays* (Salt Lake City, Utah: Peregrine Smith, Inc, 1980), 112.

Index

Page numbers for illustrations are in boldface.